MW01115176

HPCR PRACTITIONER'S HANDBOOK ON MONITORING, REPORTING, AND FACT-FINDING

Investigating International Law Violations

This book offers a portrait of the practice of monitoring, reporting, and fact-finding in the domain of human rights, international humanitarian law, and international criminal law. By analyzing the experiences of fifteen missions implemented over the course of the past decade, the book illuminates the key issues that these missions face and offers a roadmap for practitioners working on future missions. This book is the result of a five-year research study led by the Program on Humanitarian Policy and Conflict Research at Harvard University. Based on extensive interviews conducted with fact-finding practitioners, this book consists of two parts. Part I offers a handbook that details methodological considerations for the design and implementation of fact-finding missions and commissions of inquiry. Part II – which consists of chapters written by scholars and practitioners – presents a more in-depth, scholarly examination of past fact-finding practices.

ROB GRACE is Senior Associate at the Program on Humanitarian Policy and Conflict Research (HPCR) at the Harvard Humanitarian Initiative. In this role, he leads research projects on international law and humanitarian action. His writing on international law and foreign policy has been published by the *Journal of Conflict & Security Law*, the *European Society of International Law Reflections*, *Foreign Policy in Focus*, the *Foreign Policy Association*, and *Professionals in Humanitarian Assistance and Protection*. He holds an MA degree in politics from New York University and a BA degree from Vassar College.

CLAUDE BRUDERLEIN is Strategic Adviser to the President of the International Committee of the Red Cross (ICRC) and holds an adjunct faculty appointment at the Harvard T. H. Chan School of Public Health and the Harvard Kennedy School of Government. As a Swiss lawyer, Mr. Bruderlein has worked in humanitarian protection with the ICRC in the Middle East for several years as well as in Geneva as a legal adviser. In 1996, he joined the United Nations as special adviser to the Secretary General on Humanitarian Affairs. He worked particularly on humanitarian access in Afghanistan and North Korea.

HPCR PRACTITIONER'S HANDBOOK ON MONITORING, REPORTING, AND FACT-FINDING

Investigating International Law Violations

PROGRAM ON HUMANITARIAN POLICY & CONFLICT
RESEARCH (HPCR)

Harvard Humanitarian Initiative

ROB GRACE

Program on Humanitarian Policy and Conflict Research

CLAUDE BRUDERLEIN

Harvard T. H. Chan School of Public Health

CAMBRIDGE
UNIVERSITY PRESS

CAMBRIDGE
UNIVERSITY PRESS

University Printing House, Cambridge CB2 8BS, United Kingdom

One Liberty Plaza, 20th Floor, New York, NY 10006, USA

477 Williamstown Road, Port Melbourne, VIC 3207, Australia

4843/24, 2nd Floor, Ansari Road, Daryaganj, Delhi - 110002, India

79 Anson Road, #06-04/06, Singapore 079906

Cambridge University Press is part of the University of Cambridge.

It furthers the University's mission by disseminating knowledge in the pursuit of education, learning, and research at the highest international levels of excellence.

www.cambridge.org
Information on this title: www.cambridge.org/9781107164475
DOI: 10.1017/9781316687260

First published 2017

Printed in the United States of America by Sheridan Books, Inc.

A catalogue record for this publication is available from the British Library.

ISBN 978-1-107-16447-5 Hardback

CONTENTS

v

PREFACE

PHILIPPE KIRSCH

The increase in international efforts invested in monitoring, reporting, and fact-finding (MRF) on violations of human rights and humanitarian law over the recent decades starting in the 1990s and into the 2000s has been a welcome development. As international, regional, and national actors have sought to respond more robustly to allegations of violations of international law, commissions of inquiry and fact-finding missions have multiplied and played a significant role in addressing allegations of particular concern to the international community.

However, this development has also brought forth several challenges: interpreting ambiguous and sometimes politically charged mandates; developing a sound methodology for establishing and legally qualifying facts; devising means to mitigate security risks incurred by witnesses and victims due to their cooperation with an inquiry mission; adopting a strategic approach to public communication; and effectively drafting the mission's final report under tight resource, personnel, and time constraints. Lessons learned on past missions regarding these issues have not been effectively carried forward. Instead, practitioners often have had a sense of "reinventing the wheel" from mission to mission.

This state of affairs derives largely from the ad hoc nature of these missions. Typically, the team of commissioners, legal experts, and investigators is assembled on short notice so that the mission can promptly begin its work in the field and disbands once the mission has been completed. This scenario leaves little opportunity for building institutional memory or peer-to-peer professional exchanges. The current environment, which is not propitious to the use by governments of a permanent fact-finding entity, suggests that the ad hoc nature of this field is likely to persist.

In response, several initiatives have been undertaken to develop some guidance for members and staff of future commissions of inquiry on the basis of past and current experience, enabling them to operate more effectively within this ad hoc framework. The "Guidelines on International Human Rights Fact-Finding Visits and Reports" (also known as the

"Lund-London Guidelines"), updated in 2016 by the International Bar Association and the Raoul Wallenberg Institute of Human Rights and Humanitarian Law, address the needs of nongovernmental fact-finding efforts and are also relevant, in part, to missions mandated by governmental or intergovernmental entities. The 2013 *Siracusa Guidelines for International, Regional and National Fact-Finding Bodies* articulate rules and principles applicable to different types of fact-finding endeavors. "Commissions of Inquiry and Fact-Finding Missions on International Human Rights and Humanitarian Law: Guidance and Practice," published by the Office of the High Commissioner for Human Rights in 2015, provides important information about standard operating procedures and guidelines relevant to each stage of commissions of inquiry and fact-finding missions mandated by the United Nations Human Rights Council.

Nevertheless, an in-depth and specific assessment of the wealth of past MRF experiences was still needed to inform future methodological decision making. This book aims to fill this gap, building on the various efforts mentioned above but adopting a different approach. Rather than exhaustively addressing the full process of conducting MRF missions, it focuses on a select number of particularly challenging methodological issues, based on the assessment of leading practitioners and experts in this field. This exercise rests on the observations collected through a five-year research project that surveyed, in a systematic manner, over one hundred past MRF missions and reviewed most established professional standards, in order to equip current and future practitioners with the ability to draw on best professional practices.

My hope is that practitioners, researchers, and trainers engaged in the field of MRF will draw useful observations and reflections from this exercise. While this book constitutes a snapshot of the field of MRF at this particular point in time, this domain continues to evolve, and there is a need for efforts to analyze and learn lessons from past practice on an ongoing basis. Given the important role that MRF missions have come to play in responses to allegations of violations of international law, maximizing the potential impact of future missions by devoting energy to a continued assessment of MRF work will be crucial. This book is an important step in this ongoing process.

~

Introduction

CLAUDE BRUDERLEIN

This book is the product of a multi-annual research project undertaken by the Program on Humanitarian Policy and Conflict Research (HPCR) at Harvard University. Building on its experience in the development of interpretive guidelines and professional manuals,[1] HPCR launched this initiative in 2011 in response to concerns expressed by practitioners engaged in monitoring, reporting, and fact-finding (MRF) about the fragmentation of this professional domain and the lack of institutional memory that would capture the challenges, dilemmas, and strategies of past missions. In line with HPCR's mission to apply scientific research to address recurring policy dilemmas related to humanitarian assistance and protection, this project has entailed in-depth research on the operations and impacts of MRF initiatives, as well as extensive professional engagement with leading practitioners involved in MRF work.

HPCR began its work on this subject by undertaking a systematic analysis of the domain of MRF as a whole. At the time, no such study had been undertaken. Instead, existing literature reflected the fragmented nature of this domain: case studies had been produced analyzing individual missions, but little comparative analysis had been conducted on the respective experiences of different missions. As part of this study, HPCR constructed an online database that aggregated mandates and reports for over one hundred MRF missions implemented since the end of World War II.[2] Using this database as a research tool, and drawing from extensive interviews that HPCR conducted with MRF practitioners, HPCR concluded that a demand exists among practitioners for research into key areas of methodological concern, the continued development of tools of

---

[1] See generally Program on Humanitarian Policy and Conflict Research at Harvard University, *HPCR Manual on International Law Applicable to Air and Missile Warfare* (New York: Cambridge University Press, 2013).

[2] See "HPCR Digital Library of Monitoring, Reporting, and Fact-Finding," Program on Humanitarian Policy and Conflict Research, accessed June 7, 2015, http://www.hpcrresearch .org/mrf-database/.

practical guidance, and the creation of forums geared toward professional exchange.

Recognizing the need to directly involve MRF practitioners in the continuation of the research process, HPCR convened the HPCR Group of Professionals on Monitoring, Reporting, and Fact-Finding, a team of high-level practitioners in this domain who have served on recent missions in various capacities.[3] This esteemed collection of professionals played a key role in shaping the direction of HPCR's research and the elaboration of a practical handbook.

Through deliberations between HPCR and members of the Group of Professionals, the decision was made to conduct an assessment of fifteen specific MRF missions implemented over the past decade.[4] Drawing on the experience cumulated over the course of these missions, HPCR collaborated with the Group in elaborating a research agenda that proceeded in four steps. First, a desk analysis was undertaken of each of these missions' mandates and reports, as well as of relevant secondary literature. Second, HPCR conducted extensive interviews with high-level practitioners who served on these missions in various capacities. Third, based on the desk analyses and the interviews, HPCR analyzed trends in strategies and techniques of decision making in a series of six working papers produced over the project's period. Fourth, HPCR worked with the Group of Professionals to adapt the working papers into a format suitable for a practical, user-friendly document: the *HPCR Advanced Practitioner's Handbook on Commissions of Inquiry*. This process entailed a series of on-site meetings of the Group that HPCR convened between 2012 and 2014. This book presents the outcome of this exercise.

Structure and Overview of the Book

Part I   HPCR Advanced Practitioner's Handbook on Commissions of Inquiry

In this part of the book, readers will find a practical methodological approach to key issues that are emblematic of the policy challenges that MRF practitioners face. Given the research methodology described above, this *Handbook* reflects not only HPCR's assessment of the fifteen

---

[3] See Appendix A of this book for the names of the members of the Group of Professionals.
[4] Information about the fifteen selected missions, as well as a detailed explanation of the criteria used for selecting these missions, can be found in Appendix B.

selected missions but also the particular professional experiences and perspectives of the members of the Group of Professionals, who worked collaboratively with HPCR on structuring, drafting, and editing the document. Each section of the *Handbook* consists of four subsections designed to guide practitioners through the cumulated research and experiences:

I. *Background*: Provides information about the context within which the issue of the section emerges.

II. *Practical Steps*: Presents a systematic method for approaching the issue at hand.

III. *Explanation*: Offers detailed information, examples from past practice, and additional commentary regarding the practical steps to be taken.

IV. *Final Observations*: Summarizes the key methodological considerations detailed in the section and highlights particularly challenging issues.

The five particular areas that the *Handbook* addresses sequentially follow the planning and implementation of a mission.

Section 1. Mandate Interpretation presents the elements included in MRF mandates and details available modes of interpretation to determine the scope of the mission's activities. This section also addresses the extent and limits of the interpretive power of the practitioners leading the mission, and the importance of transparency in mandate interpretation.

Section 2. Establishing Facts and Applying the Law presents methodological considerations for approaching the interrelated processes of establishing facts, employing a standard of proof, and drawing legal conclusions. This section addresses the array of legal frameworks employed by MRF missions in order to make determinations on allegations of violations of international humanitarian law, international human rights law, international criminal law, and domestic law.

Section 3. Protection of Witnesses and Victims addresses the mission's responsibilities for mitigating risks to witnesses and victims that result from their exposure to the mission. It explains how practitioners can responsibly strike a balance between professional perspectives regarding an MRF mission's protective responsibilities, rooted in the notion that practitioners should *do no harm* to witnesses and victims, and the complex realities of on-the-ground implementation. To this end, this section presents the most favored practices articulated by practitioners, the challenges of implementing those practices, and practical considerations for grappling with these challenges.

Section 4. Public Communication focuses on the level of information that should or can be publicly communicated during the mission. This section presents a framework for a strategic approach to public communication while mitigating unintended negative repercussions for security and/or perceptions of the mission.

Section 5. Report Drafting offers considerations for report drafters regarding the presentation of information about the origins and operations of the mission, the mission's factual and legal findings, and the mission's recommendations. For each of these topics, this section seeks to assist in identifying the outputs to be included in the report, presenting the content, and planning the drafting process.

Part II   Selected Writings on Monitoring, Reporting, and Fact-Finding

The second part of the book supplements the *Handbook* by offering a selection of scholarly analyses of key issues undertaken by individual researchers and practitioners, based primarily on an assessment of the fifteen selected missions but incorporating lessons from other missions as well, when relevant. These chapters draw on the working papers prepared by HPCR, members of the Group of Professionals, and outside experts as part of the research efforts that led to the finalization of the *Handbook*.

Chapter 1. On the Hybrid Nature of Monitoring, Reporting, and Fact-Finding Missions, by Rob Grace, examines tensions and dilemmas that arise from the fact that MRF missions are mandated by political entities but implemented by legal and investigative professionals. As this chapter describes, many methodological issues arise in terms of design and planning from the hybrid political-technical nature of MRF missions.

Chapter 2. Selecting and Applying Legal Lenses in Fact-Finding Work, by Théo Boutruche, offers an assessment of how past missions have approached the process of selecting and applying legal frameworks. Through this analysis, the chapter demonstrates the risks that flawed or unclear legal reasoning and confused legal language can adversely impact an MRF report's credibility.

Chapter 3. Finding the Facts: Standards of Proof and Information Handling in Monitoring, Reporting, and Fact-Finding Missions, by Stephen Wilkinson, focuses on how past missions have grappled with adopting a standard of proof and handling and assessing information in order to draw factual conclusions. The chapter emphasizes the important role that articulating a standard of proof plays in clarifying the level of certainty of a report's findings, and in demonstrating the soundness of the mission's methodological approach to information analysis.

Chapter 4. Protecting Witnesses, Victims, and Staff: Sources and Implications of Professional Responsibilities, by Cynthia Petrigh, provides an in-depth examination of the sources of responsibility to protect witnesses, victims, and staff in the context of MRF missions. The chapter also analyzes the operational difficulties of realizing these responsibilities due to the typically limited capacity of MRF missions to appropriately mitigate security risks, as well as other factors.

Chapter 5. Professional Dilemmas in Public Communication and Report Drafting, by Luc Côté and Rob Grace, focuses on public communication and report drafting. The chapter analyzes both of these issues together as different manifestations of the same methodological question: how to make decisions about what to reveal publicly, and through what means, about an MRF mission's operations, composition, and findings.

Chapter 6. An Analysis of the Impact of Commissions of Inquiry, by Rob Grace, concludes this volume by offering an assessment of the impact of the fifteen selected missions by tracing the outcomes of recommendations offered in these missions' final reports.

Acknowledgments

Finally, I would like to offer my gratitude to my colleagues who made the completion of this book possible. First and foremost, the commitment of the members of the Group of Professionals to this initiative was invaluable to this research. The countless hours that the Group spent deliberating at on-site meetings on draft chapters, editing drafts, and engaging directly in the research greatly enriched the final product. Additionally, I wish to thank Rob Grace of HPCR, who served as the co-editor of this volume, the principal drafter of the *Handbook*, and the lead researcher on the project. I would also like to thank Anaïde Nahikian, Program Associate at HPCR, who provided valuable support on project coordination throughout the duration of the initiative. And last, but certainly not least, I express my deep appreciation and gratitude to the Swiss Federal Department of Foreign Affairs for their generous and continuous support of this research and production of the *Handbook*.

PART I

HPCR Advanced Practitioner's Handbook
on Commissions of Inquiry

I. BACKGROUND

The creation of a monitoring, reporting, and fact-finding (MRF) mission occurs over the course of two phases (see Table 1). The key actors involved in this process are the mandating body (which could be an intergovernmental body, a national government, or an entity such as the United Nations Secretary-General [hereafter the UNSG]) and the mandate holder (which is the MRF body itself, led, in the context of an ad hoc mission, by individuals under the title of "commissioner" or a similar denomination).

IN PHASE 1, a mandating body decides to establish an MRF mechanism for the purpose of gathering information on alleged violations of international humanitarian law (IHL) or international human rights law (IHRL) and grants a mandate that articulates the mission's broad contours. The mandate holder nominates respected individuals to fulfill the mandate.

IN PHASE 2, commissioners collectively interpret the mission's mandate to derive from the text the necessary instructions and guidance for the mandate's implementation.

TABLE 1 THE TWO PHASES OF CREATING AN MRF MISSION			
Phase	**Who**	**Doing what**	**Weighing which considerations**
PHASE 1: Mandate adoption	The mandating authority.	Adopting a mandate after consultations or negotiations.	The explicit aims of the mandate, as well as other interests, including geopolitical and security concerns.
PHASE 2: Mandate interpretation	Commissioners, in some cases in consultation with other practitioners serving on the mission, such as investigative and legal experts.	Adopting an interpretation of the mandate.	The text of the mandate; the object and purpose of the mission; widely accepted principles of professional practice, such as impartiality; and considerations of the mission's capacities (in terms of time frame and resources).

Commissioners typically play no role in drafting the mandate during Phase 1, which is commonly a process of generating political consensus undertaken by the mandating body. Additionally, the mandating body rarely influences the mandate holder's interpretation of the mandate during Phase 2, which is typically seen as a professional or technical process based on the prerogatives of the commissioners.

The independence of the mandate holder from the mandating body is essential. However, the fact that the mandate-drafting process in Phase 1 is led by political actors – rather than MRF professionals – frequently results in numerous challenges during mandate interpretation in Phase 2. For example, though the MRF mandate constitutes a closed text that the mandating body is unlikely to renegotiate, one or more elements of the mission's scope often remain ambiguous. Additionally, a mandate might authorize a broad investigation that is logistically unrealistic given the time and resource constraints of the mission, or a one-sided investigation that risks undermining the mission's credibility.

The overarching aim of mandate interpretation is to ensure that the mission can function properly and with integrity, in terms of both technical feasibility and insulating the implementation of the mandate from politicization, even when operating in a highly charged political climate.

II. PRACTICAL STEPS

The overarching aim of this section is to present a framework for how practitioners can identify the key elements of the mission's mandate. This framework draws not only on past and current professional MRF practices but also on the principles inherent in the common practice of treaty interpretation, by which, as articulated in the Vienna Convention on the Law of Treaties, "A treaty shall be interpreted in good faith in accordance with the ordinary meaning to be given to the terms of the treaty in their context and in the light of its object and purpose."[1]

The framework focuses on identifying the elements of a mission's mandate by asking two key questions.

THE *FIRST* QUESTION IS: What is the context to be examined? Answering this question entails discerning the following elements of the mandate:

Territorial scope ➤	Territorial limits of the investigation
Temporal scope ➤	Period of time under investigation
Nature and scope of incidents ➤	Nature, gravity, and scale of incidents

[1] Vienna Convention on the Law of Treaties, Article 31.1 (1969).

Most mandates make no mention of which parties are allegedly involved in the incidents relevant to the investigation's scope. Therefore, the typical MRF mission faces no issue in following the well-established professional practice that MRF practitioners should undertake comprehensive, impartial investigations. Mandates that do articulate or suggest a restriction on parties to be investigated lead to complications, as will be discussed in Step 4 of the practical steps elaborated below.

THE *SECOND* QUESTION IS: What activities and outputs are expected from the MRF mission? Answering this question entails determining the specific activities that the mission should undertake during implementation and the outputs that the mission should produce.

The practical steps presented below offer practitioners a method for answering these questions.

STEP 1: INTERPRET THE TEXT OF THE MANDATE
Using only the text of the mandate as a literal source of instruction, identify the scope of the investigation, as well as the activities and outputs of the mission.

STEP 2: CONSIDER THE OBJECT AND PURPOSE OF THE MISSION
Consider how the object and purpose of the mission should inform the mandate holder's interpretation of the key elements of the mandate.

STEP 3: IDENTIFY AND CLARIFY ANY GAPS OR AMBIGUITIES IN THE MANDATE
Review each element relevant to the scope of the mission and determine whether the mandate is silent on any of them or whether the mandate uses ambiguous terminology. If necessary, clarify ambiguous terms in the text of the mandate and fill in gaps through logical interpretation, taking into consideration the object and purpose of the mission.

STEP 4: VERIFY THAT THE MANDATE IS TECHNICALLY FEASIBLE AND IMPARTIAL
Ensure that the scope of the mandate is logistically feasible and that each key element of the mandate allows the mission to undertake the investigation in an impartial manner. If the interpretation results in a mission that is unfeasible and/or partial in nature, adjust the mission's mandate interpretation accordingly.

III. EXPLANATION

STEP 1: INTERPRET THE TEXT OF THE MANDATE

This step involves using only the text of the mandate as a literal source of instruction to identify the mandate's elements, which are the context to be examined (including the territorial and temporal scope, and the nature and scope of the relevant incidents), as well as the activities and outputs of the mission.

The operative paragraph of the mandate for the Côte d'Ivoire Commission, adopted by the United Nations Human Rights Council (UNHRC) in 2011, states that the council:

Decides to dispatch an independent, international commission of inquiry, to be appointed by the President of the Human Rights Council, taking into consideration the importance of ensuring the equal participation and full involvement of women, to investigate the facts and circumstances surrounding the allegations of serious abuses and violations of human rights committed in Côte d'Ivoire following the presidential election of 28 November 2010, in order to identify those responsible for such acts and to bring them to justice, and to present its findings to the Council at its seventeenth session, and calls upon all Ivorian parties to cooperate fully with the commission of inquiry.[2]

Assessing the mandate elements based on the information contained in the operative paragraph yields the following results:

Territorial scope ➤	"in Côte d'Ivoire"
Temporal scope ➤	"following the presidential election of 28 November 2010"
Nature and scope of incidents ➤	"serious abuses and violations of human rights"
Activities ➤	➡ "investigate the facts and circumstances"
	➡ "identify those responsible for such acts [i.e., serious abuses and violations of human rights]"
	➡ "present its findings to the Council at its seventeenth session"

---

2 United Nations Human Rights Council resolution 16/25, ¶10.

STEP 2: CONSIDER THE OBJECT AND PURPOSE OF THE MISSION

Commissioners' perceptions of the object and purpose of the mission can be shaped by two factors: (1) the text of the mandate, and (2) the intent of the mandating body, as discerned from other sources, including the overall context in which the mission was created.

Regarding *the text of the mandate*, the document that authorizes the mission sometimes includes language that references the aims of the mission. In such instances, these references can inform commissioners' decisions regarding the scope of the investigation.

> The mandate for the Côte d'Ivoire Commission explicitly mentions only human rights law but also states that a goal of the mission is "to identify those responsible for such acts and to bring them to justice."[3] The reference to "justice" implies the framework of international criminal law (ICL), which the commissioners employed in the mission's final report.[4]

Regarding *the intent of the mandating body*, commissioners can consider public statements made by members of the mandating body, records of the internal deliberations of the mandating body, and the overall context that led to the creation of the MRF mission. The scope of the mission can be informed by both the intent of the mandating authority at the moment of the mandate's adoption and the implied intent in response to shifting on-the-ground conditions.

> During the Libya Commission, when determining the scope of the mission, the commissioners considered not only the intent of the mandating body at the moment of the mandate's adoption but also how the mandating body would wish the mission to respond to developments that would occur after the adoption of the mandate.
>
> Regarding the mandating body's intent *at the moment of the mandate's adoption*, the mission's mandate articulated no temporal

---

[3] Ibid.

[4] See generally "Rapport de la Commission d'enquête internationale indépendante sur la Côte d'Ivoire," A/HRC/17/48, July 1, 2011, accessed June 14, 2015, http://www.refworld.org/docid/4ee05cdf2.html.

scope. However, the commissioners decided to focus on events related to the uprising that began in February 2011, one reason being that the commissioners perceived these incidents to constitute the mandate's implicit focus.

Regarding the mission's *response to shifting on-the-ground conditions*, the mission had to decide how the scope of the mission would be affected by the armed conflict that developed in Libya after the UNHRC adopted the mission's mandate. Specifically, the mandate specifies only "international human rights law" and does not mention IHL.

However, the commissioners concluded that examining IHL violations was consistent with the mandate and believed that if the council could have foreseen that an armed conflict would emerge, the council would have wanted the commissioners to gather information about IHL violations committed by all relevant parties. During subsequent council debates about the mission's report, no states raised objections to the use of IHL, and the June 2011 resolution that extended the mission's mandate also did not object, confirming for the commissioners that the mission had correctly gauged the council's expectations of how the mission should respond to the evolving situation.[5]

STEP 3: IDENTIFY AND CLARIFY ANY GAPS OR AMBIGUITIES IN THE MANDATE

This step first entails reviewing each element relevant to the scope of the mission and asking: Is the mandate silent about this element? Or does the mandate use ambiguous terminology that requires greater definitional specificity?

Once the mission has identified a gap or ambiguity in the mandate, it must fill in this gap or clarify the ambiguity through logical interpretation. Table 2 offers examples from past practice of missions that operated under mandates that either: (1) were silent about a certain scope element, or (2) mentioned a certain scope element in a manner that was interpreted to be ambiguous.

---

[5] For information on the commissioners' interpretation of the mandate for the Libya Commission, see Rob Grace, "The Design and Planning of Monitoring, Reporting, and Fact-Finding Missions" (working paper, Program on Humanitarian Policy and Conflict Research at Harvard University, December 2013), pp. 14–15, http://papers.ssrn.com/sol3/papers.cfm?abstract_id=2365435.

TABLE 2 CLARIFYING AMBIGUOUS MANDATES	
Scenario	**Example**
Mandate is silent about a certain element: temporal scope.	The mandate for the Darfur Commission authorized the mission "to investigate reports of violations of international humanitarian law and human rights law" but articulated no temporal scope.[6] However, the mission gleaned temporal cues from the mandate's authorization to investigate "reports of violations." The members considered when the "reports of violations" began to emerge and used this date – February 2003 – as the beginning of the mission's temporal focus.[7]
Mandate mentions temporal scope but remains ambiguous.	The mandate for the *Sri Lanka Panel* states that the mission should focus on "the final stages of the war."[8] With this provision, the mandate articulates a temporal limitation but relegates to the panel the process of logically deducing which specific dates constitute "the final stages of the war." As the panel's report states: The Panel focused on the period from September 2008 through May 2009, which encompasses the most intense and violent phase of the war during which many of the most serious violations of international law are alleged to have taken place. September 2008 corresponds to the beginning of the Government's final military offensive on the LTTE [Liberation Tigers of Tamil Eelam] de facto capital of Kilinochchi. It also coincides with the end of international observation of the war due to the Government's declaration that it could no longer ensure the security of international staff working for international organizations in the Vanni. May 2009 corresponds to the end of the fighting and the military defeat of the LTTE.[9]

STEP 4: VERIFY THAT THE MANDATE IS TECHNICALLY FEASIBLE AND IMPARTIAL

This final step entails reviewing the key elements of the mandate to ensure: (1) that the scope of the mission is technically feasible, and (2) that the investigation can be undertaken with impartiality.

In terms of *technical feasibility*, mandates sometimes can be interpreted as requesting that the mission achieve results or conduct activities that are technically impractical. Specifically, overly broad mandates cannot be fully implemented due to resource and time constraints faced by the mission. In such cases, commissioners must – keeping in mind the mission's object and purpose, as well as the limitations

---

[6] United Nations Security Council resolution 1564 (2004).

[7] Rob Grace, "Design and Planning," 21.

[8] "Report of the Secretary-General's Panel of Experts on Accountability in Sri Lanka," March 31, 2011, p. 2, accessed June 14, 2015, http://www.un.org/News/dh/infocus/Sri_Lanka/POE_Report_Full.pdf.

[9] Ibid., 4.

and obstacles facing the mission – calibrate the scope of the mission's activities with the resources available to the MRF body.

> The mandate for the Darfur Commission authorized the mission "to investigate reports of violations of international humanitarian law and human rights law in Darfur by all parties, to determine also whether or not acts of genocide have occurred, and to identify the perpetrators of such violations with a view to ensuring that those responsible are held accountable."[10]
>
> However, the commissioners did not perceive that the commission had the capacity to gather information about all of the incidents within the mandate's scope. Instead, the report states:
>
>> It was not possible for the Commission to investigate all of the many hundreds of individually documented incidents reported by other sources. The Commission, therefore, selected incidents and areas that were most representative of acts, trends and patterns relevant to the determination of violations of international human rights and humanitarian law and with greater possibilities of effective fact-finding. In making this selection, access to the sites of incidents, protection of witnesses and the potential for gathering the necessary evidence were, amongst others, of major consideration.[11]
>
> Regarding the genocide issue, the mission similarly deemed this question to fall beyond the mission's capacities. The mission concluded that Sudanese governmental policy lacked genocidal intent, and the mission's report did not "rule out the possibility that in some instances *single individuals*, including Government officials, may entertain a genocidal intent."[12] However, the mission declined to identify perpetrators, noting that "it would be for a competent court to make such a determination on a case by case basis."[13]

In terms of *impartiality*, the consensus-building process by which a mandating body adopts a mandate is political in nature (see Background portion of this section). While most resulting mandates allow for credible, impartial investigations, some may become politicized during the mandate design process.

---

[10] United Nations Security Council resolution 1564 (2004).

[11] "Report of the International Commission of Inquiry on Darfur to the United Nations Secretary-General," January 25, 2005, p. 61, accessed June 14, 2015, http://www.un.org/news/dh/sudan/com_inq_darfur.pdf.

[12] Ibid., 132.

[13] Ibid.

One manifestation of this politicization is the adoption of one-sided mandates, which articulate or suggest restrictions on which entities the mission may investigate. However, other aspects of the mandate might also raise questions about a mission's impartiality. For example, a restrictive temporal scope that includes violations committed by only one side of the conflict – as opposed to a more expansive temporal scope that would include violations committed by all sides to a conflict – could lead to a perception that the investigation is one-sided.

> The United Nations Secretary-General's Investigative Team in the Democratic Republic of the Congo (DRC) was originally mandated to gather information about incidents that had occurred since 1996. However, as the mission's final report states, the government of the DRC:
>
> > urged that the mandate be extended back to 1 March 1993, in order to include: the ethnic violence which, from that time, pitted self-styled "indigenous" Zairians, originally supported by the Forces Armées Zaïroises (FAZ), against Zairians of both Hutu and Tutsi origin, as well as subsequent developments, such as the influx of Hutu refugees from Rwanda in July 1994, following the genocide in that country; the insecurity generated, both in Zaire and in Rwanda, by armed members of the ex-Forces Armées Rwandaises (ex-FAR) and Interahamwe militia who maintained strict control over the refugees and launched raids into Rwanda; and the increasing violence to which Zairian Tutsis were subjected until the October 1996 uprising.[14]
>
> In response to the government's concerns that the original temporal scope would not allow for a thorough investigation, the UNSG extended the scope to encompass incidents that had occurred since 1993.

If any of the elements of the mandate might hinder the impartiality – real or perceived – of the investigation, the commissioners should adopt a mode of interpretation that allows the mission to correct any of the mandate's implicit or explicit biases.

Avenues available to practitioners operating under potentially one-sided mandates include: (1) seeking authorization from the mandating body to surpass restrictions on whom the mission may investigate, (2) justifying the examination of the actions of all parties by noting the necessity of doing so in order to make a proper determination about whether violations of IHL or IHRL have been committed, and (3) citing a

---

[14] "Report of the Secretary-General's Investigative Team charged with investigating serious violations of human rights and international humanitarian law in the Democratic Republic of the Congo," S/1998//581, June 29, 1998, p. 1, accessed June 1, 2015, http://ap.ohchr.org/documents/alldocs.aspx?doc_id=8840.

mandate provision that supports a balanced interpretation. See Table 3 for examples of responses to UNHRC mandates that focused on the conduct of Israel.

TABLE 3 ADDRESSING ONE-SIDED MANDATES	
Mode of Interpretation	**Example**
Seek authorization from the mandating body.	The original mandate adopted by the UNHRC for the Gaza Fact-Finding Mission focused investigative attention only on Israel. However, Justice Richard Goldstone, when approached to lead the mission, struck an agreement with the president of the council on a revised mandate that authorized the mission "to investigate all violations of international human rights law and international humanitarian law that might have been committed" relevant to the conflict.[15]
Refer to the necessity of examining all parties to make determinations about IHL or IHRL violations.	The Lebanon Commission was mandated, among other measures, "[t]o investigate the systematic targeting and killings of civilians by Israel in Lebanon."[16] The mission accepted that the mandate authorized an investigation only of the legality of Israel's – and not Hezbollah's – actions. However, the mission did gather the information about Hezbollah necessary to draw conclusions about potential Israeli IHL violations.[17] Indeed, the mission's report discusses factual findings about Hezbollah's conduct during the armed conflict.[18]
Cite a mandate provision that justifies a balanced interpretation.	The mandate of the *Beit Hanoun Fact-Finding Mission* focused solely on investigating the effects of incidents perpetrated by Israel.[19] However, the UNHRC resolution that includes the mission's mandate also "[u]rges all concerned parties to respect the rules of international humanitarian law, to refrain from violence against the civilian population and to treat under all circumstances all detained combatants and civilians in accordance with the Geneva Conventions of 12 August 1949."[20] Using the reference in this provision to "all parties" as a justification, the mission's report draws legal conclusions about the conduct not only of Israel but also of Hamas.[21]

15 "Report of the United Nations Fact-Finding Mission on the Gaza Conflict," A/HRC/12/48, September 25, 2009, p. 13, accessed June 14, 2015, www2.ohchr.org/english/bodies/hrcouncil/docs/12session/A-HRC-12-48.pdf.

16 United Nations Human Rights Council resolution S-2/1, "The grave situation of human rights in Lebanon caused by Israeli military operations," April 11, 2006, accessed June 1, 2015, www.refworld.org/docid/47bae9cd2.html.

17 See "Report of the Commission of Inquiry on Lebanon pursuant to Human Rights Council Resolution S-2/1," A/HRC/3/2, November 23, 2006, p. 3, accessed June 14, 2015, www.unrol.org/files/A.HRC.3.2.pdf, which states, "The Commission considers that any independent, impartial and objective investigation into a particular conduct during the course of hostilities must of necessity be with reference to all the belligerents involved. Thus an inquiry into the conformity with international humanitarian law of the specific acts of the Israel Defense Forces (IDF) in Lebanon requires that account also be taken of the conduct of the opponent."

18 For example, see ibid., 6, which discusses whether Hezbollah used "human shields."

19 United Nations Human Rights Council resolution S-3/1.

20 Ibid.

21 See "Report of the high-level fact-finding mission to Beit Hanoun established under Council resolution S-3/1," A/HRC/9/26, September 1, 2008, p. 6, accessed June 14, 2015, www.refworld.org/docid/48cfa3a22.html.

IV. FINAL OBSERVATIONS

The practical steps presented in this section offer MRF practitioners a framework for approaching the mandate interpretation process in a systematic manner. These steps aim to orient practitioners toward delineating, in technically feasible terms and in a manner that is impartial in nature, the scope of an MRF mission's investigation and activities.

Certain mandates may prove particularly challenging to navigate, in terms of designing a credible, comprehensive investigation. In particular, for mandates that, in terms of the literal text, are one-sided or otherwise biased, the mission is unlikely to avoid criticisms. Adhering to the mandate's literal interpretation will evoke criticisms that the mission is not evenhanded. Surpassing the mandate's limitations in an effort to obtain impartiality might not only fail to assuage these critics but also might bring forth criticisms that the mission has overstepped the boundaries of the mission's mandated authority.

Articulating in precise terms – in particular, in the mission's final report – the considerations that underpin the mission's mandate interpretation will assist efforts to present the mission as a credible exercise. By elaborating how the mission assessed the literal text of the mandate, defined the object and purpose of the mission, clarified gaps or ambiguities in the mandate, and ensured the technical feasibility and impartiality of the mission, commissioners can address uncertainties about how the mission derived its authority from the text received from the mandating body.

SECTION TWO
Establishing Facts and Applying the Law

I. BACKGROUND

The core task of MRF missions is to gather information to determine whether violations of international law have occurred. Before the initiation of fieldwork, preparing a preliminary desk analysis of information already available is an important step to help the mission prepare for its own data-gathering effort. This review entails collating and reviewing existing reports of events potentially relevant to the mission's mandate in order to identify the main incidents, actors, and locations and to establish a chronology of events. The analysis is a tool that informs the process of setting priorities and preparing an investigation plan.[1]

After this initial desk analysis, MRF practitioners implement a plan to gather firsthand information. There are commonly three main categories of evidence: testimonial, documentary, and physical. Specific types of sources that investigators can consider include witness testimony, physical evidence, documents, video material, photographs, personal observation of locations where incidents occurred, and satellite images. MRF practitioners tend to rely heavily on witness testimonies to establish facts. In practice, this task of collecting information has included conducting field visits to the territory in which the armed conflict or internal disturbance occurred or to another location where interviewees reside or can be invited for an interview, as well as remote engagement with interviewees (e.g., via Skype).[2] The mission reviews and analyzes the information gathered on an ongoing basis. This analysis informs subsequent stages of the data-gathering effort.

The processes of gathering information and drawing legal conclusions are interrelated. The mission's decisions about planning the investigation, selecting

---

[1] See Office of the High Commissioner for Human Rights, "Commissions of Inquiry and Fact-Finding Missions on International Human Rights and Humanitarian Law: Guidance and Practice," Office of the High Commissioner for Human Rights, 2015, pp. 38–39, accessed on May 26, 2015, http://www.ohchr.org/Documents/Publications/Col_Guidance_and_Practice.pdf.

[2] Additionally, when engaging with witnesses and victims, MRF practitioners grapple with issues of protection. For information about this issue, see Section 3, Protection of Witnesses and Victims in this Handbook.

legal frameworks, and adopting a standard of proof all inform one another and cannot be conducted in isolation. While the credibility of an MRF mission is commonly assessed with regard to the methodology used to establish facts, the legal interpretation and classification of the mission's factual findings are equally important and similarly require a rigorous and sound approach.

The interplay between the facts and the relevant legal norms allegedly violated is essential. The mission's analysis of the information gathered elucidates what additional pieces of information will be necessary to demonstrate that a violation of international law has occurred. Also, the data-gathering process is shaped by the relevant legal frameworks and the mission's standard of proof. For example, establishing whether an attacker adhered to IHL precautionary obligations requires collecting factual information related to the military or humanitarian factors that help determine what measures were practically possible at the time prior to the attack. In this sense, the norms themselves determine the type of factual information needed.

The soundness of the mission's methodology and the transparency with which the mission communicates the methodology adopted are crucial for the credibility of the mission. Given the delicate political environment in which MRF missions typically operate, as well as the sensitive nature of levying allegations of violations of international law, MRF missions often face criticisms relating to the manner in which the mission draws conclusions about controversial or sensitive issues. Missteps or ambiguities about the mission's information-gathering process or rationales underlying the report's interpretation of the law and legal conclusions feed such criticisms.

To inform how practitioners can approach these aspects of an MRF mission's methodology, this section focuses on the interplay between the facts, the law, and the standard of proof adopted by the mission.

II. PRACTICAL STEPS

The purpose of this section is to help practitioners proceed with establishing a clear methodology in terms of applying legal frameworks to the facts found by the mission. To this end, this section offers the following practical steps for the mission to consider when approaching this issue.

STEP 1: SELECT RELEVANT LEGAL FRAMEWORKS

To select which legal frameworks are relevant to the mission, answer the following two questions: What legal frameworks does the mandate specifically articulate or imply? What legal frameworks are relevant based on the facts established by the mission?

STEP 2: ADOPT A STANDARD OF PROOF

Decide the level of certainty that the mission will require in order to draw conclusions about its findings, bearing in mind that it lacks the mandate and resources to achieve the "beyond a reasonable doubt" or "intimate conviction" standard used by many criminal courts and tribunals.

STEP 3: LEGAL CLASSIFICATION OF FACTS

Apply legal frameworks to facts, considering the mission's standard of proof and the need to ensure the clarity of the mission's application of the law.

III. EXPLANATION

STEP 1: SELECT RELEVANT LEGAL FRAMEWORKS

An MRF mission must adopt a sound and rigorous approach to determining which legal frameworks are applicable in the context at hand. Nonetheless, disagreements, often politically charged in nature, sometimes arise on this issue.

The report of the UNSG Flotilla Panel mentions that, for the Gaza flotilla incident, which was the context of the panel's mandate, the determination of applicable legal frameworks was as controversial as conclusions about factual findings. When discussing the assertions of national investigative commissions mandated in Israel and Turkey, the panel's report states that the reports of these two national commissions "differ as widely on the applicable law as they do on what actually happened."[3]

---

[3] "Report of the Secretary-General's Panel of Inquiry on the 31 May 2010 Flotilla Incident," September 2011, p. 9, accessed June 14, 2015, http://www.un.org/News/dh/infocus/middle_east/Gaza_Flotilla_Panel_Report.pdf.

MRF reports commonly rely on the following bodies of law:

(a) IHL (including treaty law, such as the Geneva Conventions of 1949 and the Additional Protocols of 1977, and customary international humanitarian law), in contexts that reach the level of armed conflict, whether international or non-international in character;

(b) IHRL (e.g., international human rights treaties; regional human rights instruments; customary law; and soft law instruments that clarify the content of human rights law, such as United Nations General Assembly resolutions);

(c) ICL (e.g., the Statute of the International Criminal Court [ICC], interpreted and applied in jurisprudence of international criminal courts and tribunals, as well as customary international law); and

(d) Domestic law (in particular, domestic statutes relevant to the actors involved in the incidents examined by the mission).

Additionally, some MRF reports have also incorporated other relevant branches of public international law, such as *jus ad bellum* law and maritime law, as part of the mission's mandate to address specific allegations. MRF practitioners have also relied on other bodies of law – such as the law on state responsibility for wrongful acts and the law of treaties, notably the principles of treaty interpretation – in order to reach legal conclusions.

This section first presents the particularities and challenges inherent in the four legal frameworks listed above, in order to frame the method of undertaking Step 1, which will subsequently be elaborated.

A. DESCRIPTION OF LEGAL FRAMEWORKS

1 International Humanitarian Law

IHL is applicable in times of armed conflict – both international, including situations of occupation, and non-international – between states, between governmental armed forces and organized armed groups, or among different armed groups within a state or across international borders.

Determining the existence of an armed conflict and classifying a conflict as international, non-international, or a situation of occupation can itself be challenging. Such determinations should be based on facts and the established legal definition of an armed conflict or of occupation. However, there can be overlapping armed conflicts. Additionally, the threshold of a non-international armed conflict, as opposed to an internal disturbance, is often difficult to discern definitively.

> The report of the DRC Mapping Exercise discusses the challenges inherent in legally classifying complex and evolving situations of large-scale violence. The report states:
>
> > It is difficult to classify all of the various armed conflicts that affected the DRC all over its territory between 1993 and 2003. Depending on the time and place, the DRC experienced internal and international armed conflicts and internal conflicts that subsequently became international.[4]

2 International Human Rights Law

IHRL regulates the behavior of states vis-à-vis the people under their jurisdiction. A trend is also emerging regarding the recognition of human rights obligations for non-state armed groups under certain conditions, an issue that this section examines in greater detail in the context of Step 3.

A consensus exists that IHRL continues to apply during armed conflicts, except in cases of derogation under specific conditions as provided in the law. However, the interaction between IHL and IHRL has given rise to much debate. One widely accepted viewpoint conceives IHL as the *lex specialis* compared to IHRL during an armed conflict in cases of a conflict of norms between the two. In such instances, IHL – the more specialized, or specific, body of law in the context of an armed conflict – overrides IHRL. Or, IHRL may constitute the *lex specialis* compared to IHL on particular issues for which it is more specific than IHL. For example, regarding the grounds to detain someone in a non-international armed conflict, IHL is more general compared to IHRL. In other cases, no reconciliation is required because IHL and IHRL are compatible.

Different MRF reports have articulated the nature of the co-applicability between these two bodies of law in various ways.

---

[4] "Report of the Mapping Exercise Documenting the Most Serious Violations of Human Rights and International Humanitarian Law Committed within the Territory of the Democratic Republic of the Congo between March 1993 and June 2003," Office of the High Commissioner for Human Rights, August 2010, p. 262, accessed June 14, 2015, http://www.refworld.org/docid/4ca99bc22.html.

The following passages from MRF reports exhibit various ways of articulating the relationship between IHL and IHRL during armed conflict:

- "With an armed conflict having developed in late February in Libya and continuing during the Commission's operations, the Commission looked into both violations of international human rights law and relevant provisions of international humanitarian law, the *lex specialis* which applies during armed conflict." (Libya Commission, first report)[5]

- "It is now widely accepted that human rights treaties continue to apply in situations of armed conflict .... It is today commonly understood that human rights law would continue to apply as long as it is not modified or set aside by IHL. In any case, the general rule of human rights law does not lose its effectiveness and will remain in the background to inform the application and interpretation of the relevant humanitarian law rule." (Gaza Fact-Finding Mission)[6]

- "While the conduct of armed conflict and military occupation is governed by international humanitarian law, human rights law is applicable at all times, including during states of emergency or armed conflict. The two bodies of law complement and reinforce one another." (Lebanon Commission)[7]

3 International Criminal Law

ICL provides substantive definitions of the acts or omissions that can be qualified as international crimes – such as war crimes, crimes against humanity, and genocide – and also deals with individual criminal responsibility.

In some instances, an MRF mandate, or commissioners on a particular mission, will opt to reference ICL, especially the material elements of international crimes contained in international treaties, such as the Rome Statute, or the jurisprudence of international tribunals. However, it is important to note that an MRF mission lacks the mandate and resources of a court of law. It should be cautious about the types of conclusions and determinations that can be drawn in its report. Most MRF reports highlight the fact that the mission does not act as a judicial body and that,

---

[5] "Report of the International Commission of Inquiry to Investigate all Alleged Violations of International Human Rights Law in the Libyan Arab Jamahiriya," June 1, 2011, p. 14, accessed May 26, 2015, http://www2.ohchr.org/english/bodies/hrcouncil/docs/17session/A.HRC.17.44_AUV.pdf (internal citation omitted).

[6] Gaza Fact-Finding Mission report, 78.

[7] Lebanon Commission report, 24 (internal citation omitted).

therefore, a competent court would have to make its own determination based on the specific level of evidence required under criminal law.

4 Domestic Law

The choice to rely on relevant domestic legal frameworks in MRF reports has been driven by the principle that domestic courts bear the primary responsibility for accountability for international crimes.

However, when deciding whether to incorporate domestic law, MRF practitioners should consider whether international law has been sufficiently incorporated into domestic law and whether the domestic court system – both in terms of resources and political will – is capable of implementing international legal principles effectively.

> The *Timor-Leste Commission* was authorized:
>
> > To recommend measures to ensure accountability for crimes and serious violations of human rights allegedly committed during the above-mentioned period, taking into account that the Government of Timor-Leste considers that the domestic justice system, which has the participation of international judges, prosecutors and defence lawyers, should be the primary avenue of accountability for these alleged crimes and violations.[8]
>
> The commission concluded that "measures are needed to strengthen the ability of the domestic system to handle high-profile cases involving political actors in a manner that will be considered credible by the population," but that "the crimes under consideration contravene domestic law" so "should be handled within the domestic judicial sector."[9]

B. METHOD FOR DETERMINING WHICH LEGAL FRAMEWORKS ARE APPLICABLE

The task of MRF practitioners, when determining which legal frameworks are relevant, is to examine the applicability of international norms to the situation under consideration based on facts and previous interpretations of those norms.

---

[8] "Report of the United Nations Independent Special Commission of Inquiry for Timor-Leste," October 2006, p. 11, accessed June 14, 2015, http://www.ohchr.org/Documents/Countries/COITimorLeste.pdf.

[9] Ibid., 65.

In this process, the mission should weigh two considerations: (1) the mandate, and (2) the facts.

In terms of *the mandate*, the mission should answer two questions.

THE *FIRST* QUESTION IS: Which legal frameworks does the mandate specifically mention? Answering this question is the most straightforward portion of determining the legal frameworks applicable to the mission. Most mandates make explicit reference to certain bodies of law.

> The mandate for the *DRC Mapping Exercise* tasks the mission to examine "the most serious violations of human rights and international humanitarian law committed within the territory of the Democratic Republic of the Congo between March 1993 and June 2003."[10] Per this mandate, the mission had clear authorization to examine violations of IHRL and IHL.

THE *SECOND* QUESTION IS: Which legal frameworks does the mandate imply? Elements of the mandate's scope may be interpreted to imply a particular legal framework that was not necessarily intended by the drafters of the mandate but is essential to address alleged violations or disputed facts.

> The mandate for the *Georgia Fact-Finding Mission* authorizes the mission "to investigate the origins and the course of the conflict in Georgia, including with regard to international law, humanitarian law and human rights, and the accusations made in that context."[11] While the mandate explicitly mentions IHRL and IHL, the mission interpreted the mandate's reference to the "origins" of the conflict to imply also the application of *jus ad bellum* law, including the United Nations Charter and other laws regulating the resort to armed action by states.

In many situations, *the facts* inform commissioners' decisions about the relevancy of different legal frameworks. Therefore, the facts play a key role in selecting applicable legal frameworks, as well as specific norms within those frameworks.

---

[10] DRC Mapping Exercise report, 542.

[11] "Council Decision 2008/901/CFSP of 2 December 2008 concerning an independent international fact-finding mission on the conflict in Georgia," Council of the European Union, Article 1.2, accessed June 1, 2015, http://www.refworld.org/docid/4ac45cd22.html (internal citations omitted).

The mandate for the *Kyrgyzstan Commission* makes no reference to specific legal frameworks but rather calls on the mission to determine which bodies of law are relevant based on the facts found. Specifically, the mandate states that the mission should "[i]nvestigate the facts and circumstances" and "[q]ualify the violations and the crimes under international law."[12]

STEP 2: ADOPT A STANDARD OF PROOF

It is important for MRF missions to analyze information systematically. A key component of this analysis is the adoption of a standard of proof. Clarifying the level of certainty of the mission's findings in this regard is essential to the credibility of a mission's final report. Also, articulating the mission's standard of proof distinguishes the report's conclusions from those of a formal judicial process.

The standards commonly referred to by MRF missions are reasonable suspicion, reasonable grounds to believe, and balance of probabilities. In actual MRF practice, however, practitioners tend to use different standards of proof interchangeably. For example, though one mission uses "reasonable grounds to believe" while another mission uses "balance of probabilities," the two standards of proof may actually be indistinguishable, even though each standard of proof has its own specific, theoretical definition. "Reasonable suspicion" has been defined as "necessitating a reliable body of material consistent with other verified circumstances tending to show that an incident or event did happen."[13] "Reasonable grounds to believe" has been defined to mean that the information gathered "would justify a reasonable or ordinarily prudent man to believe that a suspect has committed a crime" and "raise a clear suspicion of the suspect being guilty of a crime."[14] This standard does not require that one "has double checked every possible piece of evidence, or investigated the crime personally, or instituted an enquiry into any special matter," and the evidence "need not be overly convincing or conclusive; it should be adequate or satisfactory to warrant the belief that the suspect has committed the crime."[15] "Balance of probabilities" refers to an assessment that a fact is more likely than not to be true.[16]

When approaching the issue of ascribing individual criminal responsibility, the standard practice of MRF missions is to employ particular caution. MRF practitioners do not

---

12 "Report of the Independent International Commission of Inquiry into the Events in Southern Kyrgyzstan in June 2010," n.d., p. xiv, accessed May 26, 2015, http://reliefweb.int/sites/reliefweb.int/files/resources/Full_Report_490.pdf.

13 DRC Mapping Exercise report, 4–5 (internal citation omitted).

14 Judge R. Sidhwa of the International Criminal Tribunal for the former Yugoslavia, quoted in Darfur Commission report, 12.

15 Ibid.

16 Stephen Wilkinson, "Standards of Proof in International Humanitarian and Human Rights Fact-Finding and Inquiry Missions," Geneva Academy of International Law and Human Rights, n.d., p. 49, accessed June 1, 2015, http://www.geneva-academy.ch/docs/reports/Standards%20of%20proo2f.pdf.

publicly identify alleged perpetrators out of concerns for due process for the accused (see also Section 5, Report Drafting in this Handbook). Table 4 indicates different ways that MRF reports have approached articulating the mission's standard of proof.

TABLE 4 ARTICULATING THE MISSION'S STANDARD OF PROOF		
Method	Implications	Example
Articulate a specific overarching standard of proof.	Presents a clear perspective on the level of certainty of the mission's findings.	The Timor-Leste Commission report states that "the Commission concluded that the most appropriate standard was that of reasonable suspicion. This would necessitate a reliable body of material consistent with other verified circumstances tending to show that a person may reasonably be suspected of involvement in the commission of a crime. Obviously the Commission would not make final judgements as to criminal guilt. It would make an assessment of possible suspects in preparation for future investigations and possible indictments by a prosecutor."[17]
Refer to an ad hoc standard that does not correlate to a formalized notion of standards of proof.	Conveys the ad hoc, mission-specific method by which some practitioners handle standards of proof but leaves the level of certainty of the mission's findings unclear.	The UNHRC Flotilla Fact-Finding report articulates no explicit standard of proof but states, "The Mission found the facts set out below to have been established to its satisfaction."[18]
Specify that the report's findings do not constitute a substitution for a formal judicial proceeding but make no reference to the mission's standard of proof.	Risks leaving the impression that the mission did not consider issues of standards of proof and did not apply a systematic methodology for assessing the information gathered by the mission.	The Georgia Fact-Finding Mission report makes no mention of the overarching level of certainty of the findings articulated in the report. However, the report states, "In summary, it should be noted that the factual basis thus established may be considered as adequate for the purpose of fact-finding, but not for any other purpose. This includes judicial proceedings such as the cases already pending before International Courts as well as any others."[19]

[17] Timor-Leste Commission report, 14.

[18] "Report of the International Fact-Finding Mission to Investigate Violations of International Law, Including International Humanitarian and Human Rights Law, Resulting from the Israeli Attacks on the Flotilla of Ships Carrying Humanitarian Assistance," September 27, 2010, p. 18, accessed May 26, 2015, http://www2.ohchr.org/english/bodies/hrcouncil/docs/15session/A.HRC.15.21_en.pdf.

[19] "Independent International Fact-Finding Mission on the Conflict in Georgia Report," vol. 1 (September 2009), 8.

If the Findings Fall Short of the Standard of Proof. For certain incidents under investigation, an MRF mission might be unable to corroborate adequately the information gathered. In such instances, the report should indicate that, since the mission was unable to obtain the necessary pieces of evidence, the mission was not able to draw a factual conclusion.

> Various MRF reports have indicated that the mission was not able to reach the standard of proof adopted in order to draw conclusions about certain incidents, as indicated by the below passages (emphases added):
>
> - "However, *the available evidence is not sufficient to conclude* that the death resulted from an excessive use of force." (Bahrain Commission, para. 954)
>
> - "It considers that there have been attacks on humanitarian units, though it is *not able to establish* whether intentional or not without further information." (Libya Commission, first report, para. 180)
>
> - "While the KIC [Kyrgyzstan Inquiry Commission] is *not in a position to make any conclusion* about the exact nature of that device nor its source, *its limited analysis supports the view* that at least some of the burning was at a high intensity and unlikely to have been caused by a Molotov cocktail." (Kyrgyzstan Commission, para. 260)
>
> - "The Commission is *not in a position at this stage to assess* the veracity of the information received." (Libya Commission, first report, para. 235)
>
> - "But we are *unable to conclude* whether this included live fire during the initial stages of the boarding attempt." (UNSG Flotilla Panel, para. 121)
>
> - "The Commission is *unable to conclude, barring additional explanation,* whether these strikes are consistent with NATO's [North Atlantic Treaty Organization] objective to avoid civilian casualties entirely, or whether NATO took all necessary precautions to that effect." (Libya Commission, second report, para. 89)
>
> - "The key questions on the existence within these militias of a clear command structure and their capacity to carry out real military operations *would need to be examined in more detail.*" (DRC Mapping Exercise, para. 476)
>
> - "The Commission received information about other cases of forced disappearance *which could not be verified.*" (Guinea Commission, para. 86)

One area that is emblematic of the challenges of gathering information about certain violations is sexual and gender-based violence (SGBV).[20] The following factors contribute to this difficulty:

- Families, if they are aware that a family member has suffered from SGBV, sometimes "hide" these victims; and
- Victims are frequently reluctant to provide information to MRF investigators, or do not agree to engage with an MRF mission, due to the stigma surrounding this type of violence, as well as the pressure that sometimes exists – from family members, for example – for the victim to seek financial compensation from, or even to marry, the perpetrator.

These challenges should not discourage MRF practitioners from investigating such violations. In some instances, practitioners are convinced that certain incidents have happened, based on a small number of interviews and on information otherwise available (such as previously produced human rights reports), but fall short of reaching the standard of proof adopted by the mission. In such instances, MRF missions have chosen to report the violations and to explain why the mission was unable to reach the standard of proof adopted for the report. By doing so, MRF missions bear in mind and draw attention to the cultural and psychological obstacles that often hinder information gathering about whether or not acts of SGBV have occurred.

The *Libya Commission* received unverified allegations of SGBV. However, when assessing the credibility of these allegations, the mission considered the many difficulties that arise when gathering information about such incidents. The report states:

> The number of cases reported was small. However, the Commission recognizes the difficulties in collecting evidence in cases of sexual violence, including a victim's reluctance to disclose information due to the trauma, shame and stigma linked to reports of sexual assault. In Libya, the fact that Libyan criminal law punishes by flogging sexual relations outside a lawful marriage also increases the reluctance of victims to report sexual violence. These factors thus need to be taken into account in evaluating the information received.[21]

---

[20] For a recent articulation of standards and best practices in this area, see generally "International Protocol on the Documentation and Investigation of Sexual Violence in Conflict: Basic Standards of Best Practice on the Documentation of Sexual Violence as a Crime under International Law," June 2014, accessed June 1, 2015, https://www.gov.uk/government/uploads/system/uploads/attachment_data/file/319054/PSVI_protocol_web.pdf.

[21] First Libya Commission report, 71–72 (internal citations omitted).

If the Findings Exceed the Standard of Proof. When practitioners have corroborated information to an extent that exceeds the mission's standard of proof, practitioners have calibrated the report's vocabulary to reflect the mission's high level of certainty.

Examples of passages from MRF reports that use vocabulary to express a high level of certainty appear below (emphases added):

- "The attacks on the Kasaian civilian population *were quite clearly* widespread and systematic." (DRC Mapping Exercise, para. 493)

- "This *could not have happened without* the knowledge of higher echelons of the command structure of the MoI [Ministry of Interior] and NSA [National Security Agency]." (Bahrain Commission, para. 1179)

- "These accounts were *so consistent and vivid as to be beyond question.*" (UNHRC Flotilla Fact-Finding Mission, para. 202)

- "The events of 28 September 2009 *strongly suggest* coordinated action by the red berets, the Thégboro gendarmes, the militia and, to some extent, the gendarmerie and the police." (Guinea Commission, para. 192)

STEP 3: LEGAL CLASSIFICATION OF FACTS

This step entails the classification of facts, bearing in mind the legal framework(s) identified in Step 1 and the standard of proof selected in Step 2. Regarding the application of legal frameworks to facts, certain key areas are emblematic of the challenges recurrently faced by practitioners in the domain of MRF. Some relate to difficulties in applying certain legal concepts and rules to facts. Others, due to the contested nature or content of certain norms in unsettled areas of international law, exacerbate the complexity of classifying facts. Five of these issues – all of which have challenged practitioners on recent missions and which are critical in terms of an MRF mission's credibility – are discussed below.

A. CO-APPLICABILITY OF INTERNATIONAL HUMANITARIAN LAW AND INTERNATIONAL HUMAN RIGHTS LAW

Although, as mentioned in Step 1, MRF missions have consistently embraced the notion of IHRL-IHL co-applicability, some have either devoted insufficient attention to the actual implications of this dual applicability or have articulated confused rationales when classifying violations.

While MRF practitioners cannot be expected to clarify all unsettled aspects of the complex interaction between IHRL and IHL, they should be mindful of the implications of co-applicability for the sake of their own legal determinations. A rigorous and nuanced approach is needed to avoid legal confusion.

One example is the prohibition of arbitrary deprivation of liberty (detention) in the context of a non-international armed conflict. Because relevant IHL norms do not articulate the grounds for detention and related procedures, IHRL could be applicable as the *lex specialis*. (See Step 1, Part A.2 of this section for more information about *lex specialis*.) Given the detailed and strict conditions under IHRL related to detention in this context, an MRF mission could conclude that a violation was committed under IHRL but would have to properly justify the IHRL basis for the conclusion.

Table 5 presents common issues, examples of passages from past reports that exemplify these issues, descriptions of how these passages fall short of accurately articulating the ways in which these two bodies of law interact, and possible solutions.

TABLE 5 ARTICULATING ISSUES OF IHL AND IHRL CO-APPLICABILITY			
Issue	Examples of passages from MRF reports	Description of problem	Solution
Generally presenting the manner in which IHL and IHRL interact with one another.	"[I]nternational human rights law obligations remain in effect and operate to limit the circumstances when a state actor – even a soldier during internal armed conflict – can employ lethal force."[22]	Adopts a progressive interpretation of co-applicability – in which IHRL provides additional constraints compared to IHL – but does not justify this interpretation or mention that the interpretation could be disputed.	Articulate with caution the way that IHL and IHRL interact with one another and provide legal citations to justify the approach adopted.
Mixing IHL and IHRL vocabulary.	"Parties to the conflict and their auxiliary forces have violated provisions of statutory and customary international humanitarian law, including the right to life and physical integrity of protected persons."[23]	Uses IHL and IHRL language interchangeably, such as the concepts of rights (from IHRL) and protected persons (from IHL), which may undermine the accuracy and credibility of legal determinations.	Ensure that the report respects the distinctions between IHL and IHRL and does not blend together terminology and concepts from these two bodies of law.
	"The deliberate and indiscriminate targeting of civilian houses constitutes a violation of international humanitarian law and of international human rights obligations."[24]	Uses IHL terminology ("deliberate and indiscriminate targeting") but claims that these incidents also constitute violations of IHRL.	

B. REFERENCES TO CUSTOMARY INTERNATIONAL LAW

While some rules of customary international law are firmly established, a lack of consensus exists regarding the customary status of other norms or their content. For this reason, a too-progressive approach when referring to customary international law can open the mission's interpretation of the law to criticism from certain governments or other entities. This should not discourage MRF practitioners from

22   "Report of the International Commission of Inquiry on Libya," March 2, 2012, p. 60, accessed May 25, 2015, http://www.nytimes.com/interactive/2012/03/03/world/africa/united-nations-report-on-libya.html?_r = 0.

23   Côte d'Ivoire Commission report, 18 (translated from French to English by HPCR).

24   Lebanon Commission report, 71.

citing customary international law in their reports, but they should seek to mitigate potential controversy by specifically and extensively articulating the report's legal reasoning.[25]

Practical considerations can complicate this approach. The mission may be unable to include in the report adequate documentation and references supporting and explaining the mission's legal reasoning due, for example, to a lack of time and/or personnel. Some practitioners are also concerned that an extensive description of the legal rationales underlying the report may divert attention from the mission's factual conclusions. Such considerations are especially relevant for missions that face limitations on the length of the report.

C. ASSESSING THE CONDUCT OF HOSTILITIES UNDER IHL

Some rules of IHL prove challenging due to the difficulty of establishing certain facts required for their application, and, therefore, for the determination of whether violations have been committed. Most of the rules on the conduct of hostilities contain elements that are defined *ex ante* (before an attack is launched), whereas the assessment is carried out *ex post facto* (after the attack has occurred), making it difficult to gather relevant information. In addition, these norms relate to factual aspects that pertain to different perspectives, such as that of the attacker and that of the defender, as well as the use of weapons and the nature of the target. All components of these norms need to be established in order to be able to reach a legal conclusion.

It is commonly considered that the law on targeting under IHL requires three sets of obligations before carrying out an attack. In a brief overview, they include the following steps: First, an attacker must respect the principle of distinction and direct his/her attack only against military objectives and combatants, based on the legal definition of a military objective. Second, even if the attack targets a military objective, the principle of proportionality prohibits excessive incidental effects on civilians and civilian objects compared to the military advantage anticipated from the attack. Finally, even if the first two conditions are met, all feasible precautionary measures must be taken to minimize the effect of the attack on civilians and civilian objects.

The law on targeting under IHL offers various examples of factual and legal challenges. As an illustration, under IHL, a civilian object, such as a school, can

---

[25] A valuable resource in this regard for customary international law is Jean-Marie Henckaerts and Louise Doswald-Beck, *Customary International Humanitarian Law*, vols. 1–3 (Cambridge: Cambridge University Press, 2005).

become a legitimate target if the attacker deems that the object makes an effective contribution to military action and that its total or partial destruction would offer a definite military advantage to the attacker. But, for example, investigating whether fighters were present on the roof of a school, which could justify targeting the building, is a particularly complex task, especially since MRF missions often do not arrive on the scene until long after an attack has occurred.

The dilemmas inherent in proportionality assessments also demonstrate these factual and legal difficulties. Gauging whether attacks were proportional entails comparing the concrete and direct military advantage anticipated by the attacker to the expected incidental loss of civilian life, injury to civilians, damage to civilian objects, or a combination thereof. Specifically, a proportionality assessment involves determining whether the latter is excessive compared to the former.

Finally, to assess whether the attacker fulfilled his/her obligations to undertake all feasible precautionary measures, MRF practitioners would need to take into account how "feasible" has been defined in IHL and to gather relevant information accordingly. The extent of the information that must be gathered is conveyed in the commonly agreed-upon definition of "feasible," which is: "that which is practicable or practically possible, taking into account all circumstances prevailing at the time, including humanitarian and military considerations."[26]

MRF reports need to address all of these issues (i.e., that an attacker respected the principles of distinction and proportionality and undertook all feasible precautionary measures) in order to draw legal conclusions about the conduct of hostilities. While direct evidence related to these obligations is often difficult for MRF investigators to obtain, legal conclusions can be based on inferences from the available evidence as a whole, or on circumstantial evidence.

Examples from past practice on the following pages demonstrate how different MRF reports have assessed the conduct of hostilities under IHL.

---

[26] The Program on Humanitarian Policy and Conflict Research at Harvard University, *HPCR Manual on International Law Applicable to Air and Missile Warfare* (New York: Cambridge University Press, 2013), xxiv.

1 ATTACK AGAINST CIVILIAN OBJECTS	
MRF mission	Lebanon Commission
Incident investigated	Bombing by the Israeli Air Force of a three-story building in the town of Qana, resulting in the death of twenty-nine civilians.
Sources of information	List of victims provided to the commission by the mayor of Qana; UNSG report outlining perspectives of the government of Israel and the government of Lebanon on the attack; press conference held by chief of staff of the Israeli Air Force after the attack; report of an official inquiry published by Israeli authorities; the commission's on-site visit to Qana; and interviews conducted by the commission with witnesses, Lebanese Red Cross staff, and rescuers from the United Nations Interim Force in Lebanon.
Factual assessment	"The Commission did not receive any information to suggest that the building in question was being used as a Hezbollah missile launch site, either prior to or at the time of the attack, and that it therefore may have been a legitimate military target."[27]
Conclusion	"It is the view of the Commission that the reasons advanced for its targeting are not tenable."[28]

2 ADHERING TO THE PRINCIPLE OF PROPORTIONALITY	
MRF mission	Darfur Commission
Incident investigated	Attacks by Sudanese government forces and the Janjaweed on villages in Darfur.
Sources of information	Justifications provided for the attacks by the government of the Sudan, reliable eyewitnesses interviewed by the commission during fieldwork, and unnamed secondary sources used for corroboration.
Factual assessment	"The issue of proportionality did obviously not arise when no armed groups were present in the village, as the attack exclusively targeted civilians. However, whenever there might have been any armed elements present, the attack on a village would not be proportionate, as in most cases the whole village was destroyed or burned down and civilians, if not killed or wounded, would all be compelled to flee the village to avoid further harm. The civilian losses resulting from the military action would therefore be patently excessive in relation to the expected military advantage of killing rebels or putting them *hors de combat*."[29]
Conclusion	"It is apparent from the Commission's factual findings that in many instances Government forces and militias under their control attacked civilians and destroyed and burned down villages in Darfur contrary to the relevant principles and rules of international humanitarian law."[30]

[27] Lebanon Commission report, 30 (internal citation omitted).
[28] Ibid. (internal citation omitted).
[29] Darfur Commission report, 73.
[30] Ibid.

3 OBLIGATION TO TAKE ALL FEASIBLE PRECAUTIONARY MEASURES	
MRF mission	Gaza Fact-Finding Mission
Incident investigated	Israeli attacks undertaken in the context of Operation Cast Lead.
Sources of information	Meetings with people in Gaza, press reports, Israeli military sources, and a review of the types and content of warnings provided by Israeli forces.
Factual assessment	• "Whether a warning is deemed to be effective is a complex matter depending on the facts and circumstances prevailing at the time, the availability of the means for providing the warning and the evaluation of the costs to the purported military advantage."[31] • "The effectiveness will depend on three considerations: the clarity of the message, the credibility of the threat and the possibility of those receiving the warning taking action to escape the threat."[32]
Conclusion	• "The Mission does not have sufficient information to assess the accuracy of the Israeli Government's claim that the warning shot method was used only when previous warnings (leaflets, broadcasts or telephone calls) had not been acted upon. However, in many circumstances it is not clear why another call could not be made if it had already been possible to call the inhabitants of a house."[33] • "The Mission considers that some of the leaflets with specific warnings, such as those that Israel indicates were issued in Rafah and al-Shujaeiyah, may be regarded as effective. However, the Mission does not consider that general messages telling people to leave wherever they were and go to city centres, in the particular circumstances of this military campaign, meet the threshold of effectiveness."[34] • "The Mission regards some specific telephone calls to have provided effective warnings but treats with caution the figure of 165,000 calls made. Without sufficient information to know how many of these were specific, it cannot say to what extent such efforts might be regarded as effective."[35] • "The Mission does not consider the technique of firing missiles into or on top of buildings as capable of being described as a warning, much less an effective warning. It is a dangerous practice and in essence constitutes a form of attack rather than a warning."[36]

[31] Gaza Fact-Finding Mission report, 127.
[32] Ibid., 128.
[33] Ibid., 131–132.
[34] Ibid., 132.
[35] Ibid.
[36] Ibid.

D. REFERENCES TO INTERNATIONAL CRIMINAL LAW

In order to demonstrate that a violation of ICL has occurred, an MRF mission needs to establish the existence of all the necessary elements of the crime. Table 6 presents the elements required about the status of the victim, the context in which the incident occurred, and the nature of the incident in order to legally classify certain incidents as international crimes.

While Table 6 does not detail all the nuances and complexities of establishing these crimes and also presents only a few international crimes as examples, it offers a starting point for MRF practitioners to map out the factual conclusions that the mission will need to draw in order to derive a legal conclusion about whether an international crime might have been committed.

E. ADDRESSING UNSETTLED AREAS OF INTERNATIONAL LAW: THE CASE OF NON-STATE ARMED GROUPS UNDER INTERNATIONAL HUMAN RIGHTS LAW

MRF practitioners have emphasized that missions should apply only existing law and should not aim to contribute to the development of new substantive norms of international law.[37] However, they have acknowledged that, due to the way that international law operates, MRF reports may inadvertently serve jurisprudential purposes, as lawyers and lawmakers, searching for answers to unsettled international legal issues, are likely to turn to conclusions reached by MRF bodies. MRF missions frequently do – and, in many cases, to fulfill MRF mandates, must – make determinations about unsettled rules, unclear areas of international law, or controversial legal questions.

One example is the extent to which armed groups have obligations under IHRL, a question that has been addressed in slightly different ways from mission to mission. Although different MRF reports have reached the same conclusion about this issue, these reports mention the "contested" nature of the question and the "rapidly evolving" nature of the law relevant to this area (see the examples indicated in the subsequent text box).

---

[37] Théo Boutruche, "Selecting and Applying Legal Lenses in Monitoring, Reporting, and Fact-Finding Missions" (working paper, Program on Humanitarian Policy and Conflict Research at Harvard University, October 2013), p. 21, http://papers.ssrn.com/sol3/papers.cfm?abstract_id=2337437.

	TABLE 6 DEMONSTRATING THE EXISTENCE OF A CRIME UNDER THE ROME STATUTE[38]		
Crime	Status of the Victim	Context	Nature of the Incident(s)
Genocide	Belonged to a particular national, ethnical, racial, or religious group.	A manifest pattern of similar conduct directed against a national, ethnical, racial or religious group, or conduct that could itself effect such destruction.	Any acts referred to in relevant articles of the Rome Statute (i.e., killing, causing serious bodily or mental harm, deliberately inflicting conditions of life calculated to bring about physical destruction, imposing measures intended to prevent births, and forcibly transferring children) undertaken with the intent to destroy, in whole or in part, that national, ethnical, racial, or religious group.
Murder as a crime against humanity.	Person.	Part of a widespread or systematic attack directed against a civilian population.	Murder committed by a perpetrator who had knowledge of the attack.[39]
Willful killing as a war crime (grave breach of the 1949 Geneva Conventions).	Protected person(s) under the relevant 1949 Geneva Conventions.	International armed conflict.	An incident in which a perpetrator killed one or more persons and was aware of the protected status of the victim(s).
Murder as a war crime (serious violation of Article 3 common to the four 1949 Geneva Conventions).	Persons taking no active part in hostilities, including members of armed forces who have laid down their arms and those placed *hors de combat* by sickness, wounds, detention, or any other cause.	Non-international armed conflict (of the type envisaged in Article 3 common to the four 1949 Geneva Conventions).	Murder of all kinds.

[38] The information presented in this table draws from International Criminal Court, "Elements of Crimes," 2011, accessed June 1, 2015, www.icc-cpi.int/nr/rdonlyres/336923d8-a6ad-40ec-ad7b-45bf9de73d56/0/elementsofcrimeseng.pdf.

[39] For a full description of acts that could constitute crimes against humanity, see International Criminal Court, "Elements of Crimes," 2011, Article 7.

Regarding the unsettled issue of the obligations of armed groups under IHRL, different missions have addressed this issue. The report of the Libya Commission states:

> Although the extent to which international human rights law binds non-state actors remains contested as a matter of international law, it is increasingly accepted that where non-state groups exercise de facto control over territory, they must respect fundamental human rights of persons in that territory. The Commission has taken the approach that since the NTC [National Transition Council] has been exercising de facto control over territory akin to that of a Governmental authority, it will examine also allegations of human rights violations committed by its forces.[40]

Meanwhile, the report of the Gaza Fact-Finding Mission states:

> The relationship between IHL and IHRL is rapidly evolving, in particular in relation to non-State actors' obligations, with the ultimate goal of enhancing the protection of people and to enable them to enjoy their human rights in all circumstances. In the context of the matter within the Mission's mandate, it is clear that non-State actors that exercise government-like functions over a territory have a duty to respect human rights.[41]

Many practitioners have indicated that MRF reports, when addressing an unsettled area of law, should indicate that the area is unsettled, take a stand on the issue, and provide adequate references to justify the choice adopted. However, this option, though adopted by some missions, has not yet emerged as a standard practice, indicating that a gap exists between notions of "best practice" held by professionals and actual practice.

This Handbook advises that MRF reports should be as explicit as possible when addressing an unsettled area of law, should clearly articulate the rationale underlying the report's legal conclusion, should provide references for such interpretations, and should indicate whether dissenting views exist about a particular legal issue.

---

[40] First Libya Commission report, 32–33 (internal citations omitted).
[41] Gaza Fact-Finding Mission report, 80.

IV. FINAL OBSERVATIONS

This section has proposed an approach for drawing both factual and legal conclusions in the context of an MRF mission. By breaking down this process into three distinct, though interrelated, steps, it has sought to provide practitioners with a roadmap for navigating the complexities inherent in this aspect of MRF work.

Each step discussed in this section presents unique challenges. When determining which legal frameworks apply to the mission, practitioners have found difficulty in qualifying complex contexts in which overlapping armed conflicts exist, precisely articulating the ways that IHL and IHRL interact with one another, and drawing conclusions about ICL violations while lacking the mandate and resources of a court or tribunal. In relation to standards of proof, practitioners employ evidentiary standards and strive to carefully calibrate the vocabulary in MRF reports to indicate whether, for each allegation, the standard was or was not reached, or was exceeded. And finally, the application of the law to facts is complicated by both the difficulty of applying certain legal norms and the lack of consensus that exists about certain areas of international law.

The overarching consideration is the importance that practitioners should place on a clear articulation of the reasoning underlying an MRF mission's approach to these issues. Similar to mandate interpretation, as discussed in Section 1, the methodology employed by the mission to establish facts and apply the law, and the resulting conclusions reached, are likely to be the subject of controversy, given the nature of MRF bodies as entities that levy allegations about violations of international law. However, by clearly communicating that the mission employed a sound methodology in terms of conducting legal analysis, the mission can seek to mitigate potential criticism and enhance its credibility.

SECTION THREE
Protection of Witnesses and Victims

I. BACKGROUND

While MRF operations are undertaken in order to draw attention to violations of international law, the implementation of an MRF mission can also put witnesses and victims at risk of further violations.

MRF practitioners are guided by the *do no harm* principle in that MRF missions should aim to avoid causing further harm to victims and witnesses. This fundamental principle is a well-established professional standard within MRF missions, as well as within the development and humanitarian community. It should inform all decisions taken by MRF practitioners. It refers to the mission's responsibilities not only toward individuals who come into direct contact with the mission but also toward other witnesses and victims in the same context. It means that practitioners should avoid increasing risks that witnesses and victims face, and to the extent possible, mitigate any risks that arise from the conduct of the mission. Given that the realities of on-the-ground implementation require activities that could create dangers for witnesses and victims, *do no harm*, in actuality, entails assessing what constitutes an acceptable level of risk.

For individuals with whom the mission comes directly into contact for information gathering, the risks are especially acute. For this reason, it is important for the mission to consider what protective measures in this regard can be taken by the mission to minimize those risks. The two core risks that these individuals face are described below.

1. Retaliation. Interviewees who provide information to MRF investigators often face the threat of retaliatory action as a result of their cooperation with the mission. In several instances, practitioners have reported that these threats have actually materialized. This danger arises because MRF missions are sometimes controversial in the countries in which they operate, leading certain actors to try to dissuade the local population from collaborating with the mission.

Though governments carry the primary responsibility for protection, in many cases, governments themselves are among the entities accused of committing violations. A widely held perspective is that, in such environments, MRF practitioners should do their best, to the extent possible, to fill the void of responsibility in relation to the protection of individuals who cooperate with the mission.

2. Retraumatization. The danger also exists that victims of violent incidents, who have been traumatized by these experiences, could suffer from retraumatization while retelling their stories to MRF investigators. While the risk of retaliation involves the physical security of interviewees, the risk of retraumatization involves interviewees' psychological health. A professional standard – consistent with the *do no harm* principle mentioned above – has developed that a responsible MRF process involves gathering information from interviewees in a manner that does not further exacerbate the trauma that they have experienced.

On the issue of mitigating these risks, a divide exists between the most-favorable practices that have been recommended by practitioners and policy actors and the realities of on-the-ground implementation, especially given the limited timespan and resources of the mission (see Table 7).

TABLE 7 THE CONTRASTING NATURE OF PROTECTION NEEDS AND MRF MISSIONS	
Nature of protection needs of witnesses and victims who cooperate with an MRF Mission	**Nature of MRF missions**
The mitigation of threats requires significant resources.	Budgetary, personnel, and overall resource restrictions limit the mission's operational capacity.
Witnesses and victims face recurring threats over an extended period of time.	The temporary nature of MRF missions does not allow the mission to pursue protective measures after the mission disbands.
Skills and training are needed for staff to handle correctly and in a sensitive manner the mission's protective responsibilities.	The ad hoc nature of the domain of MRF has sometimes led missions to be staffed with investigators who lacked sufficient experience in protective measures.

Because of this disparity, a methodological dilemma arises. While MRF practitioners have firm notions of most-favorable practices, practitioners have widely acknowledged that the domain of MRF cannot always live up to these expectations in the field. MRF practitioners and policymakers are then caught between a desire to promote activities that fully live up to a mission's protective responsibilities, and a reluctance to prescribe best practices that are unlikely to actually be followed, due to limitations in terms of budget, personnel, and logistical resources.

MRF practitioners must determine how far one can stray from the most-favorable practices while still maintaining responsible, professional conduct. MRF mandates rarely provide specific guidance in this regard. Though some mandates refer in broad terms to protective responsibilities, few mandates mention specific protection measures.

One example of a mandate that specifies certain protective measures to be undertaken by the mission is the mandate for the DRC Mapping Exercise, which states:

Sensitive information gathered during the mapping exercise should be stored and utilized according to the strictest standards of confidentiality. The team should develop a database for the purposes of the mapping exercise, access to which should be determined by the High Commissioner for Human Rights ....

The Mapping Team should devise a strategy concerning the tracing of witnesses. Consent of witnesses to the sharing with MONUC [United Nations Organization Mission in the Democratic Republic of the Congo] and transitional justice bodies of information provided by them must be sought.[1]

Instead, the protection procedures adopted depend more on the individual practitioners serving on the mission and the mission's resource capacities. Typically, UN missions have had a greater capacity than others for protection, given the possibilities for coordinating protection activities with relevant UN agencies. However, in all cases, a certain degree of risk remains for victims and witnesses, and practitioners are left to grapple with mitigating these risks.

II. PRACTICAL STEPS

The purpose of this section is to help practitioners design a protective framework for the witnesses and victims that the mission encounters. This method focuses on eight specific areas:

1. training and development of methodology,
2. engaging with local authorities,
3. ensuring confidentiality and obtaining informed consent,

---

[1] DRC Mapping Exercise report, 544.

4. exhibiting sensitivity during the interview process,
5. using discretion during the interview process,
6. data protection,
7. report drafting, and
8. follow-up measures.

For each of these eight areas, the mission should pursue the following steps.

STEP 1: IDENTIFY THE MOST FAVORABLE PRACTICES

Identify the practices that practitioners have noted as ideal manifestations of the professional responsibility to *do no harm* during a mission's implementation. This task could include reviewing existing guidelines, best practice documents, statements of principles, or relevant passages in past MRF reports.

STEP 2: ANTICIPATE COMPLICATING FACTORS

Assess the factors that could arise during implementation that might present obstacles for carrying out the practices identified in Step 1.

STEP 3: DEVELOP PRACTICAL SOLUTIONS

Devise measures for surmounting the potential obstacles identified in Step 2.

III. EXPLANATION

To assist practitioners in implementing the practical approach described above, this section details certain most-favored practices, complicating factors, and practical measures that can be adopted to address each of the eight areas mentioned in Section II above.

When reviewing the comments offered throughout this section, MRF practitioners should bear in mind that there is no "one-size-fits-all" solution to handling protection in a sensible and successful manner. Missions differ from one another in terms of context, capacities, and mandates. In each instance, the mission will have to determine individually how to best fulfill its protective responsibilities.

Nevertheless, the points detailed in this section offer a framework of considerations for how practitioners can develop protective measures that are both appropriate and practical in the particular circumstances of the mission.

1 TRAINING AND DEVELOPMENT OF METHODOLOGY	
Most-favored practices	• Develop a mission-wide methodology for mitigating risks for the witnesses and victims that the mission encounters while gathering information. • Design and conduct training for all commissioners and staff who will interact with interviewees.
Complicating factors	• The mandating body often does not provide specific guidance in the mandate in this regard. • The mission may lack sufficient resources and capacity to allow the mission to fulfill its protective responsibilities. • The lack of a community of practice limits the extent to which, when developing training and methodologies, MRF practitioners can learn from the experiences of past missions. • The pool of experienced and available staff is sometimes insufficient for the demands of the domain of MRF. Mission-specific trainings, though useful, cannot fully make up for lack of staff experience. • Training all staff members simultaneously is complicated by logistical factors, especially when different staff members join the mission at different times.
Practical solutions	Seek methodological and training guidance from practitioners who have served on past missions, and especially recent MRF operations, since the domain of MRF is rapidly evolving in response to the wide array of ongoing MRF activities.

2 ENGAGING WITH LOCAL AUTHORITIES	
Most-favored practices	• At the beginning of the mission, request that local authorities protect individuals who cooperate with the mission and stress that the primary responsibility for protection rests with governments. • During the mission, engage in communications to pressure governmental leaders, or other individuals, who appear to be responsible for, or threatening, retaliatory measures. • Recommend in the mission's report that local authorities and other relevant actors seek to protect the individuals who cooperated with the mission.
Complicating factors	Local authorities may be unable or unwilling to provide sufficient protective measures for witnesses and victims during and after the mission, in some instances because these authorities are themselves the perpetrators of violations.
Practical solutions	Make clear that governments bear the primary responsibility for protecting witnesses and victims but prepare to fill the void in terms of protection by pursuing the practical solutions addressed throughout this section.

3 ENSURING CONFIDENTIALITY AND OBTAINING INFORMED CONSENT

Most-favored practices	• Ensure the confidentiality of the information gathered. • Obtain informed consent from interviewees to ensure that interviewees understand how and for what purpose the mission will use the information obtained. • In general, refrain from revealing to external entities not only the identity of witnesses but also any additional information that could allow witnesses to be identified. • When sharing information with outside entities is consistent with the mission's mandate – for example, transmitting information to the ICC when the mandate is aimed at accountability – ensure that interviewees give an informed consent and understand the potential ramifications, such as the disclosure of the information to the accused in an ICC case. In particular, the mission should approach the transmission of names or other potentially identifying information with utmost caution.
Complicating factors	• Sometimes interviewees do not understand the risks inherent in granting their consent. • Even if an interviewee grants consent, the mission may determine that sharing the information provided could put the interviewee in danger. • In instances in which an MRF mission intends to share information with an outside entity, informed consent has sometimes lacked sufficient precision regarding potential addressees (e.g., the mission will need to clarify whether consent to share information with the ICC includes defense counsel). • Handing witness accounts over to the ICC risks undermining a criminal prosecution by giving the defense counsel the opportunity to highlight any discrepancies between statements offered by the same witness to an MRF mission and in the context of an ICC case.
Practical solutions	• Develop a rigorous system for evaluating whether or not the interviewee understands the consent granted. • Given that MRF practitioners are further refining informed consent procedures on an ongoing basis, seek to learn from the experiences of recent missions. • Engage in discussion within the mission about existing risks that may preclude sharing information even if consent has been granted.

4 EXHIBITING SENSITIVITY DURING THE INTERVIEW PROCESS	
Most-favored practices	• To avoid exposing interviewees to the risk of retraumatization, when selecting interviewees, if possible refrain from interviewing particularly psychologically vulnerable individuals. • Exhibit sensitivity during interviews and stop the interview if, during the interview, information relayed or behavior exhibited by the interviewee leads the interviewer to reassess the vulnerability of the witness.
Complicating factors	Sometimes MRF investigators lack sufficient skills and do not know how to appropriately deal with victims of trauma.
Practical solutions	Ensure that an experienced interviewer with a background in engaging with trauma victims is always present during interviews.

5 USING DISCRETION DURING THE INTERVIEW PROCESS	
Most-favored practices	To avoid exposing interviewees to the risk of retaliation: • Use discretion when approaching interviewees. • Conduct interviews in private. • When selecting interviewees, consider the compounded risks – specifically, in terms of the danger of retaliation – that exist for individuals who have already been interviewed by other organizations.
Complicating factors	• MRF missions are frequently high profile, complicating efforts to use discretion when approaching interviewees. • For certain contexts, such as detention centers and refugee camps, it is sometimes difficult or impossible to conduct interviews in private.
Practical solutions	• Investigators can meet interviewees in a different location (this could include providing money to interviewees to take local transportation to a nearby town or to investigators to rent anonymous-looking cars). • For victims of violations associated with a high level of stigma – for example, victims of SGBV – do not announce the types of victims for which you are looking. • For detention centers, ensure that information provided by a detainee is never transmitted to the interviewee's captors. • When a private interview is impossible, proceed only if the interviewee agrees and if doing so is unlikely to increase the risk of retaliation facing the interviewee.

6 DATA PROTECTION	
Most-favored practices	• Retain anonymity of interviewees (e.g., by using codes instead of actual names) in internal notes and reports. • Keep all data secure that contains information that could allow interviewees to be identified. • Destroy paper notes of interviews after converting to electronic format. • Use encrypted computers and secure servers to upload information gathered through interviews. • Ensure that data is kept secure after the mission's conclusion.
Complicating factors	• Some missions, particularly non-UN missions, lack comprehensive data protection capacities, such as encryption. • After a mission ends, it is sometimes unclear who will have access to the data and for what length of time the records of the mission will be kept confidential.
Practical solutions	The mission should adopt clear guidelines, consistent with the informed consent granted during the interviews, regarding who will and will not be granted access to the information gathered during and after the conclusion of the mission.

7 REPORT DRAFTING	
Most-favored practices	Do not include in the report: • Names of interviewees, and • Details that could allow interviewees to be identified.
Complicating factors	• It is not always clear what information should be omitted from the report in order to retain the anonymity of the interviewees. • Sometimes omitting these details will lead to reports that read as ambiguous.
Practical solutions	During report drafting, if ambiguities exist about which pieces of information would cause interviewees to be identifiable, practitioners should err on the side of caution in order to abide by the mission's responsibility to mitigate risks to witnesses and victims. .

8 FOLLOW-UP MEASURES

Most-favored practices	• Provide referrals to connect interviewees with other organizations that might be able to see to the interviewees' humanitarian, medical, and psychosocial needs (based on a mapping of potentially useful services that the mission conducts prior to the start of fieldwork). • Verify that referrals are effective. • Coordinate follow-up measures – in terms of protection or for other humanitarian needs – for interviewees. • Consider assisting interviewees interested in seeking asylum.
Complicating factors	• The temporary nature of MRF missions creates challenges for post-mission engagement with witnesses and victims. • Regarding the coordination of follow-up measures, sometimes other organizations, including UN agencies, lack the capacity to engage in effective follow-up activities. • Once the mission ends, the MRF team disbands and lacks the capacity, as a mission, to undertake follow-up measures. • Sometimes practitioners feel compelled to engage in an activist capacity to attend to the humanitarian needs of witnesses and victims, with the risk of bringing the impartial character of the mission into question or creating confusion locally about the mission's aims and purposes.
Practical solutions	When possible, an MRF mission should seek to build linkages with other entities able to assume a role in monitoring protection concerns related to the witnesses and victims with whom the mission engaged. This assists MRF investigators in attending to interviewees' long-term needs without compromising the impartiality of the mission.

IV. FINAL OBSERVATIONS

The goal of this section has been to assist practitioners in navigating, on the one hand, expectations regarding MRF practitioners' responsibilities to protect witnesses and victims, and on the other hand, the practical realities of undertaking an on-the-ground data-gathering effort. The core dilemma is that, while *do not harm* is a firmly established guiding principle of MRF operations, its application differs depending on the mandate, resources, and context of the mission. For this reason, there is no single protection template applicable to the diversity of MRF missions.

Given this state of affairs, the considerations outlined in this section offer not a conclusive framework for approaching protection, but rather a starting point for determining how an MRF mission can surmount common challenges that practitioners have faced in relation to this issue. MRF practitioners should also bear in mind that protection practices continue to evolve on an ongoing basis in response to lessons learned. Therefore, it is particularly important that practitioners seek to gain insight from a wide array of professionals experienced in these issues – in particular, from practitioners who have served on recent missions.

SECTION FOUR
Public Communication

I. BACKGROUND

Public communication serves a number of purposes at different stages of an MRF mission. Upon the mission's initiation, the aim of public engagement is to communicate in a transparent manner its aims, composition, and planned activities. During the investigation, public engagement can be used to respond to – and mitigate the effects of – criticisms regarding the mission's credibility, as well as to cultivate a feeling among witnesses and victims and affected communities of being heard by the international community. Upon the release of the report, the aim of public engagement shifts toward raising the visibility of the mission's findings.

Public engagement also carries risks, particularly as the mission is ongoing. If handled ineffectively, it can exacerbate an already volatile climate; fuel speculation about the credibility of the mission; or cause security risks for witnesses and victims, as well as for MRF practitioners themselves.

Public communication therefore requires careful management. It is important for MRF practitioners to adopt a strategic approach to public engagement so that the mission is poised to take a proactive – rather than reactive – approach to events as they unfold during an MRF investigation.

II. PRACTICAL STEPS

The purpose of this section is to provide practitioners with a strategic view of the objectives of public communication. This section focuses on public communication activities during three phases of an MRF mission's implementation, which are:

    A. The initiation of the mission
    B. During the investigation
    C. After the release of the report

For each of these three phases, the mission should pursue the following steps.

STEP 1: IDENTIFY THE OBJECTIVES
Identify whom the mission wishes to impact and why this aim is important to the operations of the mission.

STEP 2: STRATEGIC PLANNING
Plan the mission's public communication activities, taking into consideration the potential benefits and risks of different courses of action.

III. EXPLANATION

A. THE INITIATION OF THE MISSION

STEP 1: IDENTIFY THE OBJECTIVES

The aim of public communication during this phase is to ensure that all the relevant entities – governments, the affected population, and civil society – may have a basic understanding of the aims and operations of the mission. Measures taken toward this end can be particularly important for international missions, which have sometimes faced skepticism from local actors about their aims and intentions. When the mission operates simultaneously with other investigative mechanisms, a related objective is to make it clear that the mission is a distinct and independent exercise. For example, part of the public communications strategy of the Guinea Commission was to distinguish the mission from the national commission that had been mandated by the government of Guinea.

STEP 2: STRATEGIC PLANNING

Specific public communication measures that have been adopted at the outset of an MRF mission include:

- convening a press conference to announce the creation of the mission;
- publishing a press release that provides information about the mission's mandate and the identities of the commissioners;
- making public the mandate and modalities of the mission;
- creating a mission-specific webpage; and
- providing information about planned field visits, pending security considerations.

Security considerations are important in two respects.

First, offering detailed public information about the mission's planned field visits could create security risks for commissioners and staff, as well as for witnesses and victims, especially in complex security environments and where MRF missions are controversial. Regarding witnesses and victims, it is important that the mission use discretion when approaching interviewees, so as not to make them vulnerable to reprisals (see Section 3, Protection of Witnesses and Victims in this Handbook for more details). The mission should consider these factors when making decisions about the level of detail that the mission will publicly provide about its field visits.

Second, though the mission may publicly communicate about the number of its staff members and their roles, identities should be kept confidential (see Section 5, Report Drafting in this Handbook for an explanation of how to address this issue in the final report). In typical MRF practice, commissioners serve as the public face of the mission. Staff members are not publicly identified by name, due to the security risks for these individuals that could arise for them not only during – but also after the conclusion of – the mission.

B. DURING THE INVESTIGATION

STEP 1: IDENTIFY THE OBJECTIVES

During the investigation, the mission should normally exercise restraint in public communications. However, public engagement is sometimes required in order to defend the mission's credibility in response to criticisms and to reach out to witnesses and victims.

In the first case, given the importance of perceptions of the mission's credibility, it can be important for the mission to counter criticisms that may arise about its mandate or operations in order to defend its integrity.

In the second case, one key component of an MRF operation is to forge connections between the mission and witnesses and victims who are relevant to the mission's mandate. To this end, certain MRF missions have devised different means for the affected population to present information to the mission. Such measures could not only raise the visibility of the mission in a manner that enhances its impact but could also provide witnesses and victims with the sense that there is an opportunity to tell their stories to the international community.

Although public outreach measures tend to be presented as a means of gathering information, the information obtained tends to be of limited evidentiary value (as described in Step 2 below). For this reason, such measures should be undertaken only after careful consideration of the costs in terms of money, personnel, and time, as well as the potential security risks. (See Step 2 below for more on the issue of security risks.)

STEP 2: STRATEGIC PLANNING

(a) Defending the Mission's Credibility

It is important for the mission to respond publicly if the mission's integrity has been brought into question. However, a public misstep can further exacerbate an already tense political atmosphere and can also increase security risks for commissioners and staff members. Specifically, during an interview or press conference, a commissioner may make a comment that suggests – due to imprecise wording, a misunderstanding on the part of the interviewer, or subsequent quotation of the statement out of context – that the mission has prejudged the outcome of the investigation.

Given the unpredictability of in-person interviews and press conferences, in contexts where the mission's credibility is brought into question the mission should opt, whenever possible, to respond to these criticisms only in writing. This medium will better allow commissioners to control the message that the mission wishes to publicly convey. Table 8 presents common criticisms, how practitioners can respond, and examples from past practice.

(b) Public Outreach

Public outreach endeavors that have been undertaken by past MRF missions include holding public hearings, opening public offices, and issuing a public call for submissions to the mission. However, when deciding whether to pursue any of these avenues, MRF practitioners should consider the potential drawbacks: (1) engaging with witnesses publicly could impair witness protection, and (2) seeking information through public means is unlikely to yield information leading to factual conclusions.

In terms of *protection issues for witnesses and victims*, during field visits MRF missions usually aim to retain the anonymity of interviewees in order to avoid exposing these witnesses and victims to the risk of being further victimized by retaliatory measures (see Section 3, Protection of Witnesses and Victims in this Handbook for more details). MRF missions that pursue public engagement with witnesses and victims – for example, in the context of public hearings – will need to undertake extensive measures to mitigate this risk. Specifically, MRF missions should, throughout the implementation of the mission, monitor the situation of individuals who have publicly offered information, and if problems arise, pursue corrective measures. For example, if an individual, after providing information to an MRF mission, is detained by governmental authorities, commissioners can press for the release of the individual, either through written communication with the government or through public efforts that aim to apply pressure on these authorities.

TABLE 8 RESPONDING TO CRITICISMS OF THE MISSION'S CREDIBILITY

Criticism	Mission's Response	Example
The mandating body is biased, and thus the mission is perceived as biased.	Clarify that the mission is a technical exercise operating independently of the mandating body.	After members of the Bahraini political opposition expressed concern that the Bahrain Commission was mandated by the government of Bahrain, the very entity accused of committing violations, the chair of the commission made clear that the mission was independent and that the king of Bahrain was not in any way dictating or restricting the commission's activities.[1]
The mandate is unnecessarily restrictive and/or biased.	Emphasize that the mission has corrected any potential biases that might exist in the mandate.	One of the criticisms of the Gaza Fact-Finding Mission is that the original mandate focused solely on Israel. However, the chair of the mission, in a press conference announcing the initiation of the investigation, emphasized that the mission would operate under terms agreed to by the president of the UNHRC that would correct the one-sided nature of the original mandate and would allow for an investigation that would examine all sides of the conflict.[2]
The commissioners and/or staff are perceived as biased, to have prejudged the outcome of the investigation, or to have used selective approaches to gathering data.	Emphasize that the mission is gathering information from all sides and is evaluating the information in an impartial manner.	After the publication of the Kyrgyzstan Commission report, the Kyrgyz Parliament decried the report as one-sided, declared the chair of the commission "persona non grata," and discussed accusations that the chair of the commission accepted bribes from Uzbek separatists. In response, the chair offered public comments denying the accusations and asserting that the practitioners on the mission endeavored to conduct an impartial exercise.[3]

[1] Bahrain Center for Human Rights, "The Bahrain Independent Commission of Inquiry Statement," August 10, 2011, accessed June 1, 2015, http://www.bahrainrights.org/en/node/4499.

[2] "Near Verbatim Transcript of Press Conference by the President of the Human Rights Council, Martin Ihoeghian Uhomoibhi (Nigeria) and Justice Richard J. Goldstone on the Announcement of the Human Rights Council Fact-Finding Mission on the Conflict in the Gaza Strip," Geneva, April 3, 2009, accessed June 1, 2015, http://www.ohchr.org/EN/HRBodies/HRC/SpecialSessions/Session9/Pages/FactFindingMission.aspx.

[3] Dina Tokbaeva and Nina Muzaffariva, "'Banned' Investigator Regrets Kyrgyz Probe Response," Institute for War & Peace Reporting, June 9, 2011, accessed June 1, 2015, http://iwpr.net/report-news/banned-investigator-regrets-kyrgyz-probe-response.

After the public hearings held by the Gaza Fact-Finding Mission, the mission perceived that the detention of one of the participants might have been linked to his participation in the hearings. The mission expressed concern, in writing, about this issue to a representative of the Israeli government. As the mission's report states:

Subsequent to the public hearings in Geneva, the Mission was informed that a Palestinian participant, Mr. Muhammad Srour, had been detained by Israeli security forces when returning to the West Bank and became concerned that his detention may have been a consequence of his appearance before the Mission. The Mission wrote to the Permanent Representative of Israel in Geneva expressing its concern. In response, the Permanent Representative informed the Mission that the detention of the person concerned was unrelated to his appearance at the public hearing. Mr. Srour was subsequently released on bail. The Mission is in contact with him and continues to monitor developments.[4]

In terms of the *limited evidentiary value of information gathered through public means*, MRF missions should be mindful that information received through public forums has very rarely served as a basis for the mission's findings. Information received through public hearings, at public offices established by the mission, or in response to public calls for written submissions have not been as useful in terms of gathering data as interviews conducted during MRF fieldwork. Additionally, granting individuals and groups the ability to offer information to the mission in a public manner could lead to manipulation by outside interests who want to influence the conclusions reached by the mission.

The Sri Lanka Panel issued a public call for submissions and received over 4,000 submissions from over 2,300 senders.[5] However, the panel's final report states that, despite the large volume of submissions, the panel could not independently verify the material, and as a result, did not use this information as a direct source for its report.[6] Indeed, the report states that "a portion of submissions" consisted of "[g]eneral information, including media reports, web links and historical accounts,

---

[4] Gaza Fact-Finding Mission report, 40.
[5] Sri Lanka Panel report, 5.
[6] Ibid.

forwarded to the panel from publicly available sources."[7] The report also states of the submissions that "appeals urging the panel to act or to make specific recommendations, but containing neither fact-based information nor analysis, accounted for a large number of submissions received."[8]

Due to the witness protection risks and the low evidentiary value of the information obtained, and also in light of the costs (in terms of personnel, money, and time), public hearings should not be encouraged in MRF practice.

C. AFTER THE RELEASE OF THE REPORT

STEP 1: IDENTIFY THE OBJECTIVES

MRF policy literature, as well as practitioners themselves, emphasizes the importance of making final MRF reports public. Often, commissioners engage in public efforts to promote the findings and recommendations of the mission after the release of the report. These activities can be important to the success of the mission but should be weighed against potential security risks. (See Section 5, Report Drafting in this Handbook for more details.)

In some instances, though, mandates have been silent about whether reports should be made public, leaving the mandating body's intent unclear. For missions mandated by the UNHRC, mandates commonly do not specify that the report will be made public, though the practice of the Office of the High Commissioner for Human Rights (OHCHR), which plays a lead role in implementing such mandates, is to publish upon the conclusion of the mission.[9] In other instances, the mandating body's intention remains more ambiguous. Practitioners operating under such mandates can advocate, publicly or privately, that the mandating body publish the mission's final report, a strategy that has been successful in the past.[10] It is also important that the report is circulated widely and, if applicable, translated into different languages so that the key actors relevant to the context can read the report. (See Section 5, Report Drafting in this Handbook for more information.)

When planning the communication activities that aim to promote the final report, commissioners should consider the various audiences of MRF reports and their relevance to these audiences (see Table 9).

[7] Ibid.

[8] Ibid.

[9] Rob Grace, "Communication and Report Drafting in Monitoring, Reporting, and Fact-Finding Missions" (working paper, Program on Humanitarian Policy and Conflict Research at Harvard University, July 2014), p. 21, http://papers.ssrn.com/sol3/papers.cfm?abstract_id=2462590.

[10] Ibid.

TABLE 9 AUDIENCES OF MRF REPORTS	
Audience	**Potential Relevancy of the Report to These Entities**
The mandating body	Assists in determining how to address allegations of violations of international law relevant to an ongoing or past armed conflict or internal disturbance.
Affected populations	Can cultivate a feeling among affected communities of being heard by the international community. In some contexts, the report might constitute the only form of justice available to victims.[11]
Civil society	Serves as an authoritative document that can be incorporated into advocacy efforts to address allegations relevant to the mission's mandate.
International or national prosecutors	Findings of the mission can be used as lead evidence, or as background or contextual evidence, in future or ongoing investigations.

STEP 2: STRATEGIC PLANNING

Efforts undertaken by commissioners with the aim of promoting the mission's report have included:

- convening a press conference;
- organizing a public event to launch the report;
- providing media interviews; and
- publishing op-eds in prominent newspapers.

After the release of the report, though the mission ends and the team dissolves, some ex-commissioners remain publicly engaged by offering public statements about the adoption (or lack thereof) of the report's recommendations, authoring academic articles about the mission, or becoming directly involved in related advocacy efforts or capacity-building measures.[12]

---

[11] For details about this issue, see the Background portion of Section 5, Report Drafting in this Handbook.

[12] See OHCHR, "Guidance and Practice," 108–109, which notes that on missions mandated by the UNHRC, commissioners are bound by a declaration requested by the council that states, "I also undertake to respect, during the tenure of my mandate and subsequently, the confidentiality of all information made available to me in my capacity as a member of the Commission of Inquiry [or Fact-Finding Mission]." MRF practitioners bound by such a confidentiality pledge should ensure that any public communication activities do not compromise the declaration made.

Similar to statements made during the operation of an MRF mission, the release and promotion of the report also evoke security concerns for international staff who remain in the country. Normally, when MRF practitioners anticipate that the release of the report will lead to security issues, such as retaliatory measures undertaken by local actors, the mission will advise the UN and embassies in the country of the release date so that precautionary security measures can be taken. Or, for an interim report, a mission will ensure that the MRF team is out of the country on the day of the report's release.

Commissioners should also be aware that the delicate environment in which MRF missions operate does not end with their conclusion. Even long after the mission has ended, commissioners have been generally reluctant to offer public comments that might bring the mission's credibility into question. Though a commissioner's formal authority ends with the conclusion of an MRF mandate, statements made in the wake of the publication of an MRF report can still influence people's perceptions of the legitimacy of the mission's findings.

Public comments made by the chair of the *Gaza Fact-Finding Mission* more than one year after the release of the final report reignited debates between the mission's supporters and detractors about the legitimacy of the report's findings. In particular, the chair of the mission wrote an op-ed in 2011 that stated that, since the end of the mission, information had been made available that "indicate[d] that civilians were not intentionally targeted [by Israel] as a matter of policy,"[13] contrasting the conclusions offered in the mission's final report.[14]

The op-ed led to calls for the United Nations (UN) to retract the report. Additionally, the other three members of the mission disagreed with the chair's conclusion and wrote their own op-ed that aimed "to dispel any impression that subsequent developments have rendered any part of the mission's report unsubstantiated, erroneous or inaccurate."[15]

---

[13] Richard Goldstone, "Reconsidering the Goldstone Report on Israel and War Crimes," *The Washington Post*, April 1, 2011, http://www.washingtonpost.com/opinions/reconsidering-the-goldstone-report-on-israel-and-war-crimes/2011/04/01/AFg111JC_story.html.

[14] See Gaza Fact-Finding Mission report, 406–408.

[15] Hina Jilani, Christine Chinkin, and Desmond Travers, "Goldstone Report: Statement Issued by Members of UN Mission on Gaza War," *The Guardian*, April 14, 2011, http://www.theguardian.com/commentisfree/2011/apr/14/goldstone-report-statement-un-gaza.

IV. FINAL OBSERVATIONS

As this section has elaborated, public communication is important for the implementation of an MRF mission. First, a widely accepted principle of MRF practice dictates that, at the outset of an MRF operation – and during implementation – an MRF body should make publicly available basic information about the mandate, composition, and activities of the mission. Second, in some instances, criticisms levied at MRF missions have prompted commissioners to engage in a public defense of the credibility of the mission. Third, public outreach to the affected population can be an essential aspect of raising the visibility, and hence, perhaps the impact, of the mission. Fourth, after the conclusion of the mission, promoting the release of the final report allows commissioners to generate awareness of the mission's findings and advocate for the implementation of the mission's recommendations.

However, it is important that commissioners approach these activities in a strategic manner. The practical steps that this section presents aim to focus practitioners' attention on defining the objectives of these activities and mitigating potential unintended consequences. Strategizing about the mission's approach in this regard at the beginning of the implementation process – specifically, before the initiation of fieldwork – will position the mission to predict, and determine how to respond to, public relations issues and security concerns that emanate from negative perceptions of the mission.

SECTION FIVE
Report Drafting

I. BACKGROUND

The drafting and publication of the final report is the culmination of the implementation of an MRF mission. Since the final report constitutes the concrete outcome of the MRF mission and the main basis on which the whole work of the mission will be judged, practitioners are of the view that reports should be drafted with the utmost care.

The importance of the report arises in part from the temporary nature of MRF missions. Upon the completion of the mandate, the MRF team typically disbands, leaving the task of reviewing and acting on the mission's findings to governmental and intergovernmental actors, politicians, and civil society. The control that practitioners can exercise over the mission's impact is then limited. The report constitutes the link between the mission's activities and the advocacy efforts and political decision-making processes that occur after the conclusion of the mission.

It is also paramount to stress that the publication of an MRF mission's final report often constitutes the only factual account and recognition of violations victims suffered, and as such, the only form of justice victims will obtain. In this regard, MRF reports contribute to realizing the right of victims of serious IHRL and IHL violations to access relevant information about violations, as a component of their rights to remedy and to full and public disclosure of the truth related to such violations as a form of compensation, within their right to reparation. These rights have been reaffirmed in various international legal documents.[1]

However, the report-drafting process is challenging for several reasons. First, the need to produce a report in a relatively short time frame complicates the collaboration among the different actors engaged in the drafting process. Second, bureaucratic

---

[1] For example, see United Nations General Assembly resolution 60/147, "Basic principles and guidelines on the right to a remedy and reparation for victims of gross violations of international human rights law and serious violations of international humanitarian law," March 21, 2006, http://www.un.org/Docs/asp/ws.asp?m=A/RES/60/147.

constraints can also affect the process. In particular, for missions authorized by the UNHRC, the time needed for editing and translation could impose length limitations on the report (sometimes restricted to twenty-five pages) and require that the report be completed several weeks before its presentation to the council.[2]

Because the report is essential to the success of the mission, it is extremely important for practitioners to devise a report-drafting strategy that clearly defines the objectives, decision-making framework, and drafting process.

II. PRACTICAL STEPS

The purpose of this section is to provide practitioners with strategic considerations to inform the process of drafting the mission's final report. This section focuses on three core aspects of an MRF report: providing information about the creation and operations of the mission, presenting the mission's findings, and offering recommendations. For each of these three areas, the mission must define the output, determine how to present the content, and plan the drafting process as described in the practical steps presented below.

A. PROVIDE INFORMATION ABOUT THE CREATION AND OPERATIONS OF THE MISSION

STEP 1: DEFINE THE OUTPUT

To promote transparency about the mission, the mission should provide information about the adoption of the mandate, the commissioners and staff, and the activities and investigative methodology of the mission.

STEP 2: DETERMINE HOW TO PRESENT THE CONTENT

The mission must decide what level of detail the report will provide about each of the items mentioned in Step 1.

STEP 3: PLAN THE DRAFTING PROCESS

The mission should consider drafting this section of the report early on.

---

[2] Grace, "Communication and Report Drafting," 36.

B. PRESENT THE MISSION'S FINDINGS

STEP 1: DEFINE THE OUTPUT

Present the factual and legal findings of the mission and clarify the level of certainty of these findings, given the investigative methodology of the mission.

STEP 2: DETERMINE HOW TO PRESENT THE CONTENT

In terms of structure, the mission must decide whether to organize the report by geographic region (dividing sections according to the location where incidents occurred, presented in chronological order) or by violation type (dividing sections based on the type of incident, regardless of where the incidents occurred). The language should avoid emotive vocabulary, the tone should be consistent throughout the report, and legal vocabulary should be confined to sections on legal findings.

STEP 3: PLAN THE DRAFTING PROCESS

The mission must decide how to divide drafting responsibilities between commissioners and staff, and if possible, should employ a lead drafter/editor to ensure consistency throughout the entire report.

C. OFFER RECOMMENDATIONS

STEP 1: DEFINE THE OUTPUT

Decide what recommendations to offer and to whom the mission should direct its recommendations.

STEP 2: DETERMINE HOW TO PRESENT THE CONTENT

Determine how the mission's mandate, the intended audience of the report, and desired impact of the mission should be reflected in the recommendations.

STEP 3: PLAN THE DRAFTING PROCESS

The mission should draft recommendations that are precise and based on the mission's assessment of the situation on the ground.

III. EXPLANATION

A. PROVIDE INFORMATION ABOUT THE CREATION AND OPERATIONS OF THE MISSION

STEP 1: DEFINE THE OUTPUT

Due to the sensitive nature of levying allegations of violations of international law, providing detailed information about the way that the mission implemented its mandate can be crucial for fostering public perceptions of the credibility of the investigation (see Section 4, Public Communication in this Handbook). For this reason, it is important that the report provides details about how the mission came into being and the way that the mission implemented its mandate. (For additional details about the importance of transparency in this regard, see Section 1, Mandate Interpretation and Section 2, Establishing Facts and Applying the Law in this Handbook.)

STEP 2: DETERMINE HOW TO PRESENT THE CONTENT

MRF reports have varied in terms of the level of detail that reports have provided about the origins and operations of the mission. Those differences come from such factors as report length limitations and the commissioners' perceptions of what aspects of the mandate and the implementation process are particularly important to emphasize.

This section offers models for how the report can present: (1) information about the adoption of the mandate, (2) background on commissioners and staff, and (3) a description of the activities and methodology of the mission. For each of these areas, this section describes two possibilities: offer a basic level of detail that constitutes a minimum level of transparency, or provide more extensive details.

Commissioners on each MRF mission will need to decide what level of detail is useful or necessary, given the mandate and context of the mission. The framework presented on the following pages, based on approaches that practitioners on past missions adopted, presents examples from past practice to guide practitioners' decision making in this regard.

1 ADOPTION OF THE MANDATE		
Level of Detail	Description	Example
Include basic level of detail	Include only the operative portion of the mandate, the identity of the mandating body, and the date of the mandate's adoption.	The first report of the Libya Commission includes the name of the resolution adopted by the UNHRC, the date of adoption, and the operative portion of the mandate.[3]
Provide extensive details	Include the full text of the mandate and additional information about the creation of the mission.	The DRC Mapping Exercise report includes a two-page description of the creation of the mission; the operative portion of the overarching mandate, which was the resolution that created the United Nations Organization Mission in the Democratic Republic of the Congo; and in the annex, the full text of the mission's Terms of Reference, which were approved by the UNSG.[4]

2 BACKGROUND ON COMMISSIONERS AND STAFF		
Level of Detail	Description	Example
Include basic level of detail	Offer names and basic information about the commissioners.	The Lebanon Commission report provides only the names and nationalities of the commissioners, and states, "The members were appointed on the basis of their expertise in international humanitarian law and human rights law."[5]
Provide extensive details	Provide extensive information about the commissioners' professional backgrounds, as well as general information about the roles and responsibilities of the mission's staff.*	The Bahrain Commission report provides not only the names and nationalities of the commissioners but also, in an annex, one-page professional biographies for each commissioner, as well as a chart demonstrating the organizational link between the commissioners and the staff.[6]

* Due to the security issues that could arise, staff members should not be identified by name in the mission's report. See Section 4, Public Communication in this Handbook for details about this issue in terms of the mission's public communication activities.

[3] First Libya Commission report, 14.

[4] DRC Mapping Exercise report, 33–34 and 542–544.

[5] Lebanon Commission report, 14.

[6] "Report of the Bahrain Independent Commission of Inquiry," November 23, 2011, pp. 2, 495, and 499–503, http://www.bici.org.bh/BICIreportEN.pdf.

3 ACTIVITIES AND METHODOLOGY OF THE MISSION

Level of Detail	Description	Example
Include basic level of detail	Concisely describe activities that the mission undertook, challenges faced, and methodological considerations that underpinned the investigation, including the sources of information on which the mission relied, how the mission gathered this information, and the standard of proof adopted by the mission.	The Beit Hanoun Fact-Finding Mission report includes two paragraphs about challenges the mission faced due to lack of territorial access; four paragraphs about the mission's field visits and data-gathering methods; and in the annex, the itinerary of the mission's field visit to Gaza.[7]
Provide extensive details	Present an elaborate description of specific aspects of the mission's activities and methodology, including the decision-making framework that guided all of the mission's methodological choices.	The Darfur Commission report provides extensive information about the mission's methodology, including ten paragraphs about mandate interpretation, six paragraphs about working methods, two paragraphs about the constraints that affected the mission, six paragraphs about the mission's field visits, and fourteen paragraphs about cooperation received from the Sudanese authorities and rebel groups.[8]

STEP 3: PLAN THE DRAFTING PROCESS

Due to the hectic nature of the report-drafting process, it will benefit the mission to begin drafting the report as early on as possible during the implementation process. Since information about the creation and methodologies of the mission are available at the initial phase of the investigation, the mission can draft these sections at the beginning of the mission.

---

[7] Beit Hanoun Fact-Finding Mission report, 3–4 and 24.

[8] Darfur Commission report, 9–17.

B. PRESENT THE MISSION'S FINDINGS

STEP 1: DEFINE THE OUTPUT

Presenting the findings of the investigation is the ultimate purpose of an MRF exercise. For this reason, the findings should be drafted with care and precision and must be clear about their level of certainty (see Section 2, Establishing the Facts and Applying the Law in this Handbook). Additionally, the report should omit any content – such as names or other identifying information – that could jeopardize the protection of individuals who provided information to the mission (see Section 3, Protection of Witnesses and Victims in this Handbook) or that might raise due process concerns for allegations of criminal conduct by specific individuals.

In light of the importance of respecting *due process* and given the lower standard of evidence used by MRF bodies compared to courts, a mission required to identify alleged perpetrators should refrain from doing so publicly. Instead, the mission should compile a confidential list that can be made available in the future to any appropriate international or national prosecutors. The list should indicate the name of the individual and the specific allegation. Such documents should be lodged in a location where confidentiality can be assured. The common practice for missions mandated by the UNHRC is to hand over confidential lists to the OHCHR at the end of the mission.

STEP 2: DETERMINE HOW TO PRESENT THE CONTENT

The two main considerations regarding the presentation of the mission's findings are: (1) the language that the mission uses to describe the incidents examined, and (2) the structure of the factual and legal conclusions.

The language used in the report is important for its credibility. First, practitioners widely agree that the tone for which MRF reports should strive is authoritative impartiality. Emotive vocabulary or superfluous adjectives that can bring the objectivity of the mission into question should be avoided. Second, it is important that the mission confines legal vocabulary (e.g., describing incidents as violations) to the sections in the report that focus on legal analysis. Otherwise, the distinction between the report's factual and legal conclusions may be blurred. Third, the tone and vocabulary usage should be consistent throughout the entirety of the report. Fourth, report drafters should bear in mind the desirability of making the report readable to a wider audience. Presenting the information in a manner that is understandable and that tells a story could increase the outreach and impact of the report. Fifth, the report should always be written as if it is going to be made public, even if not clearly stipulated in the mandate.

Regarding structure, it is important that the report exhibits cohesion between the factual and legal findings of the investigation. If the report draws a legal conclusion that a violation has occurred, the report should also present all the requisite factual findings to indicate the presence of all the elements of the violation (see Section 2, Establishing Facts and Applying the Law in this Handbook). Additionally, structuring the findings in chronological order will allow for better readability.

The overarching structural components of the report's factual and legal conclusions are described below.

- *Applicable law*: Describes what laws apply to the context. Could necessitate references to certain factual conclusions; for example, to demonstrate that a situation constitutes an armed conflict for the purpose of applying IHL and for the classification of an armed conflict as a non-international conflict, the report will have to establish certain facts, such as that an armed group that is a party to the conflict exhibits a certain degree of organization.
- *Factual findings*: Describe the facts found by the mission.
- *Legal analysis*: Articulates the mission's conclusions regarding which, if any, of the applicable laws have been violated, in light of the mission's factual findings.

Decisions about structure are complicated by the fact that MRF reports often cover many types of incidents committed by various perpetrators in a wide array of locations. When deciding how to organize this information, dividing chapters by perpetrator should normally be avoided, since this structural choice risks evoking controversy about the mission's conclusions.

Based on the mandate of the mission, as well as the aspects of the mission's findings that the commissioners wish to emphasize, the mission must decide whether to favor structuring the report's factual findings by geographic region or by violation type. While no professional consensus exists regarding the desirability of one structural choice versus the other, both options have certain benefits.

Structure by *geographic region* entails, within a single chapter, providing an overview, in chronological order, of different types of violations that occurred within the same geographic region. The benefit of this structural choice is that, by describing within a single section factual findings related to different types of incidents that were part of the same attack, the report can more easily provide an overall narrative. Additionally, structuring a chapter in this manner can help the report demonstrate how different types of violations relate to one another.

The report of the Kyrgyzstan Commission, structured by geographic region, presents the mission's factual findings in a section titled, "Facts and Circumstances Relevant to Events of June 2010 in Osh and Surrounding Provinces," which is divided into three subsections.

A. *Narrative Chronology*: Presents a fifteen-page chronology that describes, in a narrative format, the factual conclusions of the mission, internally structured based on geographic area.

B. *Some Particular Issues*: Highlights factual findings related to particular issues of concern to the mission, which are the seizure, distribution, and use of weapons; the burning of buildings; and SGBV.

C. *Impact of the Events*: Addresses the impact of the violence by presenting statistics about injuries and fatalities, as well as discussing property damage and displacement.[9]

Structure *by violation type* breaks the report down by the type of violation being examined. Individual chapters can then be internally structured by geographic region, if necessary. This structural choice can help the report elucidate patterns of incidents that spanned multiple geographic regions, which can be particularly useful since some norms of international law – crimes against humanity, for example – require that the mission demonstrates the existence of a pattern of attacks.

The *Lebanon Commission* report is structured primarily based on incident types, including sections devoted specifically to:

- attacks on civilian population and objects (internally structured by geographic region: Southern Lebanon, South Beirut, and the Bekaa Valley);
- attacks on convoys of civilians;
- attacks on infrastructure and other objects;
- precautionary measures taken before attacks; and
- attacks on medical facilities.[10]

In each section, the report presents the mission's factual conclusions and legal analysis regarding the relevant violation type or thematic area.

---

[9] Kyrgyzstan Commission report, 25–46.
[10] See generally the Lebanon Commission report.

These two structural options are not mutually exclusive. Indeed, as described above, a report primarily structured based on violation type might require subsections structured by geographic region. Each mission should decide how best to find the most appropriate equilibrium between these two structural avenues, given the commissioners' determination of how the mission can most clearly respond to the mission's mandate.

STEP 3: PLAN THE DRAFTING PROCESS

The mission should decide early on in the implementation process how the mission plans to divide report-drafting responsibilities between commissioners and staff. Typically, commissioners make decisions about the content of the report and staff members prepare drafts, based on the directives of the commissioners, to be carefully reviewed, edited, and adopted by the commissioners, who ultimately bear the sole responsibility for the content of the report.

Despite being the result of a collaborative drafting process, the report must have a consistent tone. The use of a lead drafter/editor has proved useful to that effect.

C. OFFER RECOMMENDATIONS

STEP 1: DEFINE THE OUTPUT

The recommendations included in the final report play an important role in the impact of the final report in the aftermath of the mission. The objective in crafting recommendations is to provide the mission's view of how various actors – including the mandating body, parties to the conflict, UN entities such as the UNSG and the United Nations Security Council, armed groups, civil society, as well as international or national prosecutors – should respond to the mission's findings.

STEP 2: DETERMINE HOW TO PRESENT THE CONTENT

Commissioners must decide to whom recommendations should be directed and what specific measures the mission should recommend. Recommendations articulated in past MRF reports include the following:

- countries engaged in ongoing violations should cease and desist;
- accountability should be pursued by the countries involved in the context, on the international level or in other countries through universal jurisdiction;
- governments that have engaged in violations should pursue institutional reform (e.g., of the military or democratic institutions);

- reparations should be granted to victims by national and/or international actors;
- governments should ensure the protection of witnesses who provided information to the mission; and
- follow-up measures should be implemented to monitor developments. Those could include the mandating of a special rapporteur, the creation of an ad hoc panel to monitor progress on accountability, monitoring undertaken by a UN peace operation or by the OHCHR, or an extension of the mandate of the mission.[11]

When deciding on recommendations, and to whom they should be addressed, commissioners can be guided by two principal considerations. The first consideration is the *commissioners' perspective of the object and purpose of the mission*, as derived from their interpretation of the mandate. Commissioners working under mandates with a legal focus have tended to offer recommendations that focus on accountability, while missions with a focus on reducing international tensions have yielded reports with more politically oriented recommendations.

The mandate for the UNSG Flotilla Panel states that the mission should "consider and recommend ways of avoiding similar incidents in the future" and makes no mention of accountability.[12]

In response to this mandate, the panel produced a report that offered no recommendations about accountability but rather focused its recommendations on the non-repetition of incidents such as the Gaza flotilla raid, which was the focus of the panel's inquiry.[13]

The second consideration is *the desired result of the recommendations*. In this regard, when crafting recommendations, commissioners can be guided by the mission's assessment of the impact of the report on the intended audience (see Table 9 in Section 4, Public Communication in this Handbook). One cautionary note in this regard is that offering too many recommendations could render this section of the report less readable, adversely affecting its impact.

When deciding what to recommend, and to whom, commissioners should consider both short-term and long-term recommendations. Some recommendations can be undertaken in the immediate aftermath of an MRF report. Other recommendations –

---

[11] This list draws from a list of recommendation types offered in OHCHR, "Guidance and Practice," 94–99.

[12] UNSG Flotilla Panel report, 7.

[13] Ibid., 67–75.

for example, recommendations regarding accountability or institutional reform at the domestic level – necessarily require a longer period of time for implementation and may meet resistance from local authorities.

An MRF mission should not shy away from recommending important measures that may not be implemented in the short term. The mission should include such recommendations in the report in order to contribute to an environment of political pressure toward achieving these ends.

STEP 3: PLAN THE DRAFTING PROCESS

The mission should aim to draft recommendations that are precise and based on the mission's assessment of the situation on the ground. In particular, the mission should avoid letting preconceived notions of the report's recommendations influence the data-gathering effort. A scenario in which a mission makes decisions about recommendations before the data has been gathered and analyzed would bring the impartiality of the mission into question.

That being said, the process of crafting recommendations can benefit from preliminary steps taken toward the beginning of, and throughout, the implementation of the mission. For example, conducting a preliminary desk review of recommendations formulated by other organizations in previously produced MRF reports can inform the recommendation-drafting process. Also, on some missions, members of the investigative team have proposed recommendations for commissioners' consideration throughout the investigation. As long as such measures are undertaken internally and kept confidential, they can accelerate the pace of the drafting process that occurs at the end of the mission without raising questions about impartiality.

When feasible and deemed useful to the mission, during the preparation of the report commissioners may opt to discuss recommendations with relevant parties, such as the addressees of recommendations, as long as doing so does not compromise the independence of the mission. In such discussions, commissioners can offer addressees of recommendations the opportunity to correct any issues of concern, thus potentially enhancing the impact of the mission.

IV. FINAL OBSERVATIONS

As this section has highlighted, one overarching challenge frames the report-drafting process. On the one hand, the report is the definitive document that communicates to relevant audiences the mission's findings and the means by which the mission arrived at its conclusions. On the other hand, the circumstances under which practitioners draft reports are far from ideal. MRF practitioners operate under resource-scarce conditions, and often, particularly in the context of UN missions, bureaucratic obstacles also play a role in shaping the report-drafting process.

The practical steps articulated in this section offer MRF practitioners considerations for grappling with this challenging environment and approaching report drafting in a strategic manner. For many of the decisions that commissioners need to make during this process, there is no template applicable to all MRF mission types. When broaching questions such as what level of detail to include in the report about the creation and operation of the mission, or how to structure the report's factual and legal findings (i.e., by geographic region or by incident type), commissioners will need to consider the mandate and context of the mission, as well as the intended audience of the report. The elements that this section presents offer considerations drawn from past professional practice to assist in these decision-making processes.

For other issues, widespread consensus exists among practitioners about the most-favored approach. Specifically, the mission should not publish in the report names of individuals accused of responsibility for violations; should not use emotive vocabulary that could bring the mission's impartiality into question; and should not make any draft recommendations public. The near uniformity of MRF practitioners' views in relation to these issues suggests the low degree of flexibility that an MRF mission should exercise when deciding how to approach these matters.

PART II

Selected Writings on Monitoring, Reporting,
and Fact-Finding

1

On the Hybrid Nature of Monitoring, Reporting, and Fact-Finding Missions

ROB GRACE

Introduction

This chapter examines monitoring, reporting, and fact-finding (MRF) missions as hybrid entities defined by both political and technical characteristics. The technical aspects of MRF missions derive from their nature as investigative mechanisms mandated to gather and assess information relevant to alleged violations of international human rights law (IHRL) and international humanitarian law (IHL). However, political considerations are inherent to the creation of MRF missions. Indeed, the bodies that decide to establish an MRF mission and determine the mission's scope – specifically, by adopting the mandate – are usually political entities, such as the United Nations Human Rights Council (UNHRC) and the United Nations Security Council (UNSC). Thus, regardless of the technical characteristics of MRF work geared toward gathering and assessing data, the process by which MRF missions come into existence is one of political consensus building among members of the mandating body.

The ideal toward which MRF work strives is that these political and technical dimensions complement one another. As one practitioner asserts, the goal of an MRF mission when addressing a situation of armed conflict or an internal disturbance is to "use the technical to move it forward politically."[1] More specifically, the very purpose of mandating an MRF mission is to initiate a credible, technically sound information-gathering exercise, undertaken in a manner that is insulated from political forces, to produce an authoritative report to inform the future actions of the mandating body. As Philip Alston wrote about the UNSC's creation of the International Commission of Inquiry on Darfur (hereafter the Darfur

---

[1] Karen Kenny, Director, International Human Rights Network, interview conducted by HPCR, September 22, 2011.

Commission) before the UNSC referred the situation to the International
Criminal Court:

> [T]he process of establishing a Commission of Inquiry to evaluate
> whether or not a situation warrants a referral by the Security Council
> provides an appropriate filtering mechanism before the Council takes
> a decision. It ensures a thorough and systematic preliminary review of
> the facts, it provides a fully reasoned legal analysis, and it gives Coun-
> cil members the opportunity to consider alternative approaches which
> might be better suited to ensure a just outcome. The fact that a Com-
> mission will not always lead to a referral makes the process all the more
> legitimate and important.[2]

But to what extent do these two characteristics – political and technical –
succeed in complementing one another in MRF practice? This chapter
examines this question, focusing particularly on four aspects of an MRF
mission's creation: (1) the "triggering mechanism" by which the mandating body considers whether or not an MRF mission is warranted to
address a particular situation, (2) the mandate-drafting process, (3) the
selection of commissioners and staff, and (4) the mandate-interpretation
process that the commissioners undertake, typically as the first step of
their work. As this chapter describes, the political and technical dimensions of MRF missions are often not so easily kept distinct from one another, leading to professional dilemmas for practitioners in their efforts to
implement MRF mandates.

I. The Triggering Mechanism

This section provides an overview of the historical evolution of how MRF
missions have been activated. In broad terms, one can discern two tracks
that have been pursued. The first track requires that the parties to a conflict consent to the initiation of an investigation into their own behavior. The second track entails third-party actors mandating an MRF body
without first obtaining the consent of the parties to be investigated. For
missions with mandates relating to allegations of IHL and IHRL violations, the first track has largely proven to be unfeasible, except for periodic ad hoc missions to which particular governments have consented. As
a consequence, a state of affairs has emerged in which, as one practitioner

---

[2] Philip Alston, "The Darfur Commission as a Model for Future Responses to Crisis Situations," *Journal of International Criminal Justice* 3 (2005): 607, accessed June 14, 2015,
doi:10.1093/jicj/mqi053.

asserts, MRF missions tend to constitute "an intrusive act and may be resented as unwarranted interference into events deemed to be within the target states' jurisdiction."[3]

A. Consent-based Fact-Finding

One can trace modern MRF history back to 1899, when governments adopted the Convention for the Pacific Settlement of International Disputes (hereafter the 1899 Hague Convention). Though governments had previously created commissions on an ad hoc basis, with this convention, governments attempted for the first time to institutionalize a fact-finding process, albeit limited only to contexts related to "differences of an international nature involving neither honor nor vital interests, and arising from a difference of opinion on points of facts."[4] These commissions, which were to be "constituted by special agreement between the parties in conflict,"[5] would entail the active cooperation of the parties involved in the dispute. As Article 23 of the 1899 convention articulates: "The powers in dispute engage to supply the International Commission of Inquiry, as fully as they may think possible, with all means and facilities necessary to enable it to be completely acquainted with and to accurately understand the facts in question."[6]

Furthermore, the 1907 Convention for the Pacific Settlement of International Disputes (hereafter the 1907 Hague Convention) elaborated on certain procedural aspects of these mechanisms to "insur[e] the better working in practice of Commissions of Inquiry," as the convention's preamble states.[7] One can consider this institutionalized form of fact-finding to be a success; governments consented to seven commissions of inquiry that operated under these procedures.[8]

Unfortunately, though, the historical trajectory of institutionalized, consent-based fact-finding plateaued with these conventions. This

---

[3] Christine Chinkin, "U.N. Human Rights Council Fact-Finding Missions: Lessons from Gaza," in *Looking to the Future: Essays on International Law in Honor of W. Michael Reisman*, ed. Mahnoush H. Arsanjani, Jacob Katz Cogan, Robert D. Sloane, and Siegfried Wiessner (Leiden: Martinus Nijhoff Publishers, 2011), 487–488.

[4] Convention (I) for the Pacific Settlement of International Disputes (Hague I), 1899, Article 9, accessed June 30, 2015, http://avalon.law.yale.edu/19th_century/hague01.asp.

[5] Ibid., at Article 10.   [6] Ibid., at Article 12.

[7] 1907 Convention for the Pacific Settlement of International Disputes, Preamble.

[8] William I. Shore, *Fact-Finding in the Maintenance of International Peace* (New York: Oceana Publications, 1970), 15–18.

unfortunate fact began to crystalize after 1929, when efforts began – still ongoing yet thus far unsuccessful – to integrate institutionalized fact-finding into the field of IHL. The Geneva Conventions of 1864 and 1906 had included no provisions for an inquiry mechanism, but governments reached consensus on incorporating into the 1929 Geneva Conventions the following provision: "On the request of a belligerent, an enquiry shall be instituted, in a manner to be decided between the interested parties, concerning any alleged violation of the Convention; when such violation has been established the belligerents shall put an end to and repress it as promptly as possible."[9] This provision was included only "after much hesitation," one reason being that "[m]any delegates were afraid of opening a door, in the Convention, to possible sanctions against States,"[10] concerns that echoed those articulated during discussions about adopting the 1899 Hague Convention.[11] However, given the requirement that inquiries be instituted "in a manner to be decided between the interested parties," consensus between warring parties was never achieved, and this mechanism endured unused.

In light of the evident unfeasibility of reaching consensus among parties at conflict with one another about the creation of an inquiry focused on alleged IHL violations, would the parties to the Geneva Conventions agree to some other form of effective triggering mechanism? Thus far, the answer has been no. The Commission of Experts that the International Committee of the Red Cross (ICRC) convened in 1937 to consider revisions to the Geneva Conventions proposed an alternative: that any party to the convention could demand the initiation of an inquiry.[12] But governments rejected this option during the adoption of the Geneva Conventions of 1949, opting instead to retain the consent requirement included in the 1929 convention.[13] As with the mechanisms established by the 1929 convention, governments never consented to an inquiry under these procedures.

---

[9] Convention for the Amelioration of the Condition of the Wounded and Sick in Armies in the Field, July 27, 1929, Article 30.
[10] "Convention (I) for the Amelioration of the Condition of the Wounded and Sick in Armed Forces in the Field, Geneva, 12 August 1949," Commentary – Art. 52. Chapter IX: Repression of abuses and infractions, Treaties and States Parties to Such Treaties, International Committee of the Red Cross, accessed July 13, 2015, https://www.icrc.org/applic/ihl/ihl. nsf/Comment.xsp?action=openDocument&documentId=7F7849F767A4D99CC12563C D004224A7.
[11] Shore, Fact-Finding, 14–15.   [12] ICRC, "Commentary – Art. 52."
[13] Convention (I) for the Amelioration of the Condition of the Wounded and Sick in Armed Forces in the Field, August 12, 1949, Article 52.

The adoption of Additional Protocol I (AP I) to the Geneva Conventions in 1977 offered another opportunity to revisit this issue. The outcome of these negotiations was Article 90 of AP I, which established the International Humanitarian Fact-Finding Commission (IHFFC) to "enquire into any facts alleged to be a grave breach as defined in the [Geneva] Conventions and this Protocol or other serious violation of the Conventions or of this Protocol."[14] Many proponents of the IHFFC had hoped to design a commission that would have compulsory jurisdiction and the right to initiate inquiries.[15] But the attendees of the 1977 Plenary Meeting of the Diplomatic Conference on the Reaffirmation and Development of International Humanitarian Law Applicable in Armed Conflicts – which created the IHFFC – bifurcated into two groups, one that supported a strong commission and another that feared, according to the ICRC Commentary, "an intolerable encroachment on the sovereignty of States."[16] The result, according to one writer, was a commission plagued by "several unattractive birth marks reflecting the struggle that had accompanied its creation."[17] The IHFFC was not granted the right to initiate inquiries on its own,[18] and though states parties to the treaty can opt to recognize the competence of the IHFFC in advance,[19] inquiries otherwise require the consent of all parties concerned.[20] In other words, the IHFFC did relatively little to improve upon the inquiry procedures outlined in the Geneva Conventions of 1929 and 1949.

The ramifications of this gridlock between supporters and opponents of a strong, institutionalized fact-finding mechanism became clear in the 1990s. Twenty states parties had accepted the competence of the IHFFC, and hence, pursuant to Article 90.1.b of AP I, the IHFFC could finally be

---

[14] Protocol Additional to the Geneva Conventions of 12 August 1949, and Relating to the Protection of Victims of International Armed Conflicts (Protocol I), June 8, 1977, Article 90.2.c.i.

[15] Frits Kalshoven, "The International Humanitarian Fact-Finding Commission: A Sleeping Beauty?" in *Reflections on the Law of War: Collected Essays* (Boston: Martinus Nijhoff Publishers, 2007), 836.

[16] Yves Sandoz, Christophe Swinarski, and Bruno Zimmermann, eds., *Commentary on the Additional Protocols* (Geneva: Martinus Nijhoff Publishers and International Committee of the Red Cross, 1987), 1044.

[17] Kalshoven, "A Sleeping Beauty," 835.

[18] Sandoz, Swinarski, and Zimmermann, *Commentary*, 1044.

[19] Protocol Additional to the Geneva Conventions of 12 August 1949, and Relating to the Protection of Victims of International Armed Conflicts (Protocol I), June 8, 1977, Article 90.2.a.

[20] Ibid., at Article 90.2.d.

activated.[21] This moment in MRF history coincided seemingly auspiciously with the international community's burgeoning post-Cold War interest in civilian protection and international legal accountability, which had already manifested with the United Nations' (UN's) engagement to end El Salvador's twelve-year civil war. The UNSC had established the United Nations Observer Mission in El Salvador, the first UN peace operation to include an expressly mandated human rights monitoring component,[22] and the UN-brokered Chapultepec Peace Accords established the Commission on Truth for El Salvador, the first such commission funded and staffed by the UN.[23]

But in 1992, when the UNSC decided to address potential IHL violations committed in the former Yugoslavia, the UNSC ignored the IHFFC and established its own ad hoc MRF mission: the United Nations Commission of Experts on the Former Yugoslavia (hereafter the Former Yugoslavia Commission).[24] As if to accentuate the IHFFC's irrelevance, the United Nations Secretary-General (UNSG) appointed two IHFFC members, Frits Kalshoven and Torkel Opsahl, to the UNSC's commission.[25] As the international community continued to engage more deeply in the welfare of civilians in armed conflict, the IHFFC suffered the fate of its Geneva Convention inquiry procedure predecessors, and a diverse world of MRF mechanism types emerged in the wake of the IHFFC's failure.

Still, efforts continue to operationalize the IHFFC and to establish an institutionalized form of consent-based fact-finding for IHL violations. At the 31st Conference of the International Red Cross and Red Crescent Movement, held in November 2011, the government of Switzerland, along with several other countries, adopted pledge 1097, by which each

---

[21] Kalshoven, "A Sleeping Beauty," 836.

[22] See United Nations Security Council resolution 693 (1991), ¶ 2, which mandated the United Nations Observer Mission in El Salvador "to verify the compliance by the parties [the government of El Salvador and the Frente Farabundo Martí para la Liberación Nacional] with the Agreement on Human Rights signed at San José on 26 July 1990." Previous UN-mandated peace operations had included human rights-related activities, though without using explicit human rights language in the mandate. See generally Katarina Månsson, "The Forgotten Agenda: Human Rights Protection and Promotion in Cold War Peacekeeping," *Journal of Conflict & Security Law* 10, no. 3 (2005): 379–403, accessed July 13, 2015, doi:10.1093/jcsl/kri015.

[23] Priscilla Hayner, "Fifteen Truth Commissions – 1974 to 1994: A Comparative Analysis," *Human Rights Quarterly* 16, no. 4 (1994): 599, accessed July 7, 2015, http://www.jstor.org/stable/762562.

[24] Kalshoven, "A Sleeping Beauty," 838.   [25] Ibid.

country "commits itself to promote reflections on measures that would render the International Humanitarian Fact-Finding Commission (IHFFC) more operational and to continue its efforts to encourage the resort to the IHFFC in situations of armed conflicts."[26] Additionally, the conference adopted a resolution that invites the ICRC to engage in research and consultations to "enhance and ensure the effectiveness of mechanisms of compliance with international humanitarian law."[27] Pursuant to this resolution, over the course of four meetings that the government of Switzerland and the ICRC convened between 2012 and 2015, states discussed the possibility of incorporating fact-finding into a new IHL compliance mechanism. However, according to a summary of these meetings, though "many States believed [fact-finding] should be part of a future IHL compliance system," "no convergence of views emerged in relation to a possible fact-finding function," and states accepted "that the establishment of a fact-finding function will not be further examined at this stage."[28] During this dialogue, many states expressed that the issue of fact-finding should eventually be revisited, but the resistance of certain governments has thus far prevented forward motion.

Consent-based fact-finding does have a place on the current MRF landscape but occurs only in an ad hoc, rather than an institutionalized, manner. For example, the Secretary-General's Panel of Inquiry on the 31 May 2010 Flotilla Incident (hereafter the UNSG Flotilla Panel) included one representative from Turkey (Süleyman Özdem Sanberk) and one from Israel (Joseph Ciechanover Itzhar);[29] the Bahrain Independent Commission of Inquiry (hereafter the Bahrain Commission) was mandated by

---

[26] For the full text of pledge 1097 and the full list of countries that joined the pledge, see "Pledges list for this country," 31st International Conference of the Red Cross and Red Crescent, International Committee of the Red Cross, accessed July 13, 2015, https://www. icrc.org/pledges/pledgeList1.xsp?xsp=Statesdoc&option=States&section=Switzerland& outline=3&view=V_xspPledgesByPAUnikey.

[27] "31st International Conference 2011: Resolution 1 – Strengthening Legal Protection for Victims of Armed Conflicts," December 1, 2011, International Committee of the Red Cross, accessed July 13, 2015, http://www.icrc.org/eng/resources/documents/ resolution/31-international-conference-resolution-1-2011.htm.

[28] "Chairs' Conclusions," Fourth Meeting of States on Strengthening Compliance with International Humanitarian Law (IHL), Geneva, Swiss Federal Department of Foreign Affairs and the International Committee of the Red Cross, April 23–24, 2015, pp. 2, 7.

[29] See generally "Report of the Secretary-General's Panel of Inquiry on the 31 May 2010 Flotilla Incident," September 2011, accessed June 14, 2015, http://www.un.org/News/dh/ infocus/middle_east/Gaza_Flotilla_Panel_Report.pdf.

Bahraini royal decree;[30] and the Kyrgyzstan Inquiry Commission (hereafter the Kyrgyzstan Commission) was initiated only after the government
of Kyrgyzstan "endorsed" the Terms of Reference.[31] However, the more
prevalent scenario in the current domain of MRF is that third-party actors mandate an MRF mission to examine the actions of other parties engaged in violent conflict without first requiring that those parties consent
to the investigation, as the next section examines.

B. Fact-Finding as an "Intrusive" Act

As institutionalized, consent-based fact-finding efforts have failed to
gain traction over the past century, fact-finding instituted without the
consent of the relevant parties has flourished. One early example occurred in 1913, when the Carnegie Endowment for International Peace
initiated a commission of inquiry to examine the Balkan Wars of 1912
and 1913, concluding that "there is no clause in international law applicable to land war and to the treatment of the wounded, which was not
violated, to a greater or less extent, by all the belligerents."[32] Subsequently, MRF missions have been mandated by the League of Nations,[33] and
post-World War II, by various UN organs, as well as regional organizations, such as the Organization of American States, the Arab League,
the Organisation of Islamic Cooperation, and the European Union.[34]
Contrary to the institutionalized mechanisms envisaged in the Geneva
Conventions and AP I, the domain of MRF, lacking a centralized mandating body, developed in an ad hoc manner, emerging from different

---

[30] See generally Royal Order No. 28 of 2011, accessed June 25, 2015, http://www.lcil.cam.
     ac.uk/sites/default/files/LCIL/documents/arabspring/Bahrain_9_Royal_Order_No28
     .pdf.
[31] "Report of the Independent International Commission of Inquiry into the Events in
     Southern Kyrgyzstan in June 2010," n.d., p. xiv, accessed June 14, 2015, http://reliefweb.
     int/sites/reliefweb.int/files/resources/Full_Report_490.pdf.
[32] "Report of the International Commission to Inquire into the Causes and Conduct of
     the Balkan Wars," Carnegie Endowment for International Peace, 1914, p. 208, accessed
     July 11, 2015, https://archive.org/details/reportofinternat00inteuoft.
[33] See Larissa J. van den Herik, "An Inquiry into the Role of Commissions of Inquiry in
     International Law: Navigating the Tensions between Fact-Finding and Application of International Law," Chinese Journal of International Law 13, no. 3 (2014): 517–518, accessed
     July 13, 2015, doi:10.1093/chinesejil/jmu029.
[34] See "HPCR Digital Library of Monitoring, Reporting, and Fact-Finding," Program on
     Humanitarian Policy and Conflict Research at Harvard University, accessed June 7, 2015,
     http://www.hpcrresearch.org/mrf-database/, for links to mandates and reports for MRF
     missions implemented since the end of World War II.

institutional sources. The rest of this section describes several resulting challenges.

First, though the creation of these ad hoc MRF missions does not formally depend on the consent of the parties concerned, the cooperation of these parties can be essential to a mission's success. Indeed, various MRF reports have expressed that a lack of cooperation from parties relevant to the context impeded the information-gathering process.[35] Thus, a common aspect of current MRF work is diplomatic engagement with relevant governments and armed groups in order to secure access to territory and/or information. When these efforts are unsuccessful, an MRF mission must draw conclusions based on incomplete information.[36]

Second, in the absence of consent, the perception of the mission's legitimacy becomes a critical issue. Indeed, parties under investigation by an MRF body often strive to paint the mission as biased and illegitimate. As a result, commissioners leading MRF missions frequently must defend the mission's legitimacy, impartiality, and credibility. Whereas, in consent-based MRF work, agreement would exist from the beginning about the scope and methodology of the investigation, in the absence of consent, the credibility of the mandate and working methods of the mission sometimes become the subject of heated public debates, during and after the operations of the mission.[37]

Third, the decision to initiate an MRF mission hinges on the consensus of political actors within bodies such as the UNHRC and the UNSC. Consequently, the domain of MRF has no mechanism that applies objective criteria to each situation of armed conflict and internal disturbance to determine whether an MRF mission is warranted. Instead, the decision is not purely technical but rather primarily political. This state of affairs has led mandating bodies to be selective about the contexts in which they engage, since a mission can be initiated only if political consensus about the mandate can be achieved. This selectivity exposes the mandating body – as well as the mission itself, since MRF missions are often perceived to be agents of the mandating entity, even

---

[35] For example, see "Report of the high-level fact-finding mission to Beit Hanoun established under Council resolution S-3/1," A/HRC/9/26, September 1, 2008, p. 4, accessed June 14, 2015, http://www.refworld.org/docid/48cfa3a22.html.

[36] Chapter 3, Finding the Facts: Information Handling and Standards of Proof in this Handbook examines this issue in greater detail.

[37] For more information about this issue, see generally in this Handbook, Chapter 5, Professional Dilemmas in Public Communication and Report Drafting.

if in actuality the mission operates in an entirely independent manner – to accusations of bias.[38]

These challenges result directly from the inability of governments to reach consensus on devising an institutionalized fact-finding mechanism. In the absence of agreement in this regard, each MRF mission must demonstrate the credibility and legitimacy of its mandate and methodology – even in the absence of certainty that each party will cooperate with the investigation – in a politically charged environment in which the mission, by institutional design, could be deemed an "intrusion" to which the relevant parties have not previously consented.

II.   Mandate Drafting

A mandate is a crucial component of an MRF mechanism, as it forms the legal basis for the entire mission.[39] For this reason, MRF mission leaders frequently refer to their mandates at every phase throughout their work.[40] MRF actors note that successful mandates should be both "clear and flexible,"[41] articulating intelligible and manageable directives while also allowing commissioners sufficient interpretive leeway to shape their missions based on logistical, technical, and political considerations that emerge throughout the implementation process. As one MRF actor asserts, "If a mandate is clear, then the work is clear. If the mandate is murky, then it may be difficult to reconcile different positions among the

---

[38] A 2011 discussion on fact-finding co-organized by the Permanent Mission of Portugal to the United Nations and the United Nations Office for the Coordination of Humanitarian Affairs (OCHA) identified "selectivity in terms of what contexts are considered" as a key challenge of UN-mandated fact-finding activities. See Permanent Mission of Portugal to the United Nations and OCHA, "Highlights from the Workshop on Accountability and Fact-Finding Mechanisms for Violations of International Humanitarian Law and Human Rights Law: The Role of the Security Council – Past and Future," November 1, 2011, accessed July 13, 2015, http://www.missionofportugal.org/mop/images/documentos/nov0111.pdf.

[39] See United Nations General Assembly resolution 46/59, "Declaration on fact-finding by the United Nations in the field of the maintenance of international peace and security," December 9, 1991, ¶ 25, which asserts that "[f]act-finding missions have an obligation to act in strict conformity with their mandate."

[40] Confidential interview with a high-level MRF practitioner, name of interviewee on file, conducted by HPCR, Fall 2013.

[41] Kim Carter, Canadian Forces War Crimes Investigation Team Leader providing support for the United Nations Commission of Experts on the Former Yugoslavia, interview conducted by HPCR, September 29, 2011.

commissioners."[42] But as another states, "since decisions to create commissions of inquiry are political, this can lead to grey areas in the mandates that reflect political compromise rather than an effort to create a mandate that corresponds with complete precision to the situation under investigation."[43]

As these comments suggest, because of the political compromises usually necessary to reach consensus within a mandating body, and due to the relative lack of technical expertise among members of the mandating body (compared with commissioners, for example), specific details about a mission's implementation are generally best left out of the mandate. Indeed, most mandates are quite broad. For example, the mandate for the Independent, International Commission of Inquiry on Côte d'Ivoire (hereafter the Côte d'Ivoire Commission) states simply that the mission should "investigate the facts and circumstances surrounding the allegations of serious abuses and violations of human rights committed in Côte d'Ivoire following the presidential election of 28 November 2010."[44] However, this mandate provides no specific information about how the mission should gather information (e.g., field visits, use of third-party reports, or convening public hearings); what methodologies the mission should use to evaluate the information gathered (e.g., in relation to the mission's standard of proof); and how the mission should approach issues such as witness and victim protection, staff security, and public communications. But the broad nature of the mandate allows the political and technical aspects to remain distinct from one another. By not weighing too far into technical details, the political actors who adopt the mandate can empower the professionals undertaking the mission to determine these technical specifics.

Most mandates also allow for a great degree of interpretive leeway in terms of the scope of the mission's investigative focus. For example, the mandate for the Independent International Fact-Finding Mission on

---

[42] Roberto Ricci, Chief of Peace Mission Support and Rapid Response Unit, Office of the High Commissioner for Human Rights, interview conducted by HPCR, September 29, 2011. See also UNGA, "Declaration on Fact-Finding," ¶ 17, which asserts that "[t]he decision by the competent United Nations organ to undertake fact-finding should always contain a clear mandate for the fact-finding mission and precise requirements to be met by its report."

[43] Ben Majekodunmi, Chief of Human Rights Section for United Nations Stabilization Mission in Haiti, interview conducted by HPCR, October 6, 2011.

[44] United Nations Human Rights Council resolution 16/25, "Situation of human rights in Côte d'Ivoire," April 13, 2011, ¶ 10.

the Conflict in Georgia (hereafter the Georgia Fact-Finding Mission) specifically notes, "The geographical scope and time span of the investigation will be sufficiently broad to determine all the possible causes of the conflict."[45]

However, there are several ways that MRF mandates have created problems that the practitioners leading the mission have subsequently had to solve. First, some MRF mandates have appeared to prejudge the outcome of the investigation. Indeed, often MRF missions have been mandated by documents – resolutions adopted by the UNHRC, for example – that simultaneously condemn violations of IHL and/or IHRL and create an investigation into these very allegations. One example is the UNHRC resolution that mandated the Commission of Inquiry on Lebanon (hereafter the Lebanon Commission). This document, in one paragraph, "[s]trongly condemns the grave Israeli violations of human rights and breaches of international humanitarian law in Lebanon," and in a later paragraph, establishes a commission to probe these incidents.[46] In such scenarios, the fact that the mandate condemns the very acts the commission is tasked with investigating could evoke – and indeed has evoked – the concern that the purpose of the mission is merely to confirm conclusions that the mandating entity has already reached.[47]

It is also important for MRF mandates to draw clear distinctions between the terms "allegations" and "violations." A mandate that states that "violations of IHL and/or IHRL" have occurred gives the impression that the conclusion has already been drawn.[48] Conversely, a mandate that uses cautious terminology by mentioning "alleged violations" or "allegations of violations" appropriately conveys the need for an MRF mission to investigate the allegations that have emerged.

---

[45] "Report of the Independent International Fact-Finding Mission on the Conflict in Georgia," vol. 1, September 2009, p. 3.

[46] United Nations Human Rights Council resolution S-2/1, "The grave situation of human rights in Lebanon caused by Israeli military operations," August 11, 2006, ¶¶ 1, 7.

[47] For example, see "Report by UN Lebanon Inquiry Is One-Sided," press release, UN Watch, November 21, 2006, accessed May 26, 2015, http://www.unwatch.org/site/apps/nlnet/content2.aspx?c=bdKKISNqEmG&b=1316871&ct=3264691.

[48] For an example of a mission that faced this issue, see "Report of the International Fact-Finding Mission to Investigate Violations of International Law, Including International Humanitarian and Human Rights Law, Resulting from the Israeli attacks on the Flotilla of Ships Carrying Humanitarian Assistance," A/HRC/15/21, September 27, 2010, p. 3, accessed June 14, 2015, http://www2.ohchr.org/english/bodies/hrcouncil/docs/15session/A.HRC.15.21_en.pdf.

Second, the mandate might not match the task assigned to the mission with the available resources. An extreme example of one such mandate is that of the International Commission of Inquiry on Libya, which authorized the mission "to investigate all alleged violations of international human rights law in Libya" without offering any temporal restrictions.[49] It would indeed be impossible for the mission to investigate "all" of these allegations, especially since the mission was mandated to produce a report in less than four months and was able to undertake only three weeks of fieldwork.[50]

Third, when defining the scope of the mission, the mandate could, perhaps unintentionally, authorize an unbalanced investigation. In some contexts, for example, the temporal scope of the mission has become a politically charged issue. The United Nations Independent Expert on Somalia repeatedly called for a UNSC-authorized ad hoc MRF mission focused on Somalia and insisted that the temporal scope stretch back to 1991 to include massacres that followed the collapse of the government of Siad Barre.[51] A mission with a more narrow scope, he believed, "would be looked at as biased."[52] Opposition to this broad temporal scope played a role in various governments' resistance to the commission, and the proposal was never adopted.[53] MRF investigators in the Democratic Republic of the Congo (DRC) have repeatedly encountered host government resistance based in part on government concerns about the restricted nature of the temporal scope of these missions' mandates, and in 1998, the UNSG broadened his investigative team's temporal scope in an effort to gain the cooperation of the DRC government.[54]

[49] United Nations Human Rights Council resolution S-15/1, "Situation of human rights in the Libyan Arab Jamahiriya," February 25, 2011, ¶ 11.

[50] In terms of the time frame of the mission, the UNHRC adopted the mandate on February 25, 2011, and the mandate tasked the mission with presenting a report at the 17th session of the UNHRC, convened in June 2011. See also "International Commission of Inquiry investigating Human Rights Violations in Libya Ends Field Visits to Egypt, Libya and Tunisia," Office of the High Commissioner for Human Rights, May 3, 2011, accessed July 13, 2015, http://www.ohchr.org/en/NewsEvents/Pages/DisplayNews.aspx?NewsID=10982, which discusses the mission's field visits.

[51] Ghanim Al-Najjar, Former United Nations Independent Expert for Somalia, interview conducted by HPCR, November 3, 2011.

[52] Ibid.   [53] Ibid.

[54] See "Report of the Secretary-General's Investigative Team Charged with Investigating Serious Violations of Human Rights and International Humanitarian Law in the Democratic Republic of the Congo," S/1998//581, June 29, 1998, p. 1, accessed June 1, 2015, http://ap.ohchr.org/ documents/alldocs.aspx?doc_id=8840, which states that the government of

Fourth, mandates that impose restrictions on whom an MRF mission may investigate are especially problematic. Various one-sided mandates adopted by the UNHRC particularly exemplify this issue. The mandate for the Lebanon Commission (in addition to appearing to prejudge the investigation's outcome, as already mentioned) authorized the mission to focus solely on Israel. The mandate states that the tasks of the mission are

(a) to investigate the systematic targeting and killings of civilians by Israel in Lebanon;
(b) to examine the types of weapons used by Israel and their conformity with international law;
(c) to assess the extent and deadly impact of Israeli attacks on human life, property, critical infrastructure and the environment.[55]

Similarly, the mandate for the High-Level Fact-Finding Mission to Beit Hanoun established under resolution S-3/1 (hereafter the Beit Hanoun Fact-Finding Mission) includes the following one-sided task: "make recommendations on ways and means to protect Palestinian civilians against any further Israeli assaults."[56] Subsequently, in response to Israel's Operation Cast Lead in Gaza in 2009, the UNHRC adopted a resolution creating an MRF mission

> to investigate all violations of international human rights law and international humanitarian law by the occupying Power, Israel, against the Palestinian people throughout the Occupied Palestinian Territory, particularly in the occupied Gaza Strip, due to the current aggression, and calls upon Israel not to obstruct the process of investigation and to fully cooperate with the mission.[57]

---

the DRC "urged that the mandate be extended back to 1 March 1993, in order to include: the ethnic violence which, from that time, pitted self-styled 'indigenous' Zairians, originally supported by the Forces Armées Zaïroises (FAZ), against Zairians of both Hutu and Tutsi origin, as well as subsequent developments." The UNSG subsequently states in his report, "In response to the Government, I extended the period under investigation back to 1 March 1993."

[55] United Nations Human Rights Council resolution S-2/1, "The grave situation of human rights in Lebanon caused by Israeli military operations," August 11, 2006, ¶ 7.

[56] United Nations Human Rights Council resolution S-3/1, "Human rights violations emanating from Israeli military incursions in the Occupied Palestinian Territory, including the recent one in northern Gaza and the assault on Beit Hanoun," November 15, 2006, ¶ 7.

[57] United Nations Human Rights Council resolution S-9/1, "The grave violations of human rights in the Occupied Palestinian Territory, particularly due to the recent Israeli military attacks against the occupied Gaza Strip," January 12, 2009, ¶ 14.

This series of one-sided mandates focused on Israel has evoked accusations of bias on the part of the UNHRC. In 2012, after the UNHRC adopted a resolution authorizing an MRF mission "to investigate the implications of the Israeli settlements on the civil, political, economic, social and cultural rights of the Palestinian people throughout the Occupied Palestinian Territory, including East Jerusalem,"[58] Israel made a decision to cut off all ties with the UNHRC, citing not only the one-sided nature of the mandate but also the selective nature of the UNHRC's focus on Israel over time.[59]

The words of the commissioners of the Lebanon Commission particularly elucidate the detriments of operating under a one-sided mandate. As the commission's report states, "the Commission is not entitled, even if it had wished, to construe [the mandate] as equally authorizing the investigation of the actions by Hezbollah in Israel. To do so would exceed the Commission's interpretive function and would be to usurp the Council's powers."[60] However, the report continues, this restriction brought the entire nature of the mission into question.

> A fundamental point in relation to the conflict and the Commission's mandate as defined by the Council is the conduct of Hezbollah. The Commission considers that any independent, impartial and objective investigation into a particular conduct during the course of hostilities must of necessity be with reference to all the belligerents involved. Thus an inquiry into the conformity with international humanitarian law of the specific acts of IDF [Israel Defense Forces] in Lebanon requires that account also be taken of the conduct of the opponent.[61]

One legal expert notes that this limitation also hindered the mission's ability to make accurate assessments under IHL.

> In some instances the failure to consider Hezbollah's actions even undermined the Commission's consideration of Israeli conduct of hostilities, since an intricate understanding of Hezbollah's command structure, strategic objectives and military operations was essential in determining whether targets destroyed by Israel were military targets and whether the

---

[58] United Nations Human Rights Council resolution 19/17, "Israeli settlements in the Occupied Palestinian Territory, including East Jerusalem, and in the occupied Syrian Golan," March 22, 2012, ¶ 9.

[59] See "Israel Ends Contact with UN Human Rights Council," *BBC News*, March 26, 2012, accessed July 13, 2015, http://www.bbc.com/news/world-middle-east-17510668.

[60] "Report of the Commission of Inquiry on Lebanon pursuant to Human Rights Council Resolution S-2/1," A/HRC/3/2, November 23, 2006, p. 3, accessed May 26, 2015, http://www.unrol.org/files/A.HRC.3.2.pdf.

[61] Ibid.

incidental impact on civilians that resulted from the attacks was excessive in relation to the military advantage gained.[62]

For the United Nations Fact-Finding Mission on the Gaza Conflict (hereafter the Gaza Fact-Finding Mission), the impartial nature of the mission's original mandate delayed the process of finding an appropriate MRF practitioner to chair the mission. The president of the UNHRC first offered the position to Mary Robinson, but as Robinson later wrote:

> I refused to accept the invitation from the president of the Human Rights Council at the time, Ambassador Martin Uhomoibhi of Nigeria, to lead the investigation following the Human Rights Council's January 12, 2009 resolution. As a former UN High Commissioner for Human Rights, I felt strongly that the Council's resolution was one-sided and did not permit a balanced approach to determining the situation on the ground.[63]

The UNHRC president then offered the position to Richard Goldstone, who accepted the position only after the president agreed to an amended mandate drafted by Goldstone that broadened the scope of the inquiry "to investigate all violations of international human rights law and international humanitarian law that might have been committed at any time in the context of the military operations that were conducted in Gaza during the period from 27 December 2008 and 18 January 2009, whether before, during or after."[64] This revised mandate allowed the mission to produce a report that offered factual and legal conclusions about – as well as recommendations directed toward – not only Israel but also other relevant parties, including Hamas.[65] Though the UNHRC did not vote to adopt the new mandate, before the mission began, Goldstone persuaded the four ambassadors who co-sponsored the original UNHRC resolution to accept the broadened scope of the investigation.[66] Indeed, the mission encountered no resistance from any members of the UNHRC, either during the mission's implementation or after the release of the report, confirming for

[62] James G. Stewart, "The UN Commission of Inquiry on Lebanon: A Legal Appraisal," *Journal of International Criminal Justice* 5, no. 5 (2007): 1041, accessed June 14, 2015, doi:10.1093/jicj/mqm073 (internal citation omitted).

[63] Mary Robinson, "Accounting for Gaza," Project Syndicate, September 28, 2009, accessed June 27, 2015, http://www.project-syndicate.org/commentary/accounting-for-gaza.

[64] "Report of the United Nations Fact-Finding Mission on the Gaza Conflict," A/HRC/12/48, September 25, 2009, p. 13, accessed June 14, 2015, http://www2.ohchr.org/english/bodies/ hrcouncil/docs/12session/A-HRC-12-48.pdf.

[65] See ibid., 404–429.

[66] Richard J. Goldstone, "Quality Control in International Fact-Finding Outside Criminal Justice for Core International Crimes," in *Quality Control in Fact-Finding*, ed. Morten Bergsmo (Florence: Torkel Opsahl Academic EPublisher, 2013), 48.

the commissioners the sense that the renegotiated mandate legitimately operated as the authoritative mandate for the mission.[67]

However, revising the mandate did not resolve the issues of credibility and legitimacy that the original one-sided mandate brought forth. The government of Israel raised the issue of the renegotiated mandate, among other factors, to justify Israel's decision not to cooperate with the mission. As Goldstone recently wrote, reflecting on his efforts to engage with Israeli governmental authorities during the mission:

> To my regret, the Israeli Ambassador informed me that he had no authority to meet with me. I immediately sent him a letter, setting out the new mandate and requesting his government's co-operation. I offered to travel to Jerusalem to meet with the appropriate Israeli officials to seek their advice on how the mandate should be implemented by the Mission. A few days later, I received a negative response that was expressly based on the mandate contained in the HRC resolution that I had previously rejected. I responded, pointing out that I had refused the original mandate and reiterated the terms of my mandate. It took more than two months before that letter was answered. In the interim, I sent a personal letter to the Israeli Prime Minister requesting a meeting and advice. All these requests were turned down.[68]

The government of Israel assumed the position that, "as a matter of law, no statement by any individual, including the President of the Council, has the force to change the mandate of the Mission," and that "the legal basis of the proposed mission is HRC Resolution S-9/1."[69] Furthermore, this issue continued to arise in the contentious debates that developed about the mission's operations and findings, with some individuals agreeing with the government of Israel about the nature of the mandate's legal authority,[70] while other individuals found the mandate renegotiation to be not only unproblematic but also generally indicative of the mission's

---

[67] Hina Jilani, Member of the International Commission of Inquiry on Darfur and the United Nations Fact-Finding Mission on the Gaza Conflict, interview conducted by HPCR, April 24, 2013.

[68] Goldstone, "Quality Control," 47–48.

[69] "Letter from Israel Ambassador Leshno-Yaar to Goldstone," Israel Ministry of Foreign Affairs, July 2, 2009, accessed July 10, 2015, http://mfa.gov.il/MFA/InternatlOrgs/Issues/Pages/Letter_from_Israel_Ambassador_Leshno-Yaar_to_Goldstone_2-Jul-2009.aspx.

[70] See, for example, "UN Watch Calls on Goldstone Gaza Inquiry to Denounce Biased Mandate," press release, UN Watch, May 5, 2009, accessed June 17, 2015, http://www.un-watch.org/site/apps/nlnet/content2.aspx?c=bdKKISNqEmG&b=1316871&ct=6982241; and Irwin Cotler, "The Goldstone Mission – Tainted to the Core (Part I)," The Jerusalem Post, August 16, 2009, accessed June 17, 2015, http://www.jpost.com/Opinion/Op-Ed-Contributors/The-Goldstone-Mission-Tainted-to-the-core-part-I.

objective nature.[71] The prevalence of this issue in these debates suggests that mandate renegotiation is a potentially controversial avenue that might not always entirely succeed in insulating a mission from perceptions of bias that stem from the original mandate language.

Evidence indicates that the UNHRC has begun to learn from these experiences. Specifically, after Israel launched Operation Protective Edge in Gaza in 2014, the UNHRC once again mandated an MRF mission to gather information about potential violations of IHL and IHRL. However, the UNHRC resolution that mandated this mission did not single out Israel but rather articulated a scope that draws largely verbatim from the revised mandate that Goldstone crafted for the Gaza Fact-Finding Mission in 2009: "to investigate all violations of international humanitarian law and international human rights law in the Occupied Palestinian Territory, including East Jerusalem, particularly in the occupied Gaza Strip, in the context of the military operations conducted since 13 June 2014, whether before, during or after."[72]

In relation to other contexts, though, the UNHRC has repeated its past mistakes. One example is the UNHRC resolution adopted in 2014 in response to the rise of the Islamic State in Iraq and the Levant (ISIL). In this resolution, the UNHRC

> *Requests* the Office of the High Commissioner urgently to dispatch a mission to Iraq to investigate alleged violations and abuses of international human rights law committed by the so-called Islamic State in Iraq and the Levant and associated terrorist groups, and to establish facts and circumstances of such abuses and violations, with a view to avoiding impunity and ensuring full accountability.[73]

This mandate singles out ISIL and "associated terrorist groups" despite the fact that reports had already surfaced alleging that Iraqi security forces and pro-government militias had also been responsible for violations.[74]

It is important to note, however, that missions operating under unbiased mandates still sometimes elicit concerns that the mission has been,

---

[71] See, for example, "US: Ask Israel to Cooperate with Goldstone Inquiry," Human Rights Watch, May 17, 2009, accessed June 17, 2015, http://www.hrw.org/news/2009/05/17/us-ask-israel-cooperate-goldstone-inquiry.

[72] United Nations Human Rights Council resolution S-21/1, "Ensuring respect for international law in the Occupied Palestinian Territory, including East Jerusalem," July 23, 2014, ¶ 13.

[73] United Nations Human Rights Council resolution S-22/1, "The human rights situation in Iraq in the light of abuses committed by the so-called Islamic State in Iraq and the Levant and associated groups," September 1, 2014, ¶ 10.

[74] See "Iraq: Campaign of Mass Murders of Sunni Prisoners," Human Rights Watch, July 11, 2014, accessed July 7, 2015, http://www.hrw.org/news/2014/07/11/iraq-campaign-mass-murders-sunni-prisoners.

or will be, politicized. A fundamental aspect of the domain of MRF is that concerns about the political nature of the mandating body often color perceptions of the mission itself. This occurs despite the widespread practice of emphasizing the independence of the mission from the mandating body. The official names of various MRF missions – such as the Bahrain Independent Commission of Inquiry; the Independent, International Commission of Inquiry on Côte d'Ivoire; the Independent International Fact-Finding Mission on the Conflict in Georgia; and the United Nations Independent Special Commission of Inquiry for Timor-Leste – suggest this concern with demonstrating that the missions are independent.

One example that demonstrates how perceptions of the mandating entity can impact perceptions of the mission is the local response to the Bahrain Commission. Though the mission was mandated by Bahraini royal decree, the mandate text incorporated a "wish list" that the chair of the mission, M. Cherif Bassiouni, had presented to the king of Bahrain before agreeing to lead the mission.[75] The resulting mandate allowed for a balanced investigation by authorizing an investigation into "violations of international human rights norms by any participants."[76] The mandate also affirmed, "The Commission is wholly independent of the Government of Bahrain or of any other government, and the members of the Commission are acting in their personal capacity and do not represent any government, international organization, public official or any economic or political interest."[77] Additionally, during the implementation of the mandate, governmental actors never obstructed the mission, allowing the investigators to work freely as the mission proceeded.[78] In this sense, the mandate and operations of the mission appear to exemplify success in terms of an MRF mission's hybrid "political-technical" nature. The mandate offered enough specifics to frame the mission's focus while remaining sufficiently broad to allow for the implementation of a comprehensive, technically successful, and balanced investigation.

---

[75] "Cherif Bassiouni – interview," International Bar Association, n.d., accessed July 5, 2015, http://www.ibanet.org/Article/Detail.aspx?ArticleUid=e833feed-58a5-491c-987f-bbf-40c5e3e80.

[76] Royal Order No. 28 of 2011, Article 9, accessed June 25, 2015, http://www.lcil.cam.ac.uk/sites/default/files/LCIL/documents/arabspring/Bahrain_9_Royal_Order_No28.pdf.

[77] Ibid., at Article Three.

[78] See IBA, "Cherif Bassiouni – interview," in which Bassiouni states, "The flow of the investigation ran very smoothly. We didn't have any impediments whatsoever. The government cooperated with us at all levels. We had total open-doors. I mean I can tell you, this is very unusual. We had access to every prison and every hospital in the country. Our investigators could go to any prison we wanted at any time of the day or night."

However, a heated public discourse surrounding the nature of the mission nonetheless developed. Various opposition activists feared that the Bahrain Commission would serve as "a political shield for the regime," a tool for improving the regime's reputation and containing the 2011 uprising,[79] and an "excuse" for the international community to take no significant action.[80] These critiques arose, in part, in reaction to the domestic origin of the commission's mandate. As one member of Al Wefaq – one of the main opposition political parties in Bahrain – stated of the Bahrain Commission's domestic nature:

> We had a problem with the commission because it was appointed by a royal decree and it will submit its recommendations to the king himself. The body that may be tasked with implementing those recommendations may be the same body that has committed the violations. We would have preferred a UN-mandated commission to do the job.[81]

Furthermore, as argued in one Bahraini dissident electronic newspaper, the Bahraini government engaged in "no consultations of any sort" with victims or civil society organizations about the commission's creation, resulting in a mission that did "not express the national choice."[82]

In contrast to criticisms of the UNHRC-mandated Israel inquiries mentioned earlier, these concerns did not relate to a perception that the text of the mandate itself had become politicized. Instead, these criticisms focused on the identity of the mandating body and the process by which the mandate had come into being. This example suggests a perhaps inescapable dilemma: even if an MRF mandate successfully authorizes a comprehensive, feasible, balanced investigation, and even if the mission successfully operates in an independent manner, serious concerns may nonetheless still arise that the mandating body's political interests have unduly influenced the mission.

---

[79] Alaa Shehabi, "Bahrain's Independent Commission of Inquiry: A Path to Justice or Political Shield," *Jadaliyya*, November 22, 2011, accessed May 26, 2015, http://www.jadaliyya. com/pages/index/3244/bahrains-independent-commission-of-inquiry_a-path-.

[80] Maryam Alkhawaja, Twitter post, January 3, 2012, 2:53 a. m., https://twitter.com/mary-amalkhawaja/status/154153288558854144.

[81] "What is the BICI?" YouTube video, 2:49, posted by "Al Jazeera English," November 23, 2011, https://www.youtube.com/watch?v=555tcQ7Ujds&feature=relmfu.

[82] "Bahrain Mirror: Royal Fact Finding Commission: Five Fatal Breaches of the Standards of the UN High Commissioner for Human Rights," Bahrain Center for Human Rights, November 14, 2011, accessed July 10, 2015, http://www.bahrainrights.org/en/node/4846.

III.   The Selection of Commissioners and Staff

Once the mandate has been adopted, the process of assembling a team to undertake the investigation begins. The nature of MRF missions makes finding the right people critical. Since, as mentioned in the previous section, strong MRF mandates leave a significant amount of interpretive leeway to the practitioners leading the mission, an MRF investigation must be staffed with practitioners – including commissioners, investigators, interpreters, and logistical coordinators – who have the expertise and experience necessary to make sound technical decisions. Furthermore, the process of staffing the mission occurs under severe time constraints. As one MRF practitioner states, "You must be able to put trained boots quickly on the ground or you will miss the boat. Professionals trained in investigating international crimes must be the first on the ground in order to maximize the identification, collection, and preservation of the most important information and to minimize the danger to victims and witnesses."[83] But this highly time-sensitive process is complicated by the fact that staffing decisions must balance the need for technical expertise with the mission's political needs, especially since staffing decisions can also affect perceptions of a mission's impartiality and its overall legitimacy.

MRF practitioners, mandate drafters, and governmental actors widely acknowledge the importance of selecting commissioners based on legal expertise, eminence, and impartiality. Indeed, various mandates explicitly mention the importance of these criteria. The Bahrain Commission mandate states, "The Commission consists of five eminent and internationally renowned members, whose experience and reputation worldwide is well established;"[84] the Terms of Reference for the International Commission of Inquiry on Guinea (hereafter the Guinea Commission), according to the mission's report, "state that [the commission] will be composed of three members having a reputation for probity and impartiality;"[85]

---

[83] Andras Vamos-Goldman, Coordinator for Justice Rapid Response, interview conducted by HPCR, October 26, 2011.

[84] Royal Order No. 28 of 2011, Article Two, accessed June 25, 2015, http://www.lcil.cam. ac.uk/sites/default/files/LCIL/documents/arabspring/Bahrain_9_Royal_Order_No28. pdf.

[85] "Report of the International Commission of Inquiry mandated to establish the facts and circumstances of the events of 28 September 2009 in Guinea," transmitted by letter dated 18 December 2009 from the Secretary-General addressed to the President of the Security Council, S/2009/693, December 18, 2009, p. 6, accessed June 25, 2015, http://www .refworld.org/docid/4b4f49ea2.html.

and the Terms of Reference for the Kyrgyzstan Commission state that the mission

> will be composed of a panel of eminent personalities as well as a group of experts …. In the overall composition of the panel and experts, there will be the requisite expertise in human rights, conflict analysis, international humanitarian law and international criminal law; and knowledge of the country and language skills.[86]

Some mandates also specify the importance of diversity. For example, the mandate for the Côte d'Ivoire Commission states that the commissioner selection process should "tak[e] into consideration the importance of ensuring the equal participation and full involvement of women,"[87] and the Kyrgyzstan Commission's Terms of Reference state, "The need for gender and geographical diversity amongst members of the Commission will also be taken into account."[88]

However, when selecting commissioners and staff, various important aspects of professional expertise have often been overlooked. The rest of this section focuses on three of these areas: managerial expertise, investigative fieldwork experience, and knowledge of the context. The section concludes by commenting on the need to expand the pool of trained and experienced MRF practitioners.

A.   Managerial Expertise

Leadership skills are essential for effective commissioners, yet no mandate thus far has specified the importance of the managerial experience of the commission chair. But as one MRF actor states, "Leadership is important. Commissioners should know the law but should also be skilled at drafting, organizing, and managing. You want them to be involved, fighting, working until 3 AM."[89] MRF practitioners have expressed concern that the neglect of this consideration in the commissioner selection process sometimes leads to problems during implementation. For example, the mandate drafter for the 1992 Former Yugoslavia Commission writes:

---

[86] Kyrgyzstan Commission report, 2.
[87] United Nations Human Rights Council resolution 16/25, "Situation of human rights in Côte d'Ivoire," March 25, 2011, ¶ 10.
[88] Kyrgyzstan Commission report, 2.
[89] Fannie Lafontaine, Human Rights Officer/Special Assistant to the President on the International Commission of Inquiry on Darfur, interview conducted by HPCR, September 21, 2011.

The composition of the Commission quickly brought it under fire. My colleagues at the State Department made no secret of our feeling that there was too much emphasis on academic qualifications and too little on investigative or managerial skills. This sentiment was soon publicly voiced by Roy Gutman, who wrote that the Chairman of the Commission, Frits Kalshoven "tells visitors he does not know why he got the job."[90]

Two decades later, this problem persists. As one MRF practitioner states of a recent mission, "The chair plays a very critical role. He sets pace of work, moves the mission to next level of work. The chair lost time not knowing how to coordinate everybody because he did not have experience coordinating staff."[91] Another MRF practitioner stated that the chair of a different recent commission failed to exercise strong leadership on the administrative front, particularly in terms of setting deadlines.[92]

On some missions, the commissioners' lack of managerial expertise resulted in confusion over how different types of practitioners serving on the mission should collaborate on decision-making processes. On one mission, a commissioner and the head of the secretariat became engaged in a power struggle over who would control the mission's investigative decisions. This dispute – rooted in a disagreement over who had the authority to determine the mission's methodology – involved differing perceptions about how the mission's mandate should be implemented and what topics and actors the mission should investigate.[93] On another mission, the opposite problem occurred. In this case, the technical team was "deferential to the mission" and, rather than attempting to assert control over the mission, awaited instructions from the head of the mission, who was actually unclear about how best to use the professional staff provided.[94]

[90]   Michael P. Scharf, "Cherif Bassiouni and the 780 Commission: The Gateway to the Era of Accountability," An Occasional Paper of the Frederick K. Cox International Law Center, October 2006, p. 7 (internal citation omitted).
[91]   Mary Shanthi Dairiam, Commissioner, International Fact-Finding Mission to investigate violations of international law, including international humanitarian and human rights law, resulting from the Israeli attacks on the flotilla of ships carrying humanitarian assistance, interview conducted by HPCR, April 3, 2013.
[92]   Confidential interview with a high-level MRF practitioner, name of interviewee on file, conducted by HPCR, Spring 2013.
[93]   Confidential interview with a high-level MRF practitioner, name of interviewee on file, conducted by HPCR, Spring 2013.
[94]   Mary Shanthi Dairiam, HPCR interview.

B.   Investigative Fieldwork Experience

In many cases, commissioners – though skilled as academics, lawyers, or judges – have lacked investigative fieldwork experience. This issue has had particularly significant ramifications in cases in which the mission's fieldwork involved engaging with victims and witnesses who have experienced trauma. As one MRF practitioner recollects, commissioners on one mission would ask prepared questions in a specific order, though they learned throughout their fieldwork that a tension existed between what the mission wanted from the interviewees and what the interviewees wanted from the mission:

> The interviewees would not just want to go in that order. They wanted to tell their stories. They had been traumatized. Some were actually still shaking, some men actually cried. So we would say that some of the things they were saying were not relevant to the facts we needed. But there was another purpose that was being served. There was a process that was therapeutic for the individual. You need to find the space and let the victim tell their story. The commissioners had to realize this is not a courtroom.[95]

As with the lack of managerial expertise exhibited by certain mission chairpersons, this issue of lack of fieldwork experience has also arisen repeatedly. Indeed, a practitioner who served on the Former Yugoslavia Commission recounts that some interviewers on that mission did not realize, "You have to listen to what's important to the person before you ask what's important to the prosecution. You must show them that you care about them."[96]

C.   Knowledge of the Context

A final challenge in balancing political and technical staffing considerations is selecting commissioners and investigators who have in-depth prior knowledge of the context but who will not compromise the mission's actual or perceived impartiality. On the one hand, MRF practitioners emphasize the importance of prior knowledge of the context. "You can't really know what can be accomplished unless you've been to a country," asserts one MRF actor.[97] But on the other hand, as another states, "You

---

[95]   Mary Shanthi Dairiam, HPCR interview.
[96]   Confidential interview with a high-level MRF practitioner, name of interviewee on file, conducted by HPCR, Spring 2013.
[97]   Patrick Gaffney, Investigator for the International Commission of Inquiry for Burundi, interview conducted by HPCR, September 8, 2011.

can't recruit someone with a past that might allow the country under investigation to claim the person is biased or has a preconceived conclusion on the allegations to be investigated by the Commission. So you wind up recruiting people who haven't worked on the country before and who, by definition, are not experts on the country or the situation to be investigated."[98] One disadvantage of this solution, though, is that MRF practitioners "don't have much time and have to hit the ground running."[99] Hence, MRF practitioners have little time to master the background of the situation they will be investigating. Another disadvantage is that selecting individuals with no prior experience in the country can have the opposite of the intended effect and actually bring the mission's credibility into question. As Paulo Sérgio Pinheiro, who held country-specific UNHRC mandates for Burundi and Myanmar, and had no prior experience with either country, wrote:

> I remember that at my first meeting after been [sic] appointed special rapporteur with the ambassador of Myanmar in Geneva, he told me that he was surprised that a Latin American had been appointed instead of someone from Asia and asked me what could be the explanation. I delicately told him that I had not the slightest idea but that I was afraid he needed to become accustomed to me.[100]

D. Expanding the Practitioner Pool

The issues that this section has examined stem from the political origins of MRF mandates. The objective is to select commissioners whose eminence can counteract the political nature of the mandate adoption process. In theory, in this area, the mission's political and technical needs should be in alignment with one another, since the respectable professional profile of the commissioners both lends legitimacy to the mission and provides the mission with the necessary legal expertise. In actuality, managerial and leadership skills, fieldwork experience, and substantive expertise in the context at hand, though also extremely important, receive less emphasis.

---

[98] Ben Majekodunmi, HPCR interview.
[99] Martin Seutcheu, Human Rights Officer for Office of the High Commissioner for Human Rights, interview conducted by HPCR, September 23, 2011.
[100] Paulo Sérgio Pinheiro, "Being a Special Rapporteur: A Delicate Balancing Act," *The International Journal of Human Rights* 15, no. 2 (2011): 165, accessed July 13, 2015, doi:10.10 80/13642987.2011.537464.

A final important point is that all of the above challenges point to the importance of developing a substantial pool of available and experienced commissioners and investigators. As one MRF practitioner asserts, given that time pressures do not allow for learning on the job, "You need a stand-by pool, a core team of mobile investigators that can be pulled in. This would be an A-Team of investigators whose integrity and dependability had been scanned in advance."[101] Some MRF actors have taken steps to begin developing such a pool. The Office of the High Commissioner for Human Rights (OHCHR) now staffs its missions from a roster composed mostly of human rights officers with diverse investigation backgrounds.[102] Additionally, the organization Justice Rapid Response has developed a roster of trained investigators who are active-duty professionals and have understandings with their employers that allow for the investigator's rapid release – sometimes in a matter of days – as long as the employer agrees "in principle" with the deployment.[103] But as one MRF actor states, "There's a very small roster of people. It would be good to expand it,"[104] suggesting that the development of a staffing pool has fallen behind the rapid rate at which the domain of MRF has developed in recent decades. Indeed, this state of affairs is perhaps an inevitable result of the ad hoc nature of MRF missions. In the absence of a centralized, institutionalized MRF mechanism, a new investigative team, and a new set of commissioners, must be quickly pulled together every time a new MRF mandate is adopted.

IV. Mandate Interpretation

Mandate interpretation is the point in the process of creating an MRF mission when decision-making powers shift from political actors to technical practitioners. The mandating entity has determined the mission's framework, and MRF professionals, based on their interpretation of the mandate, now make choices about the specific scope of the investigation and the methodologies that the mission will employ to gather and analyze information. Though mandates do not explicitly specify this step in the process, MRF practitioners widely recognize its significance. According to one MRF actor, interpreting the mandate is "the most important

---

[101] Karen Kenny, HPCR interview.   [102] Martin Seutcheu, HPCR interview.
[103] Andras Vamos-Goldman, HPCR interview.
[104] Peggy Hicks, Global Advocacy Director at Human Rights Watch, interview conducted by HPCR, November 9, 2011.

job of the commissioner."[105] But what are the limits of commissioners' interpretive powers? During interviews conducted for this chapter, one practitioner expressed concerns about "commissioners who interpret the mandate too freely and too expansively" and who might feel inclined "to step outside the mandate."[106] This practitioner states:

> We take it for granted that judges and juries must operate within the confines of their respective mandates. That's essential to the Rule of Law. Why should commissioners view themselves as having a broader interpretive power than their mandate provides? I think it's very dangerous for two reasons: first, it might undermine their credibility, and second, it discourages governments and international bodies from resorting to this potentially useful technique for fear that they will be creating "run-away" commissions.[107]

In many instances, though, a certain degree of interpretation is necessary due to gaps or ambiguities that exist in the mandate. For example, the Guinea Commission, mandated by the UNSG to investigate the government of Guinea's crackdown on protesters in Conakry in 2009, included authorization to inquire into "related events in their immediate aftermath."[108] This language granted commissioners the temporal leeway to select incidents they deemed to be contextually appropriate. The Darfur Commission operated under a mandate that authorized the mission "to investigate reports of violations of international humanitarian law and human rights law" while remaining silent about temporal scope.[109] As one of the members of the mission states, the mandate nonetheless shaped the mission's decision to begin its investigative focus in February 2003: "We had to fix the temporal scope to the time when the reports began to occur. It was fixed keeping in view the wording of the mandate."[110]

But can and should commissioners undertake measures not envisaged at the time of the mandate's adoption? An overview of recent MRF practice reveals several instances in which commissioners did pursue this avenue. One example is the Georgia Fact-Finding Mission, which had a broad

---

[105] Luc Côté, Executive Director of the United Nations Independent Special Commission of Inquiry for Timor-Leste, the United Nations Mapping Exercise in the Democratic Republic of the Congo, and the Kyrgyzstan Inquiry Commission, interview conducted by HPCR, October 4, 2011.

[106] Confidential interview with a high-level MRF practitioner, name of interviewee on file, conducted by HPCR, Spring 2013.

[107] Ibid.   [108] Guinea Commission report, 6.

[109] United Nations Security Council resolution 1564 (2004), ¶ 12.

[110] Hina Jilani, HPCR interview.

mandate that allowed for a creative interpretation. The mission's mandate specified that the goal of the mission was "to investigate the origins and the course of the conflict" between Russia and Georgia in 2008.[111] The head of the mission interpreted this language as encompassing not only an assessment of potential violations of IHL and IHRL but also in-depth legal analyses of both parties' adherence to *jus ad bellum* law leading to the conflict, as well as Russia's passportization policy, which entailed Russia's issuing passports to numerous residents of South Ossetia and Abkhazia after granting them Russian citizenship.[112] Though the mandate explicitly mentioned neither of these issues, both areas became significant components of the mission's report.

An expansive mode of mandate interpretation can also be important in upholding the mission's impartiality and credibility, especially in relation to the parties that the mission investigates. As discussed previously in this chapter, a one-sided mandate can harm the credibility of the mission, hinder the mission's ability to draw conclusions under IHL, and evoke pushback from the parties who have been singled out by the investigation. How should MRF practitioners grapple with the challenges of operating under mandates that fall short of authorizing a balanced investigation? The aforementioned approach of the Lebanon Commission – accepting the mandate's limitations but mentioning the undesirability of these restrictions in the mission's final report – is one interpretive choice. But approaches undertaken in other contexts demonstrate that practitioners sometimes perceive that the importance of undertaking an impartial investigation outweighs the necessity of operating within the mandate's limitations.

One such example is the aforementioned mandate that the UNHRC adopted in 2014 to authorize an OHCHR-led investigation of ISIL and "associated terrorist groups" while overlooking government and pro-government forces. The final report makes clear that OHCHR did not accept this limited focus, stating that OHCHR "also verified information received on human rights violations and abuses, and violations of international humanitarian law that have been perpetrated by other parties to the conflict [specifically, the Iraqi security forces and associated armed groups] and documented them herein."[113] The report does not offer a clear

---

[111] Georgia Fact-Finding Mission report, 1: 3.
[112] Georgia Fact-Finding Mission report, 2: 147–183, 229–294.
[113] "Report of the Office of the United Nations High Commissioner for Human Rights on the human rights situation in Iraq in the light of abuses committed by the so-called Islamic State in Iraq and the Levant and associated groups," A/HRC/28/18, March 27, 2015, p. 4.

rationale for why OHCHR deemed that it had the authority to investigate these other parties in the absence of a clear mandate to do so. The only justification included in the report is a footnote stating that OHCHR undertook this task "[p]ursuant to General Assembly resolution 48/141" – the 1993 resolution that established OHCHR – but this footnote does not actually explain how this resolution could justify examining parties that are not clearly included in the mission's mandate.[114]

A similar example is the Beit Hanoun Fact-Finding Mission. The mandate for this mission, as noted earlier in this chapter, could have been interpreted as encompassing an investigation of incidents perpetrated only by Israel and not by Hamas. However, the mission's final report assesses the legality of Palestinian militants firing rockets into Israeli territory and directs recommendations to both Israel and Hamas.[115] Unlike the OHCHR mission to Iraq, however, the Beit Hanoun Fact-Finding Mission offered a more cogent rationale. In the context of the "Applicable Law" section, the final report states, "The mission's mandate also encompasses the humanitarian law obligations of other parties to the conflict, the most relevant being militants launching rockets from Gaza into Israel."[116] For this sentence, the report cites paragraph 6 of the UNHRC resolution that mandated the mission, in which the UNHRC "*[u]rges* all concerned parties to respect the rules of international humanitarian law, to refrain from violence against the civilian population and to treat under all circumstances all detained combatants and civilians in accordance with the Geneva Conventions of 12 August 1949."[117] Though this paragraph does not explicitly authorize the mission to investigate Hamas and other armed groups in Gaza, the members of the mission used this sentence to justify a balanced approach under the rationale that the UNHRC was not concerned solely with incidents perpetrated by Israel but rather with alleged violations committed by "all concerned parties."

These examples suggest the sometimes-countervailing forces that drive the mandate-interpretation process. The "Declaration on Fact-Finding by the United Nations in the Field of the Maintenance of International Peace and Security," adopted by the UNGA in 1991, elucidates this dilemma.

---

[114] Ibid.   [115] Beit Hanoun Fact-Finding Mission report, 21–23.   [116] Ibid., 6.
[117] United Nations Human Rights Council resolution S-3/1, "Human rights violations emanating from Israeli military incursions in the Occupied Palestinian Territory, including the recent one in northern Gaza and the assault on Beit Hanoun," November 15, 2006, ¶ 6.

According to this document, "[f]act-finding missions have an obligation to act in strict conformity with their mandate and perform their task in an impartial way."[118] The question of how commissioners should respond when the text of the mandate appears to impede an impartial investigation has both political and technical dimensions. In one sense, the importance of respecting the mandate's restrictions is a technical issue regarding the limitations of the legal authority of the mission. In another sense, this issue is related to the sensitive political environment in which MRF bodies operate. Straying too far from the text of the mandate could render the mission vulnerable to criticism, sometimes in a politically charged fashion. Similarly, on the one hand, impartiality as a technical issue is a firmly rooted guiding principle of MRF practice.[119] On the other hand, impartiality also relates to the relationship between the mission and the surrounding political environment. A failure to design an impartial mission gives entities opposed to the mission, in the words of one MRF practitioner, "room to maneuver, to criticize."[120] Thus, adhering to the principle of impartiality is important for mitigating criticism of the mission.

MRF practice demonstrates various approaches – all of which are in some way controversial – to dealing with tensions between the mandate text and the principle of impartiality. The commissioners on the Lebanon Commission accepted the mandate's restrictions, and critics of the mission pointed to the one-sided nature of the mandate as part of arguments aiming to discredit the mission.[121] Richard Goldstone renegotiated the mandate for the Gaza Fact-Finding Mission but still faced criticism based on the original mandate adopted by the UNHRC. The Beit Hanoun Fact-Finding Mission and the OHCHR mission to Iraq investigated parties

---

[118] UNGA, "Declaration on Fact-Finding," ¶ 25.

[119] For example, see M. Cherif Bassiouni and Christina Abraham, eds., *Siracusa Guidelines for International, Regional and National Fact-Finding Bodies* (Cambridge: Intersentia, 2013), 37; Office of the High Commissioner for Human Rights, "Commissions of Inquiry and Fact-Finding Missions on International Human Rights and Humanitarian Law: Guidance and Practice," 2015, p. 33, accessed June 14, 2015, http://www.ohchr.org/Documents/Publications/CoI_Guidance_and_Practice.pdf; and "Manual of Operations of the Special Procedures of the Human Rights Council," 2008, p. 11. Additionally, see United Nations General Assembly resolution 60/251, "Human Rights Council," April 3, 2006, which mandates the United Nations Human Rights Council and, in ¶ 4, articulates impartiality as a guiding principle.

[120] Ghanim Al-Najjar, HPCR interview.

[121] For example, see "Report by UN Lebanon Inquiry Is One-Sided," press release, UN Watch, November 21, 2006, accessed May 26, 2015, http://www.unwatch.org/site/apps/nlnet/content2.aspx?c=bdKKISNqEmG&b=1316871&ct=3264691.

not explicitly included in their mandates, a choice that risks violating the principle that MRF missions should operate "in strict conformity with their" mandates. The unlikelihood of entirely avoiding controversy suggests the importance of weighing carefully the different options and selecting the interpretive avenue most likely to serve the mission's political and technical needs.

V. Conclusion

The four steps of creating MRF missions that this chapter has examined – the triggering of an MRF mission, the drafting of the mandate, the selection of commissioners and staff, and mandate interpretation – reveal the inherent dual nature of MRF missions as political and technical entities. In the current ad hoc domain of MRF, the triggering mechanism and the mandate-drafting process are political in nature, involving negotiations and consensus building among members of the mandating body. The process of selecting commissioners and staff is driven by both political and technical factors that sometimes align and sometimes conflict with one another.

It is important to bear in mind the historical trajectory that has led to this state of affairs. As this chapter has described, the past century has seen a marked increase in governmental engagement in civilian protection during armed conflicts, and debates about the role that fact-finding should play in this regard have constituted a consistent thread in this development. The IHFFC endures as a relic of the hope that fact-finding can be implemented in a systematized manner with governmental consent. But given the apparent unfeasibility of the IHFFC's operationalization, various political bodies have assumed, in an ad hoc manner, the role of realizing the fact-finding aspirations that have been expressed during the course of MRF history. As a consequence, the governmental resistance that prevented the creation of a robust centralized fact-finding mechanism during negotiations for the Geneva Conventions and the Additional Protocols has given rise to a different mode of criticism: assailing the legitimacy of MRF missions through claims that they are not technical exercises (as they purport to be) but rather politically driven entities.

Recall the vision of MRF missions articulated in the introduction to this chapter. In this model, a political body desires an objective factual and legal evaluation of a certain context and outsources this task to an independent body so that this body's independent analysis can inform future decisions regarding which actions are warranted to promote civilian protection or accountability. As MRF missions have proliferated in recent decades, MRF practitioners have cultivated a great degree of facility in fulfilling their designated role in this scenario. But despite the efforts of even the most-skilled commissioners, investigators, and legal experts engaged in MRF work, the domain of MRF might never fully quite live up to this aspiration. Indeed, the politics of creating MRF missions often impact these missions' technical implementation. Given the likelihood that the current ad hoc state of affairs will continue, MRF practitioners are left to learn how to operate as effectively as possible – as technical implementers of MRF mandates – within the politicized institutional structure of this domain.

2

Selecting and Applying Legal Lenses in Fact-Finding Work

THÉO BOUTRUCHE

Introduction

At first, discussing issues pertaining to the identification and the application of relevant legal frameworks and norms in fact-finding work may seem to be a contradiction in terms. Fact-finding and inquiry are commonly defined as "methods of ascertaining facts,"[1] and as such, are primarily concerned with facts and factual determinations. Fact-finding revolves around answering key factual questions related to the circumstances of a particular incident or set of incidents. Despite the proliferation of monitoring, reporting, and fact-finding (MRF) bodies entrusted with multifaceted mandates,[2] this type of work is foremost about establishing facts with a reliable degree of certainty amidst often conflicting accounts. The core underlying question at the heart of this chapter, having both theoretical and practical ramifications, is the following: To what extent is it possible to properly distinguish between the task of ascertaining facts and that of applying legal norms to the facts to reach legal findings, in terms of both legal qualifications of facts and legal determinations of whether violations have occurred?

As highlighted by one scholar, unlike their historic counterparts, the mandates of contemporary commissions of inquiry, notably those created

---

[1] Karl Joseph Partsch, "Fact-Finding and Inquiry," in *Encyclopedia of Public International Law*, ed. Rudolph Bernhardt (Amsterdam: North-Holland Publishing Company, 1981), vol. 2, 343. On the definition of "fact-finding," see also Michael Bothe, "Fact-Finding as a Means of Ensuring Respect for International Humanitarian Law," in *International Humanitarian Law Facing New Challenges*, ed. Wolff Heintschel von Heinegg and Volker Epping (Berlin: Springer, 2007), 249–250.

[2] For primary documents, such as mandates and reports, as well as additional background information on MRF missions implemented since the end of World War II, see "HPCR Digital Library of Monitoring, Reporting, and Fact-Finding," Program on Humanitarian Policy and Conflict Research at Harvard University, accessed June 7, 2015, http://www.hpcrresearch.org/mrf-database/.

by the United Nations Human Rights Council (UNHRC), "have not been truly fact-oriented but have had a strong legal dimension."[3] This institutional development of fact-finding missions has attracted attention to the role of fact-finders in applying international law to the point of questioning whether these activities represent a new form of adjudication. As two scholars note:

> While many of these commissions are termed "fact-finding missions" or given the mandate to engage in fact-finding, in reality they tend to do much more than this and will often make quite detailed determinations on points of international law. These "fact-finding missions" will often make determinations on what law is applicable to the factual situations they are called to investigate .... The commissions will also make determinations on the scope of the legal norms at issue .... Other commissions have engaged in detailed discussions on whether particular acts amount to violations of IHL [international humanitarian law] or human rights law.[4]

This chapter intends to provide a broader perspective to complement that presented in Part I of this book. While Part I sketches the most prominent issues arising from current practice to identify strengths, gaps, and challenges with regard to selecting and applying international law in fact-finding work, this chapter presents a mapping of fundamental questions as they relate to the interplay between the facts and the law. It is structured on the basis of the distinction between the selection of relevant legal frameworks and the application of those legal norms. These two components of the chapter correspond to the two core stages of legal reasoning in that MRF bodies entrusted with fact-finding functions proceed typically by stating the relevant law, ascertaining the facts (focusing on specific incidents or key representative patterns), and applying the identified legal norms to the facts to reach conclusions. In analyzing the selection and application of legal lenses, one also has to examine which explicit or implicit legal rationale the MRF organ used to justify or explain the mission's legal choices. This chapter examines the articulation of these three issues: the determination of the relevant legal frameworks and how MRF commissioners undertook these assessments, the actual application and

---

[3] Larissa J. van den Herik, "An Inquiry into the Role of Commissions of Inquiry in International Law: Navigating the Tensions between Fact-Finding and International Law Application," *Chinese Journal of International Law* 13, no. 3 (2014): 508, accessed June 14, 2015, doi:10.1093/chinesejil/jmu029.

[4] Dapo Akande and Hannah Tonkin, "International Commissions of Inquiry: A New Form of Adjudication?" *EJIL: Talk!* April 6, 2012, accessed June 10, 2015, http://www.ejiltalk.org/international-commissions-of-inquiry-a-new-form-of-adjudication.

interpretation of substantive rules pertaining to a given legal framework, and the reasons underlying commissioners' decisions regarding the application of legal frameworks.

The topic of legal lenses is closely related to that of standards of proof, which can be seen as a substantive element pertaining to a certain legal framework, such as international criminal law (ICL), and which vary depending on which legal framework is relevant. Since Chapter 3 of this book elaborates in detail about standards of proof, this chapter considers the topic only when it gives rise to legal issues. Specifically, this chapter only briefly addresses the issue of standards of proof in the context of MRF bodies qualifying international crimes under ICL.

Overall, this chapter details how past commissioners have navigated distinct legal pathways, focusing specifically on IHL, international human rights law (IHRL), and ICL. However, when relevant, the chapter also addresses other key international law issues, such as the identification and use of customary law. MRF bodies also frequently apply domestic law, though very few missions focus exclusively on domestic legal frameworks, one exception being the United Nations Independent Special Commission of Inquiry for Timor-Leste.

This chapter is primarily based on a desk review, including an assessment of mandates and reports, of the fifteen MRF missions selected for this book.[5] This chapter also relies on a series of comprehensive interviews conducted by the Program on Humanitarian Policy and Conflict Research (HPCR) with experts, members, and commissioners associated with some of these MRF missions.[6] Based on the patterns of practice identified across different missions, specific areas that are emblematic of the challenges related to the legal aspects of fact-finding work, and recurring topics identified through the desk reviews and the interviews, this chapter is divided into three sections. It first spells out the various facets of the interplay between the facts and the law as background to inform the questions that follow. It then addresses the issue of the selection of legal lenses and the implications of that choice, including its relation to the mandates and Terms of Reference (TORs) of the missions. Finally, the chapter examines the application of the relevant norms in specific areas, focusing on eight distinct issues that have proved to be challenging in past MRF practice, and covers both substantive legal norms and facts underlying certain

---

[5] For detailed information about these missions, see Appendix B of this book.
[6] A special thank-you to Rob Grace, who carried out all the interviews and assisted me throughout the research.

legal issues. Each of these sections also addresses the manner in which MRF actors justified (or did not justify), from a legal standpoint, different choices, interpretations, and approaches to various issues, including unsettled areas of international law and the use of customary law.

I.   Understanding the Interplay between the Facts and the Law

Some fact-finding bodies are tasked exclusively with establishing facts. For example, United Nations (UN) boards of inquiry set up by the United Nations Secretary-General, such as the United Nations Headquarters Board of Inquiry into certain incidents that occurred in the Gaza Strip between July 8, 2014, and August 26, 2014 (hereafter the UN Gaza Board of Inquiry), are "directed not to include in its report any findings of law."[7] Similarly, the United Nations Mission to Investigate Allegations of the Use of Chemical Weapons in the Syrian Arab Republic (hereafter the UN Mission on Chemical Weapons Use in Syria) was strictly mandated to "ascertain the facts related to the allegations of use of chemical weapons."[8]

Even in these cases, however, one may question whether the law actually still plays a role in these factual determinations. While it is true that no legal findings are formally made, legal considerations might not be completely absent. First, the language used to describe facts can carry a certain legal meaning. For example, the UN Gaza Board of Inquiry report includes a factual account of the steps taken by the United Nations Relief and Works Agency for Palestinian Refugees to communicate the GPS coordinates of premises being used as designated emergency shelters to the Israeli Coordinator of the Government Activities in the Territories and the Coordination and Liaison Administration. This section of the report references the obligation to take all actions necessary to prevent any damage to UN facilities and threats to the safety and security of UN personnel,

---

[7] "Summary by the Secretary-General of the report of the United Nations Headquarters Board of Inquiry into certain incidents that occurred in the Gaza Strip between 8 July 2014 and 26 August 2014," transmitted by letter dated April 27, 2015, from the Secretary-General addressed to the President of the Security Council, S/2015/286 April 27, 2015, ¶ 4, accessed June 14, 2015, http://unispal.un.org/unispal.nsf/22f431edb91c6f548525678a0051 be1d/554e1cc298b3bfef85257e44005abd18?OpenDocument.

[8] United Nations Mission to Investigate Allegations of the Use of Chemical Weapons in the Syrian Arab Republic, "Report on the Alleged Use of Chemical Weapons in the Ghouta Area of Damascus on 21 August 2013" (September 13, 2013), 1, accessed June 14, 2015, http://www.un.org/disarmament/content/slideshow/Secretary_General_Report_of_CW_Investigation.pdf.

referring directly to IHL language on precautions in attack.[9] Second, factual descriptions may provide information that has implications for other factual elements that might not strictly be part of the fact-finding body's mission but that have legal implications. For example, the UN Mission on Chemical Weapons Use in Syria was not tasked with making factual determinations on attribution as to which party used chemical weapons. However, based on the environmental, chemical, and medical samples collected, the UN Mission concluded that there was clear and convincing evidence that chemical weapons were used, including against civilians and on a relatively large scale, on August 21, 2013, in the Ghouta area of Damascus. The report specifically established the use of surface-to-surface rockets containing the nerve agent Sarin. Based on information about the delivery systems (i.e., munitions) used to carry the chemical agents, the trajectory, and the type and density of the gas a deduction (or inference) of fact could be drawn about who used those weapons, implicitly raising the question of responsibility.[10]

The answer to the question of whether fact-finding and legal analysis can actually be divorced from one another largely depends on the scope of the mandate (which could range from identifying individual perpetrators and determining their responsibilities to the prevention of violations by states) and powers (from adopting judicial decisions to merely drafting recommendations) entrusted to fact-finding bodies. It seems, however, virtually impossible to conduct fact-finding without knowledge of the law because it is only through legal expertise that one can select the relevant facts from the huge quantity of information around a given incident. Apart from the aforementioned very specific examples (UN boards of inquiry and the UN Mission on Chemical Weapons Use in Syria), most fact-finding missions and commissions of inquiry operate under mandates that require applying international law. This is intrinsically part of their task, as they are entrusted with establishing facts on alleged violations of IHRL and IHL and at times make determinations on individual criminal responsibility by identifying alleged perpetrators. In that respect, the factual and legal dimensions of their work are inherently linked.

As part of basic legal syllogism, the facts cannot be dissociated from the legal analysis. This interplay happens in two closely connected ways.

---

[9] UN Gaza Board of Inquiry report, ¶ 13.
[10] Peter Bouckaert, "Dispatches: Yes it was Sarin, UN Report Says. Now What?" Human Rights Watch, September 16, 2013, accessed June 14, 2015, https://www.hrw.org/news/2013/09/16/dispatches-yes-it-was-sarin-un-report-says-now-what.

First, the work of establishing facts informs the selection of the relevant applicable international law norms. Second, the content of those norms determines the types of facts that need to be established in order to make legal findings as to whether violations occurred. The facts covered through the inquiry are framed by the elements of the very rule allegedly violated. Otherwise, a legal conclusion cannot be reached.[11] Investigating facts with an explicit or implicit link with a violation requires, to a certain extent, a minimum amount of legal evaluation for the mere purpose of defining the scope of the facts at stake. For fact-finding bodies mandated to address facts about alleged violations, the question would then be to what extent the two operations should be strictly independent of one another. This question touches on the core of the theory of law and legal reasoning. According to one prominent scholar, the expression "ascertaining" facts is misleading, as this term suggests that the operation is about ascertaining an objective phenomenon that would then be "confronted" with the legal norm. Rather, this author stresses the influence of law on facts in several respects; for example, he suggests that the relevance of a fact is linked to the choice of the applicable law.[12] This link is reflected in the structure of the reports issued by MRF missions explicitly mandated to ascertain facts vis-à-vis IHL and human rights violations.[13] While some variations exist, MRF reports generally contain a statement of the applicable law, followed by the fact-finding per se, and finally a legal conclusion on the violations.

The legal aspect of fact-finding work raises methodological issues as much as the factual assessment does, ranging from recruiting appropriate staff with relevant legal expertise to identifying and applying the law in a rigorous manner. Surprisingly, though, this dimension has been underexamined or overlooked when addressing the professionalization of

---

[11] Sylvain Vité, "L'expertise au service du droit: Comment la norme façonne le processus d'enquête dans la mise œuvre des droits de l'homme et du droit des conflits armés," in *Katyn et la Suisse: Experts et expertises médicales dans les crises humanitaires, 1920–2007,* ed. Delphine Debons, Antoine Fleury, and Jean-François Pitteloud (Geneva: Georg, 2009), 251–258.

[12] See Jean J.-A. Salmon, "Le fait dans l'application du droit international," in *The Collected Courses of the Hague Academy of International Law* 175 (1982): 261, 296.

[13] For examples, see generally "Report of the Commission of Inquiry on Lebanon pursuant to Human Rights Council Resolution S-2/1," A/HRC/3/2, November 23, 2006, accessed June 14, 2015, http://www.unrol.org/files/A.HRC.3.2.pdf; and "Report of the International Commission of Inquiry on Darfur to the United Nations Secretary-General," January 25, 2005, accessed June 14, 2015, http://www.un.org/news/dh/sudan/com_inq_darfur.pdf.

fact-finding work. The "Commissions of Inquiry and Fact-Finding Missions on International Human Rights and Humanitarian Law: Guidance and Practice," published by the Office of the High Commissioner for Human Rights (OHCHR), refers to this question only as part of a standard description of mandates and the main branches of applicable law.[14] This may be due, in part, to a perception that this question is intrinsically linked to the specific, day-to-day work of a fact-finding mission, and as such, is viewed not as a fundamental methodological issue but rather as a detail inherent to the task of a commission. More generally, this omission may result from the assumption that the work of lawyers contributing to the commission will naturally complement that of investigators. However, the complex and multifaceted relationship between the facts and the law deserves more extensive consideration at the earliest stage possible, as the approach to this issue may greatly impact the credibility of the fact-finding body – in particular, if an MRF report does not properly establish some of the relevant facts required to reach a legal conclusion or insufficiently justifies or explains a certain interpretation of the law that is controversial. The result might be a flawed methodology, or at least insufficient attention devoted to certain sources of information that are essential to reaching a legal conclusion.

Furthermore, fact-finding missions are increasingly subject to legal scrutiny. Following the publication of a report by a fact-finding body, it is not uncommon for scholars to respond with articles that assess the ways that the mission addressed key legal questions.[15] This increasing focus on the legal appraisals of MRF missions stems from the very nature of MRF work. MRF bodies are confronted with the challenging task of establishing facts with regard to a wide array of unsettled areas of international law, including complex IHL issues, such as the scope of "direct participation

---

[14] Office of the High Commissioner for Human Rights, "*Commissions of Inquiry and Fact-Finding Missions on International Human Rights and Humanitarian Law: Guidance and Practice,*" 2015, p. 11, accessed June 14, 2015, http://www.ohchr.org/Documents/ Publications/CoI_Guidance_and_Practice.pdf.

[15] For example, see generally Kevin Jon Heller, "The International Commission of Inquiry on Libya: A Critical Analysis," in *International Commissions: The Role of Commissions of Inquiry in the Investigation of International Crimes,* ed. Jens Meierhenrich, forthcoming, available at Social Science Research Network, accessed June 14, 2015, http://papers.ssrn .com/sol3/papers.cfm?abstract_id=2123782; Steven R. Ratner, "Accountability and the Sri Lankan Civil War," *The American Journal of International Law* 106, no. 4 (2012), accessed June 14, 2015, http://www.jstor.org/stable/10.5305; and James G. Stewart, "The UN Commission of Inquiry on Lebanon: A Legal Appraisal," *Journal of International Criminal Justice* 5, no. 5 (2007), accessed June 14, 2015, doi:10.1093/jicj/mqm073.

in hostilities," the threshold of non-international armed conflict (NIAC), determinations about whether a targeted civilian or civilian object was "protected" under IHL at the time of an attack, and determinations about whether a certain attack was proportional. While these are key theoretical questions, they are also related to various practical challenges, such as how MRF actors determine what information is necessary to reach sound legal conclusions and how report drafters articulate legal conclusions in MRF reports.

The legal dimension of an MRF mechanism, as much as the fact-finding aspect of the mission's mandate, thus becomes a credibility and legitimacy test for MRF missions. This aspect of MRF work is particularly relevant to areas of legal analysis that are open to various interpretations under existing international law. The "lawfare" critique – the use or misuse of the law as a means to achieve a military objective – against the United Nations Fact-Finding Mission on the Gaza Conflict (hereafter the Gaza Fact-Finding Mission) is a salient example of the controversial legal implications of MRF work.[16]

The underlying legal issue relevant to this question is the extent to which MRF bodies contribute to the progressive development of the law in certain areas. Recent analysis demonstrates that some of the legal findings of the Independent International Commission of Inquiry on Syria constitute a telling example.[17] The manner in which the commission has addressed questions of the obligations of armed groups under IHRL and under the Optional Protocol to the Convention on the Rights of the Child, according to one scholar, constitutes a contribution to the progressive development of IHRL.[18]

The large majority of MRF practitioners interviewed for this chapter clearly stated that, as a matter of principle, MRF bodies should not

---

[16] See generally Laurie R. Blank, "Finding Facts but Missing the Law: The Goldstone Report, Gaza and Lawfare," *Case Western Reserve Journal of International Law* 43 (2011), accessed June 14, 2015, http://law.case.edu/journals/jil/Documents/43_Blank.pdf.

[17] For additional information, including access to mandates and reports, see "Independent International Commission of Inquiry on the Syrian Arab Republic," in "HPCR Digital Library of Monitoring, Reporting, and Fact-Finding," Program on Humanitarian Policy and Conflict Research at Harvard University, accessed June 7, 2015, http://www.hpcrresearch.org/mrf-database/mission.php?id=48.

[18] See Tilman Rodenhäuser, "Progressive Development of International Human Rights Law: The Reports of the Independent International Commission of Inquiry on the Syrian Arab Republic," *EJIL: Talk!* April 13, 2013, accessed June 14, 2015, http://www.ejiltalk.org/progressive-development-of-international-human-rights-law-the-reports-of-the-independent-international-commission-of-inquiry-on-the-syrian-arab-republic/.

engage in the progressive development of international law and, specifically, should not decide on a progressive interpretation with regard to an unsettled area of international law. The interviewees stressed the critical need to apply only existing law to avoid unnecessary critiques and to ensure the credibility and legitimacy of the mission's findings. While this intention is, of course, understandable, when one looks more closely at some specific determinations that certain MRF missions have made, the extent to which MRF actors actually succeed in applying only existing law appears less obvious. Given the numerous issues addressed by MRF bodies, it may be unavoidable for MRF missions to, at times, adopt a progressive interpretation or to take a stand on a certain unsettled area of international law. Additionally, the notion was also raised in HPCR's interviews that, regardless of the intentions of MRF practitioners, due to the way that international law operates, MRF reports might sometimes inadvertently wind up serving jurisprudential purposes, as lawyers and lawmakers, searching for answers to unsettled international legal issues, are likely at points to turn to conclusions reached by MRF bodies.

The majority of the fifteen MRF missions under review addressed one or more of the unsettled areas of international law in carrying out their mandates. Some MRF bodies adopted a cautious approach, explicitly spelling out that certain legal issues remain controversial. For example, the International Commission of Inquiry on Libya (hereafter the Libya Commission) acknowledged that some issues within the applicable legal framework are not settled under international law. The mission's report stresses that "the findings and conclusions with respect to specific crimes and violations must be read in that light."[19] The report of the international fact-finding mission to investigate violations of international law, including international humanitarian and human rights law, resulting from the Israeli attacks on the flotilla of ships carrying humanitarian assistance (hereafter the UNHRC Flotilla Fact-Finding Mission), made a specific reference to the controversial status of the right of a belligerent in an armed conflict to visit, inspect, and control the destinations of neutral vessels on the high seas, irrespective of any declared blockade.[20] Similarly,

---

[19] "Report of the International Commission of Inquiry on Libya," A/HRC/19/68, March 2, 2012, p. 29, accessed June 14, 2015, http://www.nytimes.com/interactive/2012/03/03/world/africa/united-nations-report-on-libya.html?_r=0.

[20] "Report of the International Fact-Finding Mission to Investigate Violations of International Law, Including International Humanitarian and Human Rights Law, Resulting from the Israeli Attacks on the Flotilla of Ships Carrying Humanitarian Assistance,"

the Independent International Fact-Finding Mission on the Conflict in Georgia (hereafter the Georgia Fact-Finding Mission) had to deal with a number of issues or allegations that were difficult to ascertain factually or that referred to legal questions that may give rise to different interpretations. The mission, to avoid criticisms, endeavored to justify the positions taken under international law. This was particularly the case regarding the applicability of the law of occupation, which the mission addressed by way of the question of the degree and extent of the control or authority required in order to conclude that a territory is occupied.[21]

Finally, the question of the mission's standard of proof also illustrates the interplay between the facts and the law. As explained in Chapter 3 of this book, Finding the Facts: Standards of Proof and Information Handling in Monitoring, Reporting, and Fact-Finding Missions, the standard of proof is usually defined as the degree of certainty that fact-finders set and at which point they can make factual determinations – in other words, the type of threshold they use to consider whether they are convinced that an incident happened in a certain way. This is therefore a methodological imperative that lies primarily at the heart of the establishment of facts, as it explains how conclusions were reached. Therefore, fact-finders are faced with the following dilemma: They are expected to consistently rely on a standard of proof to make factual determinations. However, standards of proof are spelled out as general and abstract thresholds guiding the fact-finders' work, and when applying a given standard of proof, numerous factors may influence their ability to implement it in a consistent manner. The International Commission of Inquiry on the Central African

A/HRC/15/21, September 27, 2010, pp. 13–14, accessed June 14, 2015, http://www2.ohchr.org/english/bodies/hrcouncil/docs/15session/A.HRC.15.21_en.pdf.

21 See "Independent International Fact-Finding Mission on the Conflict in Georgia Report," vol. 2 (September 2009): 305–306, which notes, "The critical question is the degree and extent of the control or authority required in order to conclude that a territory is occupied. Two perceptions exist in this regard, which are not mutually exclusive but rather constitute two stages in the application of the law on occupation. These two stages reflect growing control by the occupying power. This means that, for a part of the law of occupation to apply, it is not necessary for the military forces of a given State to administer a territory fully …. [T]he mere fact that some degree of authority is exercised on the civilian population triggers the relevant conventional provisions of the law of occupation on the treatment of persons. In a further stage, the full application of the law on occupation comes into play, when a stronger degree of control is exercised. This is reflected in a number of military manuals, which require it to be established that 'a party to a conflict is in a position to exercise the level of authority over enemy territory necessary to enable it to discharge all the obligations imposed by the law of occupation.'" (internal citation omitted)

Republic (hereafter the CAR Commission) recognized the need for flexibility in applying a standard of proof.[22] While the standard of proof plays a role at the stage of the strict fact-finding work, it might also arise as relevant at the legal assessment stage in that it may be difficult to reach the required degree of certainty when drawing conclusions about violations of certain IHL norms, despite fact-finders' ability to conclude that a given incident occurred. For example, while fact-finders might be able to establish that an attacker undertook precautionary measures before launching an attack, the mission may still lack sufficient factual elements to conclude with the same degree of certainty that all feasible precautionary measures were undertaken, presenting difficulties for qualifying this as a violation of the relevant IHL norm.

Overall, the interviews that HPCR conducted with practitioners for this chapter reveal that sometimes a gap existed between certain practitioners' rather limited perceptions of the underlying legal questions at stake and the actual legal issues that have arisen in MRF reports. Though, as this chapter examines, MRF missions have exhibited numerous areas of problematic practice in terms of legal assessments, many interviewees did not appear to consider these issues to be problematic, provided laconic answers when pressed on certain details, or were unable to justify certain legal interpretations. While other factors – such as the composition and working methods of an MRF body and the length of time that had elapsed between the final report of a mission and the date of the interview – may have contributed to this research finding, the interview results suggest that a lack of awareness might exist among some practitioners about the implications of certain legal determinations made in MRF reports.

II.   The Selection of Legal Lenses and Their Implications

The selection of relevant legal frameworks greatly depends on the formulation of the mandate and the actual facts or situations being considered by an MRF mission. However, the desk review and the interviews on which this chapter is based suggest that the selection of legal lenses is the area in which MRF practice is actually the most consistent, despite some discrepancies regarding the legal rationales used to justify such selections.

---

[22] "The International Commission of Inquiry on the Central African Republic: Final Report," S/2014/928, December 22, 2014, pp. 11–12, accessed June 14, 2015, http://reliefweb .int/sites/reliefweb.int/files/resources/N1471229.pdf.

It is indeed critical to proceed with a sound and rigorous legal approach at the stage of selecting legal lenses. At times, at this stage, disagreement already exists between the relevant parties about what constitutes applicable law. For example, the Secretary-General's Panel of Inquiry on the 31 May 2010 Flotilla Incident (hereafter the UNSG Flotilla Panel) report notes:

> In relation to the relevant legal principles of public international law the position is similar. The Chair and Vice-Chair in the Appendix to this report set out their own account of what they believe to be the state of public international law as it applies to the incident. Both national investigations did the same. They differ as widely on the applicable law as they do on what actually happened.[23]

More surprisingly, the UNSG Flotilla Panel report also states that the legal issues "have not been authoritatively determined by the two States involved and neither can they be by the Panel" and that "[t]he Panel will not add value for the United Nations by attempting to determine contested facts or by arguing endlessly about the applicable law. Too much legal analysis threatens to produce political paralysis."[24] The UNSG Flotilla Panel concludes:

> Those issues in the reports submitted to the Panel revolve primarily around the legality of the conduct judged against the standards of public international law and what the facts were. But the legal issues, while a necessary element of the Panel's analysis, alone are not sufficient. We must probe more widely.[25]

In this case, the politically sensitive context of the Occupied Palestinian Territories and the fact that this MRF body was not mandated to make definitive legal determinations may explain this cautious approach. However, one could consider this approach to be too restrictive, especially since the clarification of international law by an MRF body with a certain degree of authority could help relevant actors move away from political considerations.

A. The Framework of the Mandate

While the wording of MRF missions' mandates may vary depending on political or institutional considerations, a trend has emerged of mandate drafters referring to human rights allegations or violations as a common overall framework of reference for the fact-finding work of the mission. This raises a number of questions.

---

[23] UNSG Flotilla Panel, p. 9.   [24] Ibid., 10.   [25] Ibid.

First, the mandate, by its general nature, does not and cannot pretend to resolve the issues of the legal frameworks. A reference to human rights violations in the document defining the mandate, while assuming IHRL to be the relevant body of norms to be applied, does not exclude the selection of other legal norms, such as IHL and ICL. In the case of commissions of inquiry created by the UNHRC, there has been a recurrent use in mandates of human rights language, even in contexts in which armed conflicts exist. For example, the report of the Independent, International Commission of Inquiry on Côte d'Ivoire (hereafter the Côte d'Ivoire Commission) referred to IHL (although this was done in a really laconic manner, as described in greater detail in Section B below), despite the mention of only IHRL in the UNHRC resolution that created the mission.[26] In theory, facts on the ground, including the evolution of a situation into an armed conflict after a mandating body has adopted an MRF mandate, as occurred in Libya, can justify the incorporation of IHL.[27] The approach of considering IHRL as a legal lens that encompasses IHL and ICL – a line of reasoning expressed in various interviews with practitioners conducted by HPCR – provides an additional conceptual legal rationale to justify the use of these other bodies of norms. Finally, specific aspects of the mandate can also dictate the incorporation of other legal frameworks. For example, though not explicitly mentioned in the mandate, ICL application can be inferred from the explicit reference in the mandate to "crimes" and "identifying those responsible."[28] Despite the repeated statements made

---

[26] See United Nations Human Rights Council resolution 16/25, ¶ 10, the mandate for the Côte d'Ivoire Commission, which authorized the mission "to investigate the facts and circumstances surrounding the allegations of serious abuses and violations of human rights committed in Côte d'Ivoire following the presidential election of 28 November 2010, in order to identify those responsible for such acts and to bring them to justice."

[27] Though the mandate for the Libya Commission authorizes the mission "to investigate all alleged violations of international human rights law in Libya, to establish the facts and circumstances of such violations and of the crimes perpetrated, and, where possible identify those responsible to make recommendations," the Libya Commission's first report states: "In the light of the armed conflict that developed in late February 2011 in the Libyan Arab Jamahiriya and continued during the commission's operations, the commission looked into both violations of international human rights law and relevant provisions of international humanitarian law, the *lex specialis* that applies during armed conflict." For the mandate, see United Nations Human Rights Council resolution S-15/1, ¶ 11. For the mission's first report, see "Report of the International Commission of Inquiry to Investigate All Alleged Violations of International Human Rights Law in the Libyan Arab Jamahiriya," A/HRC/17/44, June 1, 2011, p. 2, accessed June 14, 2015, http://www2.ohchr.org/english/bodies/hrcouncil/docs/17session/A.HRC.17.44_AUV.pdf.

[28] Libya Commission mandate, ibid.

by interviewees that the mandates and TORs of MRF missions are binding and cannot be changed by commissioners, the interpretation of the mandate to encompass IHL and ICL – when supported by legal or factual arguments – demonstrates room for flexibility.

Similarly, the question of the mandate prejudging the existence of violations and the related issue of limiting the parties or actors to be investigated also suggests some degree of flexibility. UNHRC resolutions creating commissions of inquiry in certain cases have stated that MRF bodies were established on the basis that IHRL and IHL violations had already taken place. For example, by authorizing the mission to investigate "violations" – rather than "allegations," as in the case of Libya – of international law, the UNHRC resolution that created the UNHRC Flotilla Fact-Finding Mission prejudged the question of whether violations had been committed.[29]

However, MRF practice and the interviews conducted by HPCR indicate that commissioners tend not to feel bound by such predeterminations when they are included in a mission's mandate. The report of the UNHRC Flotilla Fact-Finding Mission addresses this issue from the outset and states that the mission could not proceed with assumptions about the mission's conclusions. In particular, the report states:

> The Council, in its resolution, decided to dispatch a mission to investigate "violations" of international law, international humanitarian and human rights law, resulting from the Israeli "attacks" on the flotilla carrying humanitarian assistance. This appeared to determine that "violations" of international law, including international humanitarian and human rights law had in fact occurred prior to any investigation. The resolution also appeared to find as a fact that there had been Israeli attacks on the flotilla of ships and that the ships were carrying humanitarian assistance.

> The Mission did not interpret its task as proceeding on any such assumptions. It could not determine what its position was until the Mission came to its conclusion on the facts. The same can be said of the alleged actions by the Israeli forces.[30]

Similarly, mandates restricting the parties that the mission may assess also pose a series of challenges, including potentially hindering the ability of the MRF body to comprehensively address certain IHL rules on the conduct of hostilities that, by definition, require consideration of the acts of both the attacker and the party being attacked. In the case of the Commission of Inquiry on Lebanon (hereafter the Lebanon Commission), the

---

[29] United Nations Human Rights Council resolution 14/1, ¶ 8.
[30] UNHRC Flotilla Fact-Finding Mission report, 3.

UNHRC resolution defining the mandate specifically focuses on the conduct of Israel, excluding other parties to the conflict, notably Hezbollah, from the scope of the mission's work. The commissioners, mindful of this limitation, specifically addressed this issue in the final report, expressing concerns about the mission's lack of authority to examine the behavior of Hezbollah.[31] Though, as a way to mitigate this shortcoming, the report does make reference to the IHL and IHRL obligations of Hezbollah. Interestingly, a similar limitation contained in the UNHRC resolution creating the Gaza Fact-Finding Mission was adjusted in the letter of the UNHRC president that slightly redefined the mandate.[32] Based on this letter, which the mission considered to be the operative mandate, the mission, as the final report states, "determined that it was required to consider any actions by all parties that might have constituted violations of international human rights law or international humanitarian law. The mandate also required it to review related actions in the entire Occupied Palestinian Territory and Israel."[33]

---

[31] See Lebanon Commission report, 16, which notes, "A fundamental point in relation to the conflict and the Commission's mandate as defined by the Council is the conduct of Hezbollah. The Commission considers that any independent, impartial and objective investigation into a particular conduct during the course of hostilities must of necessity be with reference to all the belligerents involved. Thus an inquiry into the conformity with international humanitarian law of the specific acts of IDF [Israeli Defense Forces] in Lebanon requires that account also be taken of the conduct of the opponent. That said, taking into consideration the express limitations of its mandate, the Commission is not entitled, even if it had wished, to construe it as equally authorizing the investigation of the actions by Hezbollah in Israel."

[32] United Nations Human Rights Council resolution S-9/1, ¶ 14, states that the mandate is "to investigate all violations of international human rights law and international humanitarian law by the occupying Power, Israel, against the Palestinian people throughout the Occupied Palestinian Territory, particularly in the occupied Gaza Strip, due to the current aggression." However, the subsequent letter of the UNHRC president to the chair of the Mission offers a broader mandate "to investigate all violations of international human rights law and international humanitarian law that might have been committed at any time in the context of the military operations that were conducted in Gaza during the period from 27 December 2008 and 18 January 2009, whether before, during or after." See "Report of the United Nations Fact-Finding Mission on the Gaza Conflict," A/HRC/12/48, September 25, 2009, p. 13, accessed June 14, 2015, http://www2.ohchr.org/english/bodies/hrcouncil/docs/12session/A-HRC-12-48.pdf. It is reported that, following Mary Robinson's refusal to head the mission, and after the first objection by Justice Richard Goldstone, both of whom criticized the bias of the mandate, the UNHRC president widened the mandate's scope to encompass the conduct of Hamas. See Mary Robinson, "Accounting for Gaza," Project Syndicate, September 28, 2009, accessed June 27, 2015, http://www.project-syndicate.org/commentary/accounting-for-gaza.

[33] Gaza Fact-Finding Mission report, 14.

B.   Co-applicability of IHL and IHRL as a Matter
of Selecting Legal Lenses

All MRF bodies entrusted with ascertaining whether violations and abuses have been committed in the context of an armed conflict, when selecting applicable legal frameworks, are confronted with the issue of the interaction between IHL and IHRL. While this issue is not per se controversial, such determinations have implications for the legal classification of certain violations according to specific norms. This section addresses the general question of the relationship between those two bodies of law.

MRF reports commonly restate the principle of co-applicability in times of armed conflict, as reflected in international jurisprudence, though the level of detail and breadth of sources for reaffirming this complementarity varies from mission to mission. The articulation of the relationship between IHL and IHRL is also highly dependent on the specific situation or context. For example, the Georgia Fact-Finding Mission report notes:

> Two main sets of norms constitute the applicable legal framework: IHL and HRL. First, both branches of international law are applicable in times of armed conflict. Second, given that the current report covers a longer period than the duration of the armed conflict per se, human rights law is also directly relevant.[34]

The Georgia Fact-Finding Mission report stresses that "three intertwined issues [have] to do with the applicability of human rights law: in time of war, in cases of occupation and extraterritorially."[35] In the same vein, the Gaza Fact-Finding Mission recalls that:

> [i]t is now widely accepted that human rights treaties continue to apply in situations of armed conflict .... It is today commonly understood that human rights law would continue to apply as long as it is not modified or set aside by IHL. In any case, the general rule of human rights law does not lose its effectiveness and will remain in the background to inform the application and interpretation of the relevant humanitarian law rule.[36]

Similarly, the International Commission of Inquiry on Darfur (hereafter the Darfur Commission) reaffirmed the principle of complementarity – as

---

[34] Georgia Fact-Finding Mission report, 2: 298.   [35] Ibid., 2: 313.
[36] Gaza Fact-Finding Mission report, 78.

did the Lebanon Commission and the UNHRC Flotilla Fact-Finding Mission – as well as the standard of *lex specialis* to resolve conflicts of norms.[37]

In contrast, the way that the UNSG Flotilla Panel addressed this issue is rather peculiar. First, the report includes references to the international legal framework only in the report's appendix. Indeed, the appendix contains several paragraphs about the interaction between IHL and IHRL, including a description of the range of approaches among scholars as to the various types of relationships between the two bodies of law. However, since the report includes this assessment only in a distinct section at the end of the document, one fails to grasp the implications of this detailed statement of the law. For example, there is no mention in the report itself of the effects, for the matters at stake, of the conclusion that the panel reached regarding the complementarity between these two bodies of norms. The panel's report notes:

> In light of the above, it is important to stress that it is difficult to make generalized statements on the exact nature of the relationship between human rights law and international humanitarian law. Rather, the application of specific provisions of either legal area depends heavily on the factual context of the situation and has to be assessed accordingly. In any case, there cannot be gaps in the law. In line with the rationale expressed in the Martens Clause – now a part of customary law – it must be assured that minimum standards of humanitarian/human rights protection are observed at all times.[38]

---

[37] See Darfur Commission report, 41, which states, "Two main bodies of law apply to the Sudan in the conflict in Darfur: international human rights law and international humanitarian law. The two are complementary. For example, they both aim to protect human life and dignity, prohibit discrimination on various grounds, and protect against torture or other cruel, inhuman and degrading treatment. They both seek to guarantee safeguards for persons subject to criminal justice proceedings, and to ensure basic rights including those related to health, food and housing. They both include provisions for the protection of women and vulnerable groups, such as children and displaced persons. The difference lies in that whilst human rights law protects the individual at all times, international humanitarian law is the *lex specialis* which applies only in situations of armed conflict." See also Lebanon Commission report, 24, which states, "While the conduct of armed conflict and military occupation is governed by international humanitarian law, human rights law is applicable at all times, including during states of emergency or armed conflict. The two bodies of law complement and reinforce one another." (internal citation omitted) And finally, see UNHRC Flotilla Fact-Finding Mission report, 17, which states, "Indeed human rights law and international humanitarian law are not mutually exclusive but rather should be regarded as complementary and mutually reinforcing to ensure the fullest protection to the persons concerned."

[38] UNSG Flotilla Panel report, 99 (internal citations omitted).

Additional examples exist in which reports do not properly address the interplay between IHL and IHRL, a shortcoming that greatly weakens the mission's findings and creates confusion throughout the report. For example, the report of the Côte d'Ivoire Commission contains only two paragraphs related to the legal framework: one paragraph on the Constitution of Côte d'Ivoire and another general paragraph referring to the core IHRL and IHL treaties.[39]

C. *The Challenging Use of International Customary Law*

While issues regarding the use of customary law relate to the application of specific norms and the question of determining the exact content of some particular rules or concepts under international law – as examined in greater detail in Section III of this chapter – the issue warrants comment at this stage as well. HPCR's interviews with practitioners indicate a tendency among practitioners to shy away from customary law, except when they felt required to rely on this source of law due to a lack of applicable treaty provisions. Given the cautious approach to participating in the progressive development of international law, as highlighted above, this tendency is hardly surprising. But one might expect that this caution would lead MRF actors, in circumstances when MRF missions apply customary law, to support this choice with extensive legal citations. The report of the Darfur Commission is one example that meets this expectation. However, in other reports, legal references justifying the use of customary law are less extensive.[40] Although one cannot expect MRF bodies to provide extensive sources as if missions were proving the customary nature of a rule for the first time, in some cases, MRF reports, such as that of the Secretary-General's Panel of Experts on Accountability in Sri Lanka (hereafter the Sri Lanka Panel), heavily rely on the *Customary International Humanitarian Law Study* conducted by the International Committee of the Red Cross (ICRC), which is for some rules controversial.[41]

---

[39] "Rapport de la Commission d'enquête international indépendante sur la Côte d'Ivoire," A/HRC/17/48, July 1, 2011, p. 7, accessed June 14, 2015, http://www.refworld.org/docid/4ee05cdf2.html.

[40] See Second Libya Commission report, 190, which notes that states have a "duty to prosecute crimes against humanity, war crimes and genocide" under customary international humanitarian law. However, the report does not provide strong legal sources for the claim that there is a general obligation for all those international crimes.

[41] For example, one topical area of controversy relates to the study's assertion that most of the rules applicable in international armed conflict (IAC) enjoy a customary nature and are applicable in non-international armed conflict (NIAC). In this regard, one of the key

III.   The Application of Legal Norms to Facts

The fifteen MRF missions considered for this book offer an extensive array of practice in terms of addressing legal issues arising from the application of legal norms to certain facts. Although it is beyond the scope of this chapter to list all of these issues, some key elements are recurrent and emblematic of the challenges and the diversity of the practice of fact-finding bodies. Some of these issues relate to existing legal concepts, categories, and rules that pose certain challenges when trying to apply them to facts. Additional issues pertain more to unsettled areas of international law that exacerbate the complexity of ascertaining facts. For both categories, this section will examine the legal justifications (or lack thereof) offered by MRF bodies. In particular, this section focuses on eight specific areas: the co-applicability of IHL and IHRL during armed conflict, the definition and classification of an armed conflict for the applicability of IHL, the content of IHL applicable to NIACs, challenges related to certain rules on the conduct of hostilities, the legality of the use of certain weapons, the obligations of non-state actors under IHL and IHRL, definitions of international crimes and other related ICL issues, and the articulation of IHRL treaties and other sources of international law.

Before delving into an analysis of the challenges related to these issues, this section first briefly examines the tendency of MRF bodies to focus on patterns of violations. The need to identify patterns is primarily dictated by the impossibility for MRF missions to look into all particular incidents relevant to their mandates. But focusing on patterns also allows MRF missions to highlight certain recurrent types of incidents that persistently raise concerns under international law. For example, the Georgia Fact-Finding Mission pointed out key patterns of violence and related violations that characterized the conflict. The report states:

> As regards the provisions of International Humanitarian Law on the conduct of hostilities and the protection of non-combatants, the violations in question mainly concern the ill-treatment of persons, the destruction of property and forced displacement. More specifically the violations include indiscriminate attacks in terms of the type of weaponry used and their targeting.[42]

sets of rules regulating IACs that have crystalized critics has to do with the conduct of hostilities and weapons law being extrapolated to also apply in NIACs. For example, see generally David Turns, "Weapons in the ICRC Study on Customary International Humanitarian Law," *Journal of Conflict & Security Law* 11, no. 2 (2006), accessed June 14, 2015, doi:10.1093/jcsl/krl010.

[42]   Georgia Fact-Finding Mission report, 1: 27.

Similarly, the report of the Darfur Commission stresses:

> It was not possible for the Commission to investigate all of the many hundreds of individually documented incidents reported by other sources. The Commission, therefore, selected incidents and areas that were most representative of acts, trends and patterns relevant to the determination of violations of international human rights and humanitarian law and with greater possibilities of effective fact-finding.[43]

However, to avoid exposing MRF missions to potential criticisms of their methodology, it is important to ensure that MRF reports articulate how the analyses of patterns are the result of both the fact-finding work and the related legal classification of violations.

A. Implications of the Co-applicability of IHL and IHRL in Times of Armed Conflict

An analysis of the fifteen MRF missions under review suggests that, while there has been, in some ways, a consistent approach to restating the co-applicability of IHL and IHRL, MRF actors either devote insufficient attention to the actual implications of this dual regime or articulate confused rationales at the stage of classifying violations. For example, the section of the report of the Côte d'Ivoire Commission that addresses IHL violations is very terse.[44] The report simply states that the parties to the conflict violated both conventional and customary IHL. Furthermore, after this mere statement, the language used in the report mixes IHRL and IHL terminology. Specifically, the report includes a reference to violations of the right to life and right to physical integrity of "protected persons" without defining these legal terms.[45] The report also, in certain cases, asserts that summary executions occurred (i.e., IHRL language), and in other cases, such as the attacks on Duékoué, levies accusations about the use of indiscriminate use of force (i.e., IHL language).[46]

In the same vein, the report of the Lebanon Commission contains a number of statements that illustrate a blurring of the line between these two bodies of norms. For example, regarding "[a]ttacks on the civilian population and objects," the commission notes, "One of the most tragic facts of the conflict raises the question of direct and indiscriminate attacks on civilians and civilian objects and the violation of the right to life."[47] More specifically, the commission concludes that "[t]he deliberate and indiscriminate

---

[43] Darfur Commission report, 61.   [44] Côte d'Ivoire Commission report, 20.
[45] Ibid.   [46] Ibid.   [47] Lebanon Commission report, 28.

targeting of civilian houses constitutes a violation of international humanitarian law and of international human rights obligations."[48] This approach, in strict legal terms, actually contradicts the commonly agreed-upon position that IHL is the *lex specialis* of IHRL when it comes to conflicting norms regarding standards on the use of lethal force. This confused approach could weaken the credibility of the report's legal conclusions.

Another problematic case is the UNHRC Flotilla Fact-Finding Mission. The mission determined, as noted in the "applicable law" section of the report, that IHL was relevant to the interception of the flotilla.[49] As the report asserts, "Flotilla passengers were civilians and in the context of the interception of the vessels must be considered protected persons."[50] However, the entire legal analysis on the use of force by Israeli soldiers and treatment of passengers is conducted using IHRL standards.[51] Although this choice may be legally justified in the context of the law of occupation and the application of IHRL standards to law enforcement operations, the report could have articulated this legal rationale in more explicit terms. Furthermore, the conclusions of the mission are very surprising. The report concludes that the killings of some passengers amount to IHL violations ("grave breaches"), though the report does not apply IHL when analyzing those facts.[52]

Understandably, in some contexts, the overlaps between several concomitant armed conflicts of a different nature and IHRL violations not related to the conflict may render the distinction between IHL and IHRL difficult. The report of the United Nations Mapping Exercise in the Democratic Republic of Congo (hereafter the DRC Mapping Exercise) stresses that:

> [a]lthough the inventory set out … includes serious violations of both human rights and international humanitarian law, it should be noted that the vast majority of the crimes reported were committed in the context of an armed conflict, domestic or international, or a widespread or systematic attack directed against a civilian population, and can thus be classified as war crimes and crimes against humanity respectively.[53]

There is, however, a need to be rigorous about the distinctions and interplay between these two bodies of norms. There is a risk of

---

[48] Ibid., 71.   [49] UNHRC Flotilla Fact-Finding Mission report, 15–16.
[50] Ibid., 15.   [51] Ibid., 35–38.   [52] Ibid., 53.
[53] "Report of the Mapping Exercise Documenting the Most Serious Violations of Human Rights and International Humanitarian Law Committed within the Territory of the Democratic Republic of the Congo between March 1993 and June 2003," Office of the High Commissioner for Human Rights, August 2010, p. 258, accessed June 14, 2015, http://www.refworld.org/docid/4ca99bc22.html.

over-simplification when MRF missions state, as some reports do, that most IHL violations also constitute IHRL violations. For example, the Sri Lanka Panel report states, "The Panel applies the rules of international humanitarian law to the credible allegations linked to the armed conflict, recognizing that many of these will also constitute violations of human rights."[54] Practitioners indicated during the interviews conducted by HPCR that the panel chose to articulate the mission's findings in this manner under the assumption that it would be duplicative, tedious, and time-consuming to analyze the same incidents under both IHRL and IHL lenses. Such comments address only in part the various scenarios and implications of the co-applicability of IHL and IHRL. Complementarity cannot be limited to stating simply that what is a violation of IHL is also a violation of IHRL, because this overlap does not apply to all types of incidents. For example, proportionate collateral damage would be lawful under IHL but would be declared a breach of IHRL standards on the use of lethal force.

Finally, in some cases, MRF missions have drawn important conclusions from the complementary principle between IHL and IHRL. The most striking example is the final report of the Libya Commission, which stresses: "international human rights law obligations remain in effect and operate to limit the circumstances when a state actor – even a soldier during internal armed conflict – can employ lethal force."[55] By employing an approach whereby IHRL limits the use of force against legitimate lawful targets under IHL, the Libya Commission adopts a very progressive interpretation of the interplay between IHL and IHRL regarding the use of lethal force. This interpretation is currently reflected in debates among scholars on a possible common set of rules stemming from both IHL and IHRL to regulate the use of force against civilians participating directly in hostilities. This debate received more attention following the publication of the ICRC's "Interpretive Guidance on the Notion of Direct Participation in Hostilities under International Humanitarian Law," which included a controversial section on "Restraints on the Use of Force in Direct Attack." However, this approach has not been confirmed by state practice. The commission's report does not support its interpretation with any legal basis, raising the question

---

[54] "Report of the Secretary-General's Panel of Experts on Accountability in Sri Lanka," March 31, 2011, p. 53, accessed June 14, 2015, http://www.un.org/News/dh/infocus/Sri_Lanka/POE_Report_Full.pdf.
[55] Second Libya Commission report, 60.

of the possible contribution of MRF missions to the progressive development of international law.

B. Definition and Classification of an Armed Conflict for the Applicability of IHL

The determination of the existence of an armed conflict and its classification are questions to be answered based on facts examined according to a legal definition. As a matter of fact and law, though, determining the threshold of armed conflict is often a challenging question for MRF bodies. Factual situations can be extremely complex. In the case of Lebanon, for example, one may consider the qualification of the situation as an international armed conflict (IAC) to be problematic. Hezbollah cannot be considered a "High Contracting Party" according to the definition of an IAC under the Geneva Conventions, and Hezbollah's actions cannot be attributed to the state of Lebanon.[56] The report of the DRC Mapping Exercise also notes:

> It is difficult to classify all of the various armed conflicts that affected the DRC all over its territory between 1993 and 2003. Depending on the time and place, the DRC experienced internal and international armed conflicts and internal conflicts that subsequently became international.[57]

In the case of Libya, the commission took into account the NIAC definition developed in international jurisprudence and commonly accepted while also noting that "[t]he precise date for determining when this change from peace to non-international armed conflict occurred is somewhat difficult in the current circumstances."[58] The commission referred to the intensity of the conflict, the extent of relevant control of territory, and the nature of the armed group in opposition to the Government.[59]

In other cases, though, MRF reports have assessed the existence of an armed conflict without due consideration for the key legal elements. For example, the Côte d'Ivoire Commission report states that, since the conflict did not take place on the whole territory of the country, IHL applied only to the parts of the country where a NIAC was effectively ongoing.[60]

---

[56] See Andreas Paulus and Mindia Vashakmadze, "Asymmetrical war and the notion of armed conflict – a tentative conceptualization," *International Review of the Red Cross* 91, no. 873 (2009): 111–112, accessed June 14, 2015, https://www.icrc.org/eng/assets/files/other/irrc-873-paulus-vashakmadze.pdf.

[57] DRC Mapping Exercise report, 262.   [58] First Libya Commission report, 30.

[59] Ibid.   [60] Côte d'Ivoire Commission report, 20.

This appears to contradict the well-established jurisprudence of the International Criminal Tribunal for the former Yugoslavia. Specifically, in the *Tadic* case, the Appeals Chamber stressed that "the temporal and geographical scope of both internal and international armed conflicts extends beyond the exact time and place of hostilities."[61] In this case, the Appeals Chamber rejected the argument of the appellant on the grounds that IHL pertains not only to those areas where actual fighting takes place. Rather, according to the Appeals Chamber, IHL applies to the entire territory of the state involved in armed conflict. Interviewees who worked on the Côte d'Ivoire Commission were unable to explain the position adopted by the mission and generally found the mission's interpretation to be unproblematic.

C.　Content of IHL Applicable to Non-international Armed Conflicts

While state practice, jurisprudence, and numerous other sources have confirmed that IHL applicable to NIAC goes beyond Common Article 3 of the Geneva Conventions I–IV, it is still important for MRF bodies to carefully elaborate on this issue. In this respect, when demonstrating the customary nature of the IHL rules applicable in NIACs, the Darfur Commission offers a summary close to a scholarly documented research work. The report states:

> In addition to international treaties, the Sudan is bound by customary rules of international humanitarian law. These include rules relating to internal armed conflicts, many of which have evolved as a result of State practice and jurisprudence from international, regional and national courts, as well as pronouncements by States, international organizations and armed groups.[62]

Similarly, the report of the High-Level Fact-Finding Mission to Beit Hanoun established under resolution S-3/1 (hereafter the Beit Hanoun Fact-Finding Mission) notes:

> Under accepted customary international humanitarian law obligations, armed groups are bound by the obligations of common Article 3 of the Geneva Conventions. They must respect and ensure respect of the principles of distinction, proportionality and the obligation to take the necessary precautions to avoid or minimize incidental loss of civilian life, injury to

---

[61] *Prosecutor v. Tadic*, Decision on the Defence Motion for Interlocutory Appeal on Jurisdiction (International Criminal Tribunal for the former Yugoslavia, October 2, 1995), ¶ 67, accessed June 14, 2015, http://www.icty.org/x/cases/tadic/acdec/en/51002.htm.
[62] Darfur Commission report, 44.

civilians and damage to civilian objects. Aiming rockets at civilian targets is a violation of this obligation, as would be endangering Palestinian civilians by launching rockets from or near civilians (for example in residential areas).[63]

Beyond the consensus around certain general principles of the law on the conduct of hostilities, the issue of the content of IHL norms applicable to NIAC remains problematic when considering more specific rules, such as those on precautions against the effects of attacks.[64] For example, the report of the Sri Lanka Panel states that there is "some disagreement among States" over some restrictions and norms, but the report stresses that "the rules on which the Panel relies ... are all, in its view, beyond dispute as rules of customary international humanitarian law."[65]

As this section illustrates, even with regard to traditional IHL legal issues, MRF bodies run the risk of having to make determinations based on fact-finding work that require careful legal explanations and justifications to prevent unnecessary critiques.

D.   Challenges Related to Certain Rules on the Conduct of Hostilities

Fact-finding, as an activity, includes core modalities that are not specific to the application of IHL. However, by definition, fact-finding on alleged violations of certain norms of IHL raises particular issues that require adapting existing methods. Some specific challenges and issues related to the context of armed conflict, the nature or type of facts to be established, or the content of IHL norms do have some impact on those common standards and methodological principles. This is particularly the case with regard to some rules of IHL on the conduct of hostilities. This could be seen as the central feature that distinguishes human rights fact-finding from IHL fact-finding.

Although some norms on the conduct of hostilities are clearly defined, these rules often prove challenging to articulate due to the difficulty of establishing the relevant facts. This difficulty stems primarily from the fact that some of these rules contain elements that are defined *ex ante* (before

---

[63] "Report of the High-Level Fact-Finding Mission to Beit Hanoun Established Under Council Resolution S-3/1," A/HRC/9/26, September 1, 2008, p. 6, accessed June 14, 2015, http://www.refworld.org/docid/48cfa3a22.html.

[64] See, for example, Christopher Greenwood, "International Humanitarian Law and the Tadic Case," *European Journal of International Law* 7, no. 2 (1996): 279, accessed June 14, 2015, http://ejil.org/pdfs/7/2/1365.pdf.

[65] Sri Lanka Panel report, 53.

an attack is launched), whereas the assessment is carried out *ex post facto* (after the attack has occurred).

Several examples illustrate this difficulty. In particular, though IHL sometimes requires a more nuanced approach, MRF actors often need to infer that an incident amounts to a violation of IHL from the absence of contradicting information or from the significant effects of an attack. For example, the absence of information indicating the presence of combatants or military activities in a certain civilian building can play an important role in reaching a legal conclusion. Regarding the incident in Qana – in which the Israeli Air Force bombed a three-story building, killing twenty-nine civilians during the 2006 war in Lebanon – the Lebanon Commission notes that it "did not receive any information to suggest that the building in question was being used as a Hezbollah missile launch site, either prior to or at the time of the attack, and that it therefore may have been a legitimate military target."[66] In another context, the overwhelming extensive destruction to civilian objects in a given town served as a basis for the Lebanon Commission to conclude that the attacks could not have been proportionate. The report notes that "[a]s with so many other cases investigated by the Commission, the IDF [Israeli Defense Force] actions were indiscriminate and disproportionate" and that "[t]he destruction of so many civilian houses is not justifiable in terms of military necessity."[67] Yet, this type of inference may actually be insufficient for a rigorous and sound application of IHL in light of the way IHL norms on the conduct of hostilities are drafted.

As this example suggests, the principle of proportionality under IHL, in the context of the prohibition of indiscriminate attacks, is very difficult to apply in practice. Indeed, this principle requires MRF actors to assess two elements, both being per se challenging to grasp: (1) the expected incidental loss of civilian life, injury to civilians, and damage to civilian objects; and (2) the anticipated concrete and direct military advantage associated with this attack. It is then necessary to compare both elements to undertake a proportionality analysis and decide whether the former is excessive vis-à-vis the latter. Unsurprisingly, MRF bodies have faced significant challenges in applying this principle. It seems that, rather than carrying out a proportionality test in some questionable cases, MRF bodies focused on manifest and clear-cut incidents or patterns of violations of this principle. For example, the Darfur Commission report states:

---

[66] Lebanon Commission report, 30 (internal citation omitted).
[67] Ibid., 32.

The issue of proportionality did obviously not arise when no armed groups were present in the village, as the attack exclusively targeted civilians. However, whenever there might have been any armed elements present, the attack on a village would not be proportionate, as in most cases the whole village was destroyed or burned down and civilians, if not killed or wounded, would all be compelled to flee the village to avoid further harm. The civilian losses resulting from the military action would therefore be patently excessive in relation to the expected military advantage of killing rebels or putting them *hors de combat*.[68]

The principle of proportionality is the topical case of a particularly unclear IHL rule that tends to be extremely difficult to apply in practice. Not only is the collection of facts very complex but also the application of the norm to specific attacks is equally difficult.

The Georgia Fact-Finding Mission also acknowledged the challenges in ascertaining facts and making legal determinations on various key issues regarding the conduct of hostilities. The report states:

> Addressing questions such as the types of objective that have been targeted, the circumstances at the time of the attack and the exact cause of damage has proved to be very delicate. For example, many administrative buildings were attacked, as well as schools and apartment buildings. In the case of these objectives, a key fact to establish would be whether or not Ossetian combatants were present in the buildings at the time they were attacked. According to Human Rights Watch, witnesses and members of South Ossetian militias themselves "made it clear that South Ossetian forces set up defensive positions or headquarters in civilian infrastructure." There are also cases where the presence of such combatants was not substantiated.
>
> Although it appears very difficult to reach definite factual and legal conclusions on each and every specific attack, a number of facts do seem to emerge from testimonies collected on the ground by NGOs [nongovernmental organizations] and from the comparison between the military objectives and the types of weapons used.[69]

These examples illustrate how these norms require consideration of specific facts that are particularly difficult to establish, which in turn impacts the ability to make a sound legal assessment in line with the content of these norms. Fact-finding work must address all components of these rules in order for a mission to reach a legal conclusion. Such components include factual elements that pertain to various aspects and perspectives related to the way weapons were used, the nature of the target, and the effects of the attack. Most importantly, there is also a constant need to take

---

[68] Darfur Commission report, 73.
[69] Georgia Fact-Finding Mission report, 2: 323 (internal citation omitted).

into account two perspectives: that of the attacker and that of the defender. Facts are to be established not in the abstract and on the basis of the information and effects of an attack as they came to light after the attack but in relation, for instance, to what could have been reasonably known by the attacker at the time before the attack. For example, the concept of military objective depends on the plans of the attacker and the perceived conduct of the defender. Similarly, those characteristics may hamper the ability to make legal findings on whether a given incident amounts to a deliberate attack on civilians rather than an indiscriminate attack in violation of the principle of proportionality.

Furthermore, the notion of what constitutes a military objective has given rise to different interpretations. For example, the Libya Commission adopted a rather broad definition of what constitutes "effective contribution to military action" as one of the elements that defines a military objective. The commission considered that "these buildings [a school and a mosque] could be said to have taken on a military character by encouraging or supporting combat operations by *thuwar* [anti-Qaddafi forces]. As such their targeting would not necessarily violate international law."[70] However, under IHL, propaganda is not considered a use that can turn a civilian object into a military objective.

The obligations under the norms on precautions in attack illustrate additional challenges, not least because they are among the few IHL norms carrying positive obligations. The rules refer to the obligation to take only feasible precautions "to avoid, and in any event to minimize, incidental loss of civilian life, injury to civilians and damage to civilian objects."[71] Feasibility is commonly defined as what was practically possible at the time of the attack. This is essential in order to assess whether precautionary measures were required, making those obligations relative in nature. Fact-finders must therefore know that the definition of feasibility depends on both humanitarian and military considerations for which facts must be established.

E. The Legality of the Use of Certain Weapons

It goes without saying that when a treaty prohibits the use of certain weapons, the legal determination is clear. A much more complicated

---

[70] Second Libya Commission report, 155.

[71] "Rule 15. Precautions in Attack," Customary IHL, International Committee of the Red Cross, accessed June 14, 2015, https://www.icrc.org/customary-ihl/eng/docs/v1_cha_chapter5_rule15.

issue lies in looking into allegations of the use of weapons whose legality is dubious because these weapons have not yet been covered by a particular convention. An interviewee stressed, for example, that the use of white phosphorus was debated among the commissioners and that in this context the question of the status of those weapons under international customary law was unclear. As different properties of white phosphorus can serve different military purposes, and it is not prohibited by a specific IHL norm, the determination of whether it falls within any other existing specific regulation, such as that on incendiary weapons, will depend on a case-by-case analysis.

Regarding the issue of the use and legality of certain weapons, the Lebanon Commission adopted two very distinct approaches: one for cluster munitions and another for dense inert metal explosives (DIME) munitions. Regarding cluster munitions, the commission first described the characteristics of the weapons and then assessed the way they were used during the armed conflict in 2006 under the general prohibition of indiscriminate attacks.[72] However, regarding DIME munitions, while the commission did not establish the use of such munitions, the report states without much elaboration that "[i]f [DIME munitions] were effectively used … they would be illegal under international humanitarian law" based on Protocol I of the Conventional Weapons Convention, which prohibits the use of any weapon for which the primary effect is to injure by fragments that cannot be detected by X-rays.[73] However, the lack of a clear articulation regarding the application of this treaty to DIME munitions risks undermining this legal conclusion.

In the case of the Beit Hanoun Fact-Finding Mission, the mission referred to the argument put forward by the Israeli military that "if an error is caused by malfunctioning technology, there can be no causal link (and thus no responsibility) on the part of individuals, be they designing, building or operating the technology."[74] In the mission's response, however, the mission changed the perspective from a technical question to a broader evaluation of the use of artillery in urban areas, "especially in densely populated urban settings such as Gaza," which "is wholly inappropriate and likely contrary to international humanitarian and human rights law."[75] Despite the constraints and challenges illustrated by these cases, documenting facts around the use of weapons brings attention to

---

[72] Lebanon Commission report, 58–60.   [73] Ibid., 61.
[74] Beit Hanoun Fact-Finding Mission report, 12 (internal citation omitted).
[75] Ibid., 13.

weapons of dubious legality in order to call for further clarification and research on their effects.

F. Obligations of Non-state Actors under IHL and IHRL

Despite the repeated statements made by the interviewees that MRF bodies seek solely to apply existing law to facts, the context in which MRF missions operate may force practitioners to take a position on the obligations of non-state actors under IHL and IHRL, a rapidly evolving topic. The Libya Commission notes the unsettled nature of this area of law:

> Although the extent to which international human rights law binds non-state actors remains contested as a matter of international law, it is increasingly accepted that where non-state groups exercise de facto control over territory, they must respect fundamental human rights of persons in that territory. The Commission has taken the approach that since the NTC [National Transitional Council] has been exercising de facto control over territory akin to that of a Governmental authority, it will examine also allegations of human rights violations committed by its forces.[76]

One controversial question is the basis on which one considers an armed group bound by IHRL. The Lebanon Commission laconically states that "[a]s a party to the conflict, Hezbollah is also bound to respect international humanitarian law and human rights."[77] However, the commission's report lacks justification under international law with respect to how international law is binding on armed groups. The Gaza Fact-Finding Mission offers a more conceptual justification:

> The relationship between IHL and IHRL is rapidly evolving, in particular in relation to non-State actors' obligations, with the ultimate goal of enhancing the protection of people and to enable them to enjoy their human rights in all circumstances. In the context of the matter within the Mission's mandate, it is clear that non-State actors that exercise government-like functions over a territory have a duty to respect human rights.[78]

The way that MRF bodies have affirmed the obligations of non-state actors in the context of fact-finding work is unquestionably contributing to strengthening the emerging legal recognition of this norm. This relatively progressive approach may be explained by the fact that this interpretation may trigger fewer critics, compared to progressive interpretations

---

[76] First Libya Commission report, 32–33 (internal citations omitted).
[77] Lebanon Commission report, 24 (internal citation omitted).
[78] Gaza Fact-Finding Mission report, 80.

expanding the scope of state obligations, which would more obviously elicit criticisms from governments.

G. Definitions of International Crimes and Other Related ICL Issues

The way that MRF reports spell out the legal sources for the definitions of international crimes is critical, and the practice of MRF missions varies greatly in this regard from case to case. Some missions have offered a rigorous application of ICL. For example, the Kyrgyzstan Inquiry Commission (hereafter the Kyrgyzstan Commission) used a cautious formula to rely on the International Criminal Court (ICC) Statute for the purpose of the definition of international crimes, rather than stating that the crime constitutes an expression of customary international law. The report states:

> While Kyrgyzstan is not a party to the Rome Statute of the International Criminal Court (ICC), the relevant formulations adopted in the Statute can for the most part be considered for present purposes to provide a convenient and appropriate definition of the content of the relevant crimes.[79]

However, other missions have offered some rather confusing statements that suggest misunderstandings. The Lebanon Commission noted under the section of the mission's report that articulates the applicable law that "[s]erious violations of international human rights law and international humanitarian law are regulated inter alia by the Rome Statute of the International Criminal Court, as well as customary international law."[80] This statement fails to elaborate on the specificities of international criminal law as a separate body of norms and also implies that the ICC Statute regulates serious IHRL violations as international crimes, whereas this treaty merely deals with genocide, crime against humanity, and war crimes.

As suggested by the statements of the UNSG Flotilla Panel referenced earlier, in some circumstances, certain MRF actors perceive that establishing the facts may prove to be more important for an MRF body than engaging in legal debates. Additionally, certain practitioners interviewed by HPCR noted laconically that one could argue that IHRL includes IHL and ICL without having to dedicate too much time to justifying the respective applicability of those bodies of norms. However, the strength and authoritative scope of some statements made by an MRF mission classifying

---

[79] "Report of the Independent International Commission of Inquiry into the Events in Southern Kyrgyzstan in June 2010," n.d., p. 47, accessed June 14, 2015, http://reliefweb.int/sites/reliefweb.int/files/resources/Full_Report_490.pdf.

[80] Lebanon Commission report, 25.

certain acts as international crimes will depend on the legal accuracy of the arguments. The field of ICL is characterized by strict requirements.

Additionally, the application of ICL raises questions of standards of proof for MRF missions. Specifically, when classifying certain acts as crimes under international law, or when tasked to identify suspected perpetrators as part of an MRF mandate, many MRF bodies applied ICL even though these missions did not apply the standards of proof used by criminal tribunals or courts.[81]

1. Crimes against Humanity

Several interviewees pointed out that addressing the definition of crimes against humanity in the absence of an international treaty is one of the most complicated issues relevant to fulfilling MRF mandates. Extensive discussions among MRF actors during the implementation of MRF missions seem to have revolved around this question in many different MRF missions, partly because of the implications of such a legal determination for the alleged perpetrators. While MRF bodies commonly refer to the definition of crimes against humanity contained in the ICC Statute, some controversy remains over this definition, notably regarding the state policy component. Customary law and the ICC Statute differ about whether incidents must have occurred as a component of state policy in order to qualify as crimes against humanity. The ICC Statute requires an additional contextual element: the widespread or systematic attack must be carried out "pursuant to or in furtherance of a State or organizational policy to commit such attack."[82] This element is not part of the customary definition under international law. For this reason, the sources of law that an MRF mission uses to define crimes against humanity directly impact the types of facts needed and the way in which the mission must assess those facts.

To address this dilemma, the Kyrgyzstan Commission – in line with the mission's aforementioned overall cautious approach to ICL – confronted the issue of different elements and interpretations of certain elements of crimes against humanity. The report states:

> In relying upon customary international law approaches to crimes against humanity the Commission does not need to take a position on current

---

[81] For issues related to standards of proof in MRF missions, see generally Stephen Wilkinson, "Standards of Proof in International Humanitarian and Human Rights Fact-Finding and Inquiry Missions," Geneva Academy of International Law and Human Rights, n.d., accessed June 14, 2015, http://www.geneva-academy.ch/docs/reports/Standards%20 of%20proo%20report.pdf.

[82] Rome Statute of the International Criminal Court, Article 7.2.a.

debates surrounding the approach to be adopted by the ICC. Instead, in conformity with existing law it adopts below a relatively demanding standard in order to assess whether a sufficient degree of organizational policy existed in relation to the June events.[83]

One example of confused legal language regarding crimes against humanity appears in the report of the Libya Commission, which seems to draw a distinction between various degrees of the "widespread or systematic" character of an attack, despite spelling out the legal definition of this expression as an element of the crime, which makes no mention to this threshold issue.[84] The specific requirements and implications of qualifying certain acts as crimes against humanity, and the differences between the ICC framework and international customary law, highlight the necessity that MRF bodies provide clear legal arguments when addressing this question.

2. Genocide

The crime of genocide raises significant issues at the level of proving the specific intent of the alleged perpetrators through fact-finding. First, as pointed out by some of the practitioners interviewed for this research, it is extremely difficult to gather factual information and evidence to prove the intent to destroy, in whole or in part, a national, ethnic, racial, or religious group. This challenge is further illustrated when considering the "discrepancies" identified by one scholar, Patryk Labuda, in the practice of commissions of inquiry.[85] Labuda refers to the conclusion by the CAR Commission that it "has not received sufficient evidence to establish reasonable grounds to believe that the perpetrators acted with specific intent to destroy the targeted group."[86] Noting, as the commission did, that genocidal intent is extremely difficult to prove, Labuda looks into a recurring methodological approach with regard to fact-finding work on establishing genocide, that is, "whether the *mens rea* can be inferred from the *actus reus*,"[87] meaning the use of jurisprudence of international tribunals to evaluate "the extent to which attacks against a large proportion of a targeted group … can be indicative of specific intent to destroy that group."[88] In that regard, Labuda highlights that "[d]espite abundant

---

[83] Kyrgyzstan Commission report, 50.

[84] See Heller, "The International Commission of Inquiry on Libya," 33–34.

[85] Patryk I. Labuda, "What Lies Beneath the 'G' Word? Genocide-Labelling and Fact-Finding at the UN," *EJIL: Talk!* May 28, 2015, accessed June 14, 2015, http://www.ejiltalk.org/what-lies-beneath-the-g-word-genocide-labelling-and-fact-finding-at-the-un.

[86] CAR Commission report, 97.   [87] Labuda, "What Lies Beneath."

[88] CAR Commission report, 98.

evidence of widespread targeting of Muslims, [the CAR Commission] declines to make any inferences from those facts, choosing instead to fall back on the assertion that it could not find clear evidence of genocidal intent."[89] He concludes by pointing out other examples, such as the OHCHR fact-finding mission in Iraq and the DRC Mapping Exercise report that, on the contrary, relied more on the factual elements of the genocidal acts to draw conclusions on the genocidal intent, even if in the latter case the report left the legal determination open.

One explanation for these discrepancies, as indicated in HPCR's interviews with practitioners, may be due to the specific gravity and symbolic dimension of qualifying certain acts as genocide, "the crime of the crimes." MRF practitioners tend to proceed with extra caution when looking into this question. The section of the DRC Mapping Exercise report that addresses genocide is drafted in very prudent terms, leaving the final determination to a court of law.[90] Similarly, the Darfur Commission report, though concluding that genocide had not been carried out as a matter of state policy, asserts:

> One should not rule out the possibility that in some instances *single individuals*, including Government officials, may entertain a genocidal intent, or in other words, attack the victims with the specific intent of annihilating, in part, a group perceived as a hostile ethnic group. If any single individual, including Governmental officials, has such intent, it would be for a competent court to make such a determination on a case by case basis.[91]

3. War Crimes

The definitions of war crimes, though widely recognized, are nevertheless challenging to some MRF bodies that struggle to present legal definitions in a consistent manner. For example, the report of the Côte d'Ivoire Commission contains certain paragraphs about war crimes that alternatively state that the acts identified may be qualified as serious violations of Common Article 3 and then as serious violations of the law and customs of war applicable in NIAC, leaving the impression that both overlap.[92]

H. Articulating IHRL Treaties and Other Sources of International Law

A final issue relates to the interaction between the relevant treaties and other sources of international law applicable to the events under

---

[89] Labuda, "What Lies Beneath." [90] DRC Mapping Exercise report, 275–284.
[91] Darfur Commission report, 132 (internal citation omitted).
[92] Côte d'Ivoire Commission report, 20–21.

investigation by MRF bodies. For example, while noting that Bahrain is not a party to either the International Convention for the Protection of All Persons from Enforced Disappearance or the Rome Statute of the ICC, the report of the Bahrain Independent Commission of Inquiry (hereafter the Bahrain Commission) indicates that such treaties "provide an international legal framework for the assessment of alleged enforced disappearances"[93] and asserts that the mission "has used the definitions contained in those instruments as a frame of reference in its assessment of allegations of enforced disappearance."[94] The Bahrain Commission, however, concluded that it "cannot find that acts and omissions that would comprise a breach of the general international human rights law prohibition against enforced disappearance took place during the relevant period."[95] This section is problematic, since the Bahrain Commission report does not articulate the legal basis for such a general prohibition in the section on applicable law but makes a specific reference to this rule only in the report's conclusions. This specific example raises the broader issue of the articulation of the relevant general legal framework identified by an MRF body and the specific factual and legal findings.

IV. Conclusion

This overview of the interplay between the facts and the law in fact-finding, and the way that MRF practitioners select and apply international norms, not only highlights the myriad of legal issues arising in fact-finding work but also points out how such questions are at times overlooked or addressed differently in practice from mission to mission. Any effort at professionalization of MRF activities requires more focus on the legal dimensions of fact-finding. A careful and sound legal analysis is as important for the credibility of the MRF bodies as the factual determinations. Furthermore, the legal perspective must be considered throughout the entire process of mission implementation and not merely as a stand-alone stage considered only in separation from the process of establishing facts. It is therefore imperative that MRF organs pay more attention to justifying the rationales used to support their references and interpretations of international norms, such as those examined in this chapter.

[93] "Report of the Bahrain Independent Commission of Inquiry," November 23, 2011, p. 315, accessed June 14, 2015, http://www.bici.org.bh/BICIreportEN.pdf.
[94] Ibid., 316–317.   [95] Ibid., 317.

3

Finding the Facts

Standards of Proof and Information Handling in Monitoring, Reporting, and Fact-Finding Missions

STEPHEN WILKINSON

Introduction

As a growing and increasingly influential mechanism for overseeing adherence to fundamental human rights and humanitarian law standards in some of the most serious situations of conflict and violence, monitoring, reporting, and fact-finding (MRF) missions are increasingly being questioned about the standards that they apply. In the same way that courts and tribunals are asked to set out clear standards and ways of working, the following question has arisen: When making legal and factual assertions regarding violations of international law – including serious violations of human rights and humanitarian law – what level of rigor has or should have been applied by MRF processes?

The driving forces behind concerns about standards are, on the one hand, the need for credibility and certainty, and on the other hand, the desire for transparency in processes that often have serious judicial and political implications. However, establishing a clear framework for setting out the certainty of findings in such an ad hoc and generally short process is far from straightforward. Some people refer to the issue in theoretical terms, such as standards of proof, while others talk more of specific investigative methodologies, such as outlining the considerations needed to corroborate information and the specific facts needed to establish a violation of a given norm.

This chapter seeks to shed some light on the practice and application of standards of proof and offers reflections and insight into the challenges facing MRF missions in sourcing, collecting, and authenticating information.

I. Standards of Proof: Utility and Application

This section examines the importance of standards of proof, the connection between the standard adopted and the overarching aims of MRF missions, different approaches that have been adopted, the practical implications of those approaches, and the role of vocabulary that articulates the certainty of missions' findings in MRF reports. For the purposes of this chapter, a "standard of proof"

> marks a point somewhere along the line between two extremes: a mere conjecture at one end, and absolute certainty at the other. Proof furnished in support of a particular proposition must meet or surpass this point for a judicial finding in favour of the proposition to be made. In practice, this may either constitute a very explicit exercise of applying an objective standard of proof … or … [be] based upon a number of unarticulated factors concerning the evidence that has been furnished.[1]

A. The Importance of Standards of Proof

It's difficult to sleep at night because you worry that you will allege something that turns out to be disputed. At the same time, if you're too conservative, you're doing injustice to the victims.[2]

Having set standards or thresholds before assertions or decisions are made or other actions are taken plays a key role in many judicial and quasi-judicial mechanisms under domestic frameworks.[3] Hence, in the context of an MRF mission, having a discussion on the appropriate standard of proof, while not the only arbiter of the mission's transparency and credibility, can and should provide a useful framework for articulating the methodology that the mission employed.[4] However, interviews with MRF practitioners demonstrated some divergence of opinion concerning the centrality or importance of the issue of standards of proof. Many practitioners stated in strong terms the need to have standards. As one practitioner asserts:

---

[1] Katherine Del Mar, "The International Court of Justice and Standards of Proof," in *The ICJ and the Evolution of International Law: The Enduring Impact of the Corfu Channel Case*, ed. Karine Bannelier, Theodore Christakis, and Sarah Heathcote (New York: Routledge, 2012), 98 (internal citations omitted).

[2] Confidential interview with a high-level MRF practitioner, name of interviewee on file, conducted by HPCR, Summer 2013.

[3] Such as, but not limited to, an array of judicial processes (including indictment, investigation, prosecution, and conviction) as well as quasi-judicial processes (such as disciplinary boards and national commissions of inquiry).

[4] For a theoretical focus considering standards of proof and fact-finding missions, see generally Stephen Wilkinson, "Standards of Proof in International Humanitarian and Human Rights Fact-Finding and Inquiry Missions," Geneva Academy of International Humanitarian Law and Human Rights, n.d., accessed June 9, 2015, http://www.geneva-academy.ch/docs/reports/Standards%20of%20proo%20report.pdf.

Standards of proof was always an issue. What you are doing is collecting information that leads you to identify certain patterns of human rights violations, and as long as you have sufficient information – interviews, documents, a whole range of other data – if this all supports the kinds of patterns that are coming out, then you're pretty much safe.[5]

A minority of practitioners suggested that standards of proof have little utility, but the reasons for stating so did differ markedly. One MRF practitioner stated, "Conversations about standards of proof may not be as necessary if all the commissioners are lawyers,"[6] while another stated, "We are not judges. It is just a report. So we cannot bring into the report everything about standard of proof."[7]

However, it appears that any apparent chasm between these differing perceptions may come down to terminology, or a disparity in the agreed level of formality, rather than a difference between various practitioners' level of concern about producing a credible and accurate product based on a sound process.

It is also important to note that those being investigated have also used standards of proof language as a means to attack the credibility of MRF missions. For example, the government of Rwanda criticized the United Nations Mapping Exercise in the Democratic Republic of Congo (hereafter the DRC Mapping Exercise) on the grounds that the mission used a "flawed methodology" that relied on the "application of the lowest imaginable evidentiary standard" and exhibited an "overreliance on the use of anonymous sources, hearsay assertions, unnamed, un-vetted and unidentified investigators and witnesses, who lack credibility; and allegation of the existence of victims with uncertain identity."[8]

Indeed, MRF practitioners widely acknowledge the connection between the mission's methodology – including the transparency with which the mission publicly communicates this methodology – and perceptions of the report's credibility. One practitioner recommends, "When you don't have enough material to draw conclusions, admit that. Make

[5] Yakin Ertürk, Commissioner, Kyrgyzstan Inquiry Commission, interview conducted by HPCR, July 18, 2013.
[6] Confidential interview with a high-level MRF practitioner, name of interviewee on file, conducted by HPCR, Summer 2013.
[7] Confidential interview with a high-level MRF practitioner, name of interviewee on file, conducted by HPCR, Summer 2013.
[8] Republic of Rwanda, Ministry of Foreign Affairs and Cooperation, "Official Government of Rwanda Comments on the Draft UN Mapping Report on the DRC," September 30, 2010, p. 3, accessed May 26, 2015, http://rwandinfo.com/documents/DRC_Report_Comments_Rwanda.pdf.

sure not to jump to conclusions that you're not entirely sure about," and also, "Be as detailed as possible on methodology in the final report."[9] Another practitioner states, "nothing was put into the report lightly,"[10] while yet another mentions of an MRF mission on which she served, "It had to be very technically credible for the findings to be accepted."[11] These comments all suggest acknowledgment of the importance of applying some standards concerning the manner in which the mission scrutinizes and assesses information.

B.   *Understanding the Interconnection between Standards of Proof and the Role of Monitoring, Reporting, and Fact-Finding Missions*

The final outcome is not to convict people in front of a court of law. The purpose is to raise a red flag.[12]

To further comprehend the role that standards of proof play in MRF missions, it is important to understand what MRF missions are, in terms of their purposes, aims, objectives, and more specifically, their role in relation to accountability. Are MRF missions an end in themselves or merely a trigger mechanism for future action? Answers or indicators to such questions will significantly help to shape discussions on the relevance of standards of proof, and if deemed relevant, where evidentiary thresholds should be set.

The mandates of MRF missions do not typically provide a clear understanding of the missions' functions and roles, aside from articulating general notions such as "establishing facts," "identifying violations of international law," and "identifying individuals responsible." However, an assessment of MRF reports and comments made by MRF practitioners provides significant insight into how practitioners view the role of MRF missions. First, MRF reports consistently affirm that MRF missions are not tribunals or courts and that this fact directly informs the standard of

[9]   Philippe Kirsch, Commissioner, Bahrain Independent Commission of Inquiry, and Chair, International Commission of Inquiry on Libya (October 2011–March 2012), interview conducted by HPCR, July 23, 2013.

[10] Sareta Ashraph, Analyst, International Commission of Inquiry on Libya, and Associate Human Rights Officer, United Nations Fact-Finding Mission on the Gaza Conflict, interview conducted by HPCR, August 8, 2013.

[11] Mary Shanthi Dairiam, Commissioner, International Fact-Finding Mission to investigate violations of international law, including international humanitarian and human rights law, resulting from the Israeli attacks on the flotilla of ships carrying humanitarian assistance, interview conducted by HPCR, April 3, 2013.

[12] Martin Seutcheu, Human Rights Officer for the Office of the High Commissioner for Human Rights, interview conducted by HPCR, September 3, 2013.

proof adopted by the mission. The following passages from various reports are emblematic of this trend.

- "One of the major premises is that mapping remains a preliminary exercise that does not seek to gather evidence that would be admissible in court, but rather to 'provide the basis for the formulation of initial hypotheses of investigation by giving a sense of the scale of violations, detecting patterns and identifying potential leads or sources of evidence.'" (DRC Mapping Exercise)[13]
- "The Commission was not endowed with the powers of a court or prosecutor." (United Nations Independent Special Commission of Inquiry for Timor-Leste [hereafter the Timor-Leste Commission])[14]
- "The Panel is not a court." (Secretary-General's Panel of Inquiry on the 31 May 2010 Flotilla Incident [hereafter the UNSG Flotilla Panel])[15]
- "In summary, it should be noted that the factual basis thus established may be considered as adequate for the purpose of fact-finding, but not for any other purpose. This includes judicial proceedings such as the cases already pending before International Courts as well as any others." (Independent International Fact-Finding Mission on the Conflict in Georgia [hereafter the Georgia Fact-Finding Mission])[16]
- "[T]he question as to whether or not crimes were committed can be finally and conclusively resolved only by a court with the requisite jurisdictional competence." (International Commission of Inquiry for Guinea [hereafter the Guinea Commission])[17]

---

[13] "Report of the Mapping Exercise Documenting the Most Serious Violations of Human Rights and International Humanitarian Law Committed within the Territory of the Democratic Republic of the Congo between March 1993 and June 2003," Office of the High Commissioner for Human Rights, August 2010, p. 36, accessed May 26, 2015, http://www.refworld.org/docid/4ca99bc22.html (internal citation omitted).

[14] "Report of the United Nations Independent Special Commission of Inquiry for Timor-Leste," October 2006, p. 13, accessed June 14, 2015, http://www.ohchr.org/Documents/Countries/COITimorLeste.pdf.

[15] "Report of the Secretary-General's Panel of Inquiry on the 31 May 2010 Flotilla Incident," September 2011, p. 7, accessed June 14, 2015, http://www.un.org/News/dh/infocus/middle_east/Gaza_Flotilla_Panel_Report.pdf.

[16] "Independent International Fact-Finding Mission on the Conflict in Georgia Report," vol. 1 (September 2009), 8.

[17] "Report of the International Commission of Inquiry Mandated to Establish the Facts and Circumstances of the Events of 28 September 2009 in Guinea," transmitted by letter dated 18 December 2009 from the Secretary-General addressed to the President of the Security Council, S/2009/693, December 18, 2009, p. 41, accessed June 14, 2015, http://www.refworld.org/docid/4b4f49ea2.html.

- "It is understood however that in determining responsibilities the Commission will not conduct a criminal investigation; the conduct of such an investigation will remain the responsibility of the authorities of the Kyrgyz Republic." (Kyrgyzstan Inquiry Commission [hereafter the Kyrgyzstan Commission])[18]
- "The Commission emphasizes that it is not a court of law." (International Commission of Inquiry on Libya [hereafter the Libya Commission])[19]

Second, several statements expressed by practitioners provide some, if not total, clarity about the conceptual nature of MRF missions. Practitioners have stated, for example, that "the goal is to put pressure on the state to improve the situation"[20] and "to bring out the facts and trigger a political intervention to stop the human rights abuses, to build momentum toward accountability."[21] There seemed to be significant agreement across the board that MRF missions are limited – and in some cases, preliminary – mechanisms (at least compared to courts and tribunals), and as such, all subsequent discussions on standards of proof, information collection, and the weighting of sources should be viewed through this lens. Interestingly, no MRF practitioner interviewed for this chapter expressed a concern that a subsequent formal judicial process reaching different conclusions would undermine the work of the mission per se, highlighting and reinforcing that practitioners view MRF missions as an entirely distinct exercise. However, though some MRF practitioners stressed the preliminary nature of MRF exercises, this is not to say that there is a perception that there is no need to apply or adhere to clear standards. In fact, it was quite the opposite. As the next section demonstrates, MRF reports regularly refer to frameworks of standards of proof.

---

[18] "Report of the Independent International Commission of Inquiry into the Events in Southern Kyrgyzstan in June 2010," n.d., p. 2, accessed May 26, 2015, http://reliefweb.int/ sites/reliefweb.int/files/resources/Full_Report_490.pdf.

[19] "Report of the International Commission of Inquiry on Libya," A/HRC/19/68, March 2, 2012, p. 29, accessed May 25, 2015, http://www.nytimes.com/interactive/2012/03/03/ world/africa/united-nations-report-on-libya.html?_r = 0.

[20] Oscar Solera, Human Rights Officer for the Rule of Law and Democracy Section, Office of the High Commissioner for Human Rights, interview conducted by HPCR, September 29, 2011.

[21] Martin Seutcheu, Human Rights Officer for the Office of the High Commissioner for Human Rights, interview conducted by HPCR, September 23, 2011.

C. Different Approaches

The standard of evidence used was on par with what the ICC [International Criminal Court] uses for arrest warrants.[22]

There are many different standards that can be adopted regarding the degree of certainty of an MRF mission's assertions and conclusions. A recent policy paper describes different options.

- Reasonable suspicion. Grounds for suspicion that the incident in question occurred, but other conclusions are possible (40 percent). Classic expression is: May be reasonable to conclude.
- Balance of probabilities (sufficient evidence). More evidence supports the finding than contradicts it (51 percent). Classic expression is: Reasonable to conclude.
- Clear and convincing evidence. Very solid support for the finding; significantly more evidence supports the finding and limited information suggests the contrary (60 percent). Classic expression is: It is clear that.
- Overwhelming evidence. Conclusive or highly convincing evidence supports the finding (80 percent). Classic expression is: It is overwhelming; it is undeniable.
- Beyond a reasonable doubt. Specific term applied for a criminal conviction in many legal systems (90–95 percent).[23]

Looking at the work of the fifteen missions selected for this book, one can see that during implementation, as will be examined in greater detail in a different section, approaches do not always adhere rigidly to a specific standard, yet the framework set out above does seem to play a role, even if limited, in guiding MRF practice.

Many MRF reports do in fact express a positive standard of proof, though the manner, methodologies, and transparency of this standard do vary from mission to mission. The standards themselves range from: balance of probabilities (Libya Commission), to reasonable grounds to believe (Independent, International Commission of Inquiry on Côte d'Ivoire [hereafter the Côte d'Ivoire Commission]), reasonable basis to believe (Secretary-General's Panel of Experts on Accountability in Sri Lanka

---

[22] Confidential interview with a high-level MRF practitioner, name of interviewee on file, conducted by HPCR, Summer 2013.

[23] Numerical values have been added for guidance purposes only and draw from Wilkinson, "Standards of Proof," 49. For more information on the "beyond a reasonable doubt" standard, see generally Larry Laudan, "Is Reasonable Doubt Reasonable?" *Legal Theory* 9, no. 4 (2003), accessed June 14, 2015, doi:10.1017/S1352325203000132.

[hereafter the Sri Lanka Panel]), and reasonable suspicion (Kyrgyzstan Commission, DRC Mapping Exercise, Guinea Commission, Timor-Leste Commission). Some missions articulate an ad hoc standard. For example, the International Fact-Finding Mission to investigate violations of international law, including international humanitarian and human rights law, resulting from the Israeli attacks on the flotilla of ships carrying humanitarian assistance (hereafter the UNHRC Flotilla Fact-Finding Mission) "found the facts ... to have been established to its satisfaction,"[24] while the United Nations Fact-Finding Mission on the Gaza Conflict (hereafter the Gaza Fact-Finding Mission) "found that there is sufficient information to establish the objective elements of the crimes in question."[25] Several missions did not specify any standard of proof (Commission of Inquiry on Lebanon [hereafter the Lebanon Commission]; High-Level Fact-Finding Mission to Beit Hanoun established under Council resolution S-3/1 [hereafter the Beit Hanoun Fact-Finding Mission]; Bahrain Independent Commission of Inquiry [hereafter the Bahrain Commission]; UNSG Flotilla Panel). As one can see, in past practice there has been a rather mixed approach to how MRF reports address the issue of standards of proof, with some missions making a clear methodological assertion on a standard of proof or evidence, while others are less clear, and in some cases, could only be ascertained through interviews with MRF practitioners conducted as research for this Handbook.

One clear trend – in addition to the aforementioned frequent affirmations that MRF missions are not tribunals or courts – is that, when missions do articulate a standard of proof, reports appear to promote a singular standard or threshold of certainty. However, it would be worthwhile to assess the utility of employing multiple standards of proof within the same mission, although this notion was not met with a great deal of professional support when mentioned during the research interviews conducted with practitioners. This option could be formal (as used by the United Nations Commission on the Truth for El Salvador) or could merely entail a level of flexibility in the reporting process to

---

[24] "Report of the International Fact-Finding Mission to Investigate Violations of International Law, Including International Humanitarian and Human Rights Law, Resulting from the Israeli Attacks on the Flotilla of Ships Carrying Humanitarian Assistance," A/HRC/15/21, September 27, 2010, p. 18, accessed May 26, 2015, http://www2.ohchr.org/english/bodies/hrcouncil/docs/15session/A.HRC.15.21_en.pdf.

[25] "Report of the United Nations Fact-Finding Mission on the Gaza Conflict," A/HRC/12/48, September 25, 2009, p. 15, accessed May 26, 2015, http://www2.ohchr.org/english/bodies/hrcouncil/docs/12session/A-HRC-12-48.pdf.

linguistically reflect variations between the levels of certainty of individual findings.[26] Such an approach was adopted explicitly by the International Commission of Inquiry on the Central African Republic, which states in the report, "The Commission has endeavoured to apply this standard [reasonable grounds to believe] with an appropriate degree of rigor, although the feasibility of different techniques of verification, cross-checking, and corroboration inevitably differs according to the context involved."[27]

As a legal expert who served on the Georgia Fact-Finding Mission pointedly notes, standards of proof may vary based on the type of incident being examined and the type of information available:

> Even if the mission had all met together and discussed a common approach to standards of proof, we could still have wound up applying different standards, depending on the area being researched. For example, for issues such as passportization, the use of force, self-defence, and military questions, they were using specific documents or were investigating less conflicting accounts. For human rights and international humanitarian law, I would have applied a strict balance of probabilities test because the conflict in Georgia was, like many other conflicts, plagued by allegations and counter-allegations.[28]

On a broad level, a standard of proof is not sufficient on its own to provide clarity – it simply sets out a broad understanding of the threshold required to assert findings of fact and law. Even when clear standards are applied, the basis for the facts or findings asserted is not necessarily always clear. One practitioner states that standard of proof is just one consideration among many shaping the overall methodology of the mission:

> Most commissions of investigation would use existing information and would also need to confirm this information with its own investigation. The mapping exercise just needed two different sources. But two different sources doesn't mean sources exclusive to the mapping, it could be existing information, as long as you can confirm that the primary sources are different. I think you expect more from a commission of inquiry. The mapping exercise was more about the analysis of existing material than

---

26 See Wilkinson, "Standards of Proof," 27–29, for more information on the approach of the United Nations Commission on the Truth for El Salvador to standards of proof.

27 "The International Commission of Inquiry on the Central African Republic: Final Report," December 22, 2014, p. 11, accessed June 9, 2015, http://reliefweb.int/sites/reliefweb.int/files/resources/N1471229.pdf.

28 Théo Boutruche, IHL/Human Rights Expert, Independent International Fact-Finding Mission on the Conflict in Georgia, interview conducted by HPCR, August 13, 2013.

only investigations. But it still used reasonable suspicion. It's a different methodology.[29]

One additional aspect that warrants stating, though it may appear obvious to some, is that rigor and standards of proof are not the same. While standards of proof can formally be shared among several missions, the degree of rigor between missions can and always will, to some extent, differ (based on numerous factors unique to each mission – e.g., timeframe, staffing level, expertise, and capacities). Such an issue is not inherently problematic; it simply reinforces the limited utility of a stand-alone standard of proof being the ultimate barometer of rigor and thoroughness.

Nevertheless, as stated earlier, the level of transparency regarding standards of proof does play an important role in perceptions of a mission's credibility. One approach that presents risks in this regard, and for this reason should likely be avoided in the future, is that of the UNHRC Flotilla Fact-Finding Mission, which set out a less than transparent standard by stating that its findings were "established to its satisfaction." Such an approach seems open to criticisms due to the lack of transparency, and even for taking a slightly supercilious approach to the mission's work.

D. Finding the Right Standard

There are three standards. One that is too high, one that is too low and one that strikes an appropriate balance. A standard that is too high comes too close to evidentiary standards in judicial proceedings, which commissions of inquiry have neither the mandate nor the capacity to apply. A standard that is too low is not substantiated enough to serve as a proper foundation for factual conclusions.[30]

A theoretical standard, as presented in the previous section and articulated in some MRF reports, is almost meaningless without application or translation into the practical. Hence, while a clear conceptual understanding of the concepts of balance of probabilities/reasonable suspicion/reasonable grounds is an important first step, the realities of practical application are also important to consider. During the implementation of an MRF mission, adherence to a certain standard of proof might be somewhat fluid. One practitioner states:

---

[29] Luc Côté, Executive Director of the United Nations Independent Special Commission of Inquiry for Timor-Leste, the United Nations Mapping Exercise in the Democratic Republic of the Congo, and the Kyrgyzstan Inquiry Commission, interview conducted by HPCR, June 8, 2013.

[30] Philippe Kirsch, HPCR interview.

It is inevitable to have a discussion of standards of proof. But when you're involved, you apply standards of proof in practical terms, not in theoretical terms. For balance of probabilities, it is unrealistic to expect to apply mechanically a mathematical formulation. You follow more generally what you believe is a sensible approach.[31]

Practitioners do express a sense, as articulated in the quote presented at the beginning of this section, that MRF missions operate somewhere between one standard that is "too low" and another that is "too high." On the one hand, as one practitioner mentions, the standard of proof cannot be too low:

A commission cannot act with the same kind of ease that advocacy groups and international human rights organizations act. A mission has to be accountable in terms of having sound evidence on which the analysis is based. This is in part because you're set up by member states, political bodies, which obviously stand on different sides. So to be able to present an analysis that can be acknowledged, it has to stand on its feet. Lesser criteria would undermine the credibility of a commission of inquiry.[32]

On the other hand, there appears to be little value in utilizing a standard – for example, "beyond a reasonable doubt" – that simply cannot be adhered to because the standard is too high.[33]

Hence, while practitioners have asserted a general desire for standards of proof (though sometimes expressed in other terms), the question becomes: what is the appropriate standard? The answer to this question is very much informed by the "flag-raising" nature of the MRF process. The general sense that can be derived from the interviews and desk reviews on which this chapter is based is that the appropriate standard of proof is seen to be along the lines of "reasonable suspicion or grounds" or "balance of probabilities." Such an approach was clearly expressed by the following missions: the Timor-Leste Commission, the Côte d'Ivoire Commission, the DRC Mapping Exercise, the Kyrgyzstan Commission, the Guinea Commission, the Sri Lanka Panel, and the Libya Commission. In addition, the standards applied by both the Gaza Fact-Finding Mission and

---

[31] Philippe Kirsch, HPCR interview.   [32] Yakin Ertürk, HPCR interview.

[33] The application of a faux standard would not only be misleading but also could undermine the report. For example, if an MRF report asserted a standard of "beyond a reasonable doubt," and then a court process used the same theoretical standard and came to a different conclusion, then an MRF mission could be undermined. As long as an MRF mission maintains an honest and accurate standard, reflecting the limitations of timeframe, resources, and powers (or lack thereof) of the mission, then subsequent assertions through a different process pose no concern (at least in principle).

the International Commission of Inquiry on Darfur (hereafter the Darfur Commission) – "sufficient information" and "reliable body of material," respectively – seem to be very close to the two aforementioned concepts. An enhanced discussion on the specific use of the terms "balance of probabilities," "reasonable suspicion," and "reasonable grounds" would appear to be necessary to clarify any differences in terms of application.

E. The Important Role of Vocabulary

We should never write in a report that there were, for example, crimes against humanity. We should phrase it that there could be, if the facts alleged in the report are proven in a court of law.[34]

While overarching standards of proof may play a role in conveying the level of certainty regarding an MRF mission's findings, the role of vocabulary is also important. However clear and systematic the application of overarching standards can be, the certainty of finding "X" will always differ somewhat from that of finding "Y." Hence, MRF missions should be encouraged to use a broad range of vocabulary to accurately reflect the specific certainty of the given facts.

Consistent with examples of language taken from past MRF reports, with regard to high certainty, the following phrases should be adopted: "highly consistent," "so consistent and vivid as to be beyond question," "highly probable," and "strongly suggest." To express a medium level of certainty, phrases such as "may have on occasion," "indicate that," and "in the absence of an explanation to the contrary" would appear to be useful. Finally, with regard to low certainty, "unable to conclude or confirm," "has been unable to establish," and "no available evidence" would have utility to refrain from ruling out certain facts while at the same time accurately reflecting the limited certainty of the mission. It must be remembered that stating that an event "did not happen" is very different from stating that one has been "unable to establish" that the event occurred.

II. Challenges to Accessing and Assessing Information

Numerous practical challenges and limitations affect MRF missions' abilities to gather and assess information. Some of these issues are internal,

---

[34] Luc Côté, Executive Director of the United Nations Independent Special Commission of Inquiry for Timor-Leste, the United Nations Mapping Exercise in the Democratic Republic of the Congo, and the Kyrgyzstan Inquiry Commission, interview conducted by HPCR, October 4, 2011.

involving, for example, the ways in which the mission defines different roles that various staff members will play during the information-gathering effort. Other issues are external, involving issues such as the political environment in which MRF missions operate, as well as issues of security and bureaucracy. This section examines the role that these factors play in shaping the process of accessing and evaluating information.

A.   Access and Cooperation

This mission was something that I have never seen before. In a sense the king gave us the keys for the kingdom. He said you can go wherever you want, you don't need permission from anyone.[35]

Securing access has huge implications for almost every aspect of an MRF mission's work and output. Obtaining access to the territory on which alleged violations occurred increases the chances of conducting a comprehensive and impartial investigation and generally expands and enhances the availability of sources of information, granting the possibility of direct access to sites and victims. Conversely, a lack of access to the country where violations are alleged to have taken place will inherently shrink the number of sources of information available.

Of the missions assessed for this book, the vast majority (thirteen missions) were granted full or partial territorial access, though this includes the Beit Hanoun Fact-Finding Mission and the Gaza Fact-Finding Mission – both of which achieved access to Gaza but did not secure access to, or the cooperation of, Israel – and the UNHRC Flotilla Fact-Finding Mission, which similarly faced a lack of cooperation from Israel but was able to inspect the *Mavi Marmara*, the ship on which many of the alleged violations within the mission's mandate had taken place.[36] One mission that had a very high level of access, the Bahrain Commission, was able to conduct sixty-five primary site visits (with several follow-up visits), highlighting that securing access naturally facilitates extensive levels of investigation.[37]

---

[35] Khaled Ahmed, Chief Investigator, Bahrain Independent Commission of Inquiry, interview conducted by HPCR, August 2, 2013.

[36] Two missions did not have access: (1) the UNSG Flotilla Panel (though access was not necessarily required by the mandate), and (2) the Sri Lanka Panel (the clearest case of a panel that plainly had no access to the territory on which the alleged violations were committed).

[37] "Report of the Bahrain Independent Commission of Inquiry," November 23, 2011, p. 3, accessed May 29, 2015, http://www.bici.org.bh/BICIreportEN.pdf.

While securing cooperation from those being investigated is an important aspect for good fact-finding work, the likelihood of securing cooperation (as seen above with the Beit Hanoun Fact-Finding Mission, the Gaza Fact-Finding Mission, and the UNHRC Flotilla Fact-Finding Mission) from those who themselves could be held to account for their actions is somewhat of a contradictory notion. However, it can and does happen; the missions in Timor-Leste and Bahrain, in particular, received very high levels of cooperation.[38] On the other end of the spectrum, some missions have expressed the limitations that a lack of cooperation has brought forth. For example, the Beit Hanoun Fact-Finding Mission report states:

> The desire of the mission to travel via Israel was motivated by the experts' desire to meet with and hear the views of Israeli actors (government, military, and non-governmental), including individuals living in areas of southern Israel under the threat of rocket attack from Gaza …. The mission regrets that it received no formal input from the Israeli authorities, despite a number of requests.[39]

Similarly, the report of the Sri Lanka Panel states:

> Since its inception, the Panel wished to engage with the Government of Sri Lanka to discuss the implementation of its mandate and to learn more about the Government's perspectives on how it is addressing the accountability issues. Indeed, the Secretary-General stated to both the Panel and the Government his hope that the Panel could serve as a resource for the Government.[40]

Even when missions do obtain territorial access, they often face local ad hoc territorial restrictions that delay entry into certain areas, and in some cases, regional actors have adversely affected MRF missions by putting pressure on certain witnesses.[41] Hence, cooperation should not only be secured at the national level but also at the local and regional levels.

---

[38] See Timor-Leste Commission report, 15.

[39] "Report of the High-Level Fact-Finding Mission to Beit Hanoun established under Council resolution S-3/1," A/HRC/9/26, September 1, 2008, pp. 3–4, accessed May 26, 2015, http://www.refworld.org/docid/48cfa3a22.html.

[40] "Report of the Secretary-General's Panel of Experts on Accountability in Sri Lanka," March 31, 2011, p. 5, accessed May 26, 2015, http://www.un.org/News/dh/infocus/Sri_Lanka/POE_Report_Full.pdf.

[41] For example, the Darfur Commission encountered resistance at both the regional and local levels. For local and regional restrictions that arose, see "Report of the International Commission of Inquiry on Darfur to the United Nations Secretary-General," January 25, 2005, p. 16, accessed May 26, 2015, http://www.un.org/news/dh/sudan/com_inq_darfur.pdf.

B. Timeframe

The Commission was given a broad mandate with a very tight deadline requiring it and the Secretariat to work intensively and under heavy time pressure.[42]

One huge factor that should not be underestimated or forgotten is the very short timeframe that many missions have to operate. Of the fifteen missions on which this book focuses, the average time from the selection of the commissioners to the production of the report is a mere 197 days. The average time spent on the ground, for the ten missions for which data was available, is sixty-seven days. That figure, sixty-seven days, is in fact a little misleading because it is inflated by three of the ten missions that had abnormally long timeframes of operation. Once the DRC Mapping Exercise (312 days), the Bahrain Commission (126 days), and the Kyrgyzstan Commission (102 days) are removed from the equation, the average drops down to just eighteen days.

Eighteen days is an incredibly short window for investigations, especially if one considers some of the labor-intensive activities undertaken by MRF missions. When significant time is allocated, a substantial amount of data can be collected – for example, the Bahrain Commission conducted 5,188 interviews.[43] But even the Bahrain Commission – despite the mission's protracted operational timeframe and high level of cooperation received – faced limitations on how many incidents the mission could investigate due to time restrictions. As one practitioner who served on the mission recounts:

> We received 592 allegations of torture and ill-treatment. Out of these, before I decided how many forensic experts I needed, I talked to a friend in the U.S. and asked how much time it would take to examine each victim. He said it would take 6–8 hours. So I decided to pick 60 cases out of the 592.[44]

Timeframe and access are largely issues outside of the MRF mission's control, as it is for the mandating body to set the mission's parameters, including the timeframe, and for the state whose territory the mission needs to access to grant permission to do so. In this regard, one practitioner states:

[42] "Report of the International Commission of Inquiry to Investigate All Alleged Violations of International Human Rights Law in the Libyan Arab Jamahiriya," A/HRC/17/44, June 1, 2011, p. 16, accessed May 26, 2015, http://www2.ohchr.org/english/bodies/hrcouncil/docs/17session/A.HRC.17.44_AUV.pdf.
[43] Bahrain Commission report, 6.   [44] Khaled Ahmed, HPCR interview.

It's not a very good system. I don't think they should have commissions of inquiry that report so quickly. There's a political imperative to be seen to be doing something, but then they take no account of UN bureaucracy, getting visas, no account of the fact that it takes time to recruit people, your amount of time in the field is tiny and the quality of information is usually variable.[45]

While increasing the length of time that MRF missions have to operate would undoubtedly improve the process, the feasibility of ensuring this measure might be limited, taking into consideration the relevant mandating bodies.

C.   Security of Interviewees and Staff

Sometimes you read the report and it appears generic or vague on detail, but it's purely for that reason of protecting the person. I find even when writing up interview notes, I might know it's a mother and daughter who are in a detention center but I'm not going to put that in the report.[46]

When MRF missions are deployed into ongoing armed conflicts, emergency situations, or post-conflict environments, the security (or lack thereof) of those involved in the mission, but also of those providing information to the mission, can play a crucial role in establishing the scope of or limiting the activities of the mission.

The issue of security and protection is the subject of a separate chapter in this Handbook so shall not be addressed extensively here,[47] but a few key points are worth highlighting, as they affect the investigative process and ultimately influence the quality of the investigations. Even if granted territorial access, missions often encounter security issues that severely limit the mission's freedom of operation. The first report of the Libya Commission mentions that one of the "significant challenges in carrying out its mandate" was the fact that "[t]he Commission was not able to visit sites where the conflict was ongoing, such as Misrata and Ajdabiya and other locations where incidents were reported. Security considerations limited the Commission's ability to enjoy access to persons and places."[48]

[45] Confidential interview with a high-level MRF practitioner, name of interviewee on file, conducted by HPCR, Summer 2013.

[46] Erin Gallagher, Gender Adviser and Sexual Violence Investigator, International Commission of Inquiry on Libya, interview conducted by HPCR, July 31, 2013.

[47] See generally in this Handbook, Chapter 4, Protecting Witnesses, Victims, and Staff: Sources and Implications of Professional Responsibilities, by Cynthia Petrigh.

[48] First Libya Commission report, 16–17. Additionally, for a recent example of a mission that experienced security risks, see "Syria crisis: UN inspectors' Convoy Hit by Sniper Fire,"

MRF missions often also curtail their activities due to the risk, or even the feeling or fear of risk, which may be prevalent for not just victims and eyewitnesses but communities as a whole. This can result in a high level of reticence to provide information, as occurred, for example, with the Bahrain Commission, according to the mission's report: "On some occasions, complainants expressed their unwillingness to share all the information relating to their detention because they were afraid of reprisals."[49] Investigators also typically discard information that carries protection concerns. For example, one practitioner stated that if a certain piece of information was not critical to the report and could be linked to a person, he would leave it out of his internal interview reports.[50]

Additionally, due to concerns about retraumatizing certain interviewees, MRF practitioners regularly curtail their own investigative efforts if this risk arises. As one practitioner states, "We've had people write in interview notes that they chose not to press interviewees on details that would have been very useful."[51] For this reason, incidents associated with higher levels of protection risks, or that more easily risk inducing retraumatization in interviewees through retelling the story, may be fundamentally more difficult to investigate.

D. Staffing the Mission with the Appropriate Level of Expertise

> How well the commission does has everything to do with the staffing of the team and their experience level.[52]

An MRF mission can only be as good as the personnel working on the mission, and while interviews with practitioners revealed many positive experiences with regard to the strength of the teams involved in various missions, many concerns were expressed concerning certain competencies. Based on interviews with MRF practitioners conducted for this book, the abilities of staff appeared to be wide-ranging, and at times problematic. Some of the key issues were:

BBC News, August 26, 2013, accessed June 9, 2015, http://www.bbc.co.uk/news/world-middle-east-23838900.

[49] Bahrain Commission report, 291.

[50] Confidential interview with a high-level MRF practitioner, name of interviewee on file, conducted by HPCR, Summer 2013.

[51] Confidential interview with a high-level MRF practitioner, name of interviewee on file, conducted by HPCR, Summer 2013.

[52] Confidential interview with a high-level MRF practitioner, name of interviewee on file, conducted by HPCR, Summer 2013.

- disparate abilities of staff (with some lacking sufficient investigative expertise);
- different investigative "mentalities"; and
- poor or little pre-deployment training.

While many issues within a mission require a specific skill set, one trend was that "experts" in a set field, be it in sexual violence, archeology, engineering, gender, or history, sometimes didn't necessarily have the ability or experience to translate that thematic expertise into proper investigative conduct. The inability to conduct interviews in a responsible manner seemed to be a particular source of concern. On one mission, certain investigators were recruited because of their language skills, but some of these investigators struggled to translate interview notes into understandable English. Some of these practitioners also initially lacked strong knowledge of what constituted good information so would sometimes not succeed in acquiring useful information.[53] Another practitioner states:

> Most commissions are staffed by human rights officers, they may be attorneys from OHCHR [Office of the High Commissioner for Human Rights], or from their own national jurisdictions, who do fact-finding and their own legal work. They may have less experience interviewing sensitive victims or insider witnesses, probably little experience with collection of evidence.[54]

In other cases, individuals possessed superior investigative skills but lacked knowledge about how to appropriately gather information in the context of a commission of inquiry. According to one practitioner:

> One investigator was very experienced but had an NGO [nongovernmental organization] mentality – go anywhere, do anything, get the story. With a commission of inquiry, there is enormous political baggage. This individual was talented, by far the best investigator, and got the best information, but chafed against UN [United Nations] procedures, and was quite challenging from that perspective. If I had to design the perfect commission, part of that would be educating them about why life is different and why you have to do things differently.[55]

---

[53] Confidential interview with a high-level MRF practitioner, name of interviewee on file, conducted by HPCR, Summer 2013.
[54] Confidential interview with a high-level MRF practitioner, name of interviewee on file, conducted by HPCR, Summer 2013.
[55] Confidential interview with a high-level MRF practitioner, name of interviewee on file, conducted by HPCR, Summer 2013.

One problem is that getting the right people is also not so straightforward, since the best people are sometimes the hardest to get released from their permanent positions to temporarily serve on an MRF mission.[56] Hence, the question of how one can secure high-quality staff does not appear to be easy to answer, but more efficient staff selection processes and measures to build a diverse pool of professionals that can be deployed on short notice would certainly help toward this end.

E. Defining Roles and Responsibilities

Though there is an assumption that every mission knows how the secretariat can help them, my own recommendation would have been that we should have had a discussion right at the start on the role of the secretariat, what they can provide, what commissioners can expect, how best to use them.[57]

In terms of roles and responsibilities, the role of commissioners is one central issue that has been raised by practitioners. A range of concerns were expressed in this regard, from the specific role played, the level of involvement, and, at times, the influence of politics. The level of involvement that commissioners should have, and how that involvement should manifest itself, was subject to a range of viewpoints among practitioners. Some practitioners were very critical of the lack of involvement. "On a scale of 1 to 10, with 10 being the maximum level of involvement, the commissioners were a 3," states one practitioner.[58] "Some commissioners are not involved, they don't even read drafts," states another.[59] Other missions had high levels of direct commissioner involvement. For example, during the UNHRC Flotilla Fact-Finding Mission, at least one commissioner was present during all the interviews, and for the very important interviews, such as that with the captain of the *Mavi Marmara*, all three commissioners were present.[60]

One commissioner expresses the importance of commissioners involving themselves in on-the-ground operations:

---

[56] One practitioner states, "There are some phenomenally good people, the problem is that getting them released by their line managers for five months is actually pretty difficult." Philip Trewhitt, Investigation Team Leader, International Commission of Inquiry on Libya, interview conducted by HPCR, July 26, 2013.

[57] Mary Shanthi Dairiam, HPCR interview.

[58] Confidential interview with a high-level MRF practitioner, name of interviewee on file, conducted by HPCR, Summer 2013.

[59] Confidential interview with a high-level MRF practitioner, name of interviewee on file, conducted by HPCR, Summer 2013.

[60] Mary Shanthi Dairiam, HPCR interview.

I need to smell the atmosphere. It's important for commissioners to get involved and not just evaluate the information that comes to them through their investigators. There is a tendency for commissioners to become more figureheads. But the more a commissioner is involved, they will have a greater feel for how they're going to use the information that comes to them through their investigators. That linkage is very important.[61]

But another practitioner cautions that commissioners sometimes lack the necessary investigative expertise: "Commissioners are not trained investigators, they have a political role. If they get too involved they may get lost in the weeds, they may get blinded by too much information."[62] Clarifying the appropriate involvement for commissioners is challenging on many levels and is always likely to be influenced by the personalities, expertise, and experience of the commissioners themselves. Regardless of the choice adopted, the way that members of missions allocate responsibilities among themselves is sure to affect the manner in which the team evaluates the information gathered.

F. Lack of Sufficient Guidelines and Training Opportunities

There are shocking consequences of ad hoc-ery. The mechanisms should be accountable. There should be a minimum standard that they should be expected to adhere to. To send people in unprepared, making it up as they go along, is unacceptable.[63]

Many MRF practitioners have called for the development of manuals, designed and provided by experts, since, for many issues on certain missions, no specific guidelines were in place, or if they were, they were developed during the mission itself.[64] Ideally, for such measures to be useful, systematic pre-deployment training is also necessary. However, several issues surround training. One problem is logistics, as one MRF practitioner states:

The logistics of training are very difficult, and that cannot be underestimated in any way. You have different people coming in at different times. For commissions, most don't last that long. Training has been less

---

[61] Yakin Ertürk, HPCR interview.
[62] Confidential interview with a high-level MRF practitioner, name of interviewee on file, conducted by HPCR, Summer 2013.
[63] Karen Kenny, Director, International Human Rights Network, interview conducted by HPCR, September 22, 2011.
[64] HPCR interviews with practitioners revealed that, when it came to guidelines, some missions used existing guidelines, other missions created mission-specific guidelines, and some missions didn't have any guidelines at all that were used mission-wide.

successful because the whole system is not set up to let people be trained as a group. The recruitment system is bureaucratic. People come in when the paperwork is finished. They come in at different times. A military expert can't give a briefing and training because he needs to go to the field and people are arriving at different times.[65]

UN missions typically receive trainings conducted by the Methodology, Education, and Training unit of OHCHR, but during interviews conducted for this chapter, the quality of certain trainings that were offered was also raised as a topic of concern.[66]

The development of guidelines and more effective trainings should, however, not be seen as a golden bullet. "Guidelines are never going to be a replacement for getting the right people," states one practitioner.[67] Additionally, the tight timeframes of MRF missions sometimes affect methodological planning. One practitioner, when asked about how commissions of inquiry might be improved, suggested, "Give them more time and better people. Give time to recruit people and maybe 6 weeks before you expect them in the field, time to do a little bit of training and a little bit of thinking."[68]

G.   Logistics and Data Management

It's like the tail wagging the dog, it's like the bureaucracy wagging the mission.[69]

One topic that doesn't often garner much attention is that of logistics. Yet, poor logistics can almost single-handedly scupper an MRF mission. Some practitioners have mentioned that investigators sometimes had to double up with logistical tasks, so individuals who should have been running investigations wound up also running logistics, drawing energy and time away from the mission's actual investigative efforts.[70] Another rather dry but fundamental reoccurring issue was the use of a database. While some were happy with improvements in databases witnessed over time

---

[65] Sareta Ashraph, HPCR interview.
[66] Confidential interview with a high-level MRF practitioner, name of interviewee on file, conducted by HPCR, Summer 2013.
[67] Sareta Ashraph, HPCR interview.
[68] Confidential interview with a high-level MRF practitioner, name of interviewee on file, conducted by HPCR, Summer 2013.
[69] M. Cherif Bassiouni, Chair, Bahrain Independent Commission of Inquiry, and Chair, International Commission of Inquiry on Libya (March–October 2011), interview conducted by HPCR, May 3, 2013.
[70] Confidential interview with a high-level MRF practitioner, name of interviewee on file, conducted by HPCR, Summer 2013.

through working on different missions,[71] others expressed an extreme level of dissatisfaction with the databases that certain missions used.[72] Practitioners have also expressed broader concerns about data management. One investigator spoke of taking a wealth of photographs of physical evidence, but at the end of the on-the-ground investigation, there was no organized process to make sure that these materials – as well as photographs taken by other investigators – were handed in and assessed.[73] Such challenges indicate the crucial role that logistics play in terms of determining the scope of evidence that MRF missions are able to gather, organize, and analyze.

H.   The Influence of Politics

The strong countries of the world are calling up the commissioners and asking them to lunch.[74]

It should not be forgotten that many MRF missions are mandated to look into conduct that is subject to extensive media coverage and to draw conclusions that may have wide-ranging and highly significant geopolitical implications. Due to the interests involved, the risk is always present that MRF activities will be open to the influence of politics. Practitioners have specifically expressed concerns regarding the possible politicization or "political game playing" engaged in by certain commissioners, which in some cases may have threatened the actual, as well as perceived, objectivity and impartiality of the mission. As one practitioner notes:

> In a court, no state is going to hold meetings with a judge. There's a respect for the vacuum around court proceedings which cannot be pierced. In commissions, that doesn't exist. Commissioners have many diplomatic meetings. Countries are asserting political points of view.[75]

While high-level political interactions may leave commissioners vulnerable to political influence, it should not be seen as a

---

[71] For example, one practitioner stated, "There's been a tremendous evolution: how information is gathered, the intricacy of the database, the consent option, and space for investigators to mark down credibility of witnesses." Sareta Ashraph, HPCR interview.

[72] Confidential interview with a high-level MRF practitioner, name of interviewee on file, conducted by HPCR, Summer 2013.

[73] Debbie Bodkin, Investigator, International Commission of Inquiry on Darfur, interview conducted by HPCR, July 19, 2013.

[74] Confidential interview with a high-level MRF practitioner, name of interviewee on file, conducted by HPCR, Summer 2013.

[75] Sareta Ashraph, HPCR interview.

black-and-white issue, as there may also be some benefit to this aspect of the process. Due to the fact that commissioners are able to create these linkages with higher-level types of actors, commissioners possibly put themselves in a position to obtain sensitive and more credible information.

It will always be difficult to accurately assess the extent to which political considerations affect the way in which MRF missions conduct investigations and draw and articulate legal conclusions. One particularly extreme example is the International Commission of Inquiry on Burundi. The commission's mandate drafter has stated that the mission found both Tutsis and Hutus guilty of genocide, but after the government of Burundi, which was led by Tutsis, expressed disapproval of the report's release, the commission "made a political decision that the government of Burundi had to approve the report," and the commission's final report makes no "mention of Tutsis killing Hutus."[76]

III. Handling Information: Sources, Approaches, Techniques, and Weighting

While the previous section details challenges that stem from the context in which MRF missions operate, this section explores the central job with which MRF missions are tasked: collecting information, cross-checking sources, and establishing the credibility of that information. While the assessment of theoretical or conceptual standards of proof, as examined in Section I of this chapter, is an important aspect for framing the work of MRF missions, the application of a standard of proof is valueless without understanding the ways that the mission scrutinized the individual pieces of information from which the conclusions were formed. The two simply cannot be separated.

One anecdotal example that underscores this link concerns the work of an NGO coming to an investigator involved in the Darfur Commission. A representative from the NGO asserted that the organization had been able to establish "beyond a reasonable doubt" that genocide had been committed. When asked to explain how they had come to such a strong assessment, the NGO representative explained how they had collected solid and credible data through the means of a questionnaire. Regardless of the assessment of the value of a questionnaire as such, once the

---

[76] Gregory Stanton, Mandate Drafter, International Commission of Inquiry on Burundi, interview conducted by HPCR, September 14, 2011.

questionnaire was scrutinized, it was apparent that it was full of leading questions, and hence, the initial assertion of establishing genocide was meaningless, since the source material was of such a poor quality.[77] This example highlights the clear connection between standards of proof and professional and high standards of information handling and processing.

A.   Sources of Information

The mission wishes to underline the importance of its travelling to Beit Hanoun to witness first-hand the situation of victims and survivors of the shelling, in particular to comprehend the deep distress of the victims of the shelling and of the population generated by the ongoing blockade. This depth of human suffering is only partially conveyed through the third-party reports on the situation.[78]

It is far from controversial to state that MRF missions should look for as much information from as broad a range of sources as possible. This was a clear message articulated by practitioners who served on many missions. The question then comes down to feasibility, resources, and the issue of weighting and corroborating that information.

Sources of information available to MRF missions are wide-ranging and extensive. The sources highlighted by MRF practitioners interviewed for this chapter include but are not limited to:

- victims
- witnesses
- perpetrators
- parties to the conflict, including "whistleblowers"
- religious leaders
- political parties
- business leaders
- journalists
- local NGOs
- international NGOs
- UN agencies

In addition to the sources of information, the mediums in which the information is received vastly differ from one another, also affecting how

---

[77] Mohamed Ali Lejmi, Investigator, International Commission of Inquiry on Darfur, interview conducted by the author, October 2010 (while working for the Geneva Academy of International Humanitarian Law and Human Rights).

[78] Beit Hanoun Fact-Finding Mission report, 4.

one assesses veracity. Different types of information include, but are not limited to:

- direct examination of primary and secondary sites and locations;
- existing reports from other actors, such as NGOs and UN agencies;
- documentation (various forms, such as hospital records);
- statements and interviews (face-to-face, over phone or Skype, submitted electronically, or provided at public hearings);
- social media;
- radio intercepts;
- photos and other types of imagery (including satellite); and
- videos

Of all the sources of information, many practitioners have stressed the central importance of speaking to both sides of the conflict or situation. As one practitioner states, "you're better off getting some cooperation or you're better off not doing it at all."[79]

Direct observations and direct interactions with victims and witnesses are also a mainstay of MRF missions, allowing for the mission to see, hear, and gain a firmer overall feel for the facts. The importance of direct observation of facts, while not always possible, sets itself at the heart of the work of MRF missions. Sites of attacks, as well as examinations of individuals who have suffered harm, provide the foundation for clear factual declarations. For example, being able to physically examine victims can be a crucial step in order to assert findings of fact and also to assess the intent and mindset of perpetrators: "I saw burn marks on the body of a 15 year old. It was someone who had disposed a cigarette in his chest. When you see this with your own eyes you definitely conclude that there were some violations," one practitioner states.[80]

However, to conduct physical examinations properly, thoroughly, respectfully, and in a culturally sensitive manner is not only labor intensive but also requires specific expertise and experience. Guidelines on certain violations exist in this regard, one notable example being the Istanbul Protocol setting out guidelines for effective investigation on torture and other cruel, inhuman, or degrading treatment or punishment. While not all violations are so heavily dependent on physical examinations, due to the inherent sensitivities of physical examinations, any conduct involving

---

[79] Confidential interview with a high-level MRF practitioner, name of interviewee on file, conducted by HPCR, Spring 2013.
[80] Khaled Ahmed, HPCR interview.

examinations should be supported with clear guidelines and undertaken by those with the relevant expertise.[81]

B. Approaches to Assessing Information: Reliability and Credibility

The fact-finding body should adopt standards for the collection, review and evaluation of evidence and other information which provide it with a degree of certainty with regard to its findings. The fact-finding body should also adopt methods for the collection of evidence and other information sufficient to enable an assessment of the reliability of the sources of evidence and other information.[82]

For all the types of sources of information listed above, the task of an MRF mission is to assess the credibility of the information and the extent to which it can be used to form a factual basis for the mission's ultimate findings of fact and associated legal analysis. In terms of quantity alone, one mission received 8,110 complaints and statements relevant to possible abuses.[83] Sorting through this information and assessing its credibility is by far the most challenging and burdensome task for MRF missions. Unsurprisingly, one practitioner involved in the Sri Lanka Panel stated, "We spent a lot of energy sifting through all the allegations and finding out which ones were credible. We devoted more time during the implementation to that task than any other aspect of the mandate."[84]

Assessing the utility of a given piece of information will be influenced by numerous factors, and an overly academic or theoretical analysis may be of limited value. One overarching point is simply that conflict environments are not conducive to clear and consistent information. As the report of the Georgia Fact-Finding Mission states, "The views of the sides involved in the conflict have been widely divergent from the beginning, and appear to be getting more so as time goes by. Thus the truth seems increasingly difficult to ascertain and verify."[85]

Additionally, different pieces of information interact with one another in unique ways. One practitioner offers a visual explanation of how

---

[81] The Guinea Commission used a forensic medical expert who, according to the report, "confirmed that there were injuries due to electrical burns." See Guinea Commission report, 22.

[82] M. Cherif Bassiouni and Christina Abraham, eds., *Siracusa Guidelines for International, Regional and National Fact-Finding Bodies* (Cambridge: Intersentia, 2013), 43.

[83] Bahrain Commission report, 2–3.

[84] Steven Ratner, Member, Secretary-General's Panel of Experts on Sri Lanka, interview conducted by HPCR, May 1, 2013.

[85] Georgia Fact-Finding Mission report, 1: 7.

certain pieces of information relate to one another: "Is it one strand in a cable or a link in a chain? If it's one strand, you can remove it. If it's a link, you better be damn sure it's right."[86]

One policy for addressing information corroboration is an approach whereby all assertions are based on at least two sources. This option was adopted by the Guinea Commission, and the report directly tied this approach to the mission's "reasonable suspicion" standard:

> In fulfilment of its mandate, the Commission decided that in order to obtain the quality of evidence needed to establish the facts, the information received must be checked against independent sources, preferably eyewitness accounts, and independently verified evidence assembled to demonstrate that a person may reasonably be suspected of having participated in the commission of a crime .... Thus, the report does not include any testimony that has not been corroborated by at least one other source.[87]

However, a numerical approach does not provide for assurances of credibility. For instance, several practitioners have spoken of concerns that many interviewees had been "coached" or told by authorities what to say. In addition, having a uniform "two sources" approach may be inadequate in assessing certain types of violations or crimes that may by their legal structure demand a multitude of sources.

In terms of assessing the reliability of information, the DRC Mapping Exercise report set out a detailed approach that appears to be a good model and could be applied to other types of MRF missions:

> Assessing the reliability of the information obtained was a two-stage process involving evaluation of the reliability and credibility of the source, and then the pertinence and truth of the information itself. This method is known as the *admiralty scale*. Reliability of the source is determined using several factors, including the nature, objectivity and professionalism of the organisation providing the information, the methodology used and the quality of prior information obtained from the same source. The validity and authenticity of the information is assessed by comparing it to other available data relating to the same incidents to ensure that it tallies with already verified elements and circumstances. In other words, the process involves cross-checking the originally obtained information by ensuring that the corroborating elements do in fact come from a different source than the primary source that provided the information in the first place.[88]

---

[86] Lesley Taylor, Report Drafter, Kyrgyzstan Inquiry Commission, and United Nations Independent Special Commission of Inquiry for Timor-Leste, interview conducted by HPCR, July 31, 2013.

[87] Guinea Commission report, 9.   [88] DRC Mapping Exercise report, 39.

Another possibility (in addition to the more detailed DRC Mapping Exercise process) is to attempt to apply a uniform scaling system to each piece of information. For example, each source gathered by the mission could be rated as having a low, medium, or high level of credibility.

C. Challenges of Specific Sources

Transparency of the data sources and how they were interacting was clearly central to the report's overall validity.[89]

The following section will comment on a few of the most important sources to MRF missions and the challenges that they pose. These sources are: statements gathered from witnesses and victims through interviews, photographs, and videos, and reports compiled by outside actors, such as NGOs and UN agencies.

1. Statements from Interviewees

As mentioned, interviewing and interacting directly with sources of information is crucial, with missions often giving preference to eyewitness accounts. Yet, though eyewitness statements are one of the best sources of information, witness credibility is difficult to gauge. How easy is it to determine whether someone has an incentive to be deceitful or is an actual victim? One practitioner states that the process is not entirely systematic:

> It comes down to individuals. You learn to tell by the details they give you. You might get someone who's an inveterate liar about 90% of the time but 10% might be true. You might also have somebody whose credibility is an A, but on one particular instance they give you a piece of information that can't possibly be true.[90]

Also, different practitioners may gauge credibility differently. As one MRF practitioner stated, "Gauging the credibility of interviewees is up to the individual investigator."[91] Another investigator stated that her process of gauging witness credibility came from a combination of her police training and gut instinct.[92]

Such complexities further highlight the importance of MRF team members having significant professional experience – for example, as police

---

[89] "Monitoring and Documenting Human Rights Violations in Africa: A Handbook," Amnesty International and CODESRIA, 2000, p. 20, accessed June 9, 2015, https://www.amnesty.nl/sites/default/files/public/ukw_eng.pdf.
[90] Philip Trewhitt, HPCR interview.   [91] Erin Gallagher, HPCR interview.
[92] Debbie Bodkin, HPCR interview.

officers, prosecutors, defense lawyers, and so on – in assessing credibility. While the rigor applied in an MRF context should not be commensurate with that used within domestic or international investigative and prosecutorial processes, the instincts and practices of experienced individuals is invaluable to MRF work.

Additionally, certain other issues appear to constitute open questions for which different missions take contrasting approaches. One development is the prevalence of technologies such as Skype, which allow for an audio and visual interaction with a witness, regardless of the interviewee's – or the interviewer's – location. Do such new means of communication provide unique challenges? One practitioner does not discern a vast difference between in-person and Skype interviews:

> I don't think Skype interviews are less easy to assess credibility than in person. You don't really know who you're speaking to over Skype, but also this is the case when you're speaking in person. I don't think the dangers for Skype are that much different than dangers from first-person interviews.[93]

However, it may be worthwhile for MRF practitioners to engage in discussion about how such communications, coupled with the growth of social media, should be handled by MRF missions.

Another issue is how investigators should handle information gathered from interviewees who provide information anonymously. Contrasting approaches have been adopted. On one mission, anonymous sources were used, but not as evidence.[94] Of another mission, a practitioner stated, "We allow our interviewees to be anonymous. Does that increase or decrease their reliability? That's a good question. Arguments can be made for both sides."[95]

2. Videos and Photographs

With the development of mobile phone technology, the availability of both photographs and videos has significantly increased as an information source for post hoc analysis by MRF practitioners. Video data allows for MRF practitioners to see events that they could not directly witness and are then able to establish a level of certainty that would be difficult to achieve with witness statements alone. One example in the context of the

---

[93] Sareta Ashraph, HPCR interview.
[94] Christina Abraham, Chief of Staff, Bahrain Independent Commission of Inquiry, interview conducted by HPCR, July 30, 2013.
[95] Vic Ullom, Legal Adviser, International Commission of Inquiry on Libya, interview conducted by HPCR, August 8, 2013.

Bahrain Commission illustrates the clarity that video can bring: "There were videos of police going unarmed to protesters and then demonstrators began chasing police and then beating them. That is reality. That is not a video that can be misinterpreted."[96]

In addition to serving as a lead source of information, video can also help to corroborate other sources. During the Libya Commission, for example, video was important in the investigations of extrajudicial killings. There were videos shown to the commission that provided critical proof that certain prisoners had been killed in captivity.[97]

Despite the clear importance of videos, in order to consider visual information credible, MRF practitioners have stressed the huge challenges of authentication. In one example, though images of rape had been recorded on mobile phones, as a practitioner stated, "We saw some of it, but there was no authentication with it. You have no idea where or when it was taken. Most of it was totally useless."[98] As warring parties become more sophisticated in their use of technology, as exemplified by the Syrian rebels' hacking of various high-profile media sites, MRF missions' means of verification of authenticity may have to become more sophisticated and may require additional resources.

3. Reports and Data Provided by Third-Party Actors

Reports from third-party entities, such as the UN, as well as international and local NGOs, are often valuable sources of information. Such reports are typically researched and written by individuals with extensive experience and awareness of the situation in the field in the relevant context. However, these reports hold a varying level of credibility. Human Rights Watch is one NGO that was identified by several practitioners as having a high level of reliability.[99] Conversely, in many instances, MRF practitioners have expressed a wariness regarding certain local NGOs due to perceptions that these entities sometimes lack impartiality and allow their activities to be guided primarily by political agendas.[100]

---

[96] Philippe Kirsch, HPCR interview.
[97] Confidential interview with a high-level MRF practitioner, name of interviewee on file, conducted by HPCR, Summer 2013.
[98] Philip Trewhitt, HPCR interview.
[99] Confidential interview with a high-level MRF practitioner, name of interviewee on file, conducted by HPCR, Summer 2013.
[100] Rob Grace and Claude Bruderlein, "Building Effective Monitoring, Reporting, and Fact-Finding Mechanisms" (working paper, Program on Humanitarian Policy and Conflict Research at Harvard University, 2012), p. 19, accessed June 9, 2015, http://papers.ssrn .com/sol3/papers.cfm?abstract_id = 2038854.

Overall, the challenge for independently mandated MRF missions is that these entities must be able to stand by their findings. For this reason, a widespread consensus exists among practitioners that MRF missions should endeavor to independently verify the factual assertions offered in third-party reports that the mission examines. Some practitioners have made contact with individuals involved in drafting third-party reports in order to be able to sufficiently gauge the validity of the methodology employed. MRF practitioners have, in addition, specified that the level of scrutiny applied to NGO reports should also be used toward third-party UN reports, especially since, in many cases, the information collected by the UN is not always directly sourced but rather provided by local NGOs. Along these lines, a commissioner for the Côte d'Ivoire Commission stated, "Even if you have UN facts and figures, this doesn't mean you have to go along with them 100 percent. We didn't use the word corroboration as such, but there was a lot of cross-checking."[101]

Ultimately, however accurate and credible reports produced by others are, it is important to note that, as with other sources of information, these reports should not be considered in isolation. While they can serve as valuable sources of information and can help identify locations or incidents that need to be looked into, these, like other sources of information, have their limitations. Additionally, despite the consensus that MRF missions should scrutinize, rather than blindly accept, third-party findings, the issue of what exact measures should be adopted to properly scrutinize third-party reports appears to be an open question.

IV. Approaches Taken, and Inherent Challenges, to Different Types of Violations

Facts needed for different violations are inherently distinct. Nonetheless, one approach taken by the Bahrain Commission with regard to a specific violation could be developed for other violations to help ensure consistent approaches. The mission set out two general criteria for establishing the use of excessive force.

- Evidence indicating whether or not the victim was using force.
- Evidence indicating how and where the victim was shot.

---

[101] Vitit Muntarbhorn, Chair, Independent, International Commission of Inquiry on Côte d'Ivoire, interview conducted by HPCR, July 23, 2013.

This model could be expanded to other violations to provide a loose practical framework within which violations can be consistently assessed. One question posed to MRF practitioners during interviews conducted for this chapter was to what extent a standard of proof would have to change based on the legal violation addressed, be it torture, sexual violence, or the conduct of hostilities under international humanitarian law. Are accusations of persecution or genocide more "aggravated," and hence, do they demand a different approach? There was a general consensus that a standard of proof should not change on this basis, but at the same time, there was a prevailing perspective that more care should be taken with more "serious" violations. The challenge is to identify what those violations are and what "more care" in fact entails.

Certain violations pose their own unique challenges for investigators, as do the nature of the legal assertion and the type of infringement. Four particular issues will be examined below.

A. International Criminal Law

We were more careful with more serious violations because it would have more serious implications.[102]

One complex aspect of the findings of MRF missions is the appropriate approach to issues relevant to international criminal law. Can an MRF mission assert that international crimes have occurred? Some would argue that one can only go so far as stating that the material (*actus reus*) elements of a war crime have been established or simply should preface any assertion of an international crime with tentative vocabulary. As stated in a quote presented earlier in this chapter, the viewpoint has been articulated that MRF reports should not present findings regarding international criminal law in certain terms and should rather state that there "could be" crimes that were committed. Recent ICC jurisprudence confirms the complexity of this issue. In June 2013, the Pre-Trial Chamber of the ICC adjourned the hearing on the confirmation of charges in the *Prosecutor v. Laurent Gbagbo* case, stating that many of the incidents "are proven solely with anonymous hearsay from NGO Reports, United Nations reports and press articles," and hence, "the Chamber is unable to attribute much

---

[102] Confidential interview with a high-level MRF practitioner, name of interviewee on file, conducted by HPCR, Spring 2013.

probative value to these materials."[103] The Pre-Trial Chamber elaborated on the limited role that investigations with comparatively low evidentiary thresholds can play in demonstrating that violations of international criminal law have occurred:

> [T]he Chamber notes with serious concern that in this case the Prosecutor relied heavily on NGO reports and press articles with regard to key elements of the case, including the contextual elements of crimes against humanity. Such pieces of evidence cannot in any way be presented as the fruits of a full and proper investigation by the Prosecutor in accordance with Article 54(l)(a) of the Statute. Even though NGO reports and press articles may be a useful introduction to the historical context of a conflict situation, they do not usually constitute a valid substitute for the type of evidence that is required to meet the evidentiary threshold for the confirmation of charges.[104]

Additionally, there might be standard of proof implications that arise from the notion that certain charges are inherently more serious than others. As the quote presented in the beginning of this section indicates, in certain cases, MRF practitioners have adjusted the manner in which the mission evaluates, and articulates findings about, certain violations, based on the severity of the crime. However, this practice stands in contrast to the trend exemplified in the first section of this chapter, that MRF reports tend to articulate a single overarching standard that is applied throughout the entire mission, regardless of the different types of violations examined.

B.   Identification of Individuals

The Commission would obviously not make final judgments as to criminal guilt; rather, it would make an assessment of possible suspects that would pave the way for future investigations, and possible indictments, by a prosecutor.[105]

An increasingly central task of MRF missions is to identify those responsible for conduct and crimes. With the inclusion of this aim in an MRF mandate, new interests, challenges, and risks come into play. As firmly stated by one commissioner:

> We were careful not to identify individuals to attribute criminal responsibility. It would have been totally irresponsible because we didn't have the

---

[103] *Prosecutor v. Gbagbo*, ICC-02/11-01/11, decision adjourning the hearing on the confirmation of charges pursuant to Article 61(7)(c)(i) of the Rome Statute (International Criminal Court, June 3, 2013), p. 17, accessed June 9, 2015, http://www.icc-cpi.int/iccdocs/doc/doc1599831.pdf.

[104] Ibid.,16.   [105] Darfur Commission report, 12 (internal citations omitted).

information to do it. The danger is for a body in a very powerful position to damage a person for life and to do it without the beginnings of the level of information required to make a prima facie case.[106]

With such sensitivities in mind, the first question to ask is what the purpose is of identifying individuals? The obvious answer relates to accountability, but as stated earlier, and as expressed by the below quote from the Côte d'Ivoire Commission report, an MRF mission differs from a court.

> The Commission is well aware that final determinations of individual criminal responsibility must be made by a court to guarantee the rights of the persons concerned; however, the mandate of the Human Rights Council requires it to identify those responsible.[107]

A degree of discomfort can be picked up by this statement, reinforcing the notion that there must be a clear separation in the minds of both the mandating body and the practitioners between identifying individuals who should be subject to investigations and those who are criminally liable.[108] The issue becomes even more complicated when names are publicly released. The Guinea Commission, for example, did publicly list those it believed to be involved in the violations identified with varying levels of certainty: "sufficient evidence," "may also be sufficient reason to presume," and "reasonable grounds."[109]

Should public listing *ever* be done? If so, in what situations and circumstances? When answering this question, it should not be forgotten that missions that have kept names confidential have also been subject to criticisms by those advocating for more transparency and genuine accountability.[110] It would appear that clear and focused guidelines on this specific issue are needed as a matter of urgency.

---

[106] Sir Nigel Rodley, Commissioner, Bahrain Independent Commission of Inquiry, interview conducted by HPCR, April 12, 2013.

[107] "Rapport de la Commission d'enquête internationale indépendante sur la Côte d'Ivoire," A/HRC/17/48, July 1, 2011, p. 24, accessed May 26, 2015, http://www.refworld.org/docid/4ee05cdf2.html (translated from French to English by HPCR).

[108] See Kyrgyzstan Commission report, 62, which also articulates this view.

[109] Guinea Commission report, 50–55.

[110] See "World Report 2012: Côte d'Ivoire," Human Rights Watch, accessed June 9, 2015, http://www.hrw.org/world-report-2012/c-te-d-ivoire, which states of the confidential annex to the Côte d'Ivoire Inquiry report that identifies persons suspected of responsibility for certain incidents: "While this annex has been provided to the Office of the High Commissioner for Human Rights, it had not been made available to relevant Ivorian authorities at this writing, thereby failing to contribute to accountability."

C.   Sexual and Gender-based Violence

If there's a girl who is known to have been raped, she is possibly going to be disowned by her family, possibly divorced, her sisters might be divorced. In the worst case, a male family member might kill her.[111]

The specific sensitivities of sexual and gender-based violence (SGBV) make it a unique and challenging type of incident to investigate. Challenges to gathering information stem from the "[c]ultural sensitivities and associated stigma" of rape, as the Sri Lanka Panel report states,[112] and the fact that "victims face a very real threat of ostracism," as the Georgia Fact-Finding Mission report mentions.[113]

Because of this state of affairs, which persists in many contexts in which MRF missions have operated, investigating SGBV amplifies many of the challenges examined in Section II of this chapter. SGBV investigators require particular expertise, including judgment about appropriate questioning, acuity with using gender-sensitive language, and an awareness of how the body language of the investigator may communicate unintended messages to the interviewee.[114] Concerns about confidentiality are also especially crucial, due to the potential negative ramifications for victims if information given privately to the mission becomes known by other individuals in the local community.

These challenges have direct implications for standards of proof. How should MRF practitioners grapple with the fact that these types of incidents are fundamentally difficult to verify? The Libya Commission took these factors into account when evaluating information received by the mission:

> The number of cases reported was small. However, the Commission recognizes the difficulties in collecting evidence in cases of sexual violence, including a victim's reluctance to disclose information due to the trauma, shame and stigma linked to reports of sexual assault. In Libya, the fact that Libyan criminal law punishes by flogging sexual relations outside a lawful marriage also increases the reluctance of victims to report sexual violence. *These factors thus need to be taken into account in evaluating the information received.*[115]

[111] Erin Gallagher, HPCR interview.   [112] Sri Lanka Panel report, 44.
[113] Georgia Fact-Finding Mission report, 2: 356.
[114] World Health Organization, "WHO ethical and safety recommendations for researching, documenting and monitoring sexual violence in emergencies," 2007, p. 14, accessed May 29, 2015, http://www.who.int/gender/documents/OMS_Ethics&Safety10Aug07.pdf.
[115] First Libya Commission report, 71–72 (internal citations omitted; emphasis added).

The Libya Commission also indicated that the mission "received but was unable to verify individual accounts of rape."[116] This statement suggests the rather complex – from a standard-of-proof perspective – implications of SGBV. Regarding these types of incidents, MRF practitioners commonly have a sense, based on secondary or unverifiable sources, that a great number of crimes have been committed that the mission will be unable to verify. One commissioner states of SGBV, "You cannot assume that it's there but you cannot assume that it's not there. It is dangerous to over-assume," indicating the importance of caution.[117]

D. International Humanitarian Law and the Conduct of Hostilities

Anticipating the collateral damage of a particular attack in the midst of war is fraught with difficulties. For a combatant acting in good faith, the vagueness of the principle of proportionality, in practice, constitutes a problem rather than an opportunity. As suggested above, assessing proportionality before an attack is a complex judgement call. The law fails to provide an absolute standard for this judgement.[118]

For very different reasons, conduct relating to hostilities (under the framework of international humanitarian law) also poses significant and unique challenges for an investigator. The legal framework, based on a good faith assessment of the facts in the mind of the attacker at the moment of attack, is constructed in a manner that inherently weakens *post facto* third-party analysis. One statement offered by a practitioner – "If you're able to demonstrate a large number of civilian casualties, then it becomes almost assumed that the principles of distinction and proportionality were not being applied"[119] – thus appears to be oversimplified.

Charles Garraway, during a discussion at the 2013 San Remo International Humanitarian Law Roundtable, spoke of his time investigating hostilities in Lebanon. Human rights experts had deemed that, due to the fact that very precise weapons were used and that no military target was in the area, the attack was a clear violation of the prohibition of direct attacks against civilians. However, Garraway (who served as a legal adviser to the

---

[116] Ibid., 74.   [117] Yakin Ertürk, HPCR interview.
[118] "Applying the Principle of Proportionality in Combat Operations," Policy Briefing, Oxford Institute for Ethics, Law and Armed Conflict, December 2010, p. 4, accessed June 9, 2015, http://www.elac.ox.ac.uk/downloads/proportionality_policybrief_%20dec_2010. pdf.
[119] Confidential interview with a high-level MRF practitioner, name of interviewee on file, conducted by HPCR, Summer 2013.

British Armed Forces for over thirty years) believed that the very precise and expensive weapons used in fact indicated that the attacking force must have been intending to hit a high-value target. Mistakes can and do happen.

On this particular issue, it appears even more pressing to involve military experts. Furthermore, though, it has also been clearly recommended that one needs the right type of military expertise. As one practitioner states:

> There was a military advisor, who was the former head of targeting for the Pentagon, and he knew what he was looking for. Always have someone with that level of ability. In our case, he had worked specifically on targeting and had worked for Human Rights Watch and the UN in Afghanistan. It was specific expertise. The average air force colonel would have less directly applicable expertise.[120]

Specifically, when the attacking side provides no information, making an accurate finding of legal fact can be difficult. Hence, in addition to securing the right type of expertise within investigation teams, when cooperation is lacking from one of the warring parties, one way to still be able to conduct legal analysis would be to switch the burden of proof, allowing for violations to be identified until the warring party accused provides facts that would lead to a contrary position. An example of this in practice would be the Gaza Fact-Finding Mission, which stated that the mission made a finding relating to the targeting of civilians "in the absence of explanations to the contrary."[121]

V.   Conclusion

As practitioners continue to develop, apply, and improve upon methodological tools to address the central issues of standards of proof and information handling in MRF missions, practitioners will need to address theoretical concepts, but also the practical application of those concepts, in a manner that is realistic and has utility for those engaged in the difficult task of undertaking MRF activities. It is also important to revisit this broad question: why should one scrutinize the process of implementing standards of proof?

One clear answer is that this scrutiny is a necessary component of developing the level of professionalism of the growing pool of MRF

---

[120] Confidential HPCR interview with a high-level MRF practitioner, name of interviewee on file, conducted by HPCR, Summer 2013.
[121] Gaza Fact-Finding Mission report, 94.

practitioners and of improving the internal workings of future MRF missions. A second aspect concerns the appropriate level of transparency that is needed or desirable concerning public MRF reports. How transparent should MRF processes be? How far can and should reports go, especially considering the numerous limitations addressed in this chapter?

Answers to such questions should be made in light of the consideration that many MRF reports have significant political and accountability implications, raising awareness among the international community of some of the most serious violations of international human rights and humanitarian law. Hence, improving the structure and processes associated with these missions, and continually reviewing past efforts with constructive self-criticism, can only help to enhance the accuracy and credibility of future MRF work, and in turn, help to promote accountability for some of the most egregious actions of human behavior.

4

Protecting Witnesses, Victims, and Staff

Sources and Implications of Professional Responsibilities

CYNTHIA PETRIGH

Introduction

Monitoring, reporting, and fact-finding (MRF) missions are plagued by a fundamental paradox. Though MRF missions aim to promote justice for victims of violations of international humanitarian law and international human rights law, the very fact that victims and witnesses decide to come forward and contribute to the establishment of the truth can put these people at risk. Courts and other investigative bodies cannot afford to increase the exposure to danger of the individuals who have already suffered human rights violations – or the witnesses of these incidents – when the objective is to stop these violations and/or provide redress. "Victims of oppression want protection more than anything else," underlines one author.[1] This challenge is multiplied in the context of MRF missions – compared to courts and tribunals – due to the fact that MRF missions often take place in locations where the perpetrators of violations either formally remain in power or have a proven nuisance capacity, and where, in the absence of cooperation from authorities, statements from witnesses and victims constitute the core body of evidence. Furthermore, due to the enduring ad hoc nature of this field, missions are often staffed with practitioners of varying levels of experience and expertise, who may not uniformly implement existing guidelines. Additionally, existing guidelines, when they are used, as well as mission-specific procedures put in place, sometimes serve as aspirational notions that are not always realizable during an actual investigation. Given these factors, the question arises: what, in actuality, is the extent of an MRF mission's protective responsibilities?

To answer this question, this chapter proceeds in three sections. Section I focuses on the protection of witnesses and victims. This section

---

[1] Robert Elias, *The Politics of Victimization: Victims, Victimology, and Human Rights* (New York: Oxford University Press, 1986), 217.

examines, first, the sources of the obligations to protect witnesses and victims; second, the nature of the threats that have arisen and could arise; and third, the measures that have been adopted by the fifteen missions that constitute this book's focus.[2] Section II addresses the protection of staff, focusing – as in Section I – on the sources of responsibility to protect staff, the threats that exist, and protective measures that have been adopted. Section III concludes by identifying issues for which consensus has emerged among practitioners and highlighting areas for which some level of divergence remains in the methodologies and practices employed by different missions.

I.   Protection of Witnesses and Victims

A.   Sources of the Responsibility to Protect Witnesses and Victims

This section looks into the sources of responsibility regarding witness protection. As enshrined in numerous treaties, United Nations (UN) resolutions, and certain soft law international or regional instruments, a general obligation exists for states to protect victims while investigating and prosecuting human rights violations. In national and international judicial processes, this responsibility falls within the statutes of courts and tribunals. For MRF missions, this responsibility is rooted in a variety of sources. While some MRF mandates address protection, this sense of responsibility also emanates from other areas, such as general standards of professional behavior and a personal sense of responsibility held by individual practitioners.

1.   Mandates and Terms of Reference

The majority of the mandates and Terms of Reference for MRF missions make no reference to the mission's responsibility to protect witnesses and victims. Of the fifteen missions studied for the purpose of this book, only six mandates directly address this issue.[3] When mandates

---

[2] See Appendix B in this Handbook for details about the fifteen missions on which this study is based.

[3] These missions are the Bahrain Independent Commission of Inquiry; the Kyrgyzstan Inquiry Commission; the International Fact-Finding Mission to investigate violations of international law, including international humanitarian and human rights law, resulting from the Israeli attacks on the flotilla of ships carrying humanitarian assistance (in the Terms of Reference for the Mission); the United Nations Mapping Exercise in the Democratic Republic of the Congo; the Commission of Inquiry on Lebanon (in the Terms of Reference for the Mission); and the United Nations Independent Special Commission of Inquiry for Timor-Leste.

do mention protection, references are usually fairly broad. For example, the Terms of Reference for the International Fact-Finding Mission to investigate violations of international law, including international humanitarian and human rights law, resulting from the Israeli attacks on the flotilla of ships carrying humanitarian assistance (hereafter the UNHRC Flotilla Fact-Finding Mission), state, "Protection should be guaranteed of victims and witnesses and all those who are in contact with the Mission in connection with the inquiry. No such person shall, as a result of such contact, suffer harassment, threats, acts of intimidation, ill-treatment or reprisals."[4]

Certain mandates – such as that of the Bahrain Independent Commission of Inquiry (hereafter the Bahrain Commission) – offer more specific statements. Specifically, the Bahrain Commission mandate mentions the duty of both the mission and the government of Bahrain to protect the security of the mission's interviewees. The mandate states:

> [T]he Commission will be able to meet with alleged victims and witnesses of alleged violations in secrecy and in accordance with measures that it shall develop to protect the privacy and security of individuals it meets with, in line with international human rights norms …. The government shall ensure that no person or member of that person's family who has made contact with the Commission or cooperated with the Commission shall in any way be penalized, negatively affected or in any way harassed or embarrassed by any public official or representative of the government.[5]

The Terms of Reference for the United Nations Mapping Exercise in the Democratic Republic of the Congo (hereafter the DRC Mapping Exercise) go into further detail about specific protective measures. For example, the Terms of Reference state that the mission should conduct interviews confidentially, ensure at least minimal security conditions, keep sensitive information secure, and obtain witness consent for sharing witness information with other entities.[6] Additionally, the Terms of Reference

---

[4] "Report of the International Fact-Finding Mission to Investigate Violations of International Law, Including International Humanitarian and Human Rights Law, Resulting from the Israeli Attacks on the Flotilla of Ships Carrying Humanitarian Assistance," A/HRC/15/21, September 27, 2010, p. 58, accessed May 26, 2015, http://www2.ohchr.org/english/bodies/hrcouncil/docs/15session/A.HRC.15.21_en.pdf.

[5] Royal Order No. 28 of 2011, Articles 5 and 7, http://www.bici.org.bh/wp-content/uploads/2011/08/RoyalOrder28of2011.pdf.

[6] "Report of the Mapping Exercise Documenting the Most Serious Violations of Human Rights and International Humanitarian Law Committed Within the Territory of the Democratic Republic of the Congo between March 1993 and June 2003," Office of the High

state that the authorities of the Democratic Republic of the Congo should "guarantee the protection against reprisal/persecution of all persons and organizations that will have contact with the Mapping Team."[7]

Regardless of what measures mandates specify, it is a standard observation that practitioners perceive a duty to consider adopting measures to mitigate protection risks. For example, though the International Commission of Inquiry on Darfur (hereafter the Darfur Commission) mandate makes no mention of protection, the mission elaborated the need for specific protective measures. The commission's report states:

> The Commission set forth the following criteria for evaluating the degree of cooperation of both the Government and the rebels: … (iii) free access to all sources of information, including documentary material and physical evidence; (iv) appropriate security arrangements for the personnel and documents of the Commission; (v) protection of victims and witnesses and all those who appear before the Commission in connection with the inquiry and, in particular, guarantee that no such person would, as a result of such appearance, suffer harassment, threats, acts of intimidation, ill-treatment and reprisals; and (vi) privileges, immunities and facilities necessary for the independent conduct of the inquiry. A letter was sent to the Government outlining these criteria.[8]

Similarly, though the mandate for the Secretary-General's Panel of Experts on Accountability in Sri Lanka (hereafter the Sri Lanka Panel) did not reference a duty to protect witnesses and victims, this mission adopted extensive protective measures, and the report actually laments the absence of sufficient witness protection in the local inquiry mechanism, the Lessons Learnt and Reconciliation Commission. The report states:

> Accountability mechanisms exist, in large measure, to serve victims and should put them at the centre of the process. To this end, international standards provide that victims and witnesses should generally only be called upon to testify on a "strictly voluntary" basis; social work and mental health practitioners should be permitted to help victims both before and after testimony; and "expenses incurred by those giving testimony shall be borne by the State."[9]

Commissioner for Human Rights, August 2010, pp. 543–544, accessed May 26, 2015, http://www.refworld.org/docid/4ca99bc22.html.

[7] Ibid., 543.

[8] "Report of the International Commission of Inquiry on Darfur to the United Nations Secretary-General," January 25, 2005, pp. 14–15, accessed May 26, 2015, http://www.un.org/news/dh/sudan/com_inq_darfur.pdf.

[9] "Report of the Secretary-General's Panel of Experts on Accountability in Sri Lanka," March 31, 2011, p. 87, accessed May 26, 2015, http://www.un.org/News/dh/infocus/Sri_Lanka/POE_Report_Full.pdf.

This trend – according to which practitioners express the importance of protection regardless of the extent to which the mission's mandate references this duty – suggests that practitioners derive this protective responsibility from sources beyond the mandate. This more general sense of professional responsibility, and the origins of this notion, will be examined in detail below.

2. Professional Responsibility

The sense of obligation to protect witnesses and victims is evidently grounded primarily in notions of professional responsibility held by MRF mission members and investigators. The United Nations High Commissioner for Human Rights has referred to the professional experience and skills of deployed personnel:

> The human rights officer considers **whom** to interview, and in **what language**, **who** will **translate**, **where** the interview should be held in order to protect the security of the witness, **how** the interview should be **recorded** so as to protect the **security** of the information, **what** the interviewer needs to **know** before the interview ... [and] **how** to deal with **cultural differences** which inhibit communication.[10]

This professional responsibility is encapsulated by the "do no harm" imperative, which offers a broad dictum that guides practices and approaches. Statements from MRF practitioners confirm the sense that a responsible approach to protection is a key aspect of professional behavior in this field. One practitioner offers a comment that suggests the professional responsibilities that investigators bring to bear: "We were all very experienced human rights investigators. The issue of witness protection came up on day one."[11]

In many cases, even though protection procedures were not systematized mission-wide, it was evidently assumed that investigators would apply appropriate measures. One practitioner states, "I didn't receive specific training. I think they relied on the fact that I had worked at the UN before and had security training."[12] Though "there were no formal guidelines,"

---

[10] "Human Rights Investigations and Their Methodology: Lecture by Ms. Navanethem Pillay, United Nations High Commissioner for Human Rights," Office of the High Commissioner for Human Rights, February 24, 2010, accessed June 5, 2013, http://unispal.un.org/UNISPAL.NSF/0/C9222F058467E6F6852576D500574710 (emphasis in original).

[11] Confidential interview with a high-level MRF practitioner, name of interviewee on file, conducted by HPCR, Summer 2013.

[12] Théo Boutruche, IHL/Human Rights Expert, Independent International Fact-Finding Mission on the Conflict in Georgia, interview conducted by HPCR, August 13, 2013.

there was "a common understanding that I would apply security procedures."[13] Additionally, as another practitioner notes, "The quality of the
people have the biggest impact on the security of the witnesses,"[14] further
highlighting the link between the professional experience of investigators
and the mission's protective capacities.

3.   Treaties, United Nations Resolutions, Protocols, and Guidelines

The professional sense of responsibility identified in the previous section
likely arises in part from the legal architecture of investigative mechanisms. For example, the report for the United Nations Fact-Finding Mission on the Gaza Conflict (hereafter the Gaza Fact-Finding Mission)
defines the legal framework for witness protection, though of the fifteen
missions on which this book focuses, this report is the only one to do so.
The report states:

> In the implementation of its mandate the Mission has called for the protec-
> tions that are required under the Declaration on the Right and Responsi-
> bility of Individuals, Groups and Organs of Society to Promote and Protect
> Universally Recognized Human Rights and Fundamental Freedoms, bet-
> ter known as the Declaration on Human Rights Defenders, to be accorded
> to all who gave testimony at the public hearings. The Mission also was
> guided by Commission on Human Rights resolution 2005/9 which "urges
> Governments to refrain from all acts of intimidation or reprisal against ...
> those who seek to cooperate or have cooperated with representatives of
> United Nations human rights bodies, or who have provided testimony or
> information to them."[15]

The High-Level Fact-Finding Mission to Beit Hanoun established under
Council resolution S-3/1 (hereafter the Beit Hanoun Fact-Finding Mission) report shares a definition of victims derived from an international
instrument, underscoring that such sources sometimes play a direct role
in shaping practitioners' perceptions of the relationship between MRF
missions and the victims of the incidents that missions investigate:

> In identifying victims, the mission was guided by the definition of the
> Basic Principles and Guidelines on the Right to a Remedy and Reparation

[13]   Ibid.
[14]   Philip Trewhitt, Investigation Team Leader, International Commission of Inquiry on Lib-
       ya, interview conducted by HPCR, July 26, 2013.
[15]   "Report of the United Nations Fact-Finding Mission on the Gaza Conflict," A/HRC/12/48,
       September 25, 2009, p. 40, accessed May 26, 2015, http://www2.ohchr.org/english/bodies/
       hrcouncil/docs/12session/A-HRC-12-48.pdf.

for Victims of Gross Violations of International Human Rights Law and Serious Violations of International Humanitarian Law. The victims of the shelling are persons who individually or collectively suffered harm, including physical or mental injury, emotional suffering, economic loss or substantial impairment of their fundamental rights as a result of the shelling; they include the immediate family or dependents of the direct victim and persons who have suffered harm in intervening to assist victims in distress or to prevent victimization.[16]

In addition to shaping conceptions of what constitutes a "victim," the "Basic Principles and Guidelines on the Right to a Remedy and Reparation for Victims of Gross Violations of International Human Rights Law and Serious Violations of International Humanitarian Law," adopted in 2005 by the United Nations General Assembly, also establish a clear responsibility of states to protect victims of human rights violations while investigating and prosecuting these violations. A wide range of international and regional instruments establish this obligation of states and no doubt shape the environment in which MRF practitioners' notions of protection obligations arise. International legal sources include core human rights treaties, including, for example, the 1984 Convention against Torture and Other Cruel, Inhuman or Degrading Treatment or Punishment, which in Article 13 states:

> Each State Party shall ensure that any individual who alleges he has been subjected to torture in any territory under its jurisdiction has the right to complain to, and to have his case promptly and impartially examined by, its competent authorities. Steps shall be taken to ensure that the complainant

[16] "Report of the High-Level Fact-Finding Mission to Beit Hanoun Established Under Council Resolution S-3/1," A/HRC/9/26, September 1, 2008, pp. 13–14, accessed May 26, 2015, http://www.refworld.org/docid/48cfa3a22.html (internal citation omitted). For reference, see United Nations General Assembly (UNGA), Resolution 60/147, "Basic Principles and Guidelines on the Right to a Remedy and Reparation for Victims of Gross Violations of International Human Rights Law and Serious Violations of International Humanitarian Law," March 21, 2006, ¶¶ 8–9, accessed June 27, 2015, http://www.un.org/Docs/asp/ws.asp?m=A/RES/60/147, which offers the following definition of a victim: "For purposes of the present document, victims are persons who individually or collectively suffered harm, including physical or mental injury, emotional suffering, economic loss or substantial impairment of their fundamental rights, through acts or omissions that constitute gross violations of international human rights law, or serious violations of international humanitarian law. Where appropriate, and in accordance with domestic law, the term 'victim' also includes the immediate family or dependants of the direct victim and persons who have suffered harm in intervening to assist victims in distress or to prevent victimization. A person shall be considered a victim regardless of whether the perpetrator of the violation is identified, apprehended, prosecuted, or convicted and regardless of the familial relationship between the perpetrator and the victim."

and witnesses are protected against all ill-treatment or intimidation as a consequence of his complaint or any evidence given.[17]

Regional texts include a number of provisions in various instruments of the European Union, such as the Council of Europe Recommendation No. R (97) 13 Concerning Intimidation of Witnesses and the Rights of the Defence; the Council of Europe Recommendation (2005) 9 on the Protection of Witnesses and Collaborators of Justice, which notably lists criteria for a witness protection program;[18] and the European Council Framework decision of 15/03/2001, which in Article 8 stipulates:

> [E]ach member State shall ensure a suitable level of protection for victims and, where appropriate, their families or persons in a similar position, particularly as regards their safety and protection of their privacy, where the competent authorities consider that there is a serious risk of reprisals or firm evidence of serious intent to intrude upon their privacy.[19]

Interestingly, the European Union instruments assume that protective measures ought to be taken to protect witnesses from the acts of private actors (such as individuals engaged in organized crime) but not of states themselves.[20]

In Africa, the Robben Island Guidelines confer the states' responsibilities for the protection of victims and witnesses of torture. The document obliges states to:

> [e]nsure that alleged victims of torture, cruel, inhuman and degrading treatment or punishment, witnesses, those conducting the investigation,

---

[17] Convention against Torture and Other Cruel, Inhuman or Degrading Treatment or Punishment, Article 13.

[18] These criteria include: "involvement of the person to be protected (as a victim, witness, co-perpetrator, accomplice, or aider and abetter) in the investigation and/or in the case; relevance of the contribution; seriousness of the intimidation; willingness and suitability to being subject to protection measures or programmes"; assessment "whether there is no other evidence available that could be deemed sufficient to establish a case related to serious offences"; and "[p]roportionality between the nature of the protection measures and the seriousness of the intimidation of the witness/collaborator of justice."

[19] Gert Vermeulen, ed., *EU Standards in Witness Protection and Collaboration with Justice* (Ghent: Institute for International Research on Criminal Policy, 2004), 27.

[20] For example, the preamble for Council of Europe Recommendation No. R (97) 13 Concerning Intimidation of Witnesses and the Rights of the Defence notes "that there is growing recognition of the special role of witnesses in criminal proceedings and that their evidence is often crucial to securing the conviction of offenders, especially in respect of organised crime and crime in the family;" and the preamble for Council of Europe Recommendation (2005) 9 on the Protection of Witnesses and Collaborators of Justice "[c]onsider[s] that in some areas of criminality, such as organised crime and terrorism, there is an increasing risk that witnesses will be subjected to intimidation."

other human rights defenders and families are protected from violence, threats of violence or any other form of intimidation or reprisal that may arise pursuant to the report or investigation.[21]

Practitioners interviewed as part of the research for this chapter also noted several specific guidelines and protocols that have guided professional practice. These documents include the "Manual on the Effective Investigation and Documentation of Torture and Other Cruel, Inhuman or Degrading Treatment or Punishment" ("Istanbul Protocol");[22] the "Manual on the Effective Prevention and Investigation of Extra-Legal, Arbitrary and Summary Executions" ("Minnesota Protocol");[23] and the "Guidelines on International Human Rights Fact-Finding Visits and Reports" ("Lund-London Guidelines").[24]

Additionally, a recent initiative led by the International Institute of Higher Studies in Criminal Sciences has produced the *Siracusa Guidelines for International, Regional and National Fact-Finding Bodies*, intended to serve as "a practical guide for establishing and operating a fact-finding

---

[21] Jean-Baptiste Niyizurugero and Patrick Lessène, "The Robben Island Guidelines for the Prohibition and Prevention of Torture in Africa: Practical Guide for Implementation," Association for the Prevention of Torture, African Commission on Human and People's Rights and Office of the High Commissioner for Human Rights, April 2008, p. 67, accessed June 1, 2015, http://www.apt.ch/content/files_res/rig_practical_eng.pdf.

[22] See generally Office of the High Commissioner for Human Rights, "Istanbul Protocol: Manual on the Effective Investigation and Documentation of Torture and Other Cruel, Inhuman or Degrading Treatment or Punishment," 2004, accessed January 17, 2014, http://www.refworld.org/docid/4638aca62.html. In particular, see ¶¶ 107–119, which provide specific guidance concerning the protection of witnesses by commissions of inquiry.

[23] See "Manual on the Effective Prevention and Investigation of Extra-Legal, Arbitrary and Summary Executions," United Nations, 1991, accessed January 17, 2014, http://www.theadvocatesforhumanrights.org/uploads/minnesota_protocol.pdf, which states, "Witnesses should be interviewed individually, and assurance should be given that any possible means of protecting their safety before, during and after the proceedings will be used, if necessary." In a section focusing on commissions of inquiry, the manual recommends a set of procedures concerning witness protection: "(a) The Government shall protect complainants, witnesses, those conducting the investigation, and their families from violence, threats of violence or any other form of intimidation; (b) If the commission concludes that there is a reasonable fear of persecution, harassment, or harm to any witness or prospective witness, the commission may find it advisable: (i) To hear the evidence in camera; (ii) To keep the identity of the informant or witness confidential; (iii) To use only such evidence as will not present a risk of identifying the witness; (iv) To take any other appropriate measures."

[24] See "Guidelines on International Human Rights Fact-Finding Visits and Reports" ("Lund-London Guidelines"), Raoul Wallenberg Institute of Human Rights and Humanitarian Law at Lund University and the International Bar Association, n.d., accessed January 17, 2014, http://www.factfindingguidelines.org/guidelines.html.

body investigating human rights violations."[25] The document presents a wide array of guidelines on the design and implementation of, and follow-up to, fact-finding bodies, focusing specifically on protection in certain provisions, as will be addressed in greater detail later in this chapter. These guidelines – along with the numerous treaties, international and regional instruments, protocols, and other guidelines mentioned above – constitute a body of material that will likely continue to shape MRF practitioners' perceptions of the protective responsibilities that exist during mission implementation.

4. Statutes and Practices of International Courts and Tribunals

Ad hoc MRF missions stand in counterpoint to international criminal courts and tribunals. On the one hand, practitioners in both contexts feel bound by a common normative responsibility for protection. On the other hand, in MRF missions, practitioners must operate with a more limited institutional, administrative, and logistical capacity. Therefore, though these missions lack the capacity to provide the same level of protective measures as international criminal courts and tribunals, these more formal investigations provide a certain reference point that informs how practitioners can strike a balance between fulfilling professionals' protective responsibilities and operating realistically within the logistical confines of an ad hoc mission's limited capacity.

MRF missions, as well as courts and tribunals, share the quality that, without witnesses, there would be little on which to base legal findings. Hence, in order to function effectively, courts and MRF missions need to protect their sources. United Nations High Commissioner for Human Rights Navi Pillay, who also served as a judge on the International Criminal Tribunal for Rwanda, and for several years as the Tribunal's president, eloquently summarized this challenge:

> The whole capacity of a country to render justice to the victims and end impunity regarding past and current abuses could come into question if the justice system is unable to secure convictions because of failures in the production of witness evidence.[26]

---

25 M. Cherif Bassiouni, preface to *Siracusa Guidelines for International, Regional and National Fact-Finding Bodies*, xvi, ed. M. Cherif Bassiouni and Christina Abraham (Cambridge: Intersentia, 2013).

26 Office of the High Commissioner for Human Rights, "Witness Protection in Kosovo," May 8, 2012, accessed January 17, 2014, http://www.ohchr.org/EN/NewsEvents/Pages/WitnessProtectionInKosovo.aspx.

This dilemma has also been referenced in publications from a wide array of organizations, including the Office of the High Commissioner for Human Rights (OHCHR),[27] the Organization for Security and Co-operation in Europe,[28] and Human Rights Watch.[29]

Because of this challenge, protection is a mainstay in the operations of international courts and tribunals. For example, the statute for the International Criminal Court (ICC) articulates a broad perspective on the court's protective responsibilities:

> The Court shall take appropriate measures to protect the safety, physical and psychological well-being, dignity and privacy of victims and witnesses. In so doing, the Court shall have regard to all relevant factors, including age, gender as defined in article 7, paragraph 3, and health, and the nature of the crime, in particular, but not limited to, where the crime involves sexual or gender violence or violence against children. The Prosecutor shall take such measures particularly during the investigation and prosecution of such crimes.[30]

This article is more developed than similar provisions of certain international tribunals, such as Article 22 of the International Criminal Tribunal for former Yugoslavia (ICTY) statute,[31] and Articles 19.1 and 21 of the International Criminal Tribunal for Rwanda (ICTR).[32] While all provide

---

[27] "Lecture by Ms. Navanethem Pillay."

[28] Valery Perry, the acting program director of the Organization for Security and Co-operation in Europe Mission to Bosnia and Herzegovina, has stated, "Witness testimony is the lynchpin of successful prosecutions in war crimes cases, but not enough is being done to ensure that trials take place without violating the rights of victims .... These failures are jeopardising the right to life, security and privacy of witnesses, and can have particularly devastating effects on those who are also the victims in these cases." See Velma Šarić, "Bosnian Witness Protection Rapped," Institute for War & Peace Reporting, June 1, 2010, accessed September 15, 2009, http://iwpr.net/report-news/bosnian-witness-protection-rapped.

[29] See "Justice at Risk: War Crimes Trials in Croatia, Bosnia and Herzegovina, and Serbia and Montenegro," Human Rights Watch, October 2004, accessed January 17, 2014, http://www.hrw.org/reports/2004/icty1004/7.htm, which states, "The successful prosecution of war crimes cases depends on the availability of credible witnesses, which in turn requires that witnesses are confident that they can testify truthfully without fear of retribution. Achieving accountability through national war crimes trials, therefore, requires measures to protect witnesses prior to, during, and after trials. In some cases, effective witness protection requires a long-term witness protection program or resettlement in another country."

[30] Rome Statute of the International Criminal Court, Article 68.1.

[31] Article 22 of the Statute of the International Criminal Tribunal for the former Yugoslavia states, "The International Tribunal shall provide in its rules of procedure and evidence for the protection of victims and witnesses. Such protection measures shall include, but shall not be limited to, the conduct of in camera proceedings and the protection of the victim's identity."

[32] Article 19.1 of the Statute for the International Criminal Tribunal for Rwanda states, "The Trial Chambers shall ensure that a trial is fair and expeditious and that proceedings are

for the protection of witnesses, the ICC statute, which has built on the experience of its predecessors, includes specific reference to victims and witnesses of sexual or gender-based violence in the general provisions. The ICC statute specifies in Article 43.6:

> The Registrar shall set up a Victims and Witnesses Unit within the Registry. This Unit shall provide, in consultation with the Office of the Prosecutor, protective measures and security arrangements, counselling and other appropriate assistance for witnesses, victims who appear before the Court, and others who are at risk on account of testimony given by such witnesses. The Unit shall include staff with expertise in trauma, including trauma related to crimes of sexual violence.[33]

Article 54.1.b further provides that the Prosecutor shall:

> Take appropriate measures to ensure the effective investigation and prosecution of crimes within the jurisdiction of the Court, and in doing so, respect the interests and personal circumstances of victims and witnesses, including age, gender as defined in Article 7, paragraph 3, and health, and take into account the nature of the crime, in particular where it involves sexual violence, gender violence or violence against children.[34]

A similar provision is found in the ICTY statute,[35] and also in the statute for the Special Court for Sierra Leone (SCSL).[36] In an article comparing the statutes and practices of international tribunals regarding the

conducted in accordance with the rules of procedure and evidence, with full respect for the rights of the accused and due regard for the protection of victims and witnesses;" and Article 21 states, "The International Tribunal for Rwanda shall provide in its rules of procedure and evidence for the protection of victims and witnesses. Such protection measures shall include, but shall not be limited to, the conduct of in camera proceedings and the protection of the victim's identity."

[33] Rome Statute of the International Criminal Court, Article 43.6.

[34] Ibid., Article 54.1.b.

[35] See generally Office of the High Commissioner for Human Rights, "Introductory Remarks by Navanethem Pillay at the OHCHR Expert meeting on witness protection for successful investigation and prosecution of gross human rights violations and international crimes," September 29, 2009, accessed January 17, 2014, http://www.unhchr.ch/huricane/huricane.nsf/0/E5E9ACC8131CFA5AC1257643004ED6F0?opendocument. As the High Commissioner notes in her remarks, "ICTY Rule 34 set up a Victims and Witnesses Support Unit under the authority of the Registrar to: (i) recommend the adoption of protective measures for victims and witnesses, (ii) ensure that they receive relevant support, including physical and psychological rehabilitation, especially counseling in cases of rape and sexual assault; and (iii) develop short term and long term plans for their protection in the face of a threat to their life, property or family. The ICTR also created a Witness and Victims Support Section pursuant to the Tribunal's Statute and Rules of Procedure and Evidence, under the authority of the Registrar."

[36] See Article 16.4 of the Statute of the Special Court for Sierra Leone.

protection of victims of rape, Sylvia Pieslak suggests that the ICC has more comprehensive and more effective mechanisms than both the ICTY and the ICTR. She explains:

> Article 36 not only mandates an equal representation of female and male, but it also states that the court will include judges with legal expertise in areas such as violence against women. Article 54 compels the Prosecutor to consider the nature of violent crimes against women, when rendering decisions. Article 42 states that the Prosecutor will recruit expert advisers in issues such as sexual violence. Lastly, Articles 43 and 68 address female witness/victim protection services. While Article 68 requires the court to take measures necessary to protect the dignity and privacy of sex crime victims, Article 43 creates the Victims and Witnesses Unit in the Registry, requiring that the Unit have experts in trauma such as that resulting from sexually violent crimes.[37]

These provisions have had a direct consequence on the conduct of the prosecution regarding how witnesses have been handled, especially when witness testimony concerns sexual and gender-based violence:

> Other additional witness protection provisions directed at women include Rules 18 and 19 that ensure training of the Victims and Witness Unit staff regarding matters related to gender and may include experts in "gender and cultural diversity." With respect to evidentiary provisions, Rule 63 states that the court will not require corroboration in sexual violence cases. Rule 70 defines the nature of consent in rape prosecutions, in order to protect women and also stipulates that the court may not use prior sexual conduct. Additionally, Rule 71 states that the court will not admit evidence of prior or subsequent sexual conduct. Under "Section III: Witness and Victims of the ICC Rules of Procedure and Evidence," Rule 86 requires the court to take into account the needs of sexual or gender violence victims in their decisions. Under Rule 88, the court states that the court must pay attention to the views of victims, so as to order measures that might facilitate the testimony of a sexual violence victim. Thus, both the ICC Statute and the Rules of Procedure and Evidence include provisions that will allow for the effective prosecution of sexual violence crimes against women. The court might then bring those perpetrators of sexual violence crimes against women to justice.
>
> The court has crafted provisions, both specifically and generally, for the protection of female victims, when they act as witnesses in their own trials.

---

[37] Sylvia Pieslak, "The International Criminal Court's Quest to Protect Rape Victims of Armed Conflict: Anonymity as the Solution," *Santa Clara Journal of International Law* 2, no. 1 (2004): 144, accessed May 29, 2015, http://digitalcommons.law.scu.edu/scujil/vol2/iss1/5 (internal citations omitted).

These witness protection provisions are essential not only because without them a large number of female rape victims would not testify because of social norms that place shame on these women, but also because there are not enough measures to protect the witness from physical threats and from societal contempt. Therefore, the ICC has crafted several provisions that protect women during the trial process.[38]

Another category of victims and witnesses that is treated with special care is people facing risks of retraumatization because of the need to remember painful memories, which sometimes re-opens unhealed wounds. A report on a seminar held in 2010 to examine the ICC's witness protection efforts suggests the importance of conducting a prior assessment of the psychological vulnerability of the witnesses:

> To avoid potential harm where the risk is identified, the OTP [Office of the Prosecutor] established the practice of conducting a preliminary psychological assessment (i.e. prior to the investigative interview). Furthermore, OTP investigators have received training on how to identify vulnerable witnesses. It was also reported that an examination of the investigators compliance to these practices is carried out afterwards. As soon as any relevant issue is detected, the OTP informs the VWU [Victims and Witness Unit] which may then take the appropriate measures.[39]

Similarly, a report documenting the best-practice recommendations for the SCSL also notes the importance of discerning which witnesses are likely to be at risk for retraumatization. The document states as a recommendation:

> Distinguish between those witnesses whose accounts involve particularly traumatic events and those whose do not, since the former group are likely to find the whole statement-taking process considerably more difficult, and [u]se specialist interviewing techniques to assist a witness who is struggling with painful feelings, having problems recalling the details of an event, or otherwise finding the process difficult.[40]

As with the ICC, the ICTY, and the ICTR, for the SCSL, these protective responsibilities derive from the Court's mandate. The statute of the SCSL includes witness protection in Article 16, paragraph 4, which states:

---

[38] Ibid., 145–146.
[39] International Criminal Court, "Summary Report on the Seminar on Protection of Victims and Witnesses Appearing Before the International Criminal Court," n.d., ¶ 21, accessed January 17, 2014, http://www.icc-cpi.int/NR/rdonlyres/08767415-4F1D-46BA-B408-5B447B3AFC8D/0/ProtectionseminarSUMMARY.pdf.
[40] Special Court for Sierra Leone, "Best-Practice Recommendations for the Protection & Support of Witnesses," 2008, p. 13, accessed January 17, 2014, http://www.rscsl.org/Documents/WVS%20Best%20Practices.pdf (internal citation omitted).

The Registrar shall set up a Victims and Witnesses Unit within the Registry. This Unit shall provide, in consultation with the Office of the Prosecutor, protective measures and security arrangements, counselling and other appropriate assistance for witnesses, victims who appear before the Court and others who are at risk on account of testimony given by such witnesses. The Unit personnel shall include experts in trauma, including trauma related to crimes of sexual violence and violence against children.[41]

Rule 34 of the SCSL's "Rules of Procedure and Evidence" elaborates on the activities of the Victims and Witnesses Unit,[42] and as noted in the aforementioned "Best-Practice Recommendations" report, some witnesses for the court have been taken into "[t]otal protective care," which includes "[h]ousing for the witness and his/her family in a safe house; 24-hour guard from a close protection officer (case-dependent); [p]rovision of a financial subsistence allowance; [m]edical cover; [s]chooling for any minors or dependents of the witness; [t]emporary provision of a mobile phone (case-dependent), and [p]ost-testimony relocation either within Sierra Leone, or the West Africa region."[43]

Based on the practices and statutes of the various international courts and tribunals to which this chapter refers, the following list summarizes various measures offered as part of witness protection programs, which include but are not limited to:

- security risk assessment and individual risk assessment;
- 24/7 emergency call and response system;
- the protection of the witnesses' identities, including by the conduct of in-camera proceedings;
- controlling the questioning of a witness to avoid harassment and intimidation;
- no requirement for corroboration for crimes of sexual violence;
- the prosecutor may withhold evidence that is dangerous for specific witnesses and instead submit a summary of the contents;
- counseling;
- housing of the witness and family in a safe house;
- post-testimony relocation, in country or abroad; and
- assessment of the situation of victims at risk of retraumatization.

---

[41] Statute of the Special Court for Sierra Leone, Article 16.4.
[42] Special Court for Sierra Leone, "Rules of Evidence and Procedure," Rule 34, 2010, accessed May 29, 2015, https://www1.umn.edu/humanrts/instree/SCSL/Rules-of-proced-SCSL.pdf.
[43] Special Court for Sierra Leone, "Best-Practice Recommendations," 6.

Ad hoc missions typically cannot adopt such extensive measures, due to the very nature and design of these mechanisms. One practitioner pointedly remarks on the differences regarding protection between MRF missions on the one hand, and courts and tribunals on the other hand: "I don't think you can use the term witness protection for a commission of inquiry because we don't have witnesses."[44] Factors that distinguish MRF missions from courts and tribunals in this regard include:

- Nature of the work: While most international courts entail an adversarial process, thus sometimes creating conflicting obligations of ensuring witness protection and due process (rights of the defense), MRF missions work confidentially and do not share interviewee statements with suspects.
- Duration: While courts and tribunals are either permanent or work for a number of years, MRF missions are ad hoc by nature and rarely exceed a few months.
- Location: MRF missions are usually (when granted territorial access) conducted in the location where the crimes were allegedly perpetrated, which exposes the witnesses and victims but also the staff to greater risks, as the perpetrators might still be on-site. Though certain aspects of the operations of courts and tribunals (such as initial investigations of prosecutors) also have this quality, formal proceedings usually occur elsewhere.
- Capacities: While courts rely on a body of well-established professionals with recognized technical expertise (e.g., judges, prosecutors, etc.), ad hoc missions resort to a varying range of professionals and skills due to the difficulty of assembling qualified staff on short notice. Budget-wise, there are also more constraints on MRF missions, which lack the capacities to fund a full-scale witness protection program.
- Nature of the mandate: The mandates of MRF missions sometimes encompass broader aspects, such as reconciliation, and do not always focus solely on the establishment of truth, sometimes prioritizing other dimensions, such as diplomatic and political considerations.
- System versus individual approach: Courts have systems in place, while in many MRF missions, once deployed on the ground, a lot depends on professional responsibility and individual practitioners' skills and experience.

[44] Sareta Ashraph, Analyst, International Commission of Inquiry on Libya, and Associate Human Rights Officer, United Nations Fact-Finding Mission on the Gaza Conflict, interview conducted by HPCR, August 8, 2013.

Given the various factors mentioned above, how do MRF missions meet the challenges of protection while lacking the resources and procedures available to courts and tribunals? One practitioner states: "There is very little that you can provide to interviewees in terms of real witness protection as an organization, which does not mean that there's nothing to do. What you can provide them is an ethic of work that will not compromise their safety."[45] Though, as another practitioner states, regardless of the extensiveness of a certain entity's protective capacities, the common conundrum facing both MRF practitioners and professionals associated with courts and tribunals is: "It doesn't matter how many procedures you have. At the end of the day, there are always risks."[46] The next section will examine how MRF practitioners have grappled with this reality.

B.   Threats to Witnesses and Victims

The two main risks to witnesses and victims identified by MRF mission reports, interviews with practitioners conducted as research for this chapter, and relevant secondary literature are: (1) retaliation, including intimidation and threats of retaliation; and (2) retraumatization of interviewees because of the memories brought up while retelling stories of traumatic events. This section examines both of these risks in detail.

1.   Retaliation

As noted earlier, many MRF missions are conducted in contexts where violations have not ceased and where the alleged perpetrators hold a certain level of power. Victims might personally know their persecutors and might still live in the vicinity of these individuals. Because of the inherent risks in such scenarios, concerns about retaliation often lead witnesses and victims to exhibit caution about communicating with MRF missions. For example, the report of the Bahrain Commission states:

> The Commission faced a number of limitations in the conduct of its investigation. The Commission was aware that there was a degree of fear among the alleged victims and witnesses of torture. This may have resulted in individuals being reticent about providing information to the Commission

---

[45] Luc Côté, Executive Director of the United Nations Independent Special Commission of Inquiry for Timor-Leste, the United Nations Mapping Exercise in the Democratic Republic of the Congo, and the Kyrgyzstan Inquiry Commission, interview conducted by HPCR, June 8, 2013.

[46] Philip Trewhitt, HPCR interview.

or even refusing to provide information altogether. On some occasions, complainants expressed their unwillingness to share all the information relating to their detention because they were afraid of reprisals. In some cases, witnesses were able to provide evidence thus obviating the need for the alleged victim to provide information.[47]

In Darfur, there were also serious concerns about reprisals, relating to both the Sudanese national justice system and the context of the Darfur Commission. The report states:

> [M]any victims informed the Commission that they had little confidence in the impartiality of the Sudanese justice system and its ability to bring to justice the perpetrators of the serious crimes committed in Darfur. In any event, many have feared reprisals in the event that they resort to the national justice system.[48]

In some cases, fears of reprisals are brought about by specific threats issued to witnesses and/or victims. According to the Darfur Commission report:

> The Commission also wishes to stress that there have been episodes indicative of pressure put by some regional or local authorities on prospective witnesses, or on witnesses already interviewed by the Commission. For instance, in the first week of November 2004, in El Fashir (North Darfur) a government official, reportedly the chief of the local office of the National Security and Intelligence Service, gave money to some IDPs and urged them not to talk to the Commission. It was also reported to the Commission that the Sudanese authorities had deployed infiltrators posing as internally displaced persons (IDPs) into some camps such as Abushouk. In the same camp various eyewitnesses reported an episode that could be taken to amount to witness harassment.[49]

The Gaza Fact-Finding Mission also reported that witnesses had received "anonymous calls and messages on private phone numbers and e-mail addresses" and that "[t]he contents seemed to imply that the originators of these anonymous calls and messages regarded those who cooperated with the Mission as potentially associated with armed groups."[50] The report specifies that some witnesses and victims "have declined to appear before it or to provide information or, having cooperated with the Mission, have asked that their names should not be disclosed, for fear of reprisal."[51]

---

[47] "Report of the Bahrain Independent Commission of Inquiry," November 23, 2011, p. 291, accessed May 29, 2015, http://www.bici.org.bh/BICIreportEN.pdf.
[48] Darfur Commission report, 149.
[49] Ibid., 16.   [50] Gaza Fact-Finding Mission report, 40.   [51] Ibid.

Witnesses' fears of reprisals after receiving threats also affected the ability of the International Commission of Inquiry for Guinea (hereafter the Guinea Commission) to collect information:

> The Commission also noted that the hospital staff was terrified at the thought of giving it any information and that several people said they had been warned not to talk. Some people, although realizing that they were taking a risk, nonetheless agreed to share bits of information discreetly with the Commission.[52]

Quite uniquely, the Independent International Fact-Finding Mission on the Conflict in Georgia (hereafter the Georgia Fact-Finding Mission) reports that there were no problems regarding protection. In the introduction, the report states: "It should be mentioned here that there were never any attempts by any side to interfere with [the fact-finding mission's] independent mandate."[53] It is worth noting that, whether by choice or by obligation based on the mandate, some missions have interviewed very few witnesses. The Georgia Fact-Finding Mission, for certain issues addressed in the final report, largely based its research on the official correspondence of relevant governments and reports of human rights organizations.[54]

Interestingly, some MRF reports provide evidence of positive outcomes on the treatment of interviewed victims, indicating that in certain contexts the actual risks of retaliation and other forms of abuse were mitigated due to the intervention of the mission. For example, the report of the Bahrain Commission states:

> During the period from 20 July to 30 September 2011, the Chairman of the Commission and the Chief Investigator provided the Minister of Interior, the head of the NSA [National Security Agency], the Attorney General and the Military Attorney General with various accounts of mistreatment, torture and other forms of cruel, inhuman or degrading treatment or punishment. These officials took steps to stop these practices, and after 10 June 2011 the Commission received reports that mistreatment had stopped at Al Qurain prison, and conditions in all detention centres had improved significantly.[55]

---

[52] "Report of the International Commission of Inquiry mandated to establish the facts and circumstances of the events of 28 September 2009 in Guinea," transmitted by letter dated 18 December 2009 from the Secretary-General addressed to the President of the Security Council, S/2009/693, December 18, 2009, p. 54, accessed June 25, 2015, http://www.refworld.org/docid/4b4f49ea2.html.

[53] "Independent International Fact-Finding Mission on the Conflict in Georgia Report," vol. 1 (September 2009): 6.

[54] See generally Georgia Fact-Finding Mission report, vol. 2.

[55] Bahrain Commission report, 300–301.

In many cases, though, threats of retaliation have actually manifested. One observer states: "two witnesses who gave evidence to Phillip Alston [sic] in Kenya suffered lethal reprisals."[56] It was also reported that witnesses were killed in connection with testifying at the ICTR in Arusha. The nongovernmental organizations (NGOs) African Rights and REDRESS have reported several such crimes.[57] The ICTY has also experienced difficulties. As a Human Rights Watch report mentions, in several cases, it was not possible to render justice in the context of the ICTY because witnesses had been threatened and the court was not able to protect them.[58]

One important consideration regarding retaliation is that the threat can arise in many forms. Threats of retaliation can come not only from local political, military, and economic elites but also from family members and neighbors.[59] The threat of retaliation can also persist long after the conflict has ended, a particularly crucial concern for MRF missions, which, as will be examined later, typically have limited to no capacity to ensure protective measures for interviewees after the conclusion of the mission.[60] Risks are also not limited only to acts of violence. As one practitioner

---

[56] Geoffrey Robertson, "Human Rights Fact-Finding: Some Legal and Ethical Dilemmas," Thematic Paper No. 1, Human Rights Institute of the International Bar Association, May 2010, p. 17.

[57] See "Survivors and Post-Genocide Justice in Rwanda: Their Experiences, Perspectives and Hopes," African Rights and REDRESS, November 2008, p. 7, accessed January 17, 2014, http://www.redress.org/downloads/publications/Rwanda%20Survivors%2031%20Oct%2008.pdf, which offers this quotation from an individual who has worked in Rwanda: "The insecurity of genocide survivors and witnesses continues to grow from today to tomorrow. Some are murdered, others have had their livestock killed or their houses burned. They receive leaflets warning them that they will be massacred. There are many other forms of threats and intimidation, and so many examples."

[58] See Human Rights Watch, "Justice at Risk," which states, "The Norac trial, named after one of four co-accused in the case, dealt with the murder of fifty civilians near Gospic in 1991, most of them ethnic Serbs. The president of the court stated during the trial that witnesses in the trial were receiving anonymous threats. He remarked that it was 'very difficult to undertake any measures of adequate protection of witnesses from possible threats.'" The report also mentions, "The Lora trial dealt with the torture and killing of Serb civilians in 1992 in the Lora military prison in Split. Out of fear, a number of key witnesses – Lora survivors who now live in Serbia or in Bosnia – did not appear in court. Several witnesses stated at the trial that they had been threatened and, therefore, could not testify freely. All eight accused were acquitted due to lack of evidence." (internal citations omitted)

[59] "Testifying to Genocide: Victim and Witness Protection in Rwanda," REDRESS, n.d., pp. 24–29, accessed January 17, 2014, http://protectionline.org/files/2012/11/121029ProtectionReport.pdf.

[60] Anna Marie L.M. de Brouwer, *Supranational Criminal Prosecution of Sexual Violence: The ICC and the Practice of the ICTY and the ICTR* (Oxford: Intersentia, 2005), 232.

states, "It was never my sense that witnesses were under threat or in physical danger. Probably the biggest fear was some kind of material reprisal, that a witness would lose their job or status."[61]

For victims of gender-based and sexual violence, particular risks stem from the stigma commonly attached to these types of incidents in many contexts. As one interviewed practitioner states, "If there's a girl who is known to have been raped, she is possibly going to be disowned by her family, possibly divorced, her sisters might be divorced. In the worst case, a male family member might kill her."[62] The resulting challenges for investigators are underlined by Sylvia Pieslak, who asserts: "women are unwilling to testify not only because there are not enough measures to protect them from physical threats, but also because of the social norms that place shame upon raped women."[63]

2. Retraumatization

The risk that witnesses and victims could experience retraumatization through retelling stories of violent incidents is widely addressed in policy literature relevant to various investigative mechanisms. The "Best-Practice Recommendations" document produced by the SCSL emphasizes the importance of avoiding retraumatization:

> Best practice should also guard against the further traumatisation of witnesses who have experienced human rights abuses as they participate in the process. It should also ensure that the experience of testifying in a war crimes tribunal is positive and not excessively distressing, frustrating or dangerous; this will encourage future witnesses to testify.[64]

These dangers particularly affect survivors of sexual violence and torture, as documented by a study conducted by the Institute for Women's Policy Research:

> "Every time they go to testify, they are going through their trauma which will mark them until the end of their life," said Irena Antic, a journalist at Federal Radio in Sarajevo who has followed these issues closely. "In many situations, even the closest members of their family don't know what happened to them. Our society, which is still a little conservative, doesn't provide the necessary help. And what our society doesn't recognise

---

[61] Christina Abraham, Chief of Staff, Bahrain Independent Commission of Inquiry, interview conducted by HPCR, July 30, 2013.

[62] Erin Gallagher, Gender Adviser and Sexual Violence Investigator, International Commission of Inquiry on Libya, interview conducted by HPCR, July 31, 2013.

[63] Pieslak, "Anonymity as the Solution," 155 (internal citation omitted).

[64] Special Court for Sierra Leone, "Best-Practice Recommendations," 6.

is that these women need help on every level, and in some ways it's still a stigma."[65]

As with the risk of retaliation, the risk of retraumatization can also endure long after the incident has occurred. The authors of the report "Survivors and Post-Genocide Justice in Rwanda: Their Experiences, Perspectives and Hopes" underline the need, in the context of formal judicial processes, for protective measures and support systems that are not limited to the duration of the investigation/prosecution:

> The experience of testifying about the horrific events of the genocide, often before a variety of judicial bodies, exposed many survivors to retraumatisation. There is a need to strengthen domestic initiatives designed to provide witnesses with psycho-social support. Similarly, while survivors testifying before the ICTR in Arusha could receive some form of counselling while in Arusha, this has not been sustained once they returned to Rwanda. The domestic witness protection processes offer an opportunity for more sustained and engaged support. It is also necessary to take steps to avoid re-traumatisation through the training of judicial personnel in order to ensure that survivors do not find it difficult to testify.[66]

As noted earlier, MRF missions typically lack the capacity to undertake the more extensive measures adopted by courts and tribunals, but in the context of an MRF process, practitioners widely assert that the risk of retraumatization should inform the manner in which interviews are conducted. For example, the "Lund-London Guidelines" articulate this widely held notion:

> Members of the delegation should be alert to the possibility of stress or trauma experienced by interviewees and be ready to terminate the interview if necessary. Wherever possible, the delegation members should ensure that interviewees are referred to appropriate victim support services.[67]

C.   What Protective Measures Have Been Adopted

This section examines how – despite the aforementioned restraints under which MRF missions operate – practitioners activate the professional responsibility for protection to guard against the risks discussed in the

---

[65] Rachel Irwin and Velma Šarić, "Poor Protection for Balkan Trial Witnesses," Institute for War & Peace Reporting, November 22, 2012, accessed January 17, 2014, http://iw3.iwpr. net/sites/default/files/poor_protection_for_balkan_trial_witnesses_-_web.pdf.

[66] REDRESS, "Testifying to Genocide," 7.   [67] "Lund-London Guidelines," 6.

previous section. As the analysis below demonstrates, a professional consensus has emerged about numerous areas of practice. However, open
questions persist on other methodological issues.

One important point to mention before delving into this assessment
is that, for certain missions, there are discrepancies between how reports
articulate the mission's approach to protection and how individual practitioners discussed their experiences in interviews conducted for this
chapter. For example, the report for the Darfur Commission expresses
that the protection of witnesses and victims was taken very seriously at
all stages during the implementation of the mission. However, an investigator who served on the mission notes many problematic issues. This
specific practitioner stated that she did not recall any specific directive
given to all of the investigators about witness protection, and investigators were not given the name of someone to contact if there was an issue of concern. Additionally, she reported that, at times, a governmental
"humanitarian aid coordinator" followed members of the mission – even
though the team was supposed to be exempt from governmental interference – during the process of conducting fieldwork. Investigators were
told to revisit interviewees after interviews to ensure that the individuals were not harmed. However, a check-up would entail, in some cases,
driving several hours to return to a certain village, and given the time
and resource constraints of the mission, such measures were not feasible.
Furthermore, investigators told interviewees that if they encountered
harassment after speaking with the mission, interviewees should contact
the United Nations refugee agency (UNHCR), though the investigators
were not always entirely certain that UNHCR would actually be helpful
if contacted.[68]

Another aspect of protection is that there is an inconsistency between
the tools and capacities available to UN versus non-UN missions. To take
but one example, the UN has its own classification system for confidential
documents,[69] a capacity that is not available to other missions. Hence,
depending on factors such as the mandating body and the entities that
provide the mission with logistical support, MRF missions' comparative
protective capacities differ from one another.

---

[68] Debbie Bodkin, Investigator, International Commission of Inquiry on Darfur, interview
conducted by HPCR, July 19, 2013.
[69] See generally United Nations Secretariat, "Secretary General's Bulletin: Information sensitivity, classification and handling," ST/SGB/2007/6, February 12, 2007, accessed May 29,
2015, https://archives.un.org/sites/archives.un.org/files/ST_SGB_2007_6_eng.pdf.

Having underlined these inconsistencies, the rest of this section will examine the main elements of witness protection. The section examines, first, measures adopted before deployment; second, measures adopted during the interview process; third, the issue of data management; and fourth, measures geared toward protecting interviewees after interviews have concluded.

1. Before the Mission Is Deployed

Two of the most important pre-deployment measures that can be taken are designing mission-specific guidance and conducting staff trainings. Some missions do develop mission-specific guidance: as one practitioner states, "If the mandate is given by the Human Rights Council, the mission will be organized by OHCHR, which will ensure that the Terms of Reference of the mission take protection into consideration."[70] A good example of a mission that integrated protection considerations into the mission's investigation design is the DRC Mapping Exercise, which in the report states:

> A document outlining the methodology to be followed by the Mapping Team was drafted on the basis of United Nations-developed tools, in particular those of OHCHR. These methodological tools covered the following areas in particular: a gravity threshold for the selection of serious violations, standard of evidence required, identity of perpetrators and groups, confidentiality, witness protection, witness interviewing guidelines with a standardised *fiche d'entretien*, and physical evidence guidelines (including mass graves), among others.[71]

The *Siracusa Guidelines* also recommend the adoption of an "[o]perational [p]lan [that] should take account of other internal protocols of the fact-finding body, such as for witness protection, safety and security, employment procedures, the release of evidence and investigation plans."[72]

Training is another key aspect of implementing mission-specific protection methodologies. One practitioner stated that on his mission, investigators received "a very basic training," covering topics such as securing documents and taking care not to use interviewees' actual names in internal reports.[73] Another practitioner highlights that the purpose of training is primarily to build on practitioners' already existing expertise:

> The staff hired by the CoI [commission of inquiry] already had significant human rights investigative training and experience. Otherwise they

---

[70] Luc Côté, HPCR interview.   [71] DRC Mapping Exercise report, 37.
[72] Bassiouni and Abraham, *Siracusa Guidelines*, 40.   [73] Luc Côté, HPCR interview.

wouldn't have been hired. The OHCHR has a well-established methodology and the chief as well as the CoI coordinator will have ensured that the training provided was in this vein and supplemented the existent knowledge.[74]

One challenge for implementing mission-specific trainings is logistics. Since staff members often arrive on the mission at different times, it is difficult to train everyone at once.[75] Furthermore, though certain missions have successfully built on existing guidelines to develop and implement mission-specific methodologies regarding protection, the question remains as to how practitioners can pass this knowledge along to benefit future missions. One practitioner states:

> Most Commissions are a one-off, meaning when the mandate ends, the bulk of the staff go home. Later, another mandate comes up and a new Commission is formed with new people. OHCHR provides the institutional memory it can, and that knowledge is increasing as more commissions of inquiry operate. Lessons learned and Best Practices exercises are conducted as a matter of course at the end of every mandate.[76]

2.   During the Interviewing Process

A variety of measures have been adopted to protect witnesses and victims during investigations. As this section demonstrates, for some issues, consensus exists in terms of best practices. For other areas, different approaches have been adopted.

(a) **Selecting Interviewees**   MRF practitioners widely agree that, when selecting interviewees, care should be taken to avoid interviewing individuals who are at risk for retraumatization. As one MRF actor notes, interviewing a victim who has already been interviewed by

---

[74] Confidential interview with a high-level MRF practitioner, name of interviewee on file, conducted by HPCR, Summer 2013.

[75] One practitioner states, "The logistics of training are very difficult, and that cannot be underestimated in any way. You have different people coming in at different times. For commissions, most don't last that long. Training has been less successful because the whole system is not set up to let people be trained as a group. The recruitment system is bureaucratic. People come in when the paperwork is finished. They come in at different times. A military expert can't give a briefing and training because he needs to go to the field and people are arriving at different times." Sareta Ashraph, HPCR interview.

[76] Vic Ullom, Legal Adviser, International Commission of Inquiry on Libya, interview conducted by HPCR, August 8, 2013.

another organization "increases the risk for re-traumatization of the victim, therefore particular caution is needed."[77]

MRF missions typically consult with NGOs on the ground to develop methodologies for selecting and approaching interviewees, as well as for conducting interviews. For example, according to the report of the Guinea Commission:

> The members of the Commission met with representatives of Forces vives [a movement that includes opposition political parties in Guinea] and of non-governmental organizations (NGOs) working in the field of human rights in order to introduce themselves and to agree on a working method that would ensure that interviews could be conducted without endangering witnesses, victims or their families. They also met with staff of the United Nations specialized agencies with offices in Guinea.[78]

Several missions have avoided conducting interviews with individuals already interviewed by other agencies, or returning to re-interview the same witness a second or third time, for the same reason. Additionally, MRF missions have frequently chosen not to interview specific categories of people that were deemed particularly vulnerable. For example, the report for the Gaza Fact-Finding Mission states, "The Mission decided not to interview children."[79] Several guidelines and best practice documents – for example, the "Lund-London Guidelines" and the SCSL "Best-Practice Recommendations" – recommend exercising caution in this regard.[80]

(b) The Context of the Interview   Several practitioners interviewed for this chapter discussed the method of approaching an interviewee. One key concern is that practitioners should use discretion when approaching interviewees. The danger is that a big white car, for example, can attract

---

[77] Théo Boutruche, IHL/Human Rights Expert, Independent International Fact-Finding Mission on the Conflict in Georgia, interview conducted by HPCR, October 17, 2011.

[78] Guinea Commission report, 7 (internal citation omitted).

[79] Gaza Fact-Finding Mission report, 42.

[80] See "Lund-London Guidelines," 5–6, which states, "The delegation is under no obligation to advise the government of the people it intends to meet. If the government or any other party finds out this information and there are concerns as to the safety of an interviewee, then the NGO may wish to cancel the interview or to abandon the mission and should seek a guarantee from the government that the interviewee or prospective interviewee will not be persecuted, victimised or otherwise put in a worse position for having been willing to cooperate with the delegation. The same principle applies if the interviewee is threatened as a result of identification by other people." See also Special Court for Sierra Leone, "Best-Practice Recommendations," 20.

attention and give away that witnesses are actually going to meet with the UN, potentially exposing these individuals to risks of retaliation. A Human Rights Watch policy piece stresses the importance of being mindful of the types of vehicles that interviewers use:

> At the investigation stage, consideration needs to be given to ensuring that in conducting interviews and transporting people to trials, witnesses' identities are not inadvertently divulged. For instance, if investigators travel to interview witnesses in clearly marked vehicles, the entire village then knows which individuals have spoken to investigators. If witnesses who agree to provide testimony are then picked up in the same type of vehicles, and flown to testify in clearly marked aircraft, their identities have in effect been revealed.[81]

As one practitioner states, one option is to move interviewees to a different location:

> To protect people, it's a question of technique, of how you approach them. Make sure you are in a safe place for them when you take the statement. The best way to do it is to move them. So what we did most often was we managed to arrange for them to meet us in another community. It could be in another village or another city. Then, when you meet witnesses, you are certain you are not compromising security because no one sees it.[82]

In the same vein, the report of the Guinea Commission mentions:

> In light of the statement by the President of the Republic of Guinea that he could not control all members of the military, who are the alleged perpetrators of the human rights violations, and in order to better protect witnesses, the victims and their families, the Commission decided to minimize individual contact with these persons by not interviewing them at their homes or places of work.[83]

To facilitate such discretion, on one mission, investigators were given money to pay for witnesses to move from one location to another and for investigators to rent anonymous cars.[84] Such measures are particularly important for victims of sexual or gender-based violence. According to one practitioner:

---

[81] "Recommendations for an Effective Special Court for Sierra Leone," letter from Richard Dicker to legal advisers of UN Security Council member states and interested states, Human Rights Watch, March 8, 2002, accessed January 17, 2014, http://www.hrw.org/news/2002/03/07/recommendations-effective-special-court-sierra-leone.
[82] Luc Côté, HPCR interview.   [83] Guinea Commission report, 7.
[84] Luc Côté, HPCR interview.

I can't advertise that I'm looking for victims of rape. The basic lesson here is that if people know you are the SGBV [sexual and gender-based violence] specialist or that you are looking for rape victims, everyone will know what happened to the people who talk to you, further exposing the victim to public marginalization and stigma.[85]

Practitioners agree on the importance of, as the report of the International Commission of Inquiry on Libya (hereafter the Libya Commission) states, "tak[ing] all reasonable measures to meet victims, witnesses and others in confidential settings, to prevent such persons suffering any harm or reprisals."[86] This aspect is captured by the *Siracusa Guidelines*,[87] reflecting that this notion is widespread among practitioners. One practitioner specifically stresses the importance of interviewing prisoners and refugees in confidential settings, stating also that MRF practitioners should endeavor to interview newcomers in refugee camps "before they come under the sway of local camp leaders."[88] However, practitioners also recognize that privacy is not always possible:

Sometimes it is impossible to do an interview alone. One of the most difficult things is finding a quiet private place to interview people, especially in a camp. It's possible, but it takes some planning and work; it may mean kicking people out of a tent or room, it may mean many interruptions by children, family, neighbors, when you do have that privacy.[89]

Privacy concerns also arise in light of evolving perspectives about various "new technology" communication platforms that practitioners have

[85] Erin Gallagher, HPCR interview.
[86] Office of the High Commissioner for Human Rights, "Oral Update by the International Commission of Inquiry on Libya to the Human Rights Council," September 19, 2011, p. 10, accessed May 29, 2015, http://www2.ohchr.org/english/bodies/hrcouncil/docs/18session/LibyaOralStatemenHRC18.pdf.
[87] See Bassiouni and Abraham, *Siracusa Guidelines*, 46, which states, "The fact-finding body should take measures to protect the confidentiality and safety of all involved in the interview, including with respect to selecting the location of the interviews."
[88] See Robertson, "Human Rights Fact-Finding," 10, which also states, "Ideally, prisoners and refugees and all persons who may be subject to pressure from custodians or others should be interviewed alone. This is a counsel of perfection, because investigators will often need a translator present and the choice may be problematic, especially if there is no choice and the translator is officially imposed. Interviewing prisoners alone does insulate their testimony from influence, although it is important to remember that some victims – especially of sexual crime – are inhibited by the subject matter and do need support before they can bring themselves to speak freely. Many traumatised victims of rape or torture simply will not divulge their excruciating experience to a stranger. In these circumstances, there can be no hard and fast rules about interviewing witnesses without anyone else present: a friend or counsellor may be a necessary companion."
[89] Erin Gallagher, HPCR interview.

integrated into MRF processes. As one practitioner states: "We used Sky-pe and had been told by our IT colleagues that it was secure until the Snowden affair. We no longer think it's secure."[90]

As the experiences of these missions indicate, the issue of discretion when meeting and speaking with interviewees constitutes an area for which a divide exists between notions of what *should* be done and the realities of what *can* be done. A private and confidential setting is ideal, though not always feasible, leaving open the question of how, in an actual on-the-ground investigation, practitioners should gauge the level of privacy that sufficiently balances the mission's investigative needs with the mission's responsibility to "do no harm" to the witnesses and victims that the mission encounters.

(c) The Conduct of the Interview During interviews, one key risk, as mentioned earlier, is retraumatization. For practitioners with extensive backgrounds dealing with victims of trauma, the appropriate conduct for interviewers to avoid retraumatization is clear. One practitioner states:

> I think if I saw it happen, I would end the interview. I did have a situation with another investigator where we met a 13-year-old girl in the hospital. This girl had just been told two days earlier that her mother had died. We didn't have a need or desire to have her retell her story or go into any of it with her. We chatted with her, we talked a little bit, but not about the shelling, it was an easy decision for both of us, it was just not appropriate.[91]

In other instances, MRF practitioners have evidently had a less extensive professional background in dealing with trauma victims. As one commissioner states:

> [Interviewees] wanted to tell their stories. They had been traumatized. Some were actually still shaking, some men actually cried. So we would say that some of the things they were saying were not relevant to the facts we needed. But there was another purpose that was being served. There was a process that was therapeutic for the individual. You need to find the space and let the victim tell their story. The commissioners had to realize this is not a courtroom.[92]

---

[90] Vic Ullom, HPCR interview.   [91] Erin Gallagher, HPCR interview.
[92] Mary Shanthi Dairiam, Commissioner, International Fact-Finding Mission to investigate violations of international law, including international humanitarian and human rights law, resulting from the Israeli attacks on the flotilla of ships carrying humanitarian assistance, interview conducted by HPCR, April 3, 2013.

This issue has been a recurrent dilemma over the past couple of decades of MRF practice. For example, a practitioner who served on the Commission of Experts on the former Yugoslavia, mandated by the United Nations Security Council in 1993, recounts that some interviewers on that mission did not realize that "[y]ou have to listen to what's important to the person before you ask what's important to the prosecution. You must show them that you care about them."[93] However, given the realities of the ad hoc state of MRF practice – in particular, the challenges of quickly assembling a skilled team – sometimes a learning curve for a practitioner during a mission is unavoidable.

Another element of the relationship between an MRF mission and interviewees is informed consent. Standard MRF practice is that investigators have a responsibility to ensure that interviewees understand how their statements will be used, and that interviewees, based on this understanding, provide consent for this use. However, there are certain complexities that arise during the practical application of informed consent.

First, in some cases, there have actually been unintended ambiguities in the consent options offered. One practitioner recounts:

> We had a simple, straightforward consent menu that proved to be insufficient when the ICC formally requested the materials. When we covered the consent options with our interviewees, one specific question we asked was whether they would permit us to share the information with the ICC. We didn't specify, either to the interviewee or in our record of the conversation, if that consent included the ability to give both to the prosecution and the defence. When the defence later requested the information we didn't know if we could give it. We had a sense that the interviewee was hoping it would be used for prosecution, to achieve "justice." We were concerned that we would be misusing their consent. We have since amended our consent options.[94]

Second, it is often not clear whether or not interviewees actually understand the measures to which they are consenting. Some missions have developed a method for dealing with such scenarios. A practitioner mentions the forms used for informed consent, "There's a box where the investigator will write: 'I do not believe this person understood what they were consenting to.'"[95] However, it appears that these determinations are not always clear-cut. "We have had many discussions about how much

---

[93] Confidential interview with a high-level MRF practitioner, name of interviewee on file, conducted by HPCR, Spring 2013.
[94] Vic Ullom, HPCR interview.   [95] Sareta Ashraph, HPCR interview.

information you have to give the interviewee so that they're giving real informed consent," states one practitioner.[96] As these statements show, even when these risks have been foreseen and systems have been put in place, an important part of the decision-making process is left to the investigators on the ground and their team.

3. Data Management

(a) **Retaining the Anonymity of Interviewees, if Necessary for Protection**   An important element of protecting interviewees from threats of retaliation is retaining the anonymous character of interviewees' contributions to the final report. MRF missions have adopted different approaches in this regard. Some missions have used numbers, instead of names, to identify interviewees in internal and external reports. For example, in the DRC Mapping Exercise report, one can deduce from the manner that the report references witness accounts – for example: "See the witness statements of W132, W249 and W287" – that the team recorded accounts by assigning a number to each witness.[97] The Gaza Fact-Finding Mission also refers to codes in lieu of witness names in its report and mentions various protective measures taken during its implementation:

> Also in keeping with normal practice for this type of report and to continue to protect their safety and privacy, the names of the victims, witnesses and other sources are generally not explicitly referred to in the report and codes are used instead. The names of individuals who publicly testified at the hearings held by the Mission or who have explicitly agreed to be named (see below) are, however, identified.[98]

Due to the publication of certain names in the report, the Gaza Fact-Finding Mission also recommended to the government of Israel that:

> [T]he Government of Israel should refrain from any action of reprisal against Palestinian and Israeli individuals and organizations that have cooperated with the United Nations Fact-Finding Mission on the Gaza Conflict, in particular individuals who have appeared at the Public Hearings held by the Mission in Gaza and Geneva and expressed criticism of actions by Israel.[99]

---

[96] Vic Ullom, HPCR interview.
[97] DRC Mapping Exercise report, 321. The fact that the number is the sole reference also suggests that there was only one list of witnesses, even if the investigators were split into several groups.
[98] Gaza Fact-Finding Mission report, 42. For witness numbers used in the report, see, e.g., Gaza Fact-Finding Mission report, 338.
[99] Ibid., 426.

The Sri Lanka Panel adopted the policy of not naming witnesses (not even referring to a number in the final report). When providing specific evidence – for example, a photograph of a massacre of children who were IDPs – the report mentions: "Source: Submission to the Panel by the photographer."[100] The Bahrain Commission used names in the final report but only for individuals who were deceased or who were already publicly known.[101]

The Libya Commission report withholds the identities of alleged perpetrators, in part, due to concerns about the protection of interviewees: "In most cases, the Commission has withheld the names of individuals believed to hold responsibility for violations. This is partly to prevent reprisals and partly to avoid prejudicing future fair trials."[102] The Darfur Commission took a similar step, stating precisely that withholding the names not only of the witnesses but also of the alleged perpetrators can contribute to interviewee protection:

> The decision to keep confidential the names of the persons who may be suspected to be responsible for international crimes in Darfur is based on three main grounds …. The third ground for confidentiality is the need to protect witnesses heard by the Commission (as well as prospective witnesses). In many instances it would not be difficult for those who may be suspected of bearing responsibility to identify witnesses who have spoken to the Commission, and intimidate, harass or even kill those witnesses. It is for this reason that not only the name of the possible perpetrator will be withheld, but also the list of witnesses questioned by the Commission, as well as other reliable sources of probative material. These will be included in the sealed file, which, as stated above, shall only be handed over to the Prosecutor.[103]

There is also a professional consensus that missions should not mention the interview location – or any other specific details – that might allow the interviewee to be identified. However, it is evidently not always clear which facts are necessary to omit. "There were debates that you shouldn't disclose which detention center it is because that might allow the interviewees to be identified," states one practitioner.[104]

(b) **Data Protection** Practitioners have deemed data protection to be a crucial issue, both for the safety of the witnesses and for members of the

---

[100] Sri Lanka Panel report, 27.   [101] Christina Abraham, HPCR interview.

[102] See, for example, "Report of the International Commission of Inquiry on Libya," A/HRC/19/68, March 2, 2012, p. 6, accessed May 25, 2015, http://www.nytimes.com/interactive/2012/03/03/world/africa/united-nations-report-on-libya.html?_r=0.

[103] Darfur Commission report, 133–134.   [104] Ibid.

mission. Data protection measures include storing data in a secure location; using a safe for all records, notes, and pieces of evidence; favoring the use of electronic data over paper; using only specific types of computers (not connected online or with encryption systems); destroying paper copies of interview notes – when no longer needed, after being uploaded to a computer, for example – on a daily basis; and defining and tracking who has access to what type of data. One practitioner describes the very careful and sophisticated process used in order to protect data on a particular mission:

> The mission created this method where every night they went back to the hotel where they had encrypted UN computers with a link back to headquarters. The hard drive itself was encrypted. If you break it, it erases all the data. Every night they would type up notes – some days it would be 10–15 interviews – then hit synch and it synchs with a computer in Geneva, then they would erase it off the computer. They were very cognizant of keeping the witnesses as safe as they possibly could.[105]

Similarly, the report for the Bahrain Commission specifies how the mission prudently handled the data received:

> The database was located in a secure facility outside Bahrain …. During the course of the investigation, the Commission created an extensive archive of records and materials. All of these records and materials were catalogued and stored in secure safes. In addition, the records were recorded electronically and stored digitally on a highly secured server outside Bahrain.[106]

Other mission reports specifically refer to the importance of keeping to strict standards regarding data protection. The Libya Commission report states, "The Commission's records, including records of interviews, have been maintained and will be handed over to OHCHR at the end of its functioning, in accordance with established rules and procedures."[107] The Sri Lanka Panel report refers to the *Secretary-General's Bulletin on Information sensitivity, classification and handling*,[108] and confirms that "nearly

---

[105] Confidential interview with a high-level MRF practitioner, name of interviewee on file, conducted by HPCR, Summer 2013.

[106] Bahrain Commission report, 8–10.

[107] "Report of the International Commission of Inquiry to investigate all alleged violations of international human rights law in the Libyan Arab Jamahiriya," A/HRC/17/44, June 1, 2011, p. 16, accessed May 26, 2015, http://www2.ohchr.org/english/bodies/hrcouncil/docs/17session/A.HRC.17.44_AUV.pdf.

[108] See generally United Nations Secretariat, "Information sensitivity, classification and handling."

all of the Panel's substantive records will be classified as 'strictly confidential' with, in some cases, additional protections regarding future use."[109]
The DRC Mapping Exercise report specifies:

> Sensitive information gathered during the mapping exercise should be
> stored and utilized according to the strictest standards of confidentiality.
> The team should develop a database for the purposes of the mapping ex-
> ercise, access to which should be determined by the High Commissioner
> for Human Rights.[110]

(c) Storage and Use of Data after the Mission Ends   Plans for handling
data after an MRF mission's conclusion are also crucial, especially in light
of the aforementioned fact that risks of retaliation can endure long after
an investigation has ended. Many MRF reports articulate specific procedures in this regard. For example, the DRC Mapping Exercise report
states: "Phase three (15 May 2009 to 15 June 2009) saw the closing down
of the Mapping Exercise with the compilation of data, final updating of
the database, the organization, digitization and classification of all the ar-
chives and the drafting of the final version of the report."[111] The Bahrain
Commission, due to demands from the public – which expressed concerns that statements made to the mission might be used against them
someday by the government – burned all the physical evidence after the
mission had concluded.[112] The mission's report also states of the mission's
database:

> [T]he Commission will preserve its database and electronic copies of these
> records, which will be preserved electronically on a secured hard drive
> outside Bahrain. The hard drive will be stored in a locked case in a secured
> facility and will not be accessible wirelessly. The hard drive will be pre-
> served for a period of ten years, after which time it will be destroyed. The
> records stored on the server will be permanently erased.[113]

However, in other cases, the mission report mentions that internal documents will be made available to certain members of the public. For
example, the Guinea Commission report states of pieces of information
gathered by the mission: "public access to them may be granted, subject
to authorization by the Secretary-General of the United Nations and
while respecting the principles of confidentiality."[114] Such an approach

---

[109] Sri Lanka Panel report, 6.   [110] DRC Mapping Exercise report, 544.
[111] Ibid., 42.   [112] Christina Abraham, HPCR interview.
[113] Bahrain Commission report, 10 (internal citation omitted).
[114] Guinea Commission report, 9.

has direct implications for the issue of informed consent, due to the fact that this option, though the report articulates specifically who authorizes public access, leaves ambiguous which types of actors will be able to view the mission's documents. Additionally, though many missions, as noted above, have approached data handling with a great deal of caution, interviews with practitioners have revealed that many investigators retained their interview notes from on-the-ground operations.[115]

4. After Interviews

There is a widespread perception that, when possible, protection should continue even after an investigation has concluded. For investigative efforts carried out by enduring organizations, such as NGOs, these measures are possible. The "Lund-London Guidelines" state of NGO fact-finding:

> The safety of those interviewed or engaged by a fact-finding delegation should continue to be monitored by the NGO, particularly where safety concerns were already present. Any post-mission threats or hostile acts should be acted upon immediately by the NGO including, where necessary, notifying the government, assisting with protective measures and alerting the wider international community.[116]

Even in the context of ad hoc, temporary missions, follow-up measures have sometimes been put into place. As noted by the OHCHR Mission Planning and Start-Up Unit, this was the case after the conclusion of the Guinea Commission:

> OHCHR has developed operational guidelines based on experience and lessons learned which include overarching guiding principles and concrete measures and options to integrate protection considerations into the entire cycle of a commission/mission's life. Witness protection was, for example, a paramount concern that guided OHCHR actions in assisting the commission to carry out its mandate in Guinea and led to numerous precautionary steps being taken. Following the completion of the field mission, OHCHR established a post-mission protection presence in Conakry for three months to provide support and advice to persons facing threats to safety and prevent reprisals against them. A similar practice had been followed by the Darfur [Commission]. However, this practice cannot be implemented for all COI due to financial constraints.[117]

---

[115] Confidential interviews with high-level MRF practitioners, names of interviewees on file, conducted by HPCR, 2011–2014.

[116] "Lund-London Guidelines," 9.

[117] Sonia Bakar, *"On Commission of Inquiry (CoI) and Fact-Finding Missions (FFM),"* UiO/ Norwegian Centre for Human Rights, November 1, 2012, accessed January 17, 2014, http://www.jus.uio.no/smr/english/research/areas/conflict/events/conferences/fact-finding/bakar.html.

Following up generally tends to be a highly problematic area. Sometimes even courts and tribunals have great difficulties. An internal ICTY audit in 2008 found the ICTY to be insufficient in this area:

> VWS [Victims and Witnesses Section] does not ensure systematic follow up of witnesses, through phone calls, direct contact or other modes, once they have returned to the region. The attendant risk is that satisfaction levels among witnesses are likely to be low during the post testimony phase.[118]

For ad hoc missions, despite the experience of the Guinea Commission, follow-up measures are more commonly perceived by practitioners to be unfeasible, and in many contexts, entirely nonexistent. "Zero" protective measures were able to be undertaken after the release of the DRC Mapping Exercise report, for example.[119] The following statement articulates a widely held view:

> For commissions, protection of people is preventative because there is no real follow-up. Because commissions cease to exist, there's no body that necessarily would follow-up, certainly compared to tribunals .... Once interviewees leave us, it is very rare that we would know what would happen to them.[120]

Regardless, some protective measures have been adopted or suggested by mission reports and practitioners that aim to look after the needs of interviewees after interviews conclude. The rest of this section provides an overview of these avenues.

(a) **Referrals** A widespread notion is that practitioners should, when possible, endeavor to refer interviewees with particular humanitarian or medical needs to organizations that can offer assistance. As the "Lund-London Guidelines" state:

> Members of the delegation should be alert to the humanitarian needs of interviewees and, wherever possible, should ensure that interviewees are referred to appropriate humanitarian or other organisations, which might be able to meet those needs.[121]

---

[118] See "The Victims and Witnesses Section of ICTY: Gaps in psychological support and counseling and post testimony follow up should be addressed to ensure the effectiveness of support provided to witnesses," Audit Report, Internal Audit Division, Office of Internal Oversight Services, December 26, 2008, ¶ 15, accessed January 17, 2014, http://usun.state.gov/documents/organization/139317.pdf, which also references a study conducted by Eric Stover that found that witnesses had experienced a "sense of abandonment." Eric Stover's report was published in book form. See generally Eric Stover, *The Witnesses: War Crimes and the Promise of Justice in The Hague* (Philadelphia: University of Pennsylvania Press, 2005).

[119] Luc Côté, HPCR interview.   [120] Sareta Ashraph, HPCR interview.

[121] "Lund-London Guidelines," 6.

In practice, it appears from interviews conducted with practitioners as part of the research for this chapter, that although most of the missions studied did not use mental health professionals – and providing mental health services does not fall within the typical MRF mission's mandate – many actors believe MRF missions should establish referral systems that can put victims and witnesses in touch with mental health professionals, if necessary.[122] One commissioner on the Guinea Commission became involved in ensuring medical access to individuals who were dying and also assisted certain pregnant women in obtaining access to abortion services.[123]

Referrals are especially crucial for victims of sexual violence. The World Health Organization (WHO) manual, "WHO ethical and safety recommendations for researching, documenting and monitoring sexual violence in emergencies," forcefully emphasizes the importance of referring victims of sexual violence to the appropriate services:

> For these reasons, it is an ethical imperative that when conducting data collection activities that involve interviewing individuals about sexual violence, at least basic care and support services to which survivors may be referred are available.[124]

The drive to offer referrals arises in part from the tension between, on the one hand, the ad hoc nature of MRF missions, and, on the other hand, the sense that investigators hold a long-term protective responsibility for the welfare of witnesses and victims encountered by the mission. The missions, in their limited capacities, cannot themselves assume responsibility for the long-term care of witnesses and victims – indeed such activities would fall well beyond their typical mandate – but practitioners can refer these individuals to other organizations that are in a position to offer assistance.

In some instances, though, the aspiration to attend to the welfare of the mission's interviewees has pushed practitioners to engage in more of an activist capacity. For example, both the Libya Commission and the Bahrain Commission engaged in securing the release of detainees who were wrongfully detained.[125] One rationale for such actions is the strong

---

[122] Confidential interviews with high-level MRF practitioners, names of interviewees on file, conducted by HPCR, Spring 2013.

[123] Pramila Patten, Commissioner, International Commission of Inquiry for Guinea, interview conducted by HPCR, April 26, 2013.

[124] World Health Organization, "WHO ethical and safety recommendations for researching, documenting and monitoring sexual violence in emergencies," 2007, p. 15, accessed May 29, 2015, http://www.who.int/gender/documents/OMS_Ethics&Safety10Aug07.pdf.

[125] For Libya, see first Libya Commission report, 17. For Bahrain, see Bahrain Commission report, 10–11.

normative pull toward correcting human rights violations, an aim congruent with that of the mission itself. As one practitioner on the Libya Commission states:

> Was it anticipated in the mandate? No, but it wasn't inconsistent with it. I am normally very strict in textual interpretation. But in a situation like that, when you're in the field, you face unexpected circumstances. If you are in a situation where you see prisoners who are in very difficult circumstances as a direct result of human rights violations which are the core of your mandate, and you have a chance to have them released, will you not do it?[126]

A second rationale – relevant to both the Bahrain Commission and the Libya Commission – is that the mission encountered no pushback from governments or other actors while engaging in such activities.[127] In the case of the Bahrain Commission, the commission discussed the release of detainees with the king of Bahrain – who had mandated the commission – and found the king to be cooperative in this regard.[128] Similarly, the Libya Commission detailed the mission's activities relevant to detainees in the mission's first report and heard no negative comments about these actions in the subsequent debates of the United Nations Human Rights Council.[129]

A third rationale emphasizes the overall role that a mission plays in the local context. As the chair of the Bahrain Commission states:

> Here I would draw a distinction between Bahrain and Libya. A UN mission has to be fact-finding and has to be based on the mandate. You can't really be a do-gooder. So I would say that in a UN context, the line is much clearer than it is in a national commission when you know that the ultimate purpose is reconciliation. If you look at the Bahrain events and the Bahrain mandate, the whole purpose was to pave the way for national reconciliation. If that's the case, then if you can minimize the harm in the course of the process then you're advancing the overall goal of reconciliation.[130]

---

[126] Philippe Kirsch, Commissioner, Bahrain Independent Commission of Inquiry, and Chair, International Commission of Inquiry on Libya (October 2011–March 2012), interview conducted by HPCR, July 23, 2013.

[127] Ibid.

[128] Confidential interview with a high-level MRF practitioner, name of interviewee on file, conducted by HPCR, Spring 2013.

[129] Philippe Kirsch, HPCR interview.

[130] M. Cherif Bassiouni, Chair, Bahrain Independent Commission of Inquiry, and Chair, International Commission of Inquiry on Libya (March–October 2011), interview conducted by HPCR, May 3, 2013.

(b) Coordinating Follow-up Measures with Other Organizations   Some practitioners have endeavored to coordinate follow-up measures with other entities, such as UN agencies, that are also engaged in the local context. However, practitioners sometimes do not actually have much confidence in these measures. As noted earlier, investigators for the Darfur Commission referred interviewees to UNHCR in the event that incidents of harassment occurred, but it was not always clear to these practitioners that UNHCR would actually be able to provide assistance. In some cases, practitioners provided their own personal contact details to witnesses so that these individuals could contact the investigator if problems arose. However, this appeared to be more of an individual practice undertaken by certain practitioners, rather than a mission-wide policy.

(c) Seeking Asylum for Interviewees   The notion has been articulated that, in some cases, it might be appropriate for a mission to seek asylum status for certain interviewees. The Guinea Commission report references this avenue:

> The Commission, whose report is the fruit of an exhaustive search for the truth with the help of these witnesses, recommends that the African Union, ECOWAS [Economic Community of West African States], the European Union and all those States that are in a position to do so, take steps to remind the Government of Guinea of its obligations to protect victims and witnesses and to provide refuge in accordance with the provisions of international law governing asylum to all victims or witnesses who may be in danger.[131]

In the same vein, a practitioner on a different mission mentioned that this option is one that practitioners might consider in the future:

> In some cases people wanted assurances in terms of asylum status. It arose as a question but in the end we never formally dealt with it. In principle, I think it's conceivable that a panel could write a letter to the authorities stating that this person has played a role in a particular investigation. I do not believe such an action is entirely inappropriate.[132]

(d) Diplomatic Communications   MRF missions may also use diplomatic communications to address protection concerns that arise. The Gaza Fact-Finding Mission pursued this option after the Israeli security

---

[131] Guinea Commission report, 59.
[132] Confidential interview with a high-level MRF practitioner, name of interviewee on file, conducted by HPCR, Summer 2013.

forces detained an individual who had participated in the mission's public hearings. The report mentions the measures that the mission undertook to follow up on this incident:

> Subsequent to the public hearings in Geneva, the Mission was informed that a Palestinian participant, Mr. Muhammad Srour, had been detained by Israeli security forces when returning to the West Bank and became concerned that his detention may have been a consequence of his appearance before the Mission. The Mission wrote to the Permanent Representative of Israel in Geneva expressing its concern. In response, the Permanent Representative informed the Mission that the detention of the person concerned was unrelated to his appearance at the public hearing. Mr. Srour was subsequently released on bail. The Mission is in contact with him and continues to monitor developments.[133]

(e) Recommendations in Reports   Many missions, in their public reports, have recommended that various actors take certain protective measures after the conclusion of the mission. In a certain way, this measure is conceptually similar to pursuing referrals. MRF missions, as temporary mechanisms, by nature cannot meet the long-term protection needs of witnesses and victims. However, MRF practitioners can call on other entities to assume this role. The quotes below offer a sampling of report recommendations addressing protection:

- "[The Commission] further recommends a number of serious measures to be taken by the Government of the Sudan, in particular ... ensuring the protection of all the victims and witnesses of human rights violations." (Darfur Commission)[134]
- "The Commission recommends that special measures be taken to ensure the dignity and avoid the retraumatization of victims in any judicial or non-judicial processes." (United Nations Independent Special Commission of Inquiry for Timor-Leste [hereafter the Timor-Leste Commission])[135]
- "The Commission believes that the Government of Guinea has a very good opportunity to demonstrate to the international community its desire to break with a recent past that has been ugly and painful for the people of Guinea as a whole, by firmly committing to fulfil its obligations in this area and not to harm in any way whatsoever the victims

---

[133] Gaza Fact-Finding Mission report, 40.   [134] Darfur Commission report, 6.
[135] "Report of the United Nations Independent Special Commission of Inquiry for Timor-Leste," October 2006, p. 79, accessed June 25, 2015, http://www.ohchr.org/Documents/Countries/COITimorLeste.pdf.

and witnesses who have cooperated with the Commission." (Guinea Commission)[136]

II. Protection of Staff

The threats to, and the protection of, staff members of MRF missions are of a somewhat different nature than those for witnesses and victims. While the threats are similar – for example, threats to the physical security of staff and the risk that staff members, while engaged in on-the-ground operations, will suffer from secondary trauma – the nature of the protective responsibility is distinct. Whereas protection of witnesses and victims relates to the relationship of a mission to the individuals with whom the mission engages, protection of staff relates to the responsibility that the mission has to the security of its own members. As with the protection of witnesses and victims, several challenges in this area arise from the ad hoc nature, and the limited resource capacity, of MRF missions. This section addresses the sources of responsibility that MRF missions have for the security of staff members, the nature of the risks, and the measures that have been, or could be, adopted to address these risks.

A.   Sources of Responsibility to Protect Staff

Similar to the protection of witnesses and victims, for the protection of staff, the mandates of the fifteen missions studied, despite constituting the authorizing documents for these missions, often make no mention of the issue or simply address the topic with passing references. Mandates for only four of the fifteen missions analyzed in this Handbook – the DRC Mapping Exercise, the Kyrgyzstan Inquiry Commission (hereafter the Kyrgyzstan Commission), the Timor-Leste Commission, and the Secretary-General's Panel of Inquiry on the 31 May 2010 Flotilla Incident (hereafter the UNSG Flotilla Panel) – refer to the protection of staff. As this finding suggests – and as is the case with the protection of witnesses and victims – given that authorizing documents make only sparse mention of staff security, the responsibility for undertaking security measures evidently arises from other sources. Unlike the protection of witnesses and victims, however, international law does not constitute a component of the architecture of these notions. As one expert states:

---

[136] Guinea Commission report, 59.

An organisation which sends fact-finders on a mission to a dangerous country will always bear responsibility for their safety and well-being. International law offers no special protection to a member of a fact-finding mission over and above that which the member is entitled by virtue of his or her status as a civilian.[137]

Protective measures for staff evidently depend on the extent to which the deploying organization perceives a duty of care and also on organizational capacities. For this issue, as well, there appears to be a discrepancy between UN and non-UN missions. UN personnel usually enjoy insurance, as well as the security advice of a specialized agency – the United Nations Department of Safety and Security – and personnel are covered by the Convention on the Safety of United Nations and Associated Personnel, adopted in 1994 by the General Assembly.[138] Additionally, UN special rapporteurs enjoy immunity against prosecution, which was confirmed by the International Court of Justice in the *Cumaraswamy* case.[139]

Practitioners can, when possible, rely on other UN agencies. Regarding the DRC Mapping Exercise, the Terms of Reference foresee a specific role for the UN peacekeeping mission in the protection of the team's members:

> MONUC [United Nations Organization Mission in the Democratic Republic of the Congo], in consultation with the OHCHR Field Safety and Security Unit, should ensure appropriate security arrangements for members of the Mapping Team. The members of the Mapping Team should be housed in secure premises. Secure office space should therefore be identified and allocated by MONUC for the duration of the mission, both in Kinshasa and in relevant field locations.[140]

Some MRF mandates have stated, in addition to the passages regarding security mentioned above, that the members of the missions should be accorded the privileges and immunities articulated in the Convention on the Privileges and Immunities of the United Nations.[141] Of the fifteen

---

[137] Robertson, "Human Rights Fact-Finding," 19.

[138] See generally "Convention on the Safety of United Nations and Associated Personnel," Office of Legal Affairs Codification Division, n.d., accessed January 17, 2014, http://www.un.org/law/cod/safety.htm.

[139] See generally International Court of Justice, "Difference Relating to Immunity from Legal Process of a Special Rapporteur of the Commission on Human Rights," Advisory Opinion, April 29, 1999, accessed January 17, 2014, http://www.icj-cij.org/docket/files/100/7619.pdf.

[140] DRC Mapping Exercise report, 543.

[141] For the text of the convention, see United Nations General Assembly, "Convention on the Privileges and Immunities of the United Nations," February 13, 1946, accessed January 17, 2014, http://www.un.org/en/ethics/pdf/convention.pdf.

missions examined in this Handbook, mandates, Terms of Reference, and operating procedures for six missions – the Bahrain Commission, the DRC Mapping Exercise, the Timor-Leste Commission, the Kyrgyzstan Commission, the UNHRC Flotilla Fact-Finding Mission, and the Commission of Inquiry on Lebanon – reference this measure.

For UN missions, the implementation of an MRF mission mandate will entail incorporating the United Nations Minimum Operating Security Standards (MOSS) into the operations of the mission. According to MOSS, based on a Security Risk Assessment particular to the relevant country, personnel on UN missions should have access to or be provided with emergency communications systems; appropriate vehicles; sufficient training; and necessary security equipment, which in some contexts includes body armor, blast resistance film, and a trauma kit.[142] In addition to these specific measures, all other regulations already in place for the UN mission in that country (obligations regarding armed escorts, preparedness of an evacuation plan, etc.) will apply.

For non-UN missions, the development of a security procedure for the staff will have to be thought of from the start. Whereas the ad hoc, resource-scarce nature of MRF missions makes it difficult for MOSS to be implemented in UN-missions, such standards are almost impossible to meet for non-UN missions, generally leaving the staff with higher security risks and more dilemmas to solve on the ground.

B. Risk Mitigation Measures for Staff

Staff protection shares with witness and victim protection the dilemma that a divide exists between aspirational notions of best practice and the reality of what can be delivered. As mentioned earlier, the main risks for staff members are threats to physical security that arise due to the typically volatile contexts that practitioners investigate and secondary traumatization that might be experienced during or after the interviews. This section examines both of these issues.

1. Physical Safety

Physical security risks can arise from the fact that some local actors actually vilify certain international investigative entities. As the President of the UN Staff Union has said of the ICTY:

---

[142] See generally "Minimum Operating Security Standards (MOSS): Instructions for Implementation," 2002, accessed May 29, 2015, http://www.securitymanagementinitiative.org/index.php?option=com_docman&task=doc_details&gid=82.

This organisation is not seen by all as a humanitarian or nation-building one .... There are many people in the former Yugoslavia who actually perceive the ICTY as a punitive organisation. Those who work here are regarded as the enemy who contributed to arresting their national heroes. The tribunal has a social responsibility to protect these staff.[143]

In the same vein, a writer offers this valid observation:

Some human rights reporters are only too pleased to give evidence to international courts. But others, especially those still in the field, are horrified at the prospect of losing their perceived neutrality by appearing to endorse the prosecution .... Neutrality is vital to war correspondents and to human rights reporters working in war zones, and their own and their colleague's safety may be put at risk if they are perceived to be spies for the prosecutor of an international criminal court.[144]

The experience of the Bahrain Commission further highlights the risks that staff face due to the politically sensitive nature of MRF work. The Bahrain Commission became a political lightning rod during the mission's implementation, leading members of the opposition in the country, on one occasion, to force their way into the mission's office. As the mission's Chief Investigator recounts, "Our offices were stormed, they invaded the offices, took charge of everything. When we failed to deal with them, they started insulting us. I was spit on. My female staff had been insulted. They posted hatred messages on the wall."[145]

However, practitioners have indicated various types of constraints – for example, budgetary and institutional – that have limited certain missions' staff protection capacities. One practitioner mentioned that he worked on a mission that proceeded even though the conditions did not meet MOSS standards.[146] Non-UN missions have an even further reduced level of support. For example, on the Kyrgyzstan Commission, there was concern about the safety of investigators, especially since the commission was a non-UN mission, and in contrast to other contexts,

---

[143] Rick Cottam, quoted in Afua Hirsch, "War crime tribunals facing crisis as staff quit," *The Guardian*, November 28, 2008, accessed January 17, 2014 http://www.theguardian.com/world/2008/nov/29/war-crimes-tribunal-under-threat.

[144] Robertson, "Human Rights Fact-Finding," 14.

[145] Khaled Ahmed, Chief Investigator, Bahrain Independent Commission of Inquiry, interview conducted by HPCR, August 2, 2013.

[146] Confidential interview with a high-level MRF practitioner, name of interviewee on file, conducted by HPCR, Summer 2013.

there was no large UN presence on the ground. However, during the mission's implementation, no security dangers for members of the mission materialized.[147]

As for the protection of witnesses, it is advised that MRF practitioners behave in a discreet manner, take commonsense measures, and be aware that an MRF mission entails specific risks. One investigator interviewed for this chapter reported that a mission was seen as putting other UN agencies in danger by using that agency's premises.[148] The members of the team decided to conduct interviews elsewhere to avoid any potential controversies.[149]

Several missions reported that they had a security officer on staff, while this measure was not granted for the witnesses and victims. The use of armed escorts was also referred to by several practitioners, as was the use of armored cars.[150]

A complaint voiced by several practitioners is that the security assessment, when it occurs, is typically conducted remotely by security staff who are not always country experts, and their conclusions apply to large regions, though not necessarily to the whole country. This type of assessment is not always perceived to be realistic, or detailed enough. As a result, after a remotely conducted security assessment that advises a mission not to proceed, investigators are sometimes left with a dilemma: not conducting the investigation, at the risk of missing important pieces of information when, in reality, the security is not an obstacle, or breaking the security rules if practitioners perceive that the assessment is not actually relevant to the specific area they want to visit.[151]

In a worst-case scenario, a mission might need to pull out of the country in which the mission is operating. Though this measure was not necessary in any of the fifteen missions examined for this book, a framework of considerations that has shaped decisions made by the International Committee of the Red Cross could inform how MRF practitioners gauge whether this option is necessary on future missions:

[147] Confidential interview with a high-level MRF practitioner, name of interviewee on file, conducted by HPCR, Summer 2013.
[148] Confidential interview with a high-level MRF practitioner, name of interviewee on file, conducted by HPCR, Summer 2013.
[149] Ibid.
[150] Confidential interview with a high-level MRF practitioner, name of interviewee on file, conducted by HPCR, Summer 2013.
[151] Confidential interviews with high-level MRF practitioners, names of interviewees on file, conducted by HPCR, Fall 2013.

A certain level of risk is considered acceptable only if it is justified by the humanitarian impact of the operation. A balance must always be struck between the risk an action entails and its anticipated effect. It is important to assess the effects of operational activities in terms of quality rather than quantity, and regularly to ask the question whether the impact of a planned activity is worth the risk it involves. If the answer is "no," the operation should in principle be suspended, postponed or discontinued.[152]

2. Psychological Well-being

Psychological risks arise from the difficult working conditions of MRF processes. A 2007 UNHCR-commissioned external evaluation on UN-HCR staff security articulates many risk factors also applicable to MRF practitioners:

> Stress and staff security go hand in hand .... Even when not directly under fire, persons living and working in or near war zones suffer from "cumulative stress." Nor is stress limited to staff working in high security-risk operations. Many field staff assigned to remote and inhospitable areas suffer hardships which are near-intolerable: inadequate or overcrowded working and living environments, extreme and unhealthy climates, hostility of the local authorities and/or population, endemic violence and crime.[153]

In the context of an MRF mission, psychological strains also arise for investigators from perpetual engagement with victims and witnesses who have suffered from trauma. A practitioner states of one mission that the issue of secondary traumatization "definitely came up, we did have investigators who were traumatized or who were suffering from some kind of stress," but the mission did not have any formal support mechanism to deal with this issue.[154] This practitioner recommended as a best practice providing investigators with access to a mental health expert or resources that could be used to de-stress from the job, as well as preliminary training for investigators about how to mitigate the risks of secondary retraumatization.[155] Another recommendation that has been articulated is to "offer post-mission debriefing to members of the delegation and persons associated with the mission where necessary to deal with stress and

---

[152] Patrick Brugger, "ICRC operational security: staff safety in armed conflict and internal violence," *International Review of the Red Cross* 91, no. 874, (2009): 434–435, accessed June 27, 2015, https://www.icrc.org/eng/assets/files/other/irrc-874-brugger.pdf.

[153] United Nations Refugee Agency, "Staff Stress and Security: A Management Challenge for UNHCR," August 15, 1997, accessed January 17, 2014, http://www.unhcr.org/3ae68cf124.html.

[154] Christina Abraham, HPCR interview.   [155] Ibid.

psychosocial trauma that may be experienced after a mission."[156] Though practitioners widely recognize the importance of such measures, these crucial support mechanisms have not materialized consistently in actual practice.

One measure that could be pursued more aggressively and that would not have drastic resource implications is to emphasize to practitioners the importance of self-care. For example, a 2007 World Health Organization document on monitoring sexual violence recommends, "Given the potential for emotional or social harm to those collecting the information, as part of the training programme, team members should engage in candid and honest discussions about [self-care] and develop strategies to minimize such effects."[157]

III. Conclusion

As this chapter has demonstrated, unlike courts and tribunals, which according to their statutes are obligated to undertake certain protective measures, MRF missions rarely derive from mandates that articulate specific protective measures. The protective obligation arises from other sources, leading at times to ambiguity about the extent of the practitioners' responsibilities and inconsistencies across different missions. The extent to which MRF missions can and do protect witnesses, victims, and staff depends less on the mandate and more on the institutional locus (i.e., UN versus non-UN) and the personalities and professional experience of commissioners and other members of the mission. But despite the limitations of what *can* be done, for some issues consensus seems to have emerged about what *should* be done. Certain policy documents that have been produced – for example, the *Siracusa Guidelines* – reflect the shared aspirational vision of the growing community of practice for MRF practitioners. Such documents, as well as the interviews with practitioners conducted for this chapter, suggest areas of consensus, as presented below.

Before interviews, do:

- Draft protocols before the start of the mission
- Train the team on protection before deployment
- Conduct a localized security assessment before deployment
- Deploy experienced interviewers

---

[156] "Lund-London Guidelines," 9.
[157] World Health Organization, "WHO ethical and safety recommendations for researching, documenting and monitoring sexual violence in emergencies," 2007, p. 25, accessed May 29, 2015, http://www.who.int/gender/documents/OMS_Ethics&Safety10Aug07.pdf.

- Request that the local authorities, as well as other countries and embassies, protect witnesses at risk
- Consult NGOs on the ground who have already conducted investigations (to avoid re-interviewing the same person multiple times)

Do not:

- Advertise the types of interviewees for whom you are looking, especially if you are seeking individuals who might face stigmatization, such as victims of sexual and gender-based violence
- Re-interview individuals already interviewed by others, unless absolutely necessary

During interviews, do:

- Use discretion when approaching interviewees and when choosing interview locations
- Use female interviewers for female interviewees who may be victims of sexual and gender-based violence
- Be aware of special circumstances for interviews in closed places, such as prisons and refugee camps
- Show sensitivity during interviews
- Obtain, with specificity, informed consent from interviewees
- Inform the interviewee of risks
- Respect the confidentiality of interviewees
- Use secure communications (phone lines, email)
- Refer interviewees to other organizations for any humanitarian or health needs, if necessary
- Refer interviewees to other UN agencies, including peacekeeping forces, for post-interview support, if possible
- Allocate numbers for each witness in internal reports
- Maintain data security

Do not:

- Instrumentalize witnesses and victims
- Endanger other human rights, UN, and humanitarian workers
- Conduct interviews with other people in the room, especially in detention contexts

After interviews and during report drafting, do:

- Respect the confidentiality of the interviewees
- Adopt a policy regarding publishing names (e.g., publish only names and cases that are already public)

- Write the report in a way that doesn't allow the interviewee to be identified (omit interview location and other details, if necessary)

Do not:

- Mention interview location (even to the ICC) if this will allow for interviewees to be identified
- Use paper data
- Leave data behind
- Underestimate the risk of secondary trauma for staff who worked on the inquiry

Despite these areas of consensus on what could constitute witness and staff protection, open questions remain about what happens when these aspirational notions collide with the ad hoc reality of MRF mission implementation. A recurrent question throughout this research concerns the fact that, in the absence of detailed reference in the mandate, and in view of diversity of practice, much is left to personal assessment. Another unsolved dilemma concerns the very ethical foundations of MRF work: is it ethically acceptable that some persons will benefit from protection more than others? Specifically, MRF investigators often afford themselves a higher level of protection than the witnesses and victims with whom they engage. Can practitioners and the entities that mandate MRF missions be satisfied with this state of affairs, or is there more that these actors can do to ensure witness, victim, and staff protection, without unburdening states of their responsibility to protect? Measures to continue to professionalize the sector will facilitate practitioners' efforts to strike a responsible balance between aspirations and reality. But as this process proceeds, the perpetual push-and-pull between aspirational notions of practitioners' protective responsibilities and the realities of on-the-ground implementation will continue.

5

Professional Dilemmas in Public Communication and Report Drafting

LUC CÔTÉ AND ROB GRACE

Introduction

Monitoring, reporting, and fact-finding (MRF) missions are undoubtedly public in nature. Indeed, MRF missions are established by public entities through an open process, their mandates are public – generally part of a published resolution adopted by a body such as the United Nations Human Rights Council (UNHRC) – and when commissioners are appointed, their identities are publicly known. During and after an MRF investigation, there are two ways that members of an MRF mission communicate with the "outside world." One mode is direct public communication through press releases, press conferences, or public interviews with the commissioners leading the mission. The second mode is through the release of the mission's public report(s). This chapter will examine these two communication avenues, both of which need to be approached with caution, since both can contribute to a mission's success or failure.

The importance of public communication arises from the fact that MRF missions often attract a great deal of attention, both nationally and internationally. Indeed, MRF missions generally operate during or after an armed conflict or a period of violent internal unrest, in environments where opposing groups and/or factions are divided along ethnic, religious, or political lines. While there is certainly a strong demand for information about an MRF mission's operations and findings during the investigation phase, a core tension exists regarding how, when, and to what extent MRF missions should engage in public communication. On the one hand, an MRF mission's primary role is to investigate and establish facts, a function that requires strict confidentiality to preserve the integrity of the mission's investigation and to mitigate potential security risks for witnesses, victims, and MRF staff. On the other hand, MRF missions aim to deter future violations and to galvanize international political support for promoting international legal accountability for incidents relevant to the mission's mandate. These factors suggest the need for robust public engagement.

This tension between the contrasting needs for confidentiality and public communication is complicated further by the fact that MRF missions typically face various criticisms. MRF missions, as entities that levy accusations about violations of international law committed by governments, armed groups, and sometimes individuals – as noted above, often in relation to events with a highly charged political, ethnic, or religious dimension – are often controversial. Indeed, critics frequently raise questions about the legitimacy of the mission's mandate, working methods, and findings, and generally about its independence and impartiality.

One early example that presaged the types of critiques that MRF missions now frequently evoke and attempt to rebut is an inquiry undertaken by the Carnegie Endowment for International Peace to gather information about the Balkan Wars of 1912 and 1913.[1] In response to this commission's report, the government of Greece, which the report singled out as being responsible for atrocities, issued scathing criticism of the commission, claiming that the report was biased, unfair, ignored relevant information that would have led to a balanced report, and examined incidents not relevant to the mission's focus.[2]

Such lines of argument are no doubt familiar to MRF practitioners leading missions today. Indeed, the fifteen missions on which this book focuses faced claims that the entity that mandated the mission lacked legitimacy;[3] the mandate of the mission was unnecessarily restrictive or

---

[1] For the full report of this mission, see generally "Report of the International Commission to Inquire into the Causes and Conduct of the Balkan Wars," Carnegie Endowment for International Peace, 1914, https://archive.org/details/reportofinternat00inteuoft.

[2] "Greeks Denounce Carnegie Board," *The New York Times*, June 8, 1914, accessed May 26, 2015, http://query.nytimes.com/gst/abstract.html?res=F00610F73C5412738DDDA10894 DE405B848DF1D3.

[3] For example, various Bahraini opposition activists feared that the Bahrain Independent Commission of Inquiry, which was mandated by Bahraini royal decree, would serve the government's political interests. See Alaa Shehabi, "Bahrain's Independent Commission of Inquiry: A Path to Justice or Political Shield," *Jadaliyya*, November 22, 2011, accessed May 26, 2015, http://www.jadaliyya.com/pages/index/3244/bahrains-independent-commission-of-inquiry_a-path-. Additionally, the UNHRC regularly faces critiques regarding selectivity. See, for example, Herb Keinon and Tovah Lazaroff, "Israel Won't Cooperate with UN Probe of Settlements," *The Jerusalem Post*, March 23, 2012, accessed May 26, 2015, http://www.jpost.com/Diplomacy-and-Politics/Israel-wont-cooperate-with-UN-probe-of-settlements.

biased;[4] the mission was not necessary or helpful;[5] the mission, during the investigation, overstepped the boundaries of the mandate;[6] the commissioners and/or staff members were biased;[7] and the mission's findings lacked objectivity or were based on unsubstantiated claims.[8] As one modern practitioner states, "There are always critics out there who wouldn't agree with the findings or the way they conduct their work."[9] These critiques – credible or not – constitute a common aspect of the politically charged environment in which the typical MRF mission operates.

Similar challenges surround the process of drafting the mission's final report, which is an MRF mission's main tool of communication. As one policy document states, MRF reports constitute "the enduring legacy of commissions."[10] While the importance of making MRF reports public is widely acknowledged,[11] MRF practitioners, when making choices about

---

[4] See, for example, "Report by UN Lebanon Inquiry Is One-Sided," UN Watch, press release, November 21, 2006, accessed May 26, 2015, http://www.unwatch.org/site/apps/nlnet/content2.aspx?c=bdKKISNqEmG&b=1316871&ct=3264691.

[5] For example, in response to the report of the United Nations Mapping Exercise in the Democratic Republic of the Congo, the Rwandan government claimed that the mission was a "dangerous and irresponsible attempt ... to undermine the peace and stability attained in the Great Lakes region, which directly contradicts the very mission of the United Nations Organization Stabilization Mission in the Democratic Republic of the Congo (MONUSCO), and the UN generally." See Republic of Rwanda, Ministry of Foreign Affairs and Cooperation, "Official Government of Rwanda Comments on the Draft UN Mapping Report on the DRC," September 30, 2010, pp. 3–4, accessed May 26, 2015, http://rwandinfo.com/documents/DRC_Report_Comments_Rwanda.pdf.

[6] See, for example, "Report of the International Commission of Inquiry on Libya," A/HRC/19/68, March 2, 2012, p. 211, accessed May 25, 2015, http://www.nytimes.com/interactive/2012/03/03/world/africa/united-nations-report-on-libya.html?_r=0.

[7] For example, one Georgian official questioned the impartiality of one staff member of the Independent International Fact-Finding Mission on the Conflict in Georgia. See Ellen Barry, "Georgia Challenges Report That Says It Fired First Shot," *The New York Times*, September 30, 2009, accessed May 26, 2015, http://www.nytimes.com/2009/10/01/world/europe/01russia.html?_r=0.

[8] See, for example, "Sri Lanka: UN Panel Report Fundamentally Flawed and Patently Biased," Sri Lanka Ministry of Defence, April 15, 2011, accessed May 26, 2015, http://www.defence.lk/new.asp?fname=20110415_01.

[9] Rolando Gomez, Public Information Officer, Human Rights Council Branch, Office of the High Commissioner for Human Rights, interview conducted by HPCR, January 31, 2014.

[10] "Reconciliation After Violent Conflict: A Handbook," International IDEA, 2003, p. 135, accessed May 26, 2015, http://www.un.org/en/peacebuilding/pbso/pdf/Reconciliation-After-Violent-Conflict-A-Handbook-Full-English-PDF.pdf.

[11] For example, see "Commissions of Inquiry and Fact-Finding Missions on International Human Rights and Humanitarian Law: Guidance and Practice," Office of the High Commissioner for Human Rights, 2015, p. 92, accessed on May 26, 2015, http://www.ohchr.org/Documents/Publications/CoI_Guidance_and_Practice.pdf.

the structure, format, tone, and content of MRF reports, have at times adopted vastly different approaches to balancing a mission's sometimes contrasting aims of maximizing political impact, presenting an objective historical record, and giving voice to victims' experiences.

This chapter examines the dilemmas inherent in calibrating an MRF mission's approach to public communication and report drafting to the mission's strategic aims. Overall, the chapter aims to offer some answers to important issues raised by MRF practitioners – as well as the implications of different approaches – regarding public communication and transparency. Should MRF practitioners communicate directly with the public? If so, what should MRF practitioners communicate publicly? What information should be kept private? When a mission does communicate publicly, how should practitioners do so? What factors should shape practitioners' communications strategies? How should these factors influence the ways that practitioners approach drafting MRF reports? How should the public report be structured, and what information should be included to fulfill the mission's mandate? Given that the effectiveness of an MRF mission hinges on the ability of commissioners to foster positive public perceptions of the mission, these questions are crucial to the overall success of the domain of MRF.

Section I of this chapter focuses on how public communication during and after the implementation of an MRF mission can contribute to a mission's success or failure. Section II examines the process of report drafting. Section III highlights issues for further discussion by MRF practitioners and policymakers.

I. Public Communication

On the topic of public communication, one recent policy guidance document states, "[I]t is important that the commission/mission discusses [media engagement] early on and decides on a media strategy, and does not simply react to events and media pressure."[12] But what should the strategy be? The answer is not always clear. One reason is that MRF missions vary greatly from one another, specifically regarding the nature of the mandate and the context examined. For example, some MRF missions are conducted while a conflict is ongoing (e.g., the International Commission of Inquiry on Libya [hereafter the Libya Commission]), while other missions do not begin until after violent events have come to an

---

[12] Ibid., 86.

end (e.g., the Independent, International Commission of Inquiry on Côte d'Ivoire [hereafter the Côte d'Ivoire Commission]). Some missions enjoy unfettered territorial access (e.g., the Bahrain Independent Commission of Inquiry [hereafter the Bahrain Commission]), while others are prevented from accessing the territory where relevant incidents occurred (e.g., the Secretary-General's Panel of Experts on Accountability in Sri Lanka [hereafter the Sri Lanka Panel]). A sound public communication strategy will need to take all of these factors into account.

In general, MRF policy documents emphasize the context-specific aspect of a mission's communications strategy. For example, the way that the *Siracusa Guidelines for International, Regional and National Fact-Finding Bodies* address the issue of transparency suggests the *sui generis* nature of each mission. The *Siracusa Guidelines* articulate a minimum level of desired transparency by asserting that, for the duration of the mission's work and in the final report, the mission should make public the text of the mandate and the name of the mandating body.[13] However, the *Siracusa Guidelines* otherwise suggest the necessity of shaping communications strategies on a case-by-case basis by stating, "A fact-finding body should be established in a transparent manner that is appropriate to the context for which it is created."[14] The "Guidance and Practice" document published by the Office of the High Commissioner for Human Rights (OHCHR) in 2015 elucidates this point by mentioning the disparity between the approaches of different missions:

> In some cases it might be useful to adopt a low-key position, while others will call for a more public stance …. The engagement by commissions/ missions with the media during their investigations has varied. Some have chosen to maintain a general media silence; others have provided periodic public updates in the form of press releases or press conferences on their travel and meetings, but without addressing the substance of their findings and conclusions before their work was finalized; yet others, such as the Commission of Inquiry on the Syrian Arab Republic (2011–2014), have had more substantive engagements with the media in the form of regular press releases and press conferences, with question-and-answer sessions and interviews with journalists.[15]

The "Guidance and Practice" document presents several factors to consider – ensuring that the public and relevant governments are informed about the mission's work, avoiding the perception that the commission

---

[13] M. Cherif Bassiouni and Christina Abraham, eds., *Siracusa Guidelines for International, Regional and National Fact-Finding Bodies* (Cambridge: Intersentia, 2013), 37–38.
[14] Ibid., 37.   [15] OHCHR, "Guidance and Practice," 82, 84–85.

has prejudged conclusions, countering misinformation, determining the likely impact of a public statement, and responding to key events – but like the *Siracusa Guidelines*, the OHCHR document implies that there is not a "one size fits all" strategy.

One would think that the mission's mandate would provide some guidance about the desired approach. However, this is rarely the case. One exception is the Terms of Reference for the United Nations Mapping Exercise in the Democratic Republic of the Congo (hereafter the DRC Mapping Exercise), which state that the mission "should develop a communications strategy, in close cooperation with MONUC [United Nations Organization Mission in the Democratic Republic of the Congo]" and that "[t]he mapping exercise should be carried out in as discreet a manner as possible."[16] But of the fifteen missions on which this Handbook focuses, the Terms of Reference of the DRC Mapping Exercise is the only mandate to mention the issue of public engagement. As the rest of this section demonstrates, different approaches have been adopted before an MRF investigation begins, during the investigation, and after the investigation has concluded.

A.   *Before the Investigation Begins*

One relatively noncontroversial area regarding communication is the announcement of the mission. The typical practice for recent MRF missions is, at the start of a mission, to make available basic information about the mandate, commissioners, timeline, and objectives of the mission. For this reason, missions are usually launched with a press conference,[17] a press release,[18] and sometimes the creation of a mission-specific web

---

[16] "Report of the Mapping Exercise Documenting the Most Serious Violations of Human Rights and International Humanitarian Law Committed within the Territory of the Democratic Republic of the Congo between March 1993 and June 2003," Office of the High Commissioner for Human Rights, August 2010, p. 544, accessed May 26, 2015, http://www.refworld.org/docid/4ca99bc22.html.

[17] For example, M. Cherif Bassiouni gave a press conference toward the beginning of the Bahrain Independent Commission of Inquiry. See "Mahmoud Cherif Bassiouni Speaks about the Independent Commission in Bahrain," YouTube video, 3:11, posted by "FriendsofBahrain," July 7, 2011, https://www.youtube.com/watch?v=izLFMQShBnY.

[18] For examples, see "Secretary-General Establishes International Commission of Inquiry for Darfur," press release, October 7, 2004, accessed May 26, 2015, http://www.un.org/News/Press/docs/2004/sga890.doc.htm; and "United Nations Human Rights Council Panel to investigate Israeli raid on Gaza flotilla established," Office of the High Commissioner for Human Rights, accessed May 26, 2015, http://www.ohchr.org/en/NewsEvents/Pages/DisplayNews.aspx?NewsID=10230&LangID=E.

page.[19] These measures are in line with the aforementioned guideline that emphasizes the importance of informing all relevant actors about basic information regarding the establishment and operations of the mission. "The public," as the OHCHR "Guidance and Practice" document asserts, "especially in the countries concerned, has a legitimate interest in being informed of the commission/mission and its work."[20]

This first public communication also offers an opportunity to guarantee the independence and impartiality of the mission by revealing the identities of the commissioners, discussing their background and expertise, and communicating about the overall methodology that the mission will employ (e.g., field visits, document analysis, witness and victim interviews, etc.). MRF missions may also use this initial communication opportunity to explain the commissioners' interpretation of their mandate, the different issues that the mission intends to explore, the goals of the mission, and the legal framework that the mission will apply. If necessary, this first public communication may also be used to preempt some anticipated criticisms of the mission's legitimacy and impartiality by announcing specific measures to be applied to ensure that all parties to the conflict will be heard, the confidentiality and security of witnesses will be taken into account, and proper attention will be given to members of vulnerable groups.

B.   During the Investigation

After the initial announcement of the mission, the process of implementing the mandate begins, and MRF practitioners must decide if they anticipate communicating publicly during the investigation stage, and if so, what mode of public engagement will best serve the mission's priorities. Unfortunately, it appears that practitioners have in many instances devoted scarce attention to this issue at the outset of an MRF mission, and instead, have not made decisions about the communications strategy until after the beginning of the investigation. Needless to say, discussions

---

[19] For examples of websites, see the website of the Bahrain Independent Commission of Inquiry, accessed May 26, 2015, http://www.bici.org.bh/index-2.html; and the website of the United Nations Mapping Exercise in the Democratic Republic of the Congo, accessed May 26, 2015, http://www.ohchr.org/EN/Countries/AfricaRegion/Pages/RDCProjetMapping.aspx. Additionally, see OHCHR, "Guidance and Practice," 84, which states, "[I]t has become a regular practice for commissions/missions set up by the Human Rights Council to establish a web page on the Human Rights Council's section of the OHCHR website to post contact information, press releases and interim reports."

[20] OHCHR, "Guidance and Practice," 82.

about communication strategy need to be conducted at the earliest stage. The rest of this section explores the various factors that have shaped practitioners' decision-making processes about whether or not to engage in public communication during an investigation.

1.   Reasons to Engage in Public Communication

(a) **Setting Expectations**   One important way that practitioners can use public engagement is to set realistic expectations of what the mission can accomplish. Setting and managing public expectations can be especially important in ongoing conflicts or internal disturbances that lack other impactful crisis resolution initiatives. While practitioners can anticipate the need for and begin engaging in expectation management before the investigation, often expectations from the local population are voiced during the investigation and should therefore be addressed at that time. For example, the Bahrain Commission operated in tandem with a National Dialogue geared toward national reconciliation. However, the National Dialogue's legitimacy faltered during the Bahrain Commission's investigation. International efforts to intervene in the dispute between the government and the political opposition were also minimal. In the absence of other substantial international or national initiatives, local actors turned their attention toward the Bahrain Commission, which became a political lightning rod for the local population. This attention generated pressure for the mission to achieve aims related to reconciliation and correcting injustices that fell beyond the commission's fact-finding mandate.[21] For this reason, during the investigation, the chair of the mission endeavored to clarify the mission's limitations by stating, "[I]t is not part of our job to call for releasing prisoners since we are not a human rights organization."[22] The danger for an MRF mission in this regard is that an inability to manage expectations will set the public up for disappointment by creating hopes that the mission will inevitably be unable to fulfill.

---

[21]   For example, one Bahraini, reacting to the fact that the Bahrain Independent Commission of Inquiry did not free her husband from prison, proclaimed, "These commissioners let us down." See Alaa Shehabi, "Red Lines and Human Rights: An Evaluation of the Bahrain Independent Commission of Inquiry Report," *Jadaliyya*, December 8, 2011, accessed May 26, 2015, http://www.jadaliyya.com/pages/index/3453/red-lines-and-human-rights_an-evaluation-of-the-ba.

[22]   M. Cherif Bassiouni, quoted in Mahamed al Arab, "No Crimes against Humanity in Bahrain, Says Fact Finding Committee," *Al Arabiya News*, August 15, 2011, accessed May 26, 2015, http://www.alarabiya.net/articles/2011/08/15/162451.html.

Additionally, when an MRF mission works concurrently with other investigative mechanisms, such as a national commission of inquiry or an investigation of the International Criminal Court (ICC), there may be a need to distinguish the MRF mission from these other parallel investigations. For example, before the implementation of the International Commission of Inquiry for Guinea (hereafter the Guinea Commission), mandated to gather information about a government crackdown that had occurred in September 2009, the Guinean government had authorized a national investigation to investigate the exact same incident.[23] Part of the Guinea Commission's public engagement strategy was to make clear that the mission was entirely separate and distinct from the national commission.[24] This factor arises as a result of the enduring ad hoc nature of the domain of MRF. Since no permanent MRF body exists, it is common for multiple mandating entities to authorize overlapping investigations, a point made clear by various responses to the violence that occurred in South Sudan in 2014. In this context, the United Nations Mission in the Republic of South Sudan, the United Nations Secretary-General (UNSG), the United Nations Children's Fund, and the African Union have all engaged in MRF activities.[25]

Other MRF missions – for example, the Libya Commission, the Côte d'Ivoire Commission, and the DRC Mapping Exercise – have been conducted at the same time that the ICC was exercising its jurisdiction over the same events. In such contexts, it is important for MRF practitioners to clearly explain that their mandate and mission are separate and distinct from a judicial mechanism that can sanction individuals for crimes committed. Indeed, Libya Commission investigators discovered that, while Libyan interviewees were aware of the United Nations Security Council's (UNSC) referral of the Libya situation to the ICC, many interviewees were previously unaware of the Libyan Commission's existence.[26] As this example indicates, during an investigation, sometimes confusion exists in the minds of the local population. In such instances, if public

[23] "Guinea to Investigate Stadium Massacre," *RFI*, October 8, 2009, accessed May 26, 2015, http://www1.rfi.fr/actuen/articles/118/article_5421.asp.

[24] Pramila Patten, Commissioner, International Commission of Inquiry for Guinea, interview conducted by HPCR, April 26, 2013.

[25] Rob Grace, "Monitoring, Reporting, and Fact-Finding: Challenges and Opportunities," Thematic Note, Professionals in Humanitarian Assistance and Protection, February 11, 2014, accessed May 26, 2015, http://phap.org/thematic-notes/2014/february/monitoring-reporting-and-fact-finding-challenges-and-opportunities.

[26] Confidential interview with a high-level MRF practitioner, name of interviewee on file, conducted by HPCR, Winter 2012.

communications issued before the investigation do not successfully clarify the mission's aims, limitations, and methodology, subsequent public communications might be necessary as the investigation proceeds.

(b) **Rebutting Criticism**   Given the fact that an MRF mission's credibility frequently falls under assault, practitioners often strive to push back against these criticisms and advocate for the mission. "There is lots of speculation, lots of rumors," states one practitioner, "we try to nip that in the bud. It's important to contain the spread of rumors. To keep all the actors who have a role to play in the process well informed, from start to finish."[27] A commissioner who served on the Kyrgyzstan Inquiry Commission (hereafter the Kyrgyzstan Commission) describes the rationale for holding a press conference after critics had alleged that the mission was one-sided:

> We felt that we needed to show ourselves to the media and explain what we were doing. It wasn't sharing initial findings but explaining the TOR [Terms of Reference], sharing working methods. There were allegations that those on the government side were not listened to, there was propaganda material going around as well. It was really to abort that propaganda, to say: everyone will be heard. And to give our opinion about why such a commission is important.[28]

(c) **Seeking Cooperation from Governments**   Commissioners also sometimes use public engagement to pressure governments to cooperate with the mission. For example, Desmond Tutu and Christine Chinkin (who led the High-Level Fact-Finding Mission to Beit Hanoun established under Council resolution S-3/1 [hereafter the Beit Hanoun Fact-Finding Mission]) and Richard Goldstone (who led the United Nations Fact-Finding Mission on the Gaza Conflict [hereafter the Gaza Fact-Finding Mission]) were all publicly very adamant about both missions' dismay over the lack of territorial access and cooperation granted by Israel. Though this form of public advocacy was not successful in terms of securing cooperation, such measures can be an important part of the "legitimacy war" that plays out during MRF operations.

In a similar vein, calls on countries to respect their international obligations to cooperate can be part of public communication, specifically in

---

[27] Rolando Gomez, HPCR interview.
[28] Yakin Ertürk, Commissioner, Kyrgyzstan Inquiry Commission, interview conducted by HPCR, July 18, 2013.

cases in which the mission's mandate was authorized by the UNSC (pursuant to the UNSC's powers under Chapter VII of the United Nations Charter), or when the government itself initially consented to the creation of the mission. In cases of ongoing conflict, MRF practitioners have also called on all parties to the conflict to respect international humanitarian law and international human rights law. Examples include a press statement issued by the chair of the Libya Commission during the operation of the mission that said, "It is extremely important that the National Transitional Council (NTC) and all armed groups in Libya ensure that all detainees under their control, irrespective of their affiliations, are treated with due respect for their human rights in accordance with international standards."[29] Similarly, during the implementation of the mandate of the Independent International Commission of Inquiry on the Syrian Arab Republic, the mission issued a press statement to remind "all parties to the conflict that the use of chemical weapons is prohibited in all circumstances under customary international humanitarian law."[30]

(d) General Call for Information from Witnesses and Victims   There are some examples of MRF missions making public calls to gather information from witnesses and victims. These calls can serve a public outreach objective by establishing an open-door policy and promoting the mission as an evenhanded initiative. For example, the Kyrgyzstan Commission, in order to show that the mission was open to receiving information from both sides, opened public offices where witnesses could provide information directly to the mission.

However, these endeavors can also lead to security issues for the witnesses and can lead the mission to be flooded with one-sided testimonies, depending on the political situation in the country. This occurred with the Sri Lanka Panel, which issued a public call for written submissions that was posted on the mission's website. The panel's report describes this measure as a part of the panel's "outreach to the broader public."[31] Indeed,

[29] Philippe Kirsch, quoted in "UN Panel Urges Libya to Probe Detainee Violations, Commit to Human Rights," *UN News Centre*, October 25, 2011, accessed May 26, 2015, http://www.un.org/apps/news/story.asp?NewsID=40198#.VUj5Io08bew.

[30] "Press release from the Commission of Inquiry on Syria (chemical weapons)," Office of the High Commissioner for Human Rights, May 6, 2013, accessed May 26, 2015, http://www.ohchr.org/EN/NewsEvents/Pages/DisplayNews.aspx?NewsID=13298&LangID=E.

[31] "Report of the Secretary-General's Panel of Experts on Accountability in Sri Lanka," March 31, 2011, p. 5, accessed May 26, 2015, http://www.un.org/News/dh/infocus/Sri_Lanka/POE_Report_Full.pdf.

this measure was particularly important given that the panel did not have access to the territory where the incidents relevant to the panel's mandate occurred. The response to this public call was massive. The panel received over four thousand submissions from over two thousand senders.[32] However, the panel's final report states that, while some of the information was helpful in terms of corroboration, the submissions actually had limited probative value.[33]

(e) **Public Hearings** Public hearings have commonly been used by truth and reconciliation commissions (TRCs), which are distinct from other MRF mechanism types because, for truth and reconciliation commissions, the information-gathering process is directly linked to the objective of national reconciliation. Indeed, giving voice to victims is a vital component of serving a TRC's national reconciliation aims. Therefore, public outreach is a key element of a TRC, and public hearings are valuable tools toward this end. As one handbook on TRCs states:

> Public outreach by a truth commission is critically important. The nature and the extent of a commission's outreach efforts will profoundly affect its access to information, its effectiveness in addressing the needs of victims, its ability to manage public expectations and its general reputation in the eyes of the public. Some of these efforts can be carried out directly by the commission through holding public information meetings and through the preparation, publication and dissemination of pamphlets, videos and publications in popular form about the role and mandate of the commission. The commission can also achieve its outreach goals by engagement with and effective use of NGOs, local grass-roots organizations and the media. Relations with civil society and the media can, however, be complicated by the fact that they will often play a dual role vis-à-vis the commission, working simultaneously as partner to it and as a critical watchdog of its procedures and actions.[34]

But what role can and should public hearings play in other MRF mechanism types, such as fact-finding missions and commissions of inquiry? Only two such missions – the Gaza Fact-Finding Mission and the Commission of Inquiry on Human Rights in the Democratic People's Republic of Korea (hereafter the DPRK Commission) – have used public hearings.

---

[32] Ibid.
[33] See ibid., which states, "Submissions could not be individually verified by the Panel and, therefore, were not used as a direct source to meet the Panel's threshold of credibility for the allegations."
[34] International IDEA, "Handbook," 133.

The objective of these public hearings was evidently not primarily to gather information but mainly to raise the visibility of the mission. As Richard Goldstone – who, as noted earlier, led the Gaza Fact-Finding Mission – said of the public hearings held during the Gaza Fact-Finding Mission, "The purpose of the public hearings in Gaza and Geneva is to show the faces and broadcast the voices of victims – all of the victims."[35] And as the Gaza Fact-Finding Mission's final report states:

> The purpose of the public hearings, which were broadcast live, was to enable victims, witnesses and experts from all sides to the conflict to speak directly to as many people as possible in the region as well as in the international community. The Mission is of the view that no written word can replace the voice of victims. While not all issues and incidents under investigation by the Mission were addressed during the hearings, the 38 public testimonies covered a wide range of relevant facts as well as legal and military matters.[36]

Similarly, one practitioner comments on the significance of the public hearings held during the DPRK Commission:

> The DPRK commissioner started to hold public hearings, carefully chose the witnesses who realized the risks they were taking and spelled out their stories, harrowing accounts of violations taking place in North Korea. Public hearings are one important way to expose a story and to generate awareness and hopefully create some sort of response.[37]

In general, though, public hearings are not an efficient way to gather evidence. As the OHCHR "Guidance and Practice" document stipulates, "Public hearings in the context of international human rights fact-finding and investigations mechanisms are a **complementary**, rather than an exclusive, information-gathering method."[38]

A cost-benefit analysis of public hearings as an efficient investigative tool would discourage this practice since the complexity, the costs, and more importantly, the security risks of publicly exposing witnesses and victims seem to outweigh the evidentiary value of information garnered. Indeed, during the Gaza Fact-Finding Mission, Israeli security forces

---

[35] Richard Goldstone, quoted in Rory McCarthy, "UN Public Hearing in Gaza Broadcasts Accounts of War Victims," *The Guardian*, June 28, 2009, accessed May 26, 2015, http://www.theguardian.com/world/2009/jun/28/inquiry-gaza-palestine-israel-war.

[36] "Report of the United Nations Fact-Finding Mission on the Gaza Conflict," A/HRC/12/48, September 25, 2009, p. 44, accessed May 26, 2015, http://www2.ohchr.org/english/bodies/hrcouncil/docs/12session/A-HRC-12-48.pdf.

[37] Rolando Gomez, HPCR interview.

[38] OHCHR, "Guidance and Practice," 55 (emphasis in original).

detained one Palestinian who had participated in the public hearings in Geneva, and the mission perceived that the detention might have been linked to this individual's cooperation with the mission, though Israeli officials denied this connection.[39] In the case of the DPRK Commission, the strategy of raising the visibility of individual victims backfired when, after the publication of the mission's report, one of the individuals who testified during the mission's public hearings recanted part of his testimony, leading to the risk that his recantation could bring the legitimacy of many of the mission's findings into question.[40] These examples suggest that MRF practitioners should seriously consider the risks of public hearings when deciding whether to pursue this avenue.

2.   Reasons Not to Engage in Public Communication

The main reason not to engage in public communication during an investigation derives from the core mandate of all MRF missions to ascertain relevant facts relating to serious violations of international humanitarian and/or human rights law. Most investigation activities are per se of a discreet, non-public nature, in order to preserve the security of witnesses, to ensure the efficient and smooth collection of evidence, and to preserve the MRF mission's integrity and credibility.[41] For these reasons, as one practitioner notes, "Discretion at times is absolutely necessary."[42] Although, as noted earlier, there may be good reasons to engage in public communication during an MRF investigation, the danger always exists that public statements will backfire. Various practitioners have commented on the need for restraint in this regard:

- "If you talk to the media, you control your presentation but not the questions. Sooner or later, questions will be asked that are deliberately provocative. They will put you on the spot on your approach, for example, to the responsibility of certain people. As an investigation is

---

[39] Gaza Fact-Finding Mission report, 40.
[40] Anna Fifield, "Prominent N. Korean Defector Shin Dong-hyuk Admits Parts of Story Are Inaccurate," *The Washington Post*, January 17, 2015, accessed May 26, 2015, http://www.washingtonpost.com/world/prominent-n-korean-defector-shin-dong-hyuk-admits-parts-of-story-are-inaccurate/2015/01/17/fc69278c-9dd5-11e4-bcfb-059ec-7a93ddc_story.html.
[41] See OHCHR, "Guidance and Practice," 34, which states, "The commission/mission is required to respect the confidentiality of persons who cooperate with it and of the information it gathers. In addition to the protection it affords, confidentiality enhances the credibility of the commission/mission, the integrity of its information-gathering activities and the effectiveness of its work."
[42] Yakin Ertürk, HPCR interview.

ongoing, I think it is unwise to give interviews because you may make a mistake in answering a question, or in any event the chances are high that something you say will be taken out of context. That may give an impression, however unwarranted, of lack of impartiality, which may in turn affect the access and overall credibility of the mission. I have seen this happen."[43]

- "I don't think it's helpful to have running commentaries. You don't want to say something and then roll back. It's better just to keep quiet."[44]
- "There's a sense that the report speaks for itself. If you allow people to speak freely, you can get people to divulge information they shouldn't."[45]

In particular, security considerations often weigh heavily against developing a strong public presence during implementation. Many missions have adopted a discreet approach, as evidenced by the below passages from various MRF reports:

- "[The commission] also decided to limit its contacts with the media to providing factual information about its visits. On 9 April 2011, the Chair of the Commission, together with the two other members held a press conference in Geneva informing about its mandate and the planned visit to Libya. On 3 May 2011, the Commission issued a press statement informing about its field missions." (Libya Commission)[46]
- "The Commission agreed to carry out its mandate in confidentiality and, in particular, to limit its contacts with the media to factual information about its visits to Lebanon." (Commission of Inquiry on Lebanon [hereafter the Lebanon Commission])[47]

---

[43] Philippe Kirsch, Commissioner, Bahrain Independent Commission of Inquiry, and Chair, International Commission of Inquiry on Libya (October 2011–March 2012), interview conducted by HPCR, July 23, 2013.

[44] Philip Trewhitt, Investigation Team Leader, International Commission of Inquiry on Libya, interview conducted by HPCR, July 26, 2013.

[45] Confidential interview with a high-level MRF practitioner, name of interviewee on file, conducted by HPCR, Summer 2013.

[46] "Report of the International Commission of Inquiry to Investigate All Alleged Violations of International Human Rights Law in the Libyan Arab Jamahiriya," A/HRC/17/44, June 1, 2011, pp. 14–15, accessed May 26, 2015, http://www2.ohchr.org/english/bodies/hrcouncil/docs/17session/A.HRC.17.44_AUV.pdf.

[47] "Report of the Commission of Inquiry on Lebanon Pursuant to Human Rights Council Resolution S-2/1," United Nations Human Rights Council, November 23, 2006, p. 15, accessed May 26, 2015, http://www.unrol.org/files/A.HRC.3.2.pdf.

- "The Commission agreed at the outset that it would discharge its mission in strict confidentiality. In particular, it would limit its contacts with the media to providing factual information about its visits to the Sudan." (International Commission of Inquiry on Darfur [hereafter the Darfur Commission])[48]

One danger is that an MRF mission, particularly in the context of an ongoing armed conflict or internal disturbance, could become a target for violence. Thus, as one practitioner states, "There are other times that we have to be a bit quieter for security reasons."[49] Additionally, the security of witnesses and victims can be jeopardized. Interviewees face the risk of retaliation for cooperating with the mission, and missions usually operate in a discreet manner during on-the-ground operations to mitigate this risk.[50] The use of non-confidential forums, such as public hearings, during MRF processes presents a particular risk in this regard, as suggested by the aforementioned security concerns expressed after public hearings in the context of the Gaza Fact-Finding Mission.

C.   The Release of the Report

Upon the release of the mission's final report, the tensions between the needs for confidentiality and publicity mostly dissipate. Instead, consensus has emerged among practitioners about the importance of shedding as much light as possible on the report's findings and recommendations.[51] Indeed, most MRF reports are released initially to the mission's mandating body in a public meeting and therefore become publicly available. Typically, after the presentation of the report to the mandating body, the members of the mission strive forcefully to bring the mission's report into the public eye. Commissioners commonly hold press conferences and

---

[48] "Report of the International Commission of Inquiry on Darfur to the United Nations Secretary-General," January 25, 2005, p. 11, accessed May 26, 2015, http://www.un.org/news/dh/sudan/com_inq_darfur.pdf.

[49] Rolando Gomez, HPCR interview.

[50] See generally in this Handbook, Chapter 4, Protecting Witnesses, Victims, and Staff: Sources and Implications of Professional Responsibilities, by Cynthia Petrigh.

[51] For example, see Bassiouni and Abraham, *Siracusa Guidelines*, 51, which states, "The report, along with any recommendations, should be published, translated if necessary, and widely disseminated." Additionally, see OHCHR, "Guidance and Practice," 92, which states, "Reports of commissions/missions should generally be **public**. The public nature of these reports is important for them to contribute to the historical recording of events, strengthen the calls for accountability and promote implementation of the recommendations" (emphasis in original).

grant interviews.[52] The heads of the Gaza Fact-Finding Mission and the Independent International Fact-Finding Mission on the Conflict in Georgia (hereafter the Georgia Fact-Finding Mission) both published op-eds in *The New York Times* upon the release of the mission's report.[53] The report of the Bahrain Commission was released with a public ceremony during which the chair of the mission officially presented the report to the king of Bahrain.[54]

Conversely, one reason for exercising discretion at this stage is concern for the security of UN and other international staff who remain in the country. Normally, when MRF practitioners anticipate that the release of the report will lead to security issues – such as retaliatory measures undertaken by local actors – the mission advises the UN and embassies in the country of the release date so that precautionary security measures can be taken. Or, for an interim report, a mission will ensure that the MRF team is out of the country on the day of the report's release.

Additionally, external pressures sometimes exist to keep reports confidential. The report for a commission of inquiry mandated at the national level in Zimbabwe in 1985 has not been published due to concerns that releasing the report could lead to an outbreak of ethnic violence in the country.[55] The report of a commission of inquiry mandated in 2004 to examine incidents in Côte d'Ivoire has not been released publicly either, though various NGOs and other UN entities – including the United Nations Operation in Côte d'Ivoire and the 2011 Côte d'Ivoire Commission – have argued that this decision contributes to an environment of

---

[52] For example, see "Press Conference by Archbishop Desmond Tutu and Christine Chinkin on Report of High-Level Fact-Finding Mission to Beit Hanoun (Gaza) to the Human Rights Council," September 18, 2008, accessed May 26, 2015, http://www2.ohchr.org/english/bodies/hrcouncil/docs/9session/BeitHanoun_PC_18Sept08.pdf.

[53] For the Gaza Fact-Finding Mission op-ed, see Richard Goldstone, "Justice in Gaza," *The New York Times*, September 17, 2009, accessed May 25, 2015, http://www.nytimes.com/2009/09/17/opinion/17goldstone.html?adxnnl=1&adxnnlx=1383688412-VB8iBp/Aj0+Ajb6A9n3vQA. For the Georgia Fact-Finding Mission op-ed, see Heidi Tagliavini, "Lessons of the Georgia Conflict," *The New York Times*, September 30, 2009, accessed May 26, 2015, http://www.nytimes.com/2009/10/01/opinion/01iht-edtagliavini.html?_r=0&adxnnl=1&adxnnlx=1383686542-DmN+dP5xC9k6Ay6bky8sfw.

[54] For a description of the public event at which the Bahrain Commission report was presented to the king, see Brian Dooley, "Bassiouni Report Takes Bahrain Back to Square One," *Huffington Post*, November 25, 2011, accessed May 26, 2015, http://www.huffingtonpost.com/brian-dooley/bassiouni-report-takes-ba_b_1112991.html.

[55] Priscilla Hayner, "Fifteen Truth Commissions – 1974 to 1994: A Comparative Analysis," *Human Rights Quarterly* 16, no. 4 (1994): 617, http://www.jstor.org/stable/762562.

impunity.[56] A debate about this issue has also played out in the context of the Monitoring and Reporting Mechanism (MRM) on children and armed conflict.[57] The disagreement stems from differing perceptions about what the MRM should aim to accomplish and how the mechanism should strategically pursue these ends. As one policy piece states of the MRM in Sri Lanka:

> Some UN agencies see the MRM as a way to improve the capacity of government institutions to monitor and report on human rights violations while others see the MRM as a substitute human rights monitoring mechanism in the absence of a UN human rights monitoring mission which the GoSL [Government of Sri Lanka] has consistently blocked. Furthermore, while many donor governments and NGOs see the MRM as a way to publicly advocate at the national level for the improved protection of children, diplomats from a few donor governments are hesitant to use the MRM for public advocacy, believing that closed-door sessions with parties to the conflict are more effective.[58]

More recently, the African Union's Peace and Security Council decided to keep confidential the report of the Commission of Inquiry on South Sudan, which the Council had mandated, due to concerns that the

[56] See "Council Hears Reports on Côte d'Ivoire and Syria, Holds General Debate on Human Rights Situations That Require Its Attention," *UN News & Media*, June 15, 2011, accessed May 26, 2015, http://www.ohchr.org/EN/NewsEvents/Pages/DisplayNews. aspx?NewsID=11159&LangID=E; and Côte d'Ivoire (UNOCI), "January 2006 Monthly Forecast," posted December 22, 2005, accessed May 26, 2015, http://www.securitycouncil-report.org/monthly-forecast/2006-01/lookup_c_glKWLeMTIsG_b_1313229.php, which states, "The failure to consider and make public the 2004 report of the international commission of inquiry on serious violations of human rights has led to questions being raised on the ground, especially by members of civil society, about the value of UN investigations and UN's commitment to transparency."

[57] United Nations Security Council resolution 1612 (2005) established the MRM to monitor and report on the following six violations against children in armed conflict: killing or maiming of children, recruitment or use of child soldiers, rape and other forms of sexual violence against children, abduction of children, attacks against schools or hospitals, and denial of humanitarian access to children. Originally, the 1612 MRM monitored all six violations but only in countries in which "recruitment and use of child soldiers" had occurred, thus allowing this violation to function as a "trigger." United Nations Security Council resolution 1882 (2009) added both "killing and maiming of children" and "rape and other sexual violence against children" to the list of triggers. United Nations Security Council resolution 1998 (2011) added "attacks on schools and/or hospitals" to the list of triggers.

[58] "Getting It Done and Doing It Right: Implementing the Monitoring and Reporting Mechanism on Children and Armed Conflict in Sri Lanka," Watchlist on Children and Armed Conflict, 2008, p. 3, accessed March 26, 2015, http://www.watchlist.org/reports/pdf/sri-lanka-v6-web.pdf.

publication of the report would adversely affect the ongoing peace process in the country.[59]

To preempt the effect of these pressures, some mandates specify that the report should be made public. The mandate for the Bahrain Commission states, "The Commission's final report, to be submitted to His Majesty no later than 30 October 2011, shall be made public in its entirety."[60] Similarly, the Terms of Reference for the DRC Mapping Exercise specify, "The report should be made public."[61] And the Terms of Reference for the Kyrgyzstan Commission state, "The Commission will make the report, with the comments of the Government, public by presenting it to the United Nations (UN), the Organization for Security and Cooperation in Europe (OSCE), the European Union (EU) and the Commonwealth of Independent States (CIS)."[62]

It is interesting to note that many mandates make no reference at all to the production of a public report. The mandates for missions mandated by the UNHRC – including the Libya Commission; the Côte d'Ivoire Commission; the International Fact-Finding Mission to investigate violations of international law, including international humanitarian and human rights law, resulting from the Israeli attacks on the flotilla of ships carrying humanitarian assistance (hereafter the UNHRC Flotilla Fact-Finding Mission); the Gaza Fact-Finding Mission; the Beit Hanoun Fact-Finding Mission; and the Lebanon Commission – are completely silent on this issue. However, for missions mandated by the UNHRC, which operate with the leadership and cooperation of OHCHR, there is an implicit understanding, though not an explicit policy, that missions will culminate in a report that will be released publicly.[63]

One example for which the fate of the final report was unclear from the beginning was the Sri Lanka Panel, which was given a peculiar mandate by the UNSG: "to advise the Secretary-General on the modalities, applicable international standards and comparative experience relevant

---

59 David K. Deng, "The Silencing of the AU Commission of Inquiry on South Sudan," *Sudan Tribune*, February 6, 2015, accessed May 26, 2015, http://www.sudantribune.com/spip .php?article53903.

60 Royal Order No. 28 of 2011, Article 9, accessed June 25, 2015, http://www.lcil.cam.ac.uk/ sites/default/files/LCIL/documents/arabspring/Bahrain_9_Royal_Order_No28.pdf.

61 DRC Mapping Exercise report, 544.

62 "Report of the Independent International Commission of Inquiry into the Events in Southern Kyrgyzstan in June 2010," n.d., p. 7, accessed May 26, 2015, http://reliefweb.int/ sites/reliefweb.int/files/resources/Full_Report_490.pdf.

63 Sonia Bakar, Peace Mission Support, Rapid Response Section, Office of the High Commissioner for Human Rights, interview conducted by HPCR, January 20, 2014.

to the fulfillment of the joint commitment [between the UNSG and the President of Sri Lanka] to an accountability process, having regard to the nature and scope of alleged violations."[64] The members of the panel felt strongly that the report should be made public, were concerned due to past UN reports that were kept confidential, and wrote a confidential letter to the UNSG urging that he make the report public.[65] In the end, the report was indeed released publicly. This example demonstrates that, in situations in which the report could conceivably be kept confidential, advocacy on the part of MRF practitioners might play a role in persuading decision makers to release the report.

One reason why practitioners emphasize the importance of publishing reports is the perception that MRF missions strive ultimately to impact the relevant context, either by influencing the behavior of parties engaged in violent conflicts or by building support among international actors to address the situation. As one practitioner states, MRF mechanisms are designed "to bring out the facts and trigger a political intervention to stop the human rights abuses, to build momentum toward accountability," ends that obviously cannot be achieved if reports are kept from the public.[66] For many missions, these aims are implicit, though the report of the DRC Mapping Exercise explicitly states that the mission "was aimed at providing a key advocacy tool *vis-à-vis* the Government and Parliament, as well as the international community regarding the establishment of appropriate transitional justice mechanisms and to encourage concerted efforts to combat impunity in the DRC."[67]

In order to serve these ends, though, the report must not only be made public but must also be distributed widely. The OHCHR "Guidance and Practice" document elaborates on the importance of both dissemination and translation:

> Some commissioners/missions have arranged for unofficial translations of their report into the main language of the country concerned (for example, Arabic or Tetum) for distribution within the country at the time of its release or at a later stage, a practice that is strongly encouraged to allow for greater dissemination of these findings and assessment among the people who are most directly concerned.[68]

---

[64] Sri Lanka Panel report, 2.

[65] Steven Ratner, Member, Secretary-General's Panel of Experts on Sri Lanka, interview conducted by HPCR, May 1, 2013.

[66] Martin Seutcheu, Human Rights Officer for the Office of the High Commissioner for Human Rights, interview conducted by HPCR, September 23, 2011.

[67] DRC Mapping Exercise report, 33.   [68] OHCHR, "Guidance and Practice," 92.

Many missions have emphasized the importance of translating reports into languages readable by relevant audiences. The report of the Kyrgyzstan Commission "urges the Government of the Kyrgyz Republic to prepare translations of the Executive Summary in the Kyrgyz and Uzbek languages, and arrange for the broad dissemination of both the Executive Summary and the report in its entirety throughout Kyrgyzstan in the print and electronic media."[69] The Côte d'Ivoire Commission took the step of publishing the full report in French – while also publishing only a short extract in English – so that the people of Côte d'Ivoire, where the official language is French, could read and use the report.[70]

D.   After the Mission Ends

After the release of the report, the mission ends, the team dissolves, and the responsibility shifts to international actors, governments, and members of civil society to use the report as an advocacy tool and to allow the report to inform decision-making processes. Some commissioners remain publicly engaged by offering public statements about the adoption (or lack thereof) of the report's recommendations,[71] authoring academic articles about the mission,[72] or becoming directly involved in advocacy efforts or capacity-building measures related to the context.[73] However, on missions mandated by the UNHRC, commissioners are limited by a declaration that UNHRC requests commissioners to sign, that states, "I also

---

[69] Kyrgyzstan Commission report, 89.

[70] See generally "Rapport de la Commission d'enquête internationale indépendante sur la Côte d'Ivoire," A/HRC/17/48, July 1, 2011, accessed May 26, 2015, http://www.refworld .org/docid/4ee05cdf2.html.

[71] For example, see "Bahrain: Promises Unkept, Rights Still Violated," Human Rights Watch, November 22, 2012, accessed May 26, 2015, http://www.hrw.org/news/2012/11/22/bahrain-promises-unkept-rights-still-violated.

[72] For example, see generally M. Cherif Bassiouni, "Appraising UN Justice-Related Fact-Finding Missions," *Washington University Journal of Law & Policy* 5, no. 35 (2001), accessed June 20, 2015, http://law.wustl.edu/harris/documents/p_35_Bassiouni.pdf; Théo Boutruche, "Credible Fact-Finding and Allegations of International Humanitarian Law Violations: Challenges in Theory and Practice," *Journal of Conflict & Security Law* 16, no. 1 (2011), accessed June 20, 2015, doi:10.1093/jcsl/krq027; and Steven R. Ratner, "Accountability and the Sri Lankan Civil War," *The American Journal of International Law* 106, no. 4 (2012), accessed June 20, 2015, http://www.jstor.org/stable/10.5305.

[73] For example, Yasmin Sooka, Member of the Sri Lanka Panel, has remained engaged in advocacy regarding accountability in Sri Lanka. See "Sooka and Sheeran Join Sri Lanka Campaign," Sri Lanka Campaign for Peace & Justice, August 22, 2012, accessed May 26, 2015, http://blog.srilankacampaign.org/2012/08/sooka-and-sheeran-join-sri-lanka.html.

undertake to respect, during the tenure of my mandate and subsequently, the confidentiality of all information made available to me in my capacity as a member of the Commission of Inquiry [or Fact-Finding Mission]."[74]

Interviews conducted for this chapter reveal a tendency among practitioners to hold positive perceptions of the missions on which they served. This tendency is reflected by the fact that when commissioners speak publicly about past MRF work, they are generally reluctant to offer comments that might bring the mission's credibility into question.

There is, however, one famous exception. In April 2011, Richard Goldstone, who, as noted earlier, had led the Gaza Fact-Finding Mission in 2009, wrote an op-ed published in *The Washington Post* that stated that, since the conclusion of the mission, information had been published that "indicates that civilians were not intentionally targeted [by Israel] as a matter of policy,"[75] contrasting the conclusions offered in the mission's final report.[76] Such a comment should theoretically be uncontroversial, since the possibility that new information revealed after an MRF mission's conclusion could lead a subsequent investigation to reach a different conclusion is in no way remote or unusual. Practitioners interviewed for this book understood this to be an inherent aspect of MRF work and articulated no concern that such a scenario would harm the credibility of an MRF mission.[77] The situation had previously arisen with the Darfur Commission, which had concluded "that the Government of Sudan has not pursued a policy of genocide,"[78] while the Pre-Trial Chamber of the ICC subsequently issued an arrest warrant for Sudanese President Omar al-Bashir that included three counts of genocide.[79] Despite this development, practitioners still perceive the Darfur Commission to be a valuable exercise that can serve as a model for future MRF work.

---

[74] OHCHR, "Guidance and Practice," 108–109.

[75] Richard Goldstone, "Reconsidering the Goldstone Report on Israel and War Crimes," *The Washington Post*, April 1, 2011, accessed May 26, 2015, http://www.washingtonpost.com/opinions/reconsidering-the-goldstone-report-on-israel-and-war-crimes/2011/04/01/AFg111JC_story.html.

[76] See Gaza Fact-Finding Mission report, 406–408.

[77] Confidential interviews with high-level MRF practitioners, names of interviewees on file, conducted by HPCR, Spring 2013.

[78] Darfur Commission report, 131.

[79] Though the first arrest warrant issued by the ICC for President al-Bashir did not include a genocide charge, the decision to exclude genocide was overturned by the Appeals Chamber, and the Pre-Trial Chamber then issued a second arrest warrant. See *Prosecutor v. Bashir*, ICC-02/05-01/09, Second Warrant of Arrest for Omar Hassan Ahmad Al Bashir (International Criminal Court, July 12, 2010), accessed May 26, 2015, http://www.icc-cpi.int/iccdocs/doc/doc907140.pdf.

However, for the Gaza Fact-Finding Mission, Goldstone's op-ed reignited debates about the credibility of the mission, leading to calls for the
UN to retract the report.[80] Additionally, the other three members of the
mission disagreed with Goldstone's conclusion and wrote their own op-ed
that aimed "to dispel the impression that subsequent developments have
rendered any part of the mission's report unsubstantiated, erroneous or
inaccurate."[81] The "legitimacy war" that had been fiercely waged between
the mission's supporters and detractors was revived.

Furthermore, one could argue that the *functus officio* doctrine applies
to such a scenario. This doctrine dictates that, once arbitrators have fully exercised their authority to adjudicate the issues submitted to them,
"their authority over those questions is ended," and "the arbitrators have
no further authority, absent agreement by the parties, to redetermine
that issue."[82] However, the fact that the credibility of MRF missions
hinges directly on the eminence of the commissioners leads to a tenuous
relationship, at least in terms of perception, between MRF missions and
this doctrine. When a mission concludes, though the formal authority
endowed to the commissioners by the mandate terminates, subsequent
comments made by commissioners could feed into the perception that
a re-evaluation of the mission's findings is necessary. Indeed, the Goldstone op-ed episode highlights the fact that the delicate environment in
which MRF missions operate endures long after the conclusion of the
mission.

E.   *Mitigation Measures*

While public communication plays an important role in MRF missions,
the factors examined above suggest the importance of reserve and caution. Though advocating for the mission can be crucial for promoting

---

[80]   For example, see "Goldstone U.N. Report Retraction Spurned by Co-authors," *CNN*, April
14, 2011, accessed May 26, 2015, http://www.cnn.com/2011/WORLD/meast/04/14/israel.
goldstone.report/; and Richard Falk, "Goldstone Breathes New Life into Gaza Report,"
Al Jazeera, April 20, 2011, accessed May 26, 2015, http://www.aljazeera.com/indepth/
opinion/2011/04/2011417115920432106.html.

[81]   Hina Jilani, Christine Chinkin, and Desmond Travers, "Goldstone Report: Statement
Issued by Members of UN Mission on Gaza War," *The Guardian*, April 14, 2011, accessed
May   26,   2015,   http://www.theguardian.com/commentisfree/2011/apr/14/goldstone-
report-statement-un-gaza.

[82]   For example, see *McGregot ven DE Moere, Inc. v. Paychex, Inc.*, United States District
Court for the Western District of New York, June 10, 1996, accessed May 26, 2015, http://
www.geigroth.com/decisions/dec29.htm.

perceptions of the mission's legitimacy, a public misstep can further exacerbate an already tense political atmosphere and increase security risks for the staff. Given the unpredictability of in-person interviews and press conferences, one practitioner recommends that missions communicate publicly primarily through writing.[83] The concern is that, during an interview or press conference, a commissioner might make a comment that insinuates – either due to imprecise wording, a misunderstanding on the part of the interviewer, or subsequent commentators who take the statement out of context – that the mission has prejudged the outcome of the investigation.

Another measure that can be taken to mitigate the risks of public communication is to nominate only one spokesperson for the mission. While MRF missions are typically led by numerous commissioners, having only one spokesperson will help ensure the propagation of a uniform and coherent public position, preventing divergences of opinion between commissioners from becoming public and being exploited to the detriment of the mission's aims.

II. Report Drafting

The mission's final report is the primary channel of communication by which the commissioners' work enters the public domain. The report is, ultimately, the only concrete outcome of the MRF mission and the main basis on which the whole work of the MRF mission will be judged. Therefore, the report should be drafted with the utmost caution.

As with the overall issue of public communication, report drafting is also concerned with the question of who constitutes the report's intended audience. While the report is primarily directed to the mandating body, the actual intended audience is much larger. Is the report for affected populations to have a historical record of the events that occurred? For governments and other actors in the international community as a means of generating support for accountability or for some other political intervention to resolve an ongoing conflict? For international and national prosecutors to use as lead evidence for formal investigations? What specific objectives is the mission aiming to meet? The way that MRF practitioners answer these questions shapes decision making during the report drafting process, as this section will demonstrate.

---

[83] Philippe Kirsch, HPCR interview.

A. *The Drafting Process*

Drafting a report in an MRF context is difficult. The process involves many people collaborating under tight time constraints, and practitioners have stated of their report drafting processes that "the time pressure was enormous"[84] and that the process was "very painful."[85] One practitioner notes that, for UN missions, the time constraints are compounded by the fact that "the report needs to be submitted six weeks before you'll be presenting it. This also affects how much time the mission has."[86]

These far-from-ideal circumstances often lead to MRF reports that are peppered with typographical errors,[87] though these small mistakes, and the frustration that practitioners have expressed with the report-drafting process, have not translated into dissatisfaction with the overall outcome of the report. One practitioner states, sharing a widely held sentiment, "The one message I want to send is the sense that, to the extent that it has merit, it's remarkable, given the circumstances under which we had to put it together. In terms of resources, time, scope of the inquiry, it's just a very very difficult exercise."[88]

---

[84] Confidential interview with a high-level MRF practitioner, name of interviewee on file, conducted by HPCR, Summer 2013.

[85] Confidential interview with a high-level MRF practitioner, name of interviewee on file, conducted by HPCR, Summer 2013.

[86] Vic Ullom, Legal Adviser, International Commission of Inquiry on Libya, interview conducted by HPCR, August 8, 2013.

[87] For example, the footnotes of the DRC Mapping Exercise report do not line up correctly with the paragraphs to which they are supposed to refer. Many of the paragraphs in the report's footnotes are off by 40, suggesting that footnotes were not updated after edits were made to earlier drafts of the report. See, for example, footnotes 881 and 882, which mention ¶¶ 121 and 122, while the information referred to in these footnotes actually correlates to ¶¶ 161 and 162. Also, the report does not have a footnote 108. Instead, the footnotes jump from 107 to 109. And, in the body of the report, two paragraphs in a row are both numbered 95. The Darfur Commission report contains two different annexes that are both labeled "Annex 3," and the heading for Annex 2 misspells "Sudan." The first report of the Libya Commission contains a footnote citing a news story about a survey on sexual violence, but the figures that the footnote provides do not match those that appear in the news story cited. Specifically, in the first Libya Commission report, ¶ 215 states, "A psychologist in Benghazi informed the Commission that out of 60,000 persons responding to a survey, 259 reported cases of sexual abuse." The footnote for this sentence, footnote 287, cites the following article: "Psychologist: Proof of Hundreds of Rape Cases during Libya's War," *CNN*, May 23, 2011, accessed May 26, 2015, http://edition.cnn.com/2011/WORLD/africa/05/23/libya.rape.survey.psychologist/. However, this article states that 50,000 (not 60,000) people responded to the survey and that 295 (not 259) respondents admitted that they had been raped.

[88] Sir Nigel Rodley, Commissioner, Bahrain Independent Commission of Inquiry, interview conducted by HPCR, April 12, 2013.

In light of these difficulties, the report-drafting process should begin as early as possible. Report structure, main topics to be examined, and suggested length can all be discussed by the commissioners in the early stage of the operations of the mission. Furthermore, at this early stage, the mission can identify a lead drafter for the report.

Still, different missions have grappled with these challenges in different ways. This section examines trends in MRF practice regarding report-drafting processes. The section focuses first on different ways that practitioners have divided responsibilities while report drafting, and second, on complications that arise from the need to keep the report-drafting process confidential.

1.   Division of Labor

While ultimately the final report is the sole responsibility of the commissioners, it is common practice that other members of the MRF team are directly involved in preparing drafts of the report. Therefore, it is important to organize the division of labor right from the start.

There are different ways to divide responsibilities during report drafting. On the Darfur Commission, one of the mission's members recalls the beneficial effect of different members of the mission working in one physical location:

> The environment allowed us to have this consultation. We were all in Geneva, sitting in one office, which means we were all there. People were not working from different countries. We were all there in the morning, everyone getting together. That kind of environment helps to have a better consultation and collaboration in the report drafting.[89]

In contrast, the Georgia Fact-Finding Mission is a unique example of a mission that lacked a unified collaborative process. On this mission, the investigators and drafters of different chapters of the report had no contact with one another, and according to one practitioner, "This was the most problematic aspect. It limited the full picture of international law we were looking at."[90]

Some missions have relied on a lead drafter. One practitioner states, "I tend to think that reports read better if there is a primary drafter. There

---

[89]   Hina Jilani, Member of the International Commission of Inquiry on Darfur and the United Nations Fact-Finding Mission on the Gaza Conflict, interview conducted by HPCR, April 24, 2013.

[90]   Confidential interview with a high-level MRF practitioner, name of interviewee on file, conducted by HPCR, Fall 2013.

is one voice. But this drafter must also be very open to the suggestions of others. It needs to be a very collaborative process. I don't know if there's a correct way to do it."[91]

In another context, a drafter was brought in toward the end of the drafting process to serve as a fresh eye:

> In the end, we were maybe a month away from the deadline, we still didn't have a report that we felt comfortable releasing publicly. We got someone fresh who had been involved in writing a similar report. We assigned her the task of being a fresh eye. By then, those involved were too deep in to see very objectively. It helped to have someone say what to make shorter and what to expand.[92]

Though the use of a lead drafter has not necessarily become a standard practice, the fact that a lead drafter can ensure uniformity across different sections of the report suggests the benefits of employing a lead drafter on future missions. Having a lead drafter who also acts as the legal adviser of the mission may also engender better cohesion between the legal framework, the level of evidence, and the way the facts are presented in the report. A lead drafter is also in a good position to ensure that the length of the report is kept on track with what the mission initially planned.

As noted above, report drafting should begin at the early stage of the mission. All the material on the creation of the mission, commissioner selection and background, the mandate and its interpretation, the methodology adopted, and the legal framework applicable are available during the early stages of the mission's work. Having these sections of the report drafted early on can avoid rushing at the end and can allow for more time to work on the results of the investigation. Even the report's recommendations can be the subject of early draft exercises and then can be refined and reformulated toward the end of the process.

Finally, the last draft of the report will have to be reviewed carefully by the commissioners, who will bear the sole responsibility for the whole report. This last phase of final review concludes with the adoption of the final report by the commissioners.

---

[91] Lesley Taylor, Report Drafter, Kyrgyzstan Inquiry Commission, and United Nations Independent Special Commission of Inquiry for Timor-Leste, interview conducted by HPCR, July 31, 2013.

[92] Confidential interview with a high-level MRF practitioner, name of interviewee on file, conducted by HPCR, Summer 2013.

2. Confidentiality

One risk during the report-drafting process is that the report, or certain sections of it, might be leaked before the report's publication. Indeed, the reports for the Darfur Commission,[93] the DRC Mapping Exercise,[94] the Secretary-General's Panel of Inquiry on the 31 May 2010 Flotilla Incident (hereafter the UNSG Flotilla Panel),[95] and the Sri Lanka Panel were all leaked – in whole or in part – before the intended publication date.[96] On one mission, concerns about leaks led to caution from commissioners about sharing drafts with the mission's experts.[97] This danger is particularly concerning, given the sensitive nature of materials that MRF missions produce. For example, a widespread reluctance exists among practitioners to publicly disclose the names of alleged perpetrators identified by the mission, primarily because of due process concerns for the suspects.[98] For this reason, many missions have opted to compile lists that identify names of alleged perpetrators but to keep these documents confidential.[99]

Sometimes the need for confidentiality conflicts with the need to consult outside experts. Specifically, practitioners have sometimes felt compelled to share certain sections of the report with external scholars or analysts who were in a position to assist in sharpening the report's analysis for certain issue areas. However, when engaging in this practice, it is important to share only sections of the report that are not contentious and that do not include any information about the mission's findings. For example, seeking the views of an outside international law expert on the report's "applicable law" section could allow the mission to receive valuable

---

[93] "UN Rules out Genocide in Darfur," *BBC News*, February 1, 2005, accessed May 26, 2015, http://news.bbc.co.uk/2/hi/africa/4224757.stm.

[94] "DR Congo: UN Releases Most Extensive Report to Date on War Massacres, Rapes," *UN News Centre*, October 1, 2010, accessed May 26, 2015, http://www.un.org/apps/news/story.asp?NewsID=36306#.UykMSa1dVU3.

[95] Neil MacFarquhar and Ethan Bronner, "Report Finds Naval Blockade by Israel Legal but Faults Raid," *The New York Times*, September 1, 2011, accessed May 26, 2015, http://www.nytimes.com/2011/09/02/world/middleeast/02flotilla.html?pagewanted=all.

[96] "UN Expert Panel Report on Sri Lanka Leaked to Local Media," *ColomboPage*, April 16, 2011, accessed May 26, 2015, http://www.colombopage.com/archive_11/Apr16_1302928062CH.php.

[97] Confidential interview with a high-level MRF practitioner, name of interviewee on file, conducted by HPCR, Fall 2011.

[98] See Rob Grace, "The Design and Planning of Monitoring, Reporting, and Fact-Finding Missions" (working paper, Program on Humanitarian Policy and Conflict Research at Harvard University, December 2013), pp. 33–40, http://papers.ssrn.com/sol3/papers.cfm?abstract_id=2365435.

[99] Ibid.

outside feedback without increasing the risk that the mission's findings could be made public prematurely.

B.   *The Format and Content of the Report*

MRF reports vary from one another in terms of length and format. Regarding length, of the fifteen missions on which this book focuses, the longest report is the Georgia Fact-Finding Mission report, totaling 1,129 pages, and the shortest is the Beit Hanoun Fact-Finding Mission report, totaling just 24 pages. Perhaps the most significant factor shaping report length is one imposed by UN bureaucracy. For missions authorized by the UNHRC, length limitations are based on the time needed for editing and translation.[100] For some missions, this could mean that the report cannot exceed twenty-five pages. For the Côte d'Ivoire Commission, which abided by the length limitation, there was much more information that the commissioners wanted to put into the report but could not due to the space restriction.[101]

The length limitation also played a role in the second Libya Commission report. As one practitioner states of this report, "Some of our biggest fights would be whether an incident that someone put hours of research into gets cut purely for space reasons."[102] However, the Libya Commission learned that the mission could place a longer report online by including an extended version in the report's annex. Consequently, the mission drafted a long report and then cut this version down to an abridged version that was printed, translated, and circulated to governments leading up to the presentation of the report to the UNHRC.[103]

Many MRF reports also include certain visual elements, such as maps, charts, tables, and photographs. Charts and tables are helpful to summarize data relevant to the mission's mandate. For example, the Bahrain Commission report includes a pie chart detailing percent loss of income for businesses during the events of February/March 2011, based on a survey conducted by the Bahrain Chamber of Commerce.[104]

---

[100] Sonia Bakar, HPCR interview.
[101] Confidential interview with a high-level MRF practitioner, name of interviewee on file, conducted by HPCR, Spring 2013.
[102] Vic Ullom, HPCR interview.
[103] Confidential interview with a high-level MRF practitioner, name of interviewee on file, conducted by HPCR, Summer 2013.
[104] "Report of the Bahrain Independent Commission of Inquiry," November 23, 2011, p. 343, accessed June 14, 2015, http://www.bici.org.bh/BICIreportEN.pdf.

Similarly, maps can be very useful tools to help the reader identify regions or sites where events occurred, to illustrate which parties to the conflict controlled different regions, and to visualize the movement of troops. One note about the use of maps is that the source of the map can affect perceptions of the legitimacy of the information included. For example, the Sri Lanka Panel deliberately used maps pulled from the website of the Ministry of Defense of Sri Lanka so that Sri Lankan officials would have a more difficult time attempting to dispute information derived from these maps.[105] The concern about the perceived legitimacy of the information contained in MRF reports suggests that the mission should be transparent about the sources of the maps included in its report. However, some maps included in MRF reports provide no information about who drafted the maps.[106]

Regarding photographs, of the fifteen missions on which this book focuses, only one mission – the Sri Lanka Panel – took the step of including photographs throughout the body of the report. For the source of these photographs, each photograph is labeled: "submission to the Panel by the photographer."[107] The captions for these photographs are:

- "IDP settlement near Putumattalan Hospital in second No Fire Zone, March 2009."[108]
- "IDP shelter destroyed by shelling in second No Fire Zone, April 2009."[109]
- "Putumattalan Hospital, March 2009."[110]
- "Infant amputee in second No Fire Zone, March 2009."[111]
- "Civilian deaths in second No Fire Zone, May 2009."[112]
- "Child in hospital in second No Fire Zone, April 2009."[113]

As these captions suggest, some of the images are quite gruesome. For example, the image titled "Infant amputee in second No Fire Zone, March 2009," shows a baby missing a right arm, with bandages wrapped around the head, arms, and right leg. It seems the panel opted to include visuals to have an impact that extended beyond what written descriptions of violations could accomplish. The reasons that most MRF missions do not incorporate photographs include the fact that the source of photographs – by

---

[105] Confidential interview with a high-level MRF practitioner, name of interviewee on file, conducted by HPCR, Summer 2013.
[106] For example, see Kyrgyzstan Commission report, xii–xiii.
[107] For example, see Sri Lanka Panel report, 27.
[108] Ibid.   [109] Ibid., 29.   [110] Ibid., 31.   [111] Ibid., 33.
[112] Ibid., 35.   [113] Ibid., 39.

whom, when, and where the photograph was taken – is often difficult to establish. Additionally, showing a photograph for one incident and not another could evoke criticisms that the mission has been selective regarding the depth of attention devoted to different incidents. For these reasons, it is unusual for a UN report to incorporate photographs, though the practice is quite common for NGO reports.

C. Presenting Background on the Creation and Operation of the Mission

Practitioners have deemed transparency regarding the mission's formation and operations to be an important element of MRF reports. This notion is encapsulated in the *Siracusa Guidelines*, which state: "The Report should present the purpose, formation, operations and method of work of the fact-finding body, as well as evidence and other information compiled during the investigation."[114] The following section provides an overview of how different reports have presented information about the mission's mandate and Terms of Reference, the commissioners and staff, and funding. As noted earlier in this chapter, drafting these sections early on could allow the mission more time at the end to focus practitioners' energies on drafting the sections of the report that present the mission's factual and legal findings.

1. The Formation of the Mission

MRF reports nearly universally provide information about the mandate of the mission and the identity of the mandating entity. The DRC Mapping Exercise report contains two pages describing how the report came into being.[115] Both Libya Commission reports, the Côte d'Ivoire Commission report, the UNHRC Flotilla Fact-Finding Mission report, the Beit Hanoun Fact-Finding Mission report, and the Lebanon Commission report reference the UNHRC resolutions that created these missions.[116]

---

[114] Bassiouni and Abraham, *Siracusa Guidelines*, 49.

[115] DRC Mapping Exercise report, 2–3.

[116] See first Libya Commission report, 14; second Libya Commission report, 5; Côte d'Ivoire Commission report, 6; "Report of the International Fact-finding Mission to Investigate Violations of International Law, Including International Humanitarian and Human Rights Law, Resulting from the Israeli Attacks on the Flotilla of Ships Carrying Humanitarian Assistance," A/HRC/15/21, September 27, 2010, p. 3, accessed May 26, 2015, http://www2. ohchr.org/english/bodies/hrcouncil/docs/15session/A.HRC.15.21_en.pdf; "Report of the High-Level Fact-Finding Mission to Beit Hanoun established under Council resolution S-3/1," A/HRC/9/26, September 1, 2008, p. 3, accessed May 26, 2015, http://www .refworld.org/docid/48cfa3a22.html; and Lebanon Commission report, 2.

The Darfur Commission report references the UNSC resolution that authorized the mission.[117] The reports for the Sri Lanka Panel, the Guinea Commission, the United Nations Independent Special Commission of Inquiry for Timor-Leste (hereafter the Timor-Leste Commission), and the UNSG Flotilla Panel, all of which were established by the UNSG, provide information about how and why the UNSG created the mission.[118] The report for the Bahrain Commission includes in the annex the full text of the two royal orders that constitute the mission's mandate.[119] And the beginning of the report for the Georgia Fact-Finding Mission presents a full copy of the Council of the European Union decision that created the mission.[120]

In some cases, though, even a lengthy description of the mission's creation can leave some ambiguities. For example, the Kyrgyzstan Commission report includes a paragraph about the formation of the mission that provides a good deal of background but also remains vague about certain pieces of information. The report states:

> Following the violent events in June 2010 in southern Kyrgyzstan, numerous calls were made for an international investigation. An initiative by the Nordic countries was accepted by the President of the Kyrgyz Republic, H.E. Ms. Roza Otunbayeva. On 6 July 2010, the President asked Dr. Kimmo Kiljunen, Special Representative for Central Asia, OSCE Parliamentary Assembly, to coordinate the preparation process for the International Independent Commission for Inquiry into "tragic events that have taken place in the South of the Region of the Kyrgyz Republic (KIC)". In a letter from the Ministry of Foreign Affairs addressed to the United Nations (UN) on 21 July 2010, the Government of the Kyrgyz Republic requested the UN Secretary General to support the International Independent Commission of Inquiry headed by K. Kiljunen. There was broad consultation with numerous international organizations and entities including the UN,

---

[117] Darfur Commission report, 9.

[118] "Report of the International Commission of Inquiry mandated to establish the facts and circumstances of the events of 28 September 2009 in Guinea," transmitted by letter dated 18 December 2009 from the Secretary-General addressed to the President of the Security Council, S/2009/693, December 18, 2009, pp. 5–6, accessed June 25, 2015, http://www.refworld.org/docid/4b4f49ea2.html; "Report of the United Nations Independent Special Commission of Inquiry for Timor-Leste," October 2006, pp. 10–11, accessed June 25, 2015, http://www.ohchr.org/Documents/Countries/COITimorLeste.pdf; and "Report of the Secretary-General's Panel of Inquiry on the 31 May 2010 Flotilla Incident," September 2011, p. 7, accessed June 14, 2015, http://www.un.org/News/dh/infocus/middle_east/Gaza_Flotilla_Panel_Report.pdf.

[119] Bahrain Commission report, 481–485.

[120] "Independent International Fact-Finding Mission on the Conflict in Georgia Report," vol. 1 (September 2009): 3.

the OSCE, the EU and the CIS. Finally, after discussion with the office of the UN High Commissioner for Human Rights as to the appropriate terms of reference for such an exercise, the Government officially informed UN Secretary-General Ban Ki-Moon in its letter of 29 September 2010 that it had endorsed the proposed terms of reference which include a mandate calling upon the KIC "*to investigate the facts and circumstances of these events [the outbreak of violence in June 2010].*"[121]

The above description mentions that the initiative arose from certain "Nordic countries" but does not specify which countries were involved; it states that the government of Kyrgyzstan requested the support of the UNSG but does not specify whether the UNSG acted on this request; and it states that the terms of reference were discussed with OHCHR and "endorsed" by the government of Kyrgyzstan without providing information about how, or if, these terms of reference legally authorize the mission. In contrast, the report for the DRC Mapping Exercise, which also had a complicated genesis that involved many different entities, makes clear that the Terms of Reference, which were approved by the UNSG, fell under the umbrella of MONUC and that MONUC's mandate served as the legal basis for the mission.[122]

Another somewhat confusing example is the Gaza Fact-Finding Mission. In this case, lack of clarity about the authorization for the mission arises from the fact that the mandate under which the mission operated differed from the original mandate adopted by the UNHRC. The original mandate, UNHRC resolution S-9/1, authorized an investigation only of Israel,[123] but Richard Goldstone renegotiated the mandate with the President of the UNHRC to encompass all sides of the conflict and to expand the temporal and territorial scope of the investigation.[124] The report of the Gaza Fact-Finding Mission provides the text of the renegotiated mandate and mentions the original mandate, but does not comment on whether or not any aspects of the original mandate still hold relevance in terms of the mission's legal basis.

2.   Commissioners and Staff

Reports for all of the fifteen missions of focus state clearly the names of the commissioners who worked on the mission in order to give more

---

[121]   Kyrgyzstan Commission report, xiv (internal citations omitted; emphasis in original).
[122]   DRC Mapping Exercise report, 33.
[123]   United Nations Human Rights Council resolution S-9/1, ¶ 14.
[124]   See Tomer Zarchin, "Goldstone to Haaretz: US Does Not Have to Protect Israel Blindly," *Haaretz*, November 13, 2009, accessed May 26, 2015, http://www.haaretz.com/print-edition/news/goldstone-to-haaretz-u-s-does-not-have-to-protect-israel-blindly-1.4211.

credibility to the mission and the report. However, staff members typically receive less attention. Security concerns factor into this decision, since staff members can sometimes be more vulnerable than commissioners. However, as one practitioner states, transparency in this regard, if possible, can be helpful to the mission:

> I am, in principle, in favor of having more information on staff in the report. In the mind of most people, what's important is the commissioners because they are the face of the mission, but staff are no less important. It would be beneficial to indicate what type of skills and background people had, and whether they were used for jobs for which they were ready. Staff changes are also relevant. Too many staff changes lead to a lack of continuity. Transparency in that area as in others helps the credibility of the report.[125]

Indeed, some reports, while not providing names of staff members, do present an overview of the types of experts who served on the mission. The Timor-Leste Commission report states:

> The secretariat was established and assisted by the Office of the United Nations High Commissioner for Human Rights (OHCHR) and located in the former United Nations House, Rua de Caicoli, Dili, Timor-Leste. The secretariat consisted of criminal investigators, human rights monitors, legal advisers, a political adviser, an expert in military sector reform, an expert in police sector reform, a data-management officer, security officers and other administrative support staff. The secretariat was headed by an Executive Director assisted by an executive assistant, who both arrived in Dili with a few other staff members on 7 July 2006, marking the official beginning of the work of the Commission.[126]

Similarly, the report for the Kyrgyzstan Commission states:

> As provided by the TOR, the Secretariat was established by the Crisis Management Initiative (CMI), a Finnish non-governmental organisation based in Helsinki. The main office of the KIC Secretariat was located in Osh, in southern Kyrgyzstan. The Secretariat consisted of experts in political science, ethnic relations, human rights, international law and gender based violence as well as military and media issues.[127]

Additionally, the Kyrgyzstan Commission report is transparent about the nationalities of the mission's international staff and the ethnic identity of the mission's local staff, in order to rebut any accusation of being partial in such a divided conflict situation. The report states:

---

[125] Philippe Kirsch, HPCR interview.   [126] Timor-Leste Commission report, 12.
[127] Kyrgyzstan Commission report, 3 (internal citation omitted).

Experts came from Armenia, Australia, Austria, Belgium, Canada, Finland, France, Germany, Kazakhstan, Tajikistan, Russia, United Kingdom and United States of America. The local assistants and support staff were from different ethnic backgrounds: Kyrgyz 8, Uzbek 4, Russian 4, Kazakh 1, Korean 1 and Tatar 1.[128]

Two of the reports from the fifteen missions of focus were unusually transparent about the staff of the mission. One report, that of the Georgia Fact-Finding Mission, identifies the names and nationalities of all the military experts, legal experts, historians, and political analysts who worked on the mission, as well as the names, nationalities, and current and former roles of members of the mission's Senior Advisory Board.[129] Another report, that of the Bahrain Commission, does not provide the names of staff members but, in the report's annex, presents an organizational chart that shows different staff members' roles and their organizational relationships with one another.[130]

3. Funding

MRF reports rarely provide detailed information about the mission's funding since most of them are funded by UN organizations from their regular budget. The Kyrgyzstan Commission report states that the mission "was financially supported by the EU, the United States, Finland, Norway, Germany, Switzerland, Sweden, Denmark, Turkey, Estonia and France" but provides no information about the size of the budget.[131] The report of the Sri Lanka Panel includes the mission's Terms of Reference, which state, "The Panel shall be funded from the Secretary-General's unforeseen budget."[132] However, the report offers no other details. The report for the DRC Mapping Exercise offers a bit more information:

> It was decided that OHCHR would lead the Mapping Exercise and the project was funded by the voluntary contributions of ten interested partners. The UNDP [United Nations Development Programme] Country Office in the DRC was responsible for the financial administration of the Mapping Exercise and MONUC provided logistical support. The three parties signed an agreement defining their respective rights and obligations. The continued and overwhelming support of these three bodies for the Mapping Exercise should be mentioned at this juncture.[133]

---

[128] Ibid.   [129] Georgia Fact-Finding Mission report, 1: 40–41.
[130] Bahrain Commission report, 495.   [131] Kyrgyzstan Commission report, 7.
[132] Sri Lanka Panel report, 2.
[133] DRC Mapping Exercise report, 34–35 (internal citations omitted).

This report also mentions the ten parties – Austria, Belgium, Canada, Germany, the Netherlands, the Republic of Korea, the United Kingdom, Sweden, Switzerland, and the MacArthur Foundation – that contributed funds, but it does not mention the size of the budget.[134]

The reports for the Georgia Fact-Finding Mission and the Bahrain Commission – as with transparency regarding the mission's staff – are also unusually transparent regarding funding. The text of the mandate for the Georgia Fact-Finding Mission, included in the beginning of the final report, contains a section devoted solely to the mission's finances.[135] And the Bahrain Commission report not only provides specific information about the salaries of the commissioners and staff members but also states of the mission's finances:

> The Commission enjoyed full financial autonomy from the GoB [Government of Bahrain]. This was achieved by the allocation of 1.3 million USD to the Commission's independent bank account, to which it had exclusive access. In addition to this budgeted amount from the Royal Court, the Commission received contributed support in the form of air travel and hotel expenses, ground transport in Bahrain and the use of two villas for its offices. These services were contributed directly to the Commission but their cost was charged to the Royal Court. All other expenses were paid by the Commission and recorded by an independent accounting firm. The Commission's accounts will be audited by a second, independent accounting firm to ensure accuracy and transparency. The report of the Commission's accountant and the subsequent audit will be posted to the Commission's website on 16 December 2011.[136]

The widespread concerns that exist about perceptions of a mission's credibility suggest the desirability of greater transparency regarding funding. One common perception is that governments can exert political pressure that can affect the operations and findings of the mission. Control of funding could be one way that a government might influence a mission. This issue is particularly relevant for non-UN missions, though for UN missions, a good practice would be to annex the budget – which is public information but might otherwise be difficult to find – to the mission's final report in order to preempt any criticisms that might arise about the mission's funding sources.

---

[134] Ibid., 34.   [135] Georgia Fact-Finding Mission report, 1: 3.
[136] Bahrain Commission report, 9–10 (internal citation omitted).

D.   Presenting the Mission's Findings

The aforementioned fact that MRF work deals with events that are by nature highly political and controversial heightens the importance of being, and appearing to be, impartial. Impartiality connotes the absence of preconceived ideas, prejudices, or biases. However, in order to appear impartial, MRF practitioners tend to strive to present a balanced account, crafting a narrative that emphasizes that serious violations were committed by multiple parties to the conflict. Such a balanced account does not mean reporting on an equal number of events by each party to a conflict, nor does it suggest a "moral equivalence" between different parties or an "equivalence of blame" for violations. Rather, this approach merely stresses that serious violations of international law were committed by all sides.

This need for balance can lead to an "impartiality paradox," by which, in order to appear impartial, when making decisions about what to investigate and how to convey a mission's findings in the final report, practitioners consider factors that might be seen as biased by suspects and the political, religious, or ethnic groups to which those suspects belong. Specifically, MRF practitioners, in order to promote the perception that the mission is balanced, will actually deliberately take into account criteria related to victims' or suspects' affiliations with certain groups. A commissioner for the Bahrain Commission, in an interview conducted after the conclusion of the mission, offered comments that nicely express this dilemma. This practitioner stated, "Let's put it this way, we would never have distorted the truth for the sake of balance but certainly we needed balance as a dimension of the truth."[137] As these comments suggest, there are twin objectives that sometimes conflict with one another. On the one hand, the report aims to present the mission's findings in an impartial manner. On the other hand, the report aims to present the mission's findings in a way that also gives the *appearance* of objectivity. These two aims are not always congruent with one another, a situation that can be described as the "impartiality paradox."

The rest of this section will examine how this consideration, as well as others, affect two factors – structure and tone – during the MRF report-drafting process.

---

[137] "Interview with BICI Commissioner Sir Nigel Rodley – Part 2," Bahrain Justice and Development Movement, June 27, 2012, accessed May 26, 2015, http://bahrainjdm.hopto. org/2012/06/27/exclusive-interview-with-bici-commissioner-sir-nigel-rodley-part-2/.

1. Structure

Report structure is inherently linked to the mandate. The Bahrain Commission serves as an obvious example of the mandate determining the report's structure. Article Nine of Royal Order No. 28 of 2011, which authorized the mission, outlines ten areas of focus for the mission, and these ten areas roughly correlate to the chapters of the mission's final report.[138] Regardless of the mandate, though, the typical MRF report will include the following structural elements.

- Introduction
  - Information about the establishment of the mission
  - Names and biographical information about the commissioners
  - Presentation of the mission's interpretation of the mandate
  - Details about the methodology adopted (e.g., types of sources, standard of proof used, information about the mission's site visits)
  - Information about the operations of the mission (e.g., challenges faced and level of cooperation provided by relevant governments and armed groups)
- Background
  - Historical information about the country and about the specific conflict being examined
  - Information about relevant institutions in the context examined (e.g., the composition of military forces in the country where alleged violations occurred)
- Factual conclusions (presented, e.g., chronologically, geographically, or by type of violation)
- Legal classifications (i.e., presentation of the mission's perspective on the relevant legal framework and the mission's assessment of which laws have been violated)
- Responsibility (i.e., if called for in the mandate, an assessment of individual and institutional responsibility, in legal and/or political terms, for the events examined)
- Additional areas called for in the mandate (e.g., some missions have been mandated to assess the domestic legal system in the country of focus)
- Recommendations
- Annex

---

[138] Royal Order No. 28 of 2011, Article 9, accessed June 25, 2015, http://www.lcil.cam.ac.uk/sites/default/files/LCIL/documents/arabspring/Bahrain_9_Royal_Order_No28.pdf.

The public perception factor can also shape decisions about what to include and exclude. For one MRF body, genocide was not specifically mentioned in the mandate, but the practitioners examined the issue and concluded that genocide had not occurred.[139] The practitioners decided to leave this conclusion out of the report, because, given the inflammatory nature of the issue, the practitioners figured that if the report mentioned genocide, no matter what the report said, it was likely to be misinterpreted.[140]

Structure can also be used to accentuate or de-emphasize certain findings. On one mission, violations committed by a certain government were deliberately not presented in a single chapter but rather were included throughout the report in multiple chapters to reduce the risk of inflaming tensions in the country and throughout the region.[141] Structuring the report based on different groups involved in the perpetration of violations may have the effect of singling out one party to the conflict more than another, fostering the impression of unbalance. Conversely, the Libya Commission report devotes a chapter that focuses solely on the North Atlantic Treaty Organization (NATO), a choice that avoids the appearance of suggesting that NATO is on par with the Qaddafi-loyalist and rebel forces fighting in the country.

One key question facing report drafters is whether to structure the report by violation (so that each section addresses all of the mission's findings about a specific violation) or by geographical region (which allows a single section to discuss different types of violations that occurred in the same location). While structuring the report by violation facilitates the integration of the legal classification and analysis with the actual fact-finding elements, a geographical and chronological structure puts the emphasis more on the narrative aspect, leaving the legal questions to a specific and subsequent part of the report.

Some practitioners prefer the "violation" approach. As one practitioner states:

> I think that a report should be really well organized and preferably constructed symmetrically. The presentation of each violation, for example, should be structured the same way. That facilitates the reader's access to and understanding of the report, helps you maintain clarity in your own analysis and creates a perception of a systematic and professional approach.[142]

---

[139] Steven Ratner, HPCR interview.   [140] Ibid.
[141] Confidential interview with a high-level MRF practitioner, name of interviewee on file, conducted by HPCR, Fall 2013.
[142] Philippe Kirsch, HPCR interview.

Other practitioners have emphasized the benefits of the "geographic" approach. For example, discussion about the respective merits of the "violation" approach and the "geographic" approach played out during the Libya Commission. One practitioner who served on the mission states, "We decided by violations because that was in line with the mandate. It wasn't without discussion. Some people said it would be better to do it by geography because it's easier to tell a story of what happened."[143] During the process of finalizing the report, on the day before the report was due, one of the commissioners suggested restructuring the report to present the information temporally, as opposed to structuring the report by violation type.[144] However, the practitioners on the mission concluded that there was not enough time to execute the restructuring process successfully.[145]

Another factor that practitioners have considered when determining structure is readability. This factor played a role in the decision of the UNSG Flotilla Panel to place the mission's legal analysis in the report's annex. The main body of the report makes no mention of international law, and the annex presents only an analysis of the applicable law without analyzing the report's factual findings through these legal lenses. The decision was made to relegate the legal analysis to the annex because the analysis of the applicable law was deemed "too exhaustive," and the goal was to "place more emphasis on factual findings and what should happen next."[146]

One particularly important aspect of MRF reports is that, when presenting facts that will serve as a basis for a legal conclusion, the text needs to address all of the elements relevant to specific violations or crimes. For crimes against humanity, for example, the report should provide information indicating whether or not the attacks were widespread or systematic. For international humanitarian law, the report should demonstrate whether or not an armed conflict exists and should provide information about the behavior of both the alleged perpetrator and the victim. For all types of violations, the report should answer basic questions about where and when each incident occurred, should exhibit uniformity in terms of the standard of proof, and should use vocabulary appropriate to the

---

[143] Vic Ullom, HPCR interview.
[144] Confidential interview with a high-level MRF practitioner, name of interviewee on file, conducted by HPCR, Summer 2013.
[145] Confidential interview with a high-level MRF practitioner, name of interviewee on file, conducted by HPCR, Summer 2013.
[146] Sir Geoffrey Palmer, Chair, Secretary-General's Panel of Inquiry on the 31 May 2010 Flotilla Incident, interview conducted by HPCR, April 4, 2013.

extent of evidentiary corroboration (e.g., the use of the word "alleged" if information has not been corroborated and the use of more affirmative vocabulary if the information has been corroborated). However, reports have not always succeeded in demonstrating cohesion between factual findings and legal conclusions. For example, the UNHRC Flotilla Fact-Finding Mission report states in the "applicable law" section that international humanitarian law applies, and concludes later in the report that international humanitarian law violations had been committed. However, the legal analysis section does not actually analyze the facts through the lens of this body of law.[147]

2. Tone

Tone, similar to structure, can be used to draw attention to – or away from – certain findings. Additionally, tone can play a role in perceptions of a report's objectivity. Similar to structure, the question of how to strike the correct tone in an MRF report is linked to the tension between an MRF mission's apolitical and political aspects. In most cases, the incidents described are so horrific that they speak for themselves with no need for emotive vocabulary. Many practitioners emphasize this perspective:

- "Well, it's not an NGO, not an advocacy document. It should be measured. I think we got the tone about right, it's fairly conservative, dry, and sober. No hyperbole at all. We erred on the side of caution. I think that's right. You don't want people to say, 'Well, I think they're making it up.'"[148]
- "A report should be drafted in a neutral tone. No diatribes. It should give an image of impartiality to the commission. It should be written in descriptive and dispassionate terms, even at the level of conclusion and recommendations. To say that the commission feels strongly about something, for example, may create the impression of a personal rather than professional approach to issues."[149]
- "There is no chance for future peace without the facts being presented in a sober and neutral manner."[150]

---

[147] Théo Boutruche, "Selecting and Applying Legal Lenses in Monitoring, Reporting, and Fact-Finding Missions" (working paper, Program on Humanitarian Policy and Conflict Research at Harvard University, October 2013), p. 19, http://papers.ssrn.com/sol3/papers.cfm?abstract_id=2337437.

[148] Philip Trewhitt, HPCR interview.   [149] Philippe Kirsch, HPCR interview.

[150] Heidi Tagliavini, quoted in Ellen Barry, "Georgia Challenges Report."

Additionally, as with structure, readability is also an issue. One practitioner states, "I would like to make it easier for people who are non-lawyers
to read and understand while maintaining very apolitical and uprightness
in legal writing. One tries to be fairly forensic about it but not write it in a
way that's utterly uninteresting."[151] And as another practitioner writes of
the many ends that an MRF report might be meant to serve:

> The final rule for a human rights report is to make it readable. It will often
> be written by lawyers, who must remember that it will not be read only
> by lawyers: to achieve its objective, it must be comprehensible to a wide
> range of people involved in civil society programmes, to journalists and
> politicians and diplomats, to victims and even to perpetrators. Some read-
> ers will not have English as a first language, and will not have the benefit
> of translation. The art is to be simple without becoming simplistic: let the
> facts speak for themselves, and confine legislation or technical details to
> appendices.[152]

One danger is that, in an effort to read as "apolitical" and "dry" – as various practitioners have stated as the desired tone – the report may undercut itself. One practitioner states that the ideal tone for MRF reports
is "authoritative impartiality."[153] This practitioner asserts, "I don't think
it's at all useful to apologize for writing a report to undercut your own
conclusions. It should be direct, clear."[154] Another practitioner speaks of a
mission that fell victim to the danger of couching conclusions in tentative
terms:

> I think the Georgia exercise is a good example as something that went well.
> At the same time, one has to admit that because everything was drafted so
> cautiously and carefully that in terms of the political impact of the report,
> it has been somewhat limited. When you read between the lines, you un-
> derstand that, for instance, the Georgian armed forces fell into a trap. They
> took an initiative that they should not have taken. But it's said in a very
> careful way. So you don't have an article in the press. It did not trigger the
> major re-evaluation. It was said so softly that nobody had an interest in
> dotting the "I's." It systematically avoided any statements that could lead
> to some polemics.[155]

---

[151] Confidential interview with a high-level MRF practitioner, name of interviewee on file,
conducted by HPCR, Summer 2013.
[152] Geoffrey Robertson, "Human Rights Fact-Finding: Some Legal and Ethical Dilemmas,"
Thematic Paper No. 1, Human Rights Institute of the International Bar Association, May
2010, p. 21.
[153] Lesley Taylor, HPCR interview.   [154] Ibid.
[155] Confidential interview with a high-level MRF practitioner, name of interviewee on file,
conducted by HPCR, Summer 2013.

The opposite danger, though, is that emotive vocabulary could discredit the report. Despite the consensus of practitioners interviewed for this chapter that an MRF report should strive for an unemotional tone, some MRF reports do contain emotive passages.[156] The evident paradox, based on this assessment of practitioners' perspectives, is that a report must sometimes be written in a manner that appears apolitical in order to maximize the report's political impact. The challenge, it seems, is writing a report that captures the experiences of victims without using emotive terminology that discredits the mission; presents the mission's factual and legal findings in a manner that is legally sound but also readable for a wider audience; and strives for a neutral tone without couching the report's findings in a manner that, by its tentativeness, fails to draw attention to the allegations examined. The delicacy and importance of tone in this regard constitutes another reason that a lead drafter can be useful. A lead drafter, or at least an editorial reviewer, can ensure that clarity, readability, spelling, verb tense, and formatting remain consistent across the entire report.

III. Conclusion

Public communication and report drafting both require caution and the balancing of competing goals: witness, victim, and staff security; political impact; and the mission's impartiality, for example. However, MRF practice appears to reveal no framework for matching the communications strategy to the context. Instead, the incentives and risks of public engagement more often push against one another, and an MRF mission's hybrid nature – as both an investigation that calls for confidentiality and a political exercise aiming to foster perceptions of the mission's credibility and pressure governments and groups to alter behavior – leads different practitioners toward distinct avenues, depending greatly on the preferences and personalities of commissioners. Though consensus exists about the importance of avoiding statements that might lead the public to perceive that the mission has prejudged the outcome of the investigation, the mission, in response to critiques, is placed in the difficult position of

---

[156] For example, see the Beit Hanoun Fact-Finding Mission report, 4, which states, "The mission felt it had to go to Gaza, even if reluctantly through Egypt, to express through its presence the solidarity of the international community with the suffering people, very much like the prophet Ezekiel sitting dumbfounded with his compatriots in their exile in Babylon, or the friends of Job in his suffering."

having to defend its credibility and comment on the methodology used to highlight the mission's impartiality while avoiding missteps that could further inflame the situation.

Furthermore, this chapter's assessment of recent MRF practice suggests that decisions about communication and report drafting are complicated by the fact that MRF work aims to influence different audiences in different ways. The way that the mission prioritizes its aims will affect the decisions that the mission makes about the level of public engagement during implementation and about issues such as tone and structure during the report-drafting process. These audiences and aims include:

- governments and other entities in the international community, for use as an authoritative document to serve as a basis for determining how to address an ongoing or past armed conflict or internal disturbance;
- governments and groups engaged in violent conflict, to urge these entities to abide by international law and to pursue accountability for past violations;
- international or national prosecutors, for use as evidence (or as leads) in investigations;
- civil society, for use as advocacy tools; and
- affected populations, so victims and affected communities feel heard by the international community.

Finally, one should remember that MRF missions are unlikely to be able to avoid criticisms entirely. The strategic public engagement aim – in terms of dealing with criticisms – is not one of prevention but rather mitigation. In this sense, there are sensible steps that an MRF mission can take. For example, responding to criticisms in writing rather than through in-person interviews reduces the likelihood that a public misstep will occur, and nominating one spokesperson for the mission can ensure that disagreements between commissioners will be kept confidential. In terms of report drafting, beginning the process early on in the mission helps the mission with time management toward the end, and using a single report drafter or editor presents a greater possibility that the report will have a consistent overall style and tone.

6

An Analysis of the Impact of Commissions
of Inquiry

ROB GRACE

Introduction

Commissions of inquiry that investigate alleged violations of international humanitarian law (IHL) and human rights law are impermanent entities. Under a mandate granted by governmental actors, commissioners and other practitioners undertake an information-gathering process with the goal of producing a report. Once the mandate is completed – usually just a few months after the commission's creation – the team disbands, leaving the task of reviewing and ensuring the implementation of the commission's recommendations to governmental actors, politicians, and civil society. Due to this ad hoc, temporary nature of commissions of inquiry – as well as of other types of monitoring, reporting, and fact-finding (MRF) mechanisms – a tension exists around how the impacts of MRF missions should be viewed and assessed. On the one hand, one could judge the success of an MRF mission simply by how well the practitioners on the mission fulfilled their mandate. On the other hand, one could argue that the measure of a mission's value is related to the role the mission plays in influencing the behavior of different actors relevant to the context at hand. As one MRF practitioner writes, although simply fulfilling the mission's mandate is a challenging and worthwhile end in itself, the domain of MRF is ultimately oriented toward more long-term impacts:

> On one level, the mission can be deemed a success for the Human Rights Council: it was able to fulfill all parts of its mandate, including an on-site visit and making recommendations …. But, more importantly, writing in early 2009 what is only too apparent is that it has not contributed positively to peace and security within the region, to any peace process, to an improvement in the protection of human rights for people in the Gaza Strip or Southern Israel, or to enforcement of international humanitarian law. The primary objectives of fact-finding – international dispute resolution, contribution to peace and security, change in behavior

279

and human rights compliance by all relevant parties – have not been accomplished.[1]

What impacts have MRF missions actually had? This chapter provides an answer to this question. The particular methodology that this chapter employs is to examine the actions taken – or not taken – by various entities to which MRF reports have addressed recommendations, focusing, in particular, on four emblematic types of recommendations that have appeared in MRF reports. Part I of the chapter provides an overview of different perspectives on assessing impact and also highlights a few analytical caveats relevant to the methodology that this chapter employs. Part II presents an assessment of the actions taken in the wake of the fifteen MRF missions that constitute the focus of this book.[2] Part III offers concluding remarks.

I.   Assessing Impact: Importance and Dilemmas

This section first offers an overview of the importance that MRF practitioners have placed on impact as a measure of success for MRF missions. Second, the section examines the role that recommendations play in influencing the surrounding political environment in the aftermath of an MRF mission. Third, the section addresses several complications to assessing impact.

A.   Professional Perspectives on Impact

To what extent are MRF practitioners concerned with the impact of the missions on which they serve? On the one hand, a fairly standard notion articulated about MRF work, though a peculiar factor in terms of assessing outcomes is that practitioners do not always link measures of success to actual impact. This belief – that MRF work has value even in contexts where results are difficult, or even impossible, to achieve – is not uncommon within the field of human rights. As stated in a document summarizing discussions that occurred during the 2005 conference,

---

[1] Christine Chinkin, "U.N. Human Rights Council Fact-Finding Missions: Lessons from Gaza," in *Looking to the Future: Essays on International Law in Honor of W. Michael Reisman*, ed. Mahnoush H. Arsanjani, Jacob Katz Cogan, Robert D. Sloane, and Siegfried Wiessner (Leiden: Martinus Nijhoff Publishers, 2011), 493.
[2] See Appendix B of this book for detailed information about these missions.

"Measuring Impact in Human Rights: How Far Have We Come, and How Far to Go?":

> Furthermore, other participants argued, even if the war were never won, the battles would still be worth fighting on purely principled grounds. To do otherwise would be to sacrifice the movement's most deeply held beliefs. There is value even in fighting "losing battles," they argued, and any self-assessment system needs to account for that. We need ways to ensure for ourselves that our "strategies are maximally effective even if they don't succeed" in achieving their goals. We need a way to keep track of long-term goals, as well as a way to register smaller, incremental and subtle changes that may help make those long-term goals more likely in the future.[3]

On the other hand, the prevalent view among MRF practitioners is that the overarching strategic objective of MRF reports is to effect change regarding the behavior of actors relevant to an ongoing or past armed conflict or internal disturbance. As one author writes, "producing a report is 'only a means to an end,' whereby disseminating information can further other human rights goals, such as raising awareness, preventing violations, influencing global human rights policy debates, implementing universal standards, and conveying the truth."[4] Indeed, several practitioners, when questioned about the added value of MRF missions, have focused on specific outcomes in terms of changing governmental behavior. One practitioner stated of the overall benefits of MRF missions, "I think the great value of them is, one, that when they're set up, it puts nations on their guard that they have to behave because there might be some accountability, and two, it does clarify what is a very murky situation. When you get an objective panel looking at it, you get greater clarity."[5] This practitioner also asserted of MRF missions, "They are proliferating, you do get some greater degree of accountability than you got before because nations are not a law unto themselves in these matters. This is the way in which international law is developing."[6] Another practitioner takes this view further, stating that MRF missions can make up for deficiencies in the enforceability of international criminal law:

> [B]oth monitoring and institutional fact-finding are expressions of a new relationship existing in the world society between each individual state and

---

[3] "Measurement & Human Rights: Tracking Progress, Assessing Impact," A Carr Center Project Report, 2005, pp. 41–42.

[4] Louise Mallinder, "Law, Politics and Fact-Finding: Assessing the Impact of Human Rights Reports," *Journal of Human Rights Practice* 2, no. 1 (2010): 166, accessed June 14, 2015, doi:10.1093/jhuman/hup027 (internal citations omitted).

[5] Sir Geoffrey Palmer, Chair, Secretary-General's Panel of Inquiry on the 31 May 2010 Flotilla Incident, interview conducted by HPCR, April 4, 2013.

[6] Ibid.

the whole society. Each state is no longer master of his own, but strongly depends on multilateral relations and is subject to the pressure and weight of the collectivity. True, the world legal order does not have yet the various means available in each domestic legal system to centralize authority. To induce compliance with international standards it cannot therefore resort to compulsory judicial determination let alone to collective enforcement. Monitoring and institutional fact-finding are thus the best way of bringing the weight of the community to bear on each member state (and other international legal subjects).[7]

Indeed, MRF reports can directly influence the behavior of government actors, as one article mentions of fact-finding work undertaken by nongovernmental organizations (NGOs):

> The strategy – promoting change by reporting facts – is almost elegant in its simplicity. And there is growing evidence that it works. Governments frequently have adopted reforms in response to critical reports by NGOs, and former political prisoners who had been subjects of AI [Amnesty International] letter writing campaigns have often attributed their release from detention to AI. Country reports prepared by the more prominent NGOs often receive front page news coverage abroad, and in the United States, such reports have prompted Congress to adopt legislation suspending foreign aid or conditioning future aid on a country's compliance with international human rights standards.[8]

A salient example of direct impact is the Bahrain Independent Commission of Inquiry (hereafter the Bahrain Commission), which, as the mission's report notes, led to immediate improvement in the treatment of detainees:

> During the period of the Commission's work, the Commission took steps to address existing situations of human rights violations and particular attention was given to cases of humanitarian concern. This was accomplished by communicating with GoB [Government of Bahrain] officials where immediate intervention by GoB agencies was required to alleviate burdens suffered by individuals who were in detention, in hospitals, as well as in situations involving dismissal of private and public sector employees and the expulsion of students from universities and the suspension of their scholarships.
>
> Subsequently, more than 300 detainees were released by the GoB and special medical attention was provided to injured persons. Hundreds of

---

[7] Antonio Cassese, "Fostering Increased Conformity with International Standards: Monitoring and Institutional Fact-Finding," in *Realizing Utopia: The Future of International Law*, ed. Antonio Cassese (Oxford: Oxford University Press, 2012), 303.

[8] Diane F. Orentlicher, "Bearing Witness: The Art and Science of Human Rights Fact-Finding," *Harvard Human Rights Journal* 3 (1990): 84 (internal citations omitted).

dismissed public and private sector employees and suspended students were reinstated.

The establishment of the Commission resulted in a significant change in the policies and practices of several GoB agencies. The Commission was able to secure visitation rights by relatives of detainees. Following the Commission's efforts, certain criminal charges against certain persons, particularly medical personnel, were dropped.[9]

Additionally, Special Procedures mandate holders of the United Nations Human Rights Council (UNHRC) can claim many successes in terms of altering the conduct of governments. One special rapporteur reported on a confidential agreement between Indonesia and Malaysia that would have empowered employers in Malaysia to confiscate identify documents from Indonesian migrant workers; after the release of the report, the agreement was annulled.[10] In 2004, President Hamid Karzai released 534 Afghan and Pakistani detainees after the United Nations Independent Expert on Afghanistan discovered detainees living in intolerable conditions and reported this information to the Afghan Minister of Justice.[11] In 2003, a United Nations special rapporteur recommended that Spain install video cameras in Spanish interrogation rooms, a recommendation that the government of Spain eventually undertook.[12]

But despite these examples of positive impact, practitioners have also expressed wariness about the potential "dark side" of the domain of MRF. This concern emanates from the risk that an MRF mission can serve the exact opposite of the mission's expressly stated function. A national commission mandated by the government of Uganda in the 1970s is the salient example of this risk, as one scholar describes:

> It should also be recognised that a government might establish a truth commission in order to manipulate the public perception of its own tarnished image, to promote a more favourable view of the country's human rights policies and practices. There are examples where abuses by government forces have continued even while a truth commission undertakes an investigation into the past …. [F]rom Uganda, where Idi Amin set up a commission in 1974 to investigate hundreds of disappearances that took place under his rule – and then rejected the commission's conclusions, only worsening his abuses in the ensuing years – we learn that a truth commission can sometimes be set up as a whitewash, projecting the image of a

---

[9] "Report of the Bahrain Independent Commission of Inquiry," November 23, 2011, pp. 10–11, accessed June 14, 2015, http://www.bici.org.bh/BICIreportEN.pdf.
[10] Ted Piccone, *Catalysts for Change* (New York: The Brookings Institution, 2012), 27–28.
[11] Ibid., 28.   [12] Ibid., 30.

concern for rights, satisfying the donors who provide aid, but representing no will to change.[13]

Along the same lines, various MRF practitioners have asserted, "Commissions of inquiry should not be an alibi for global inaction,"[14] and "Commissions of inquiry should not be used as a fig leaf when urgent international action is required to stop large-scale killings or similar international crimes."[15] Though, some actors have claimed that the actual point of many MRF missions – from the perspective of the mandating authority – is to allow governments to maintain the appearance of remaining engaged while actually taking no significant action. One author, discussing the League of Nations' creation of the Lytton Commission, which examined the outbreak of hostilities between Japan and China in the 1930s, states:

> Finally, a mechanism was devised for doing nothing at all. It took the form of a fact-finding mission – the standard device for diplomats signaling that inaction is the desired outcome. Such commissions take time to assemble, to undertake studies, and to reach a consensus – by which point, with luck, the problem might even have gone away.[16]

Furthermore, the publication of an MRF report could further exacerbate an already tense situation. Specifically, accusations levied in MRF reports could lead domestic actors, concerned about legal ramifications, to pass amnesty legislation, as occurred in Afghanistan in 2005 after the publication of a Human Rights Watch report;[17] could embolden domestic opposition, which could prompt further governmental crackdowns;[18] and could, rather than produce an authoritative historical record, cause

---

[13] Priscilla B. Hayner, "Commissioning the Truth: Further Research Questions," *Third World Quarterly* 17, no. 1 (1996): 22–24, accessed June 14, 2015, http://www.jstor.org/stable/3992990.

[14] Remarks delivered by Vitit Muntarbhorn, Commissioner, Independent, International Commission of Inquiry on Côte d'Ivoire, at "Meeting on International Commissions of Inquiry and Fact-Finding Missions on Violations of International Human Rights Law and International Humanitarian Law," Palais des Nations, November 19, 2013.

[15] Remarks delivered by Peter Bouckaert, Emergency Director, Human Rights Watch, at "Meeting on International Commissions of Inquiry and Fact-Finding Missions on Violations of International Human Rights Law and International Humanitarian Law," Palais des Nations, November 19, 2013.

[16] Henry Kissinger, *Diplomacy* (New York: Simon & Schuster, 1994), 286–287.

[17] Mallinder, "Law, Politics and Fact-Finding," 167.

[18] Emilie M. Hafner-Burton, "Sticks and Stones: Naming and Shaming the Human Rights Enforcement Problem," *International Organization* 62, no. 4 (2008): 692, accessed June 14, 2015, doi.org/10.1017/S0020818308080247.

contrasting views of history to calcify, thus actually increasing tensions.[19] The prevalence of these risks suggests the importance of conducting an assessment of the impact of past MRF missions in order to illuminate the extent to which MRF activities have actually succeeded in supporting accountability and civilian protection aims.

B. The Function of Recommendations

Practitioners, activists, and scholars alike have proclaimed the importance of recommendations that appear in MRF reports. Various authors have commented that an MRF mission "seems unlikely to have much of an impact unless they produce recommendations,"[20] and that recommendations "are key to a commission affecting real change"[21] and "can provide pressure points around which the civilian society or the international community can push for change in the future."[22] One example of incorporating MRF recommendations into advocacy efforts is a study conducted in 2012 by the Project on Middle East Democracy (POMED) about the implementation of the Bahrain Commission's recommendations. "[E]ven the full implementation of the BICI [Bahrain Independent Commission of Inquiry] recommendations would fall well short of resolving the current political impasse in Bahrain," the report concludes, "[b]ut such moves are essential to national reconciliation and genuine political reform."[23]

This widely perceived importance of recommendations is reflected by the trend of practice that has emerged by which MRF reports include recommendations, even without explicit authorization to do so in the mission's mandate. For example, the mandates for the Independent, International Commission of Inquiry on Côte d'Ivoire (hereafter the Côte d'Ivoire Commission), the United Nations Fact-Finding Mission on the Gaza Conflict (hereafter the Gaza Fact-Finding Mission), the Independent International Fact-Finding Mission on the Conflict in Georgia (hereafter the Georgia Fact-Finding Mission), the Commission of Inquiry on Lebanon (hereafter the Lebanon Commission), and the International Commission of Inquiry

[19] Eric Brahm, "Uncovering the Truth: Examining Truth Commission Success and Impact," *International Studies Perspectives* 8, no. 1 (2007): 20, accessed June 14, 2015, doi:10.1111/ j.1528-3585.2007.00267.x.
[20] Ibid., 21.   [21] Hayner, "Commissioning the Truth," 24.   [22] Ibid., 22.
[23] Stephen McInerney, introduction to "One Year Later: Assessing Bahrain's Implementation of the BICI Report," Project on Middle East Democracy, November 2012, accessed June 14, 2015, http://pomed.org/wp-content/uploads/2013/12/One-Year-Later-Assessing-Bahrains-Implementation-of-the-BICI-Report.pdf.

on Darfur (hereafter the Darfur Commission) made no mention of recommendations whatsoever. However, all of these missions' reports include
recommendations, indicating the professional view that the articulation of
recommendations is an integral aspect of MRF work.

Still, many practitioners have expressed dissatisfaction with the responses to MRF recommendations. According to one practitioner, "Another frustration is what happens after you hand in the report. It's frustrating when you write one of these reports and think very carefully about
what the recommendations are. What's frustrating is that you write the
report and then it's out of your hands as to what action UN [United Na-
tions] officials will take on it."[24] In the same vein, a commissioner who
served on the International Commission of Inquiry for Guinea (hereafter
the Guinea Commission) focuses on the lack of sufficient capacity on the
part of international actors to engage in effective follow-up:

> I'm not very happy with the lack of engagement with the ICC [International
> Criminal Court]. That is frustrating for a commissioner. I also see a lack of
> involvement of commissioners in the follow up to the commission and the
> implementation of recommendations. I think if fact-finding missions are to
> become an important tool, something must come out of it in terms of follow
> up and implementation. I'm looking at the added value from the perspective
> of the weaknesses of the Special Procedures and the treaty body system.[25]

The core dilemma to which these comments allude is that, after the production of a mission's final report, commissioners have no formal capacity to participate in the process of implementing the report's recommendations. Instead, two interrelated factors constitute key determinants of
impact. The first factor is political will. As one writer notes, since MRF
missions are "temporary bodies with relatively weak powers … they rely
on moral suasion, pressure from civil society and the international community, and the political will of politicians to see most of their impact
realized."[26] A lack of political will, one policy paper states, constitutes
"[o]ne of the main causes of non-implementation" of a mission's recommendations.[27] One study of the recommendations offered by the Commission

---

[24] Steven Ratner, Member, Secretary-General's Panel of Experts on Sri Lanka, interview
conducted by HPCR, May 1, 2013.
[25] Pramila Patten, Commissioner, International Commission of Inquiry for Guinea, interview conducted by HPCR, April 26, 2013.
[26] Brahm, "Uncovering the Truth," 28–29.
[27] "Reconciliation After Violent Conflict: A Handbook," International IDEA, 2003, p. 137,
accessed June 14, 2015, http://www.un.org/en/peacebuilding/pbso/pdf/Reconciliation-
After-Violent-Conflict-A-Handbook-Full-English-PDF.pdf.

on Truth for El Salvador finds a correlation between the recommendations that were adopted and the issues for which international actors exerted significant political pressure. The author of the study concludes:

> It should be noted that the implementation of some of the Commission's recommendations owed much to the lobbying efforts of the international community. For example, significant pressure had to be exerted on the Salvadorean government before high ranking officials from the armed forces who had been implicated in serious human rights violations by the Truth Commission were removed from office. Significantly, there was very little international pressure calling for the compensation of families of the victims of human rights violations or the other reconciliation measures, and none of these elements of the Commission's recommendations have been implemented.[28]

A second relevant factor – related to political will – is the extent to which domestic and international actors engage in follow-up monitoring of the implementation of recommendations. Various types of entities typically assume this role. Members of civil society, including NGOs, are key actors in this regard, as noted by one scholar:

> Tracing the implementation record of reforms is an important first step, but this does not necessarily mean that the new rules are followed. Fortunately, local and international human rights NGOs have often been important watchdogs providing periodic updates on whether countries are adhering to human rights commitments. Truth commission reports often serve as benchmarks to which NGOs hold governments accountable.[29]

In terms of monitoring that has been implemented at the international level, a study that focuses on the Special Procedures system of the UNHRC describes the limitations in resources and institutional capacity that have impeded the initiation of effective follow-up measures. These factors, described in detail below, are also applicable to the broader domain of MRF:

> In only a few cases, usually when additional resources are available, has a special rapporteur methodically reported on a state's implementation of recommendations. And only rarely had a current or successor rapporteur carried out visits to the same country two or more years later with the express purpose of tracking progress on previous recommendations .... The lack of follow-up to rapporteur visits was widely viewed as the Achilles' heel of the mechanism. As one European diplomat put it, "Special

---

[28] Mike Kaye, "The Role of Truth Commissions in the Search for Justice, Reconciliation and Democratisation: The Salvadorean and Honduran Cases," *Journal of Latin American Studies* 29, no. 3 (1997): 712, accessed June 14, 2015, http://www.jstor.org/stable/158356 (internal citation omitted).

[29] Brahm, "Uncovering the Truth," 27.

procedures visits will exacerbate a sore tooth for a little while, but then it goes away again." According to an African official, "It's like a vaccine shot – once the report is done, you forget about it." ... Given the significant investment of resources devoted to country visits and the important contribution they can make toward advancing human rights at the national level, the lack of any systematic mechanism to follow up on such visits is glaring and an embarrassment to the UN human rights system.[30]

But is it appropriate to focus on recommendation implementation as a barometer of an MRF mission's impact? First, the belief that assessing the result of recommendations can serve as a useful measure of an MRF mission's success is prevalent throughout academic literature focusing on truth and reconciliation commissions.[31] Second, practitioners interviewed for this chapter also articulated this view both explicitly and implicitly. For example, several practitioners, when questioned about their thoughts on whether the missions on which they served were successful, answered the question by referencing recommendations that had been undertaken.[32] Indeed, assessing recommendations provides, at the very least, a useful starting point for gauging the impact of MRF missions, even despite the various inherent analytical challenges that the next section will describe.

C. Analytical Limitations

What limitations exist for assessing the impact of MRF missions? Especially given the risk of unintended consequences, how can one parse out the positive impacts from the potentially negative ramifications of MRF work? This section examines four factors that complicate efforts to assess the outcomes of an MRF mission. These factors are: (1) the contrasting conclusions reached through quantitative versus qualitative analysis, (2) the impossibility of establishing causality between a mission and subsequent developments that occur in the relevant context, (3) the fact that in many cases impact is long-term, and (4) the fact that the less tangible outcomes of MRF work are difficult to measure.

---

[30] Piccone, *Catalysts for Change*, 32–33, 99, 123 (internal citations omitted).
[31] For example, see Brahm, "Uncovering the Truth," 24; and Margaret Popkin and Naomi Roht-Arriaza, "Truth as Justice: Investigatory Commissions in Latin America," *Law & Social Inquiry* 20, no. 1 (1995): 101, accessed June 14, 2015, doi:10.1111/j.1747-4469.1995. tb00683.x.
[32] Confidential interviews with high-level MRF practitioners, names of interviewees on file, conducted by HPCR, 2011–2013.

1.   Quantitative versus Qualitative Approaches

The divide between quantitative and qualitative approaches that exists among practitioners and researchers in the domain of MRF is an outgrowth of tensions that exist throughout the broader field of social science. Some scholars devote energy to empirically grounded comparative analyses based on quantitative criteria while other analysts focus on qualitative case studies.[33] Indeed, quantitative and qualitative methodologies emphasize different aspects of an MRF mission's impact. As one assessment of these contrasting research practices notes:

> The qualitative scholars' case studies involve close-to-the-ground scrutiny of the twists and turns in human rights behavior, giving researchers insight into the political nuts and bolts of change. In contrast, the statistical analyses that quantitative researchers use are resoundingly macroscopic; from up high, the twists may appear as minor deviations.[34]

Because of these differing emphases, these two methods of evaluating impact lead quantitative and qualitative researchers to reach contrasting conclusions. According to two scholars, "Those working in the more established case study tradition tend toward greater optimism, while those working in the newer quantitative genre are more skeptical."[35] Given the various desired impacts of MRF work, it is unsurprising that qualitative case studies, by adapting the research methodology based on the nuanced differences between various contexts, are better able to find evidence of success. Some missions can point to tangible outcomes, such as a definitive change in government behavior, but, as one paper on the subject states, "intangible impacts, such as changes in perceptions, attitudes, or value systems at the individual or societal levels … are inherently difficult to measure and report on, yet absolutely central to the mission of most human rights organizations."[36]

Still, the past few decades have seen increased attention devoted to quantitative assessments of global human rights developments. The enjoyment and protection of human rights has been measured by

---

[33] See generally Henry E. Brady and David Collier, eds., *Rethinking Social Inquiry* (Lanham: Rowan & Littlefield Publishers, Inc., 2004).

[34] Emilie M. Hafner-Burton, "Human Rights Institutions: Rhetoric and Efficacy," *Journal of Peace Research* 44, no. 4 (2007): 381, accessed June 14, 2015, doi:10.1177/0022343307078941.

[35] Emilie M. Hafner-Burton and James Ron, "Seeing Double: Human Rights Impact through Qualitative and Quantitative Eyes," *World Politics* 61, no. 2 (2009): 363, accessed June 14, 2015, http://journals.cambridge.org/abstract_S0043887109000136.

[36] Carr Center, "Assessing Impact," 42.

benchmarks and indicators,[37] as well as by various indices and other modes of collating cross-national data, including the Freedom House Democracy Index, the Human Freedom Index that appears in Human Development Reports published by the United Nations Development Programme, the Humana Index, the Physical Quality of Life Index, the Political Terror Scale, and the Cingranelli and Richards Index.[38] Though some analysts have argued that quantitative metrics should be explored further,[39] during interviews with MRF practitioners conducted for this study, no practitioners emphasized the importance of quantitative assessments. Instead, while several practitioners expressed an interest in seeing more research about impacts, practitioners appear to have more interest in qualitative assessments.

2.   The Impossibility of Establishing Causality

One core issue is the impossibility of establishing causality. Though a great deal of academic literature focuses on assessing the impact of truth and reconciliation commissions, as one scholar asserts, "[S]eldom is a causal chain between truth commission and the outcome of interest carefully traced. Rather, correlations are often equated with causation."[40] Positive changes that occur after the publication of an MRF report could be entirely unrelated to the MRF mission's work.[41] Additionally, the environments in which MRF missions operate are typically flooded with many other fact-finding and advocacy initiatives, making it difficult to determine which specific endeavor has been most instrumental in effecting change. Practitioners interviewed for this chapter indicated that the purpose of MRF missions is actually to operate in concert with other initiatives to gradually shape an environment conducive to greater respect for accountability.[42] Given this conception of MRF missions, one cannot very easily gauge the impact of a single mission.

---

[37] See generally Maria Green, "What We Talk About When We Talk About Indicators: Current Approaches to Human Rights Measurement," *Human Rights Quarterly* 23, no. 4 (2001), accessed June 14, 2015, doi:10.1353/hrq.2001.0054.

[38] Ibid. Also, see generally Hafner-Burton and Ron, "Seeing Double."

[39] See, for example, Todd Landman, "Measuring Human Rights: Principle, Practice and Policy," *Human Rights Quarterly* 26, no. 4 (2004): 931, accessed June 14, 2015, doi:10.1353/hrq.2004.0049.

[40] Eric Wiebelhaus-Brahm, *Truth Commissions and Transitional Societies* (New York: Routledge, 2010), 22.

[41] James C. Franklin, "Shame on You: The Impact of Human Rights Criticism on Political Repression in Latin America," *International Studies Quarterly* 52 (2008): 192, accessed June 14, 2015, doi:10.1111/j.1468-2478.2007.00496.x.

[42] Confidential interviews with high-level MRF practitioners, names of interviewees on file, conducted by HPCR, 2011–2013.

Establishing causality is made more difficult by the fact that practitioners themselves sometimes have an interest in avoiding public statements that connect specific initiatives to specific outcomes. As one report states:

> For example, in certain contexts it may be imprudent for an organisation to publicly lay claim to certain activities let alone their impacts. A number of participants noted that on many occasions they had been unable to publicise, sometimes even to donors, a certain impact because it would have endangered a specific individual or a group. Indeed, tactically, human rights advocates often encourage others to claim primary credit for changes secured, since this "co-opts" others into the process of ownership and may prove useful in fully embedding change .... OHCHR [Office of the High Commissioner for Human Rights] recognises that human rights results are the outcome of a combination of factors and of the work of many diverse actors; consequently, OHCHR rarely speaks of attribution and prefers to highlight its collaborative contribution to the achievement of results, and those of its partners, in its reporting.[43]

Governments also have an interest in obfuscation. One author writes about the Special Procedures of the UNHRC, "[A] direct connection between recommendations of a rapporteur and government action is hard to prove. In part this is because the relevant national authorities are unlikely to give credit to a UN mechanism for their actions or are motivated by other domestic political factors."[44] Indeed, governmental behavior related to alleged violations of international law, as noted by another author, "is often intentionally ambiguous, dilatory, or confusing, and frequently takes place under conditions in which verification of compliance is difficult."[45]

A related issue is that, even if a report's recommendations are not adopted, the recommendations may still produce a positive outcome. As two authors state of the report of the Commission on Truth for El Salvador, "Despite the refusal to accept the report, some recommendations initially rejected have had a significant effect. For example, although the Supreme Court refused to step down before the end of its term, no member of that Court was reelected by the legislature in June 1994."[46]

---

[43] "No Perfect Measure: Rethinking Evaluation and Assessment of Human Rights Work," Report of a Workshop, International Council on Human Rights Policy, 2012, p. 9.
[44] Piccone, *Catalysts for Change*, 28.
[45] Beth A. Simmons, "Compliance with International Agreements," *Annual Review of Political Science* 1 (1998): 78–79, accessed June 14, 2015, http://scholar.harvard.edu/files/bsimmons/files/Simmons1998.pdf.
[46] Popkin and Roht-Arriaza, "Truth as Justice," 103.

3.   Short-term versus Long-term Impacts

An additional complicating factor is that impact often takes a great deal of time. The quotes presented below from various practitioners and commentators elucidate the perspective that one should consider the long-term impacts that MRF missions can yield:

- "Bearing witness, collecting the stories, recording them and putting them there for future use can sometimes bear fruit a little later."[47]
- "No, the effects of a truth commission are not seen in a day. Perhaps next year, when the all-important final report and recommendations have been submitted, published, read, and implemented, we shall be able to say more. Yet by what criterion is 'success' to be judged? Truth? Justice? Reconciliation? Closure? Healing? National unity? Prevention of future abuses? And of course we will never know what would have happened if the truth commission had never been."[48]
- "Human rights change is aimed at challenging and sometimes overturning current power relationships and therefore indicators need to be long-term and qualitative."[49]
- "A human rights project can have little effects in the short-term, although it may have important long-term impact. Awareness-raising campaigns that give little immediate gains may have positive effects in the long-run."[50]

Conversely, some missions might produce only short-term gains, appearing effective only in the mission's immediate aftermath without actually producing significant long-term changes. For example, governmental leaders accused of human rights violations might alter their behavior when faced with increased media attention, and then when attention fades, might once again escalate the perpetration of violations.[51] This

---

[47] Michael Kirby, quoted in Peter Walker, "North Korea Human Rights Abuses Resemble Those of the Nazis, Says UN Inquiry," *The Guardian*, February 18, 2014, accessed June 14, 2015, http://www.theguardian.com/world/2014/feb/17/north-korea-human-rights-abuses-united-nations.

[48] Timothy Garton Ash, "True Confessions," *The New York Review of Books*, July 17, 1997, p. 10, accessed June 14, 2015, http://www.nybooks.com/articles/archives/1997/jul/17/true-confessions/.

[49] "No Perfect Measure," 8.

[50] Bård Anders Andreassen and Hans-Otto Sano, "What's the Goal? What's the Purpose? Observations on Human Rights Impact Assessment," *The International Journal of Human Rights* 11, no. 3 (2007): 281, accessed June 25, 2015, doi:10.1080/13642980701443483.

[51] Franklin, "Shame on You," 206.

factor raises the question of how long one must wait before making a valuable assessment of an MRF mission's effectiveness.

4.   The Difficulty of Assessing Intangible Effects

As various scholars and practitioners have stated, MRF reports, by producing an authoritative historical record, can "provide a form of recognition and acknowledgement to victims;"[52] "provide victims with official acknowledgment of their suffering that, many argue, is empowering and/or cathartic;"[53] help victims "regain some part of the human dignity that had been denied them by the perpetrators of the crimes inflicted upon them;"[54] generate "an honest account of the violence [that] prevents history from being lost or rewritten, and opens the possibility for a society to learn from its past in order to prevent the return of such violence in the future;"[55] and "serve to counter the fictitious or exaggerated accounts of the past."[56]

How can such impacts be measured? One possible research methodology would be to conduct an assessment of local actors – including witnesses and victims – in contexts where MRF missions have been undertaken. Such an undertaking could survey perspectives of witnesses and victims, as well as other relevant actors, about the value of MRF missions in achieving the objectives described above. While an assessment methodology along these lines might produce valuable data, the assessment would not only be expensive and time consuming – potentially requiring resources comparable to the MRF exercise itself – but also would bring forth questions and dilemmas regarding the protection of the witnesses and victims involved. These concerns would not necessarily preclude the implementation of such an assessment, but these factors do highlight the difficulties of gathering data about the more intangible objectives of MRF work.

II.   Recommendation Implementation: An Assessment

This section assesses the impact of fifteen MRF missions by focusing on the actions that have been taken in the wake of the reports' recommendations. The section focuses specifically on four categories of recommendations:

---

52 Mallinder, "Law, Politics and Fact-Finding," 175.
53 Brahm, "Uncovering the Truth," 20 (internal citations omitted).
54 Christian Tomuschat, "Clarification Commission in Guatemala," *Human Rights Quarterly* 23, no. 2 (2001): 242, accessed June 14, 2015, doi:10.1353/hrq.2001.0025.
55 Hayner, "Commissioning the Truth," 21.
56 International IDEA, "Reconciliation after Violent Conflict," 125.

(1) accountability at the domestic level, (2) the signing and ratification of treaties and/or enactment of domestic law that incorporates international law, (3) accountability at the international level, and (4) follow-up monitoring measures. Of course, MRF reports also include a wide array of other recommendation types. Many reports have issued recommendations that address improving the treatment of detainees; fostering national reconciliation; paying reparations; reducing international tensions; ceasing the perpetration of ongoing violations; initiating institutional reforms; and providing monetary support, capacity-building measures, and technical assistance to domestic actors. The recommendation types examined in this section constitute a first step toward assessing trends across different missions.

Before launching into this assessment, an analytical note of caution is important to bear in mind. Namely, this section considers the factors examined in the previous section, and specifically, the challenge of establishing causality and the fact that many effects of MRF missions are long-term. Though a government might undertake an action recommended in an MRF report, this correlation does not necessarily insinuate causation. Other factors might have played a role in the recommendation being undertaken. Conversely, even if recommendations were not undertaken, the mission might have had other significant impacts that one should not overlook. Though assessing the implementation of a report's recommendations does not capture the full story, the aim of this assessment, by offering a valuable reference point for discerning trends across different missions, is to further our understanding about which recommendations are likely to be undertaken and which recommendations are likely to face greater resistance.

A. Accountability at the Domestic Level

Of the fifteen missions on which this study focuses, eleven missions directed recommendations regarding the implementation of accountability measures at the domestic level toward actors engaged in the conflict. Relevant portions from these reports include the following passages:

- "The commission calls on the Government of the Libyan Arab Jamahiriya … [t]o conduct exhaustive, impartial and transparent investigations into all alleged violations of international human rights law and international humanitarian law, and in particular to investigate, with a view to prosecuting, cases of extrajudicial, summary or arbitrary executions, disappearances and torture, with full respect for judicial guarantees." (First report of the International Commission of Inquiry on Libya [hereafter the Libya Commission])[57]

- "The commission calls on the National Transitional Council ... [t]o conduct exhaustive, impartial and public investigations into all alleged violations of international human rights law and international humanitarian law, and in particular to investigate, with a view to prosecuting, cases of extrajudicial, summary or arbitrary executions and torture, with full respect for judicial guarantees." (Libya Commission, first report)[58]

- "The Commission calls upon the interim Government of Libya to ... [i]nvestigate all violations of international human rights law and international humanitarian law set out in this report and to prosecute alleged perpetrators, irrespective of their location or affiliation, while affording them all their rights under international law." (Libya Commission, second report)[59]

- "[T]he commission recommends ... that the Ivorian Government ... [s]ee to it that those responsible for violations of human rights and international humanitarian law are brought to justice; the inquiries that have been launched must be conducted exhaustively, impartially and transparently." (Côte d'Ivoire Commission)[60]

- "The Commission makes the following *general* recommendations .... To establish a national independent and impartial mechanism to determine the accountability of those in government who have committed unlawful or negligent acts resulting in the deaths, torture and mistreatment of civilians with a view to bringing legal and disciplinary action against such individuals, including those in the chain of command, military and civilian, who are found to be responsible under international standards of 'superior responsibility.'" (Bahrain Commission)[61]

- "In light of the allegations found credible by the Panel, the Government of Sri Lanka, in compliance with its international obligations and

---

57 "Report of the International Commission of Inquiry to Investigate All Alleged Violations of International Human Rights Law in the Libyan Arab Jamahiriya," A/HRC/17/44, June 1, 2011, p. 9, accessed June 14, 2015, http://www2.ohchr.org/english/bodies/hrcouncil/docs/17session/A.HRC.17.44_AUV.pdf.

58 Ibid.

59 "Report of the International Commission of Inquiry on Libya," A/HRC/19/68, March 2, 2012, p. 23, accessed June 15, 2015, http://www.nytimes.com/interactive/2012/03/03/world/africa/united-nations-report-on-libya.html?_r=0.

60 "Report of the Independent, International Commission of Inquiry on Côte d'Ivoire," A/HRC/17/48 (Extract), June 6, 2011, p. 3, accessed June 14, 2015, http://www2.ohchr.org/english/bodies/hrcouncil/docs/17session/A.HRC.17.48_Extract.pdf.

61 Bahrain Commission report, 422.

with a view to initiating an effective domestic accountability process, should immediately commence genuine investigations into these and other alleged violations of international humanitarian and human rights law committed by both sides involved in the armed conflict." (Secretary-General's Panel of Experts on Accountability in Sri Lanka [hereafter the Sri Lanka Panel])[62]

- "The State should conduct thorough, independent and impartial investigations into crimes, without reference to the ethnicity of alleged perpetrators, and ensure that prosecutions conform with international fair trial standards." (Kyrgyzstan Inquiry Commission [hereafter the Kyrgyzstan Commission])[63]

- "The perpetrators of the more serious crimes, being masked, cannot be identified without the assistance of the Israeli authorities. They reacted in a violent manner when they thought that anyone was attempting to identify them. The Mission sincerely hopes that there will be cooperation from the Government of Israel to assist in their identification with a view to prosecuting the culpable and bringing closure to the situation." (International Fact-Finding Mission to investigate violations of international law, including international humanitarian and human rights law, resulting from the Israeli attacks on the flotilla of ships carrying humanitarian assistance [hereafter the UNHRC Flotilla Fact-Finding Mission])[64]

- "The Government of the DRC [Democratic Republic of the Congo] must abide by its obligations under international law, namely to prosecute crimes under international law committed on its territory." (United Nations Mapping Exercise in the Democratic Republic of the Congo [hereafter the DRC Mapping Exercise])[65]

---

[62] "Report of the Secretary-General's Panel of Experts on Accountability in Sri Lanka," March 31, 2011, p. 120, accessed June 14, 2015, http://www.un.org/News/dh/infocus/Sri_Lanka/POE_Report_Full.pdf.

[63] "Report of the Independent International Commission of Inquiry into the Events in Southern Kyrgyzstan in June 2010," n.d., p. 86, accessed June 14, 2015, http://reliefweb.int/sites/reliefweb.int/files/resources/Full_Report_490.pdf.

[64] "Report of the International Fact-Finding Mission to Investigate Violations of International Law, Including International Humanitarian and Human Rights Law, Resulting from the Israeli Attacks on the Flotilla of Ships Carrying Humanitarian Assistance," A/HRC/15/21, September 27, 2010, p. 54, accessed June 14, 2015, http://www2.ohchr.org/english/bodies/hrcouncil/docs/15session/A.HRC.15.21_en.pdf.

[65] "Report of the Mapping Exercise Documenting the Most Serious Violations of Human Rights and International Humanitarian Law Committed within The Territory of the Democratic Republic of the Congo between March 1993 and June 2003," Office of the High Commissioner for Human Rights, August 2010, p. 22, accessed June 14, 2015, http://www.refworld.org/docid/4ca99bc22.html.

- "The Mission notes that the responsibility to investigate violations of international human rights and humanitarian law, prosecute if appropriate and try perpetrators belongs in the first place to domestic authorities and institutions. This is a legal obligation incumbent on States and State-like entities." (Gaza Fact-Finding Mission)[66]
- "International law should continue to be respected and observed in its entirety. All tendencies to accept the erosion or a selective application of some of its principles, such as the respect of territorial integrity, must not be tolerated. Particular attention should be paid to upholding the rule of the non-use of force together with the non-use of the threat of force. Multilateral and negotiated solutions must continue to be given preference over unilateral action, and conflict prevention must continue to be a prevailing consideration." (Georgia Fact-Finding Mission)[67]
- "The Commission of Inquiry therefore recommends the Government of the Sudan to ... end the impunity for the war crimes and crimes against humanity committed in Darfur." (Darfur Commission)[68]

Additionally, the report of the United Nations Independent Special Commission of Inquiry for Timor-Leste (hereafter the Timor-Leste Commission), following the request in the mission's mandate, offers a list of names of individuals that the mission recommends for prosecution and/ or further investigation.[69] Of the fifteen missions, only the Timor-Leste Commission and the Guinea Commission publicly identify names of potential perpetrators. However, the Guinea Commission report, unlike the Timor-Leste Commission report, does not offer specific recommendations linked to these names, but rather states more broadly, "The Commission also recommends that the Government of Guinea should be firmly enjoined to ... [p]rosecute those responsible and provide compensation to the victims."[70]

[66] "Report of the United Nations Fact-Finding Mission on the Gaza Conflict," A/HRC/12/48, September 25, 2009, pp. 421–422, accessed June 14, 2015, http://www2.ohchr.org/english/bodies/hrcouncil/docs/12session/A-HRC-12-48.pdf.
[67] "Independent International Fact-Finding Mission on the Conflict in Georgia Report," vol. 1 (September 2009): 36.
[68] "Report of the International Commission of Inquiry on Darfur to the United Nations Secretary-General," January 25, 2005, p. 163, accessed June 14, 2015, http://www.un.org/news/dh/sudan/com_inq_darfur.pdf.
[69] "Report of the United Nations Independent Special Commission of Inquiry for Timor-Leste," October 2006, pp. 46–52, accessed June 14, 2015, http://www.ohchr.org/Documents/Countries/COITimorLeste.pdf.
[70] "Report of the International Commission of Inquiry Mandated to Establish the Facts and Circumstances of the Events of 28 September 2009 in Guinea," transmitted by letter dated

In terms of implementation of these recommendations, in the wake of the publication of the reports of these eleven missions, domestic actors undertook accountability measures only to a limited extent or in a manner that has raised questions about the effectiveness, independence, and impartiality of the resulting judicial processes. In several countries – such as Libya, Côte d'Ivoire, and Kyrgyzstan – justice has been one-sided. Regarding Libya, the second report of the Libya Commission states that, after the government of Qaddafi fell, under the successor government, "the law has not been applied consistently or equally,"[71] and that "the absence of a functioning court system prevents perpetrators being held accountable."[72] More recent assessments include a report published by International Crisis Group (ICG) in April 2013 that states of former rebel fighters, "Rather than being investigated, those suspected of such acts often are hailed as national heroes."[73] Additionally, ICC Prosecutor Fatou Bensouda said in November 2013 that Libya's aspirations to observe the rule of law and hold violators of international law accountable, "while genuine and praiseworthy, are yet to be fully realized."[74] Concerns about impunity for acts including arbitrary detention, torture, forcible displacement, and attacks against civilians and civilian property have persisted as large-scale violence has escalated throughout Libya since early 2014.[75] In Côte d'Ivoire, since the inauguration of President Ouattara in May 2011, over 150 individuals have been charged in military and civilian courts with crimes committed during the 2011 post-election crisis, but none of these cases have been against pro-Ouattara forces.[76] Regarding

---

18 December 2009 from the Secretary-General addressed to the President of the Security Council, S/2009/693, December 18, 2009, p. 60, accessed June 25, 205, http://www.ref-world.org/docid/4b4f49ea2.html.

[71] Second Libya Commission report, 20.   [72] Ibid.

[73] "Trial by Error: Justice in Post-Qadhafi Libya," Middle East/North Africa Report No. 140, International Crisis Group, 2013, p. 28, accessed June 14, 2015, http://www.crisisgroup.org/~/media/Files/Middle%20East%20North%20Africa/North%20Africa/libya/140-trial-by-error-justice-in-post-qadhafi-libya.

[74] Fatou Bensouda, quoted in "Efforts by Libya, International Partners Vital to Close Impunity Gap, Says ICC Prosecutor," UN News Centre, November 14, 2013, accessed June 14, 2015, https://www.un.org/apps/news/story.asp?NewsID=46491&Cr=Libya&Cr1=.

[75] Richard Dicker, "Letter to the ICC Prosecutor Regarding Accountability for Serious Crimes in Libya," Human Rights Watch, November 11, 2014, accessed June 18, 2015, http://www.hrw.org/news/2014/11/11/letter-icc-prosecutor-regarding-accountability-serious-crimes-libya.

[76] "Turning Rhetoric Into Reality: Accountability for Serious International Crimes in Côte d'Ivoire," Human Rights Watch, 2013, p. 1, accessed June 14, 2015, http://www.hrw.org/sites/default/files/reports/CDI0413_ForUpload.pdf.

Kyrgyzstan, as the United Nations High Commissioner for Human Rights has stated, "Criminal investigations into the June 2010 violence appear to have been marred by discriminatory practices against ethnic minorities,"[77] and more specifically, "around 75 percent of those killed were Uzbek, while some 77 percent of those arrested and charged with crimes relating to the violence were also Uzbek."[78]

In other contexts – including Bahrain, the DRC, and Israel and the Occupied Palestinian Territories (in relation to Operation Cast Lead) – there has been a reluctance to investigate senior officials. In Bahrain, though some actors involved in the 2011 crackdown have faced prosecution, these cases have focused on low-ranking officials, and publicly available information indicates that no member of the military has been investigated or prosecuted.[79] Similarly, in the DRC, domestic prosecutions have shied away from senior-level figures and have focused on lower-level actors, though the government of the DRC has indicated a commitment to denying amnesty for perpetrators of violations of IHRL and IHL.[80] In

[77] "Report of the United Nations High Commissioner for Human Rights on Technical Assistance and Cooperation on Human Rights for Kyrgyzstan," A/HRC/20/12, April 3, 2012, p. 8, accessed June 27, 2015, http://www.ohchr.org/Documents/HRBodies/HRCouncil/RegularSession/Session20/A-HRC-20-12_en.pdf.

[78] "Opening remarks by UN High Commissioner for Human Rights Navi Pillay at a press conference during her mission to Kyrgyzstan Bishkek," Office of the High Commissioner for Human Rights, July 10, 2012, accessed June 14, 2015, http://www.ohchr.org/en/News-Events/Pages/DisplayNews.aspx?NewsID=12338&LangID=E.

[79] As one commentator stated on the third anniversary of the 2011 uprising in Bahrain, "To be fair, the authorities did investigate and prosecute some low-ranking security officials in connection with cases of alleged torture and unlawful killings. However, no high-ranking official at the Ministry of Interior or at the National Security Agency have so far been held responsible for alleged unlawful or negligent acts resulting in the mistreatments, torture and deaths of civilians. No official from the Bahrain Defence Forces is known to have been investigated, although the military played a leading role in the 2011 campaign of repression. As such, nobody with the legal authority to make the decision for these things to happen, or to punish their having happened, has ever been charged, let alone prosecuted or convicted." See Niccoló Figa-Talamanca, "Bahraini Uprising's Third Anniversary: Accountability for past and present human rights violations must take centre stage," No Peace Without Justice, February 15, 2014, accessed June 14, 2015, http://www.npwj.org/ICC/Bahraini-Uprising%E2%80%99s-third-anniversary-accountability-past-and-present-human-rights-violations-mu. Also, see generally POMED, "One Year Later."

[80] See "Report of the United Nations High Commissioner for Human Rights on the Situation of Human Rights and the Activities of her Office in the Democratic Republic of the Congo," A/HRC/24/33, Office of the High Commissioner for Human Rights, July 12, 2013, p. 16, accessed June 14, 2015, http://www.ohchr.org/EN/HRBodies/HRC/RegularSessions/Session24/Documents/A-HRC-24-33_en.pdf; and "Democratic Republic of Congo: UPR Submission September 2013," Human Rights Watch, September 24, 2013, accessed June 18, 2015, http://www.hrw.org/news/2013/09/24/democratic-republic-congo-upr-submission-september-2013.

2014, the parliament of the DRC approved an amnesty law relevant to acts committed since 2006 that specifically excludes amnesty for acts of genocide, crimes against humanity, and war crimes, but human rights groups have expressed concerns about the will of the government of the DRC to follow through with efforts to combat impunity.[81] Regarding accountability for the context of the Gaza Fact-Finding Mission's mandate, the follow-up committee established by the UNHRC to monitor Israeli and Palestinian accountability efforts undertaken in the wake of Operation Cast Lead found that "there is no indication that Israel has opened investigations into the actions of those who designed, planned, ordered and oversaw 'Operation Cast Lead.'"[82] Additionally, the committee noted that it "had not received any information to indicate that criminal investigations or prosecutions were actually under way in the West Bank"[83] and expressed concerns that mechanisms initiated by Hamas did not address in an in-depth manner the recommendations of the Gaza Fact-Finding Mission,[84] raised concerns about impartiality and credibility, and "sought to explain away allegations of serious violations of IHL."[85]

In other instances – for example, Sri Lanka and Israel (regarding both the 2006 Beit Hanoun shelling and the 2010 Flotilla raid) – domestic investigations found no wrongdoing but were criticized by international actors. In Sri Lanka, the government established a court that concluded that Sri Lankan armed forces were not responsible for any civilian casualties that occurred during the civil war. However, OHCHR has stated that Sri Lanka's efforts "lack the independence and impartiality required to inspire confidence."[86] In a recent OHCHR report, the High Commissioner states "that military courts of inquiry do not have the necessary

---

[81] Kenneth Roth, "DR Congo: Letter to President Joseph Kabila on Prosecuting M23 Leaders and Others for Serious Abuses," Human Rights Watch, January 29, 2014, accessed June 18, 2015, http://www.hrw.org/news/2014/01/29/dr-congo-letter-president-joseph-kabila-prosecuting-m23-leaders-and-others-serious-a.

[82] "Report of the Committee of Independent Experts in International Humanitarian and Human Rights Laws to Monitor and Assess Any Domestic, Legal or Other Proceedings Undertaken by both the Government of Israel and the Palestinian side, in the Light of General Assembly Resolution 64/254, Including the Independence, Effectiveness, Genuineness of these Investigations and their Conformity with International Standards," A/HRC/15/50, September 23, 2010, p. 23.

[83] Ibid., 20.   [84] Ibid., 20–21.   [85] Ibid., 21–22.

[86] "Report of the Office of the United Nations High Commissioner for Human Rights on Advice and Technical Assistance for the Government of Sri Lanka on Promoting Reconciliation and Accountability in Sri Lanka," A/HRC/22/38, Office of the High Commissioner for Human Rights, February 11, 2013, p. 1, accessed June 14, 2015, http://www.ohchr.org/Documents/HRBodies/HRCouncil/RegularSession/Session22/A-HRC-22-38_en.pdf.

impartiality and independence to inspire confidence" and notes that "[t]he Commander of the Army who established the courts was also the commander of the security forces in the main battle zone of the conflict, and was actively engaged in the overall military planning and operations there."[87]

Regarding Beit Hanoun, before the publication of the report of the High-Level Fact-Finding Mission to Beit Hanoun established under Council resolution S-3/1 (hereafter the Beit Hanoun Fact-Finding Mission), Israel had already undertaken an investigation of the shelling there. This investigation – deemed to be "flawed" by the Beit Hanoun Fact-Finding Mission – found no wrongdoing on the part of Israeli forces.[88] Regarding the flotilla raid, by the time the UNHRC Flotilla Fact-Finding Mission completed its final report, Israel had already initiated a commission at the national level. This commission – the Public Commission to Examine the Maritime Incident of May 31, 2010 (commonly referred to as the Turkel Commission, after retired Israeli Supreme Court Judge Jacob Turkel, who chaired the commission) – concluded that Israeli forces had committed no violations of international law during the raid.[89] Based on the Turkel Commission's findings, no further accountability actions were taken within Israel against Israeli security forces related to this context. However, various critics expressed skepticism about the validity of the Turkel Commission's conclusions.[90]

Regarding the two contexts in which MRF reports named names – Timor-Leste and Guinea – implementation of the reports' recommendations has proved to be a struggle. For example, in Timor-Leste, Rogerio Lobato, whom the commission had recommended for prosecution for "illegal possession, use and movement of PNTL [Polícia Nacional de Timor-Leste] weapons," was sentenced to seven and a half years in

[87] "Promoting reconciliation and accountability in Sri Lanka," A/HRC/25/23, Office of the High Commissioner for Human Rights, February 24, 2014, pp. 10–11.

[88] "Report of the High-Level Fact-Finding Mission to Beit Hanoun established under Council resolution S-3/1," A/HRC/9/26, September 1, 2008, p. 23, accessed June 14, 2015, http://www.refworld.org/docid/48cfa3a22.html.

[89] For information about this commission, see "The Public Commission to Examine the Maritime Incident of 31 May 2010," HPCR Digital Library on Monitoring, Reporting, and Fact-Finding, Program on Humanitarian Policy and Conflict Research, accessed June 14, 2015, http://www.hpcrresearch.org/mrf-database/mission.php?id=27.

[90] Edmund Sanders, "Deadly Commando Raid on Gaza Flotilla Did Not Violate Law, Israeli Panel Says," Los Angeles Times, January 24, 2011, accessed June 14, 2015, http://articles.latimes.com/2011/jan/24/world/la-fg-israel-gaza-flotilla-20110124.

prison, but his sentence was commuted.[91] Four members of the F-FDTL [Forças Armadas de Defesa de Timor-Leste] were convicted in 2007 of manslaughter in a civilian court but were detained "in an *ad hoc* military prison" and continued to receive military salaries, which, according to a report of the United Nations Mission in Timor-Leste, "gives the impression that those convicted are not subject to the rule of law."[92] Vicente da Conceição, whom the Timor-Leste Commission report recommended for prosecution, was sentenced to prison for illegal weapons distribution, but not until 2010 and only for two years and eight months.[93] As a 2012 ICG report states:

> The most fundamental risk factor remains the near-complete impunity for political violence. In those few cases that result in prosecution and sentencing, the convicted are generally offered remanded sentences by the current president. He has worked hard to "close" the chapter of the country's history that included the 2006 crisis and the events that led to his shooting in February 2008; he declared a handful of pardons passed down at the end of 2011 would "close definitively one of the dark periods of our recent history."[94]

In Guinea, though the Guinean Minister for Justice appointed a panel of judges to investigate the government crackdown of September 2009 – the context on which the Guinea Commission focused – this panel has struggled due to a lack of political will and sufficient resources.[95] As an OHCHR report states, "the people named in the final report of the International Commission of Inquiry as having criminal responsibility have yet to be prosecuted; indeed, some of them still hold office."[96]

---

[91] "Report on Human Rights Developments in Timor-Leste: The security sector and access to justice 1 September 2007–30 June 2008," United Nations Mission in Timor-Leste, 2008, pp. 12–13, accessed June 14, 2015, http://www.ohchr.org/Documents/Countries/UNMIT200808.pdf.

[92] Ibid., 12.

[93] "Railos Sentenced to 2 Years 8 Months Imprisonment for Role in 2006 Illegal Weapons Distribution," *East Timor Law and Justice Bulletin*, January 12, 2010, accessed June 14, 2015, http://www.easttimorlawandjusticebulletin.com/2010/01/railos-sentenced-to-2-years-8-months.html.

[94] "Timor-Leste's Elections: Leaving Behind a Violent Past?" Asia Briefing No. 134, International Crisis Group, February 21, 2012, pp. 11–12, accessed June 14, 2015, http://www.crisisgroup.org/~/media/Files/asia/south-east-asia/timor-leste/b134-timor-lestes-elections-leaving-behind-a-violent-past.pdf (internal citations omitted).

[95] "Report of the United Nations High Commissioner for Human Rights on the situation of human rights in Guinea," A/HRC/19/49, January 17, 2012, p. 8, accessed June 14, 2015, http://www.ohchr.org/Documents/HRBodies/HRCouncil/RegularSession/Session19/A-HRC-19-49_en.pdf.

[96] Ibid., 9.

The context of Sudan further demonstrates the difficulties of pursuing accountability at the domestic level. Despite the recommendation of the Darfur Commission that the government of the Sudan should "end the impunity for the war crimes and crimes against humanity committed in Darfur," accountability remains an enduring problem in the country. As a report of the independent expert on the situation of human rights in the Sudan states, immunity laws have stood in the way of accountability:

> Legislations granting immunities to security personnel have effectively prevented the prosecution of security personnel in the regular courts. Immunities continue to exist for law enforcement and security agents under various laws, including the Police and Armed Forces Acts and NSS [National Security Service] Act. While the Government has maintained these immunities are only procedural and could easily be lifted when the need arises, practice has shown that the waiver of such immunities is very cumbersome and time consuming, and very often requires decisions from authorities in Khartoum.[97]

As the above assessment indicates, in terms of domestic accountability, no unqualified success story exists for these MRF missions. Though, there is, of course, no way to know for certain the counterfactuals. Progress in combating impunity has been slow and has faced many obstacles, but it is possible that the MRF missions implemented in these contexts have contributed to the progress that *has* been made. Regardless of the analytical difficulties of establishing causality, the definitive conclusion of this assessment is that MRF recommendations focusing on domestic accountability are likely to face a great deal of resistance.

B.   *The Signing and Ratification of Treaties and/or Enactment of Domestic Law that Incorporates International Law*

Related to the recommendations examined in the previous section are recommendations that focus on enacting legislation to accede to international treaties and to incorporate international law into domestic law. While the previous section focused on accountability for violations previously committed, the importance of this category of recommendations

---

97 "Report of the Independent Expert on the Situation of Human Rights in the Sudan on the Status of Implementation of the Recommendations Compiled by the Group of Experts to the Government of the Sudan for the Implementation of Human Rights Council Resolution 4/8, Pursuant to Council Resolutions 6/34, 6/35, 7/16, 11/10 and 15/27," A/HRC/18/40/Add.1, August 22, 2011, p. 9, accessed June 14, 2015, http://www2.ohchr.org/english/bodies/hrcouncil/docs/18session/A-HRC-18-40-Add1_en.pdf.

relates to violations that might be perpetrated in the future. By encouraging countries to incorporate international law into domestic law, MRF missions aim not only toward creating an environment that encourages non-repetition of past violations but also toward the adoption of a legal framework for pursuing accountability at the domestic level if future violations do occur. The following recommendations address this issue:

- "The commission calls on the Government of Libya ... [t]o bring all Libya's laws and policies into conformity with international human rights standards." (Libya Commission, first report)[98]
- "The Commission calls upon the NTC [National Transition Council] and the future Constituent Assembly to ... [e]nsure that the future Constitution of Libya incorporates international human rights law defined in the human rights treaties ratified by Libya," "[u]ndertake legislative reform to incorporate international crimes into the Libyan Criminal Code and repeal any statutory limitations applying to such crimes," and "[r]eform all laws to bring them into conformity with Libya's obligations under international law." (Libya Commission, second report)[99]
- "In this context, the commission recommends ... that the Ivorian Government ... [t]ake all urgent and appropriate measures for the prompt ratification of the Rome Statute, the African Charter on Democracy, Elections and Governance, the Protocol to the African Charter on the Rights of Women in Africa, the African Charter on the Rights and Welfare of the Child, the African conventions on refugees, displaced persons and asylum-seekers, and the Convention for the Elimination of Mercenarism." (Côte d'Ivoire Commission)[100]
- "The Government should incorporate crimes against humanity in the Criminal Code of Kyrgyzstan," "should either ratify the Rome Statute or accept the jurisdiction of the International Criminal Court as a non-party state," and should "[a]ccede to the European Convention for the Prevention of Torture and Inhumane or Degrading Treatment or Punishment." (Kyrgyzstan Commission)[101]
- "The most crucial and urgent of the reforms that aim to prevent repetition of these crimes are those pertaining to improvements to the judicial system, adoption of a law to implement the Rome Statute, and the vetting of the security services." (DRC Mapping Exercise)[102]

---

[98] First Libya Commission report, 83.   [99] Second Libya Commission report, 24.
[100] Côte d'Ivoire Commission report (Extract), 3–4.
[101] Kyrgyzstan Commission report, 87–88 (internal citation omitted).
[102] DRC Mapping Exercise report, 29.

- "Israel should initiate a review of the rules of engagement, standard operating procedures, open fire regulations and other guidance for military and security personnel. The Mission recommends that Israel should avail itself of the expertise of the International Committee of the Red Cross, the Office of the United Nations High Commissioner for Human Rights and other relevant bodies, and Israeli experts, civil society organizations with the relevant expertise and specialization, in order to ensure compliance in this respect with international humanitarian law and international human rights law. In particular such rules of engagement should ensure that the principles of proportionality, distinction, precaution and non-discrimination are effectively integrated in all such guidance and in any oral briefings provided to officers, soldiers and security forces, so as to avoid the recurrence of Palestinian civilian deaths, destruction and affronts on human dignity in violation of international law." (Gaza Fact-Finding Mission)[103]
- "The Mission recommends that the Palestinian Authority should issue clear instructions to security forces under its command to abide by human rights norms as enshrined in the Palestinian Basic Law and international instruments." (Gaza Fact-Finding Mission)[104]
- "It is essential that Sudanese laws be brought in conformity with human rights standards through *inter alia* abolishing the provisions that permit the detention of individuals without judicial review, the provisions granting officials immunity from prosecution as well as the provisions on specialized courts." (Darfur Commission)[105]

As with the recommendations examined in the previous section, an assessment of actions undertaken related to the above recommendations suggests the tortuous path to accountability that typically exists in the wake of armed conflicts and internal disturbances. In Libya, positive steps taken by the government include a draft law proposing that rape during armed conflict constitute a war crime.[106] However, amendments made to Libya's Constitutional Declaration have been criticized for being contrary to "the fundamental principles of both human rights and

---

[103] Gaza Fact-Finding Mission report, 426.   [104] Ibid., 427.
[105] Darfur Commission report, 163.
[106] "Efforts by Libya, International Partners Vital to Close Impunity Gap, Says ICC Prosecutor," *UN News Centre*, November 14, 2013, accessed June 14, 2015, https://www.un.org/apps/news/story.asp?NewsID=46491&Cr=Libya&Cr1.

the rule of law."[107] Côte d'Ivoire ratified the Rome Statute in February 2013 but has not pursued ratifying the other treaties recommended by the Côte d'Ivoire Commission report.[108] Kyrgyzstan did not incorporate crimes against humanity into the country's criminal code, took no action to engage with the ICC, and did not accede to the European Convention for the Prevention of Torture and Inhumane or Degrading Treatment or Punishment.[109] In the DRC, steps have been taken to apply a law that criminalizes torture, but parliament has not yet adopted legislation to incorporate the Rome Statute into national law.[110] The follow-up committee to the Gaza Fact-Finding Mission noted that Israel adopted new procedures for protecting civilians during urban warfare, a New Order Regulating the Destruction of Private Property for Military Purposes, and new orders about the use of white phosphorous.[111] However, concerns persist that Israeli forces have not adhered to principles of IHL.[112] Sudan has

---

[107] "Lawyers for Justice in Libya Condemns the GNC's Amendments to Libya's Constitutional Declaration," Lawyers for Justice in Libya, April 17, 2013, accessed June 14, 2015, http://www.libyanjustice.org/news/news/post/74-lawyers-for-justice-in-libya-condemns-the-gncs-amendments-to-libyas-constitutional-declaration.

[108] The only exception to this statement is the African Charter on the Rights and Welfare of the Child. The Côte d'Ivoire Commission report recommends ratification, but Côte d'Ivoire had already ratified this convention, an apparent error made by the commission. For a list of countries that have ratified the African Charter on the Rights and Welfare of the Child, see "Ratification Table: African Charter on the Rights and Welfare of the Child," African Commission on Human and People's Rights, accessed June 14, 2015, http://www.achpr.org/instruments/child/ratification/. For information about Côte d'Ivoire's ratification of the Rome Statute, see "Côte d'Ivoire Ratifies the Rome Statute," International Criminal Court, February 18, 2013, accessed June 14, 2014, http://www.icc-cpi.int/en_menus/icc/press%20and%20media/press%20releases/Pages/pr873.aspx.

[109] See generally "Kyrgyzstan: Dereliction of Duty," Amnesty International, 2012, accessed June 14, 2015, http://www2.ohchr.org/english/bodies/hrc/docs/ngos/AI_Kyrgyzstan_HRC108.pdf.

[110] "Report of the United Nations High Commissioner for Human Rights on the situation of human rights and the activities of her Office in the Democratic Republic of the Congo," A/HRC/24/33, July 12, 2013, pp. 7, 16, accessed June 14, 2015, http://www.ohchr.org/EN/HRBodies/HRC/RegularSessions/Session24/Documents/A-HRC-24-33_en.pdf.

[111] Gaza Follow-up Committee report, 12–13.

[112] See, for example, "Report of the United Nations High Commissioner for Human Rights on the Implementation of Human Rights Council Resolutions S-9/1 and S-12/1," A/HRC/19/20, December 13, 2011, pp. 17–18, accessed June 14, 2015, http://www.ohchr.org/Documents/HRBodies/HRCouncil/RegularSession/Session19/A-HRC-19-20_en.pdf; "Report of the United Nations High Commissioner for Human Rights on the Implementation of Human Rights Council Resolutions S-9/1 and S-12/1," A/HRC/22/35, March 6, 2013, p. 17, accessed June 14, 2015, http://www.securitycouncilreport.org/atf/cf/%7B65BFCF9B-6D27-4E9C-8CD3-CF6E4FF96FF9%7D/a_hrc_22_35.pdf; and see generally "This is How We Fought in Gaza: Soldiers' Testimonies and Photographs from Operation 'Protective Edge,'" Breaking the Silence, 2014, accessed June 18, 2015, http://www.breakingthesilence.org.il/pdf/ProtectiveEdge.pdf.

enacted a bill of rights and a ten-year plan to improve the human rights situation in the country, but, as noted in the previous section, impunity remains a serious problem in the country.[113]

C.   Accountability at the International Level

This section focuses on recommendations that address pursuing accountability at the international level, specifically through the involvement of the ICC, universal jurisdiction, or hybrid measures that involve international and domestic judicial actors operating in concert with one another. Due to the resistance to accountability experienced at the domestic level – as examined in the previous two sections – measures taken at the international level sometimes constitute the only viable route for pursuing justice. Of the fifteen missions, four reports recommended ICC involvement. The relevant passages appear below:

• "Given the lack of progress in the fight against impunity in the DRC, it would seem to be of primary importance that the ICC maintain and indeed increase its commitment. The ICC must address in particular the most serious crimes, which could be difficult to prosecute in the DRC because of their complexity, for example networks that fund and arm the groups involved in these crimes. Persons allegedly involved in these activities appear to benefit from political, military and economic support and are sometimes outside the DRC and hence beyond the reach of national justice. It would therefore appear important that the ICC's Prosecutor pay particular attention to these cases, in order that they be brought to justice." (DRC Mapping Exercise)[114]

• "The Commission also recommends that where, in accordance with the conclusions contained in this report, there is a strong presumption that crimes against humanity were committed, the cases against the individuals concerned should be referred to the International Criminal Court." (Guinea Commission)[115]

• "To the Prosecutor of the International Criminal Court, with reference to the declaration under Article 12 (3) received by the Office of the Prosecutor of the International Criminal Court from the Government of Palestine, the Mission considers that accountability for victims and the interests of peace and justice in the region require that the

---

[113] "Report of the Independent Expert on the situation of human rights in the Sudan, Mashood A. Baderin," A/HRC/24/31, September 18, 2013, pp. 6–7.

[114] DRC Mapping Exercise report, 30–31.   [115] Guinea Commission report, 60.

Prosecutor should make the required legal determination as expeditiously as possible." (Gaza Fact-Finding Mission)[116]
- "With regard to the judicial accountability mechanism, the Commission strongly recommends that the Security Council should refer the situation in Darfur to the International Criminal Court, pursuant to Article 13(b) of the Statute of the Court." (Darfur Commission)[117]

Among these recommendations, one can more easily find examples of success. The ICC has been engaged in some capacity in all of the four contexts mentioned above. The United Nations Security Council's (UNSC) decision to refer the Darfur situation to the ICC is particularly notable. As the head of the Darfur Commission writes, after the publication of the mission's report, "certain members of the Security Council who had previously displayed strong antagonism to the ICC judiciously toned down their opposition and abstained from voting."[118] Another MRF actor states, the Darfur Commission "succeeded in persuading sceptical members of the Security Council to permit a referral of the situation to the International Criminal Court" and constitutes "a major contribution to the evolution of a practice which has the potential to maximize the value of the Court."[119]

Additionally, in 2012, the ICC issued the court's first conviction: of Thomas Lubanga for conscripting child soldiers, an issue examined by the DRC Mapping Exercise (though this trial had already begun before the completion of the Mapping Exercise).[120] The ICC also, as of July 2015, has five open cases related to the situation in the DRC.[121] Regarding Guinea, the recommendation in the report is phrased in the passive voice – "the cases against the individuals concerned should be referred to the International Criminal Court" – but the insinuation is a UNSC referral. Despite the mission's recommendation, the UNSC has not referred the situation to

---

[116] Gaza Fact-Finding Mission report, 424.   [117] Darfur Commission report, 162.

[118] Antonio Cassese, "Is The ICC Still Having Teething Problems?" *Journal of International Criminal Justice* 4, no. 3 (2006): 436, accessed June 14, 2015, doi:10.1093/jicj/mql033.

[119] Philip Alston, "The Darfur Commission as a Model for Future Responses to Crisis Situations," *Journal of International Criminal Justice* 3 (2005): 601 and 607, accessed June 14, 2015, doi:10.1093/jicj/mqi053.

[120] See DRC Mapping Exercise report, 234–235. For the ICC decision, see generally *Prosecutor v. Lubanga*, ICC-01/04-01/06, Judgment pursuant to Article 74 of the Statute (International Criminal Court, March 14, 2012), accessed June 14, 2015, http://www.icc-cpi. int/iccdocs/doc/doc1379838.pdf.

[121] See "Situation in Democratic Republic of the Congo," International Criminal Court, accessed June 14, 2015, http://www.icc-cpi.int/EN_Menus/ICC/Situations%20and%20 Cases/Situations/Situation%20ICC%200104/Pages/situation%20index.aspx.

the ICC but rather has urged that action be taken at the domestic level.[122] Regardless, the ICC prosecutor has opened a preliminary examination but, as with the UNSC, is awaiting the outcome of ongoing domestic investigations.[123] In the context of Gaza, the ICC prosecutor initiated a preliminary investigation into "acts committed on the territory of Palestine since 1 July 2002."[124] The ICC prosecutor stated in 2012 that the United Nations Secretary-General (UNSG) – with, if necessary, the consultation of the United Nations General Assembly (UNGA) – must determine whether Palestine meets the requirements to be considered a state, a precondition necessary for the ICC to exercise the court's jurisdiction.[125] In November 2012, the UNGA admitted Palestine as a "non-member observer state,"[126] and after the collapse of Israeli-Palestinian peace talks in 2014, the Palestinian president signed the Rome Statute, and the Palestinian Authority officially acceded to the treaty.[127] However, the ICC's jurisdiction stretches back only to 2014 so does not encompass Operation Cast Lead.[128]

Other accountability recommendations directed toward international actors have not been as impactful. For example, the Timor-Leste Commission specifically recommended the creation of a hybrid system in Timor-Leste that would include an international deputy prosecutor general, but Timor-Leste did not undertake this option.[129] Additionally, the DRC Mapping Exercise and the Gaza Fact-Finding Mission are, of the fifteen

---

[122] "Statement by the President of the Security Council," S/PRST/2010/3, United Nations Security Council, February 16, 2010, accessed June 14, 2015, http://www.securitycouncil-report.org/atf/cf/%7B65BFCF9B-6D27-4E9C-8CD3-CF6E4FF96FF9%7D/Guinea%20S%20PRST%202010%203.pdf.

[123] "Statement of the Prosecutor of the International Criminal Court, Fatou Bensouda, on the occasion of the 28 September 2013 elections in Guinea," International Criminal Court, September 27, 2013, accessed June 14, 2015, http://www.icc-cpi.int/en_menus/icc/structure%20of%20the%20court/office%20of%20the%20prosecutor/reports%20and%20statements/statement/Pages/statement-OTP-27–09–2013.aspx.

[124] "Situation in Palestine," International Criminal Court, April 3, 2012, p. 1, accessed June 14, 2015, http://www.icc-cpi.int/NR/rdonlyres/9B651B80-EC43-4945-BF5A-FAFF5F334B92/284387/SituationinPalestine030412ENG.pdf.

[125] Ibid., 1–2.

[126] Ruth Tenne, "The Way Ahead: Taking Israel to the ICC," *Redress Information & Analysis*, March 18, 2014, accessed June 14, 2015, http://www.redressonline.com/2014/03/the-way-ahead-taking-israel-to-the-icc/.

[127] Laura Smith-Spark, "Palestinians Join International Criminal Court, Permitting War Crimes Inquiries," *CNN*, April 1, 2015, accessed June 18, 2015, http://www.cnn.com/2015/04/01/middleeast/palestinians-icc-membership/.

[128] David Luban, "Palestine and the ICC – Some Legal Questions," *Just Security*, January 2, 2015, accessed June 18, 2015, http://justsecurity.org/18817/palestine-icc-legal-questions/.

[129] Timor-Leste Commission report, 68.

missions on which this book focuses, the only missions that recommended that other states use universal jurisdiction to initiate prosecutions.[130] Before and after the publication of the Gaza Fact-Finding Mission report, some efforts were launched to initiate prosecutions through universal jurisdiction, though none have succeeded.[131] Universal jurisdiction has also not been successfully used to prosecute individuals for allegations included in the DRC Mapping Exercise report.

D. Follow-up Monitoring Measures

Follow-up monitoring measures have assumed many forms, including mandating special rapporteurs, publishing OHCHR reports, monitoring in the context of peace operations, and, as occurred after the Gaza Fact-Finding Mission, creating an independent follow-up mechanism to gather information about and report on relevant developments. This section first presents recommendations that MRF reports have offered regarding follow-up monitoring. Specifically, the section focuses on recommendations directed to the UNHRC, as well as the United Nations Commission on Human Rights, the predecessor to the UNHRC; OHCHR; the UNSC; national governments; and miscellaneous international, regional, national, and nongovernmental entities. The section then assesses the actions undertaken in the aftermath of these recommendations.

Recommendations directed toward either the UNHRC or the United Nations Commission on Human Rights include:

- Extend the mandate of the mission or establish a succeeding mechanism (Libya Commission, first report).
- Establish a mechanism to monitor the implementation of recommendations (Libya Commission, second report, and Côte d'Ivoire Commission).
- Endorse the report's recommendations, take action to implement recommendations, and review implementation in future sessions (Gaza Fact-Finding Mission).
- Submit the report to the ICC prosecutor, the UNGA, and human rights bodies, and consider a review of implementation progress during Universal Periodic Review (Gaza Fact-Finding Mission).

---

[130] See Gaza Fact-Finding Mission report, 427; and DRC Mapping Exercise report, 461–464.

[131] Jennifer Barnette, "Initial Reactions to the Goldstone Report and Reflections on Israeli Accountability," in *Is There a Court for Gaza? A Test Bench for International Justice,* ed. Chantal Meloni and Gianni Tognoni (The Hague: Asser Press, 2012), 139.

- Request that the UNSG submit the report to UNSC (Gaza Fact-Finding Mission).
- Establish a procedure on the recovery of reparations (Lebanon Commission).
- Establish a procedure to monitor the human rights situation in the country (Lebanon Commission).
- Consider re-establishing a country-specific rapporteur (Darfur Commission).

Recommendations directed toward OHCHR include:

- Monitor the situation with a significant presence in the country (Guinea Commission).
- Monitor the situation of persons who cooperated with the mission (Gaza Fact-Finding Mission).
- Give attention to the mission's recommendations in periodic reporting (Gaza Fact-Finding Mission).

Recommendations directed toward the UNSC include:

- Remain seized of the situation (Guinea Commission).
- Establish a mechanism to monitor legal proceedings undertaken and, after a six-month review, refer the situation to the ICC, if necessary (Gaza Fact-Finding Mission).

Recommendations directed toward national governments include:

- Establish a mechanism to follow up on and implement recommendations – directed to the government of Bahrain (Bahrain Commission).
- Request OHCHR to evaluate progress in implementing recommendations – directed to the government of Kyrgyzstan (Kyrgyzstan Commission).

Recommendations directed toward miscellaneous international, regional, national, and nongovernmental actors include:

- Monitor the implementation of recommendations – directed to the United Nations Mission in Libya (Libya Commission, second report).
- Establish a mechanism to monitor the implementation of recommendations – directed to the African Commission on Human and Peoples' Rights (Libya Commission, second report).
- Establish a mechanism to monitor the domestic accountability process, investigate allegations, and collect and safeguard relevant information – directed to the UNSG (Sri Lanka Panel).

- Request the UNSC to report on accountability measures taken, including implementation of recommendations – directed to the UNGA (Gaza Fact-Finding Mission).
- Establish an environmental monitoring program – directed generally to the UN, with no particular entity specified (Gaza Fact-Finding Mission).
- Monitor the progress of cases – directed to the Office of the Provedor for Human Rights and Justice in Timor-Leste, the United Nations Mission in Timor-Leste, and NGOs (Timor-Leste Commission).

An analysis of the implementation of the above recommendations reveals a significant opportunity for impact through follow-up monitoring. Indeed, various UN bodies have undertaken a wide array of follow-up monitoring and reporting activities. Measures carried out by the UNHRC (and, before the creation of the UNHRC, by the United Nations Commission on Human Rights) include decisions to:

- Extend the mandate of the Libya Commission,[132]
- Establish the independent expert on the situation of human rights in Côte d'Ivoire,[133]
- Establish an independent follow-up committee to monitor progress on accountability in Israel and Palestine,[134]
- Request that OHCHR consult with the government of Lebanon on the report of the Lebanon Commission, including the report's findings and recommendations,[135] and
- Re-establish the independent expert on the situation of human rights in the Sudan.[136]

Additionally, as the Guinea Commission recommended, the UNSC remained seized of the situation in Guinea.[137] The United Nations Mission in Timor-Leste and the United Nations Mission in Libya, as the Timor-Leste Commission and Libya Commission respectively recommended, issued reports assessing the human rights situation in these missions'

---

[132] United Nations Human Rights Council resolution 17/L.3.
[133] United Nations Human Rights Council resolution 17/21.
[134] United Nations Human Rights Council resolution 13/9.
[135] United Nations Human Rights Council resolution 3/3.
[136] United Nations Human Rights Council resolution 11/10.
[137] "Security Council Press Statement on Guinea," United Nations Security Council, SC/10992-AFR/2607, April 29, 2013, accessed June 14, 2015, http://www.un.org/News/Press/docs//2013/sc10992.doc.htm.

countries of operation.[138] Follow-up monitoring measures undertaken by OHCHR, including reporting on the human rights situation in Guinea and providing periodic updates on the situation in Gaza, have addressed not only the security of individuals who cooperated with the Gaza Fact-Finding Mission but also progress on implementing the Gaza Fact-Finding Mission's recommendations.[139]

Still, MRF missions have not been universally successful with respect to accountability or follow-up monitoring. For example, regarding the Sri Lanka Panel, despite the fact that the purpose of the mission was "to advise the Secretary-General on the modalities, applicable international standards and comparative experience relevant to the fulfillment of the joint commitment [of the UNSG and the President of Sri Lanka] to an accountability process,"[140] the UNSG adopted none of the report's recommendations related to accountability or follow-up monitoring. Based on publicly available information, the only recommendation that the UNSG undertook was initiating a review of the UN's humanitarian and civilian protection response during the final stages of the Sri Lankan Civil War.[141] Furthermore, though the Gaza Fact-Finding Mission advocated for UNSC involvement in accountability for Operation Cast Lead, the UNHRC did not formally request that the UNSG refer the report to the UNSC.[142]

[138]   For the United Nations Mission in Timor-Leste, see generally, for example, UNMIT, "Report on Human Rights Developments in Timor-Leste." For the United Nations Support Mission in Libya, see generally, for example, "Reports of the Secretary-General on the United Nations Support Mission in Libya," United Nations Support Mission in Libya, accessed June 14, 2015, http://www.unsmil.unmissions.org/Default. aspx?tabid=3549&language=en-US.

[139]   For a report on Guinea, see generally, for example, "Report of the High Commissioner for Human Rights on the Situation of Human Rights in Guinea," A/HRC/16/26, February 25, 2011, accessed June 14, 2015, http://www2.ohchr.org/english/bodies/hrcouncil/docs/16session/A.HRC.16.26_en.pdf. For a report on Gaza, see generally, for example, "Progress Report of the United Nations High Commissioner for Human Rights on the Implementation of Human Rights Council Resolution 19/18," A/HRC/20/36, May 21, 2012, accessed June 25, 2015, http://www.ohchr.org/Documents/HRBodies/HRCouncil/RegularSession/Session20/A.HRC.20.36_En.PDF.

[140]   Sri Lanka Panel report, 2.

[141]   Robert Mackey, "Leaked Report on Sri Lanka Critical of U.N.," The Lede, The New York Times, November 13, 2012, accessed June 14, 2015, http://thelede.blogs.nytimes.com/2012/11/13/leaked-report-on-sri-lanka-critical-of-u-n/?_php=true&_type=blogs&_r=0.

[142]   "Progress made in the implementation of the recommendations of the Fact-Finding Mission by all concerned parties, including United Nations bodies, in accordance with paragraph 3 of section B of Human Rights Council resolution S-12/1," A/HRC/21/33, September 21, 2012, pp. 3–4.

Two missions – the Kyrgyzstan Commission and the Bahrain Commission – recommended that national actors engage in some capacity in follow-up monitoring measures. However, the results have not been as successful as those that have occurred at the international level. The government of Kyrgyzstan rejected the findings of the Kyrgyzstan Commission and did not request OHCHR to monitor the implementation of the report's recommendations.[143] OHCHR, at the request of the UNHRC, provides technical assistance to Kyrgyzstan but does not monitor the implementation of the report's recommendations. In response to the Bahrain Commission's recommendation "[t]o establish an independent and impartial national commission … to follow up and implement the recommendations of this Commission,"[144] the government of Bahrain did establish two national commissions that produced reports in 2012 and 2013. However, many commentators and activists have criticized these Bahraini-mandated follow-up mechanisms. For example, the POMED assessment of the Bahraini government's recommendation implementation record states that one can consider that the recommendation for creating a national commission has "only been partially implemented, as the original commission and its derivative appear to lack both the independence and impartiality specified by the BICI."[145]

III. Conclusion

This assessment of recommendations indicates that the direct impact of an MRF mission can be more readily detected at the international level. Recommendations directed toward actors engaged in large-scale violence have not proved to be likely to produce immediate and unqualified results. However, recommendations directed toward other governments and UN entities have been more impactful. This research finding suggests that the more readily discernible value of MRF missions is that these mechanisms play a role in drawing governments into a process of monitoring global developments regarding accountability during and after armed conflicts and internal disturbances.

This finding does not necessarily mean that MRF reports should not bother to direct recommendations to domestic actors. Indeed, at the

---

[143] "Head of Commission on Kyrgyz Violence Declared Persona Non Grata," *Radio Free Europe Radio Liberty*, May 26, 2011, accessed June 14, 2015, http://www.rferl. org/content/head_of_commission_on_kyrgyz_violence_declared_persona_non_ grata/24205930.html.

[144] Bahrain Commission report, 422.   [145] POMED, "One Year Later," 6.

domestic level, MRF reports may yield a less tangible but nonetheless important impact on efforts to achieve accountability, institutional reform, and reconciliation. Furthermore, even if the surrounding political environment is not conducive to change, many actors have proclaimed the value of MRF work in presenting the mere "possibility" of contributing to greater attention to accountability. Conversely, though, MRF missions that do not advocate for additional follow-up monitoring and other accountability measures at the international level might be missing a key opportunity that aligns with MRF missions' most likely area of impact. In some cases, MRF efforts can push open an already cracked window of political opportunity among international actors, as occurred in the situation of Darfur with the UNSC referral, and in the many other examples previously mentioned.

APPENDIX A
HPCR GROUP OF PROFESSIONALS ON
MONITORING, REPORTING, AND FACT-FINDING

The Program on Humanitarian Policy and Conflict Research (HPCR) at Harvard University undertook the research presented in this Handbook and drafted the HPCR Advanced Practitioner's Handbook on Commissions of Inquiry in collaboration with the HPCR Group of Professionals on Monitoring, Reporting, and Fact-Finding. This team of high-level practitioners met at five on-site meetings that HPCR convened between 2012 and 2014. Throughout the duration of this initiative, the Group of Professionals steered the direction of HPCR's research, offered comments on draft versions of the chapters that appear in this Handbook, and collaborated on drafting and editing the Handbook.

Mr. Claude Bruderlein (Group Chair)
Lecturer, Harvard T. H. Chan School of Public Health; Affiliate Faculty, Harvard Kennedy School of Government; Senior Researcher, Program on Humanitarian Policy and Conflict Research at Harvard University; Strategic Adviser to the President, International Committee of the Red Cross

Ms. Karen AbuZayd
Commissioner, Independent International Commission of Inquiry on the Syrian Arab Republic; Former Commissioner-General of the United Nations Relief and Works Agency for Palestine Refugees in the Near East

Dr. Théo Boutruche
Independent Consultant in International Human Rights and Humanitarian Law; Former Post-Conflict Legal Adviser at REDRESS and Researcher on the Democratic Republic of Congo at Amnesty International; Former IHL and Human Rights Expert, Independent International Fact-Finding Mission on the Conflict in Georgia

Mr. Luc Côté
Director of Rule of Law, United Nations Stabilization Mission in Haiti; Former Executive Director of the United Nations Mapping Exercise in the Democratic Republic of Congo, the Kyrgyzstan Inquiry Commission, and the United Nations Independent Special Commission of Inquiry for Timor-Leste

Ms. Hina Jilani
Advocate, Supreme Court of Pakistan; Former United Nations Special Representative on Human Rights Defenders; Former Member of the United Nations Fact-Finding Mission on the Gaza Conflict and the International Commission of Inquiry on Darfur

Judge Philippe Kirsch
Former Chairman, International Commission of Inquiry on Libya; Former Commissioner, Bahrain Independent Commission of Inquiry; Former President, International Criminal Court

Ms. Beatrice Mégevand-Roggo
Special Representative for Syria, HD Centre for Humanitarian Dialogue; Former Head of Middle East Operations, International Committee of the Red Cross

Ms. Cynthia Petrigh
Founder, Beyond (peace); Former Human Rights and IHL Expert, International Monitoring Team in Mindanao; Former Human Rights Expert, Kyrgyzstan Inquiry Commission

Dr. Paulo Sérgio Pinheiro
Chairman, Independent International Commission of Inquiry on the Syrian Arab Republic; Former Chairman, United Nations Independent Special Commission of Inquiry for Timor-Leste

APPENDIX B
SELECTED MISSIONS

Both parts of this Handbook – the *Handbook* in Part I and the supplemental scholarly analyses that appear in Part II – draw on the experiences of recent MRF missions. The Program on Humanitarian Policy and Conflict Research (HPCR) at Harvard University – in collaboration with the HPCR Group of Professionals on Monitoring, Reporting, and Fact-Finding – undertook an extensive review of fifteen missions mandated and implemented over the past decade. When selecting these fifteen missions, HPCR chose missions that reflect the diversity that exists within the domain of MRF.

First, HPCR focused on missions that would demonstrate the wide array of bodies that have created MRF mechanisms. In this regard, HPCR deemed it important to include missions mandated by various international entities – such as the UNHRC, UNSC, and the UNSG – as well as missions authorized at the regional and national levels. The significance of this diversity is that, depending on the mandating entity, the experiences of MRF missions have varied in terms of institutional memory capturing lessons learned from past missions; operational, methodological, and personnel support provided to the mission; and opportunities for coordination with other entities involved on the ground in the same context.

Second, HPCR selected missions that reflect the distinct contexts in which MRF missions operate, from protracted armed conflicts to relatively brief internal disturbances. By drawing from these experiences, HPCR has sought to present information relevant to the diversity of environments on which future MRF missions are likely to focus.

Third, HPCR was interested in selecting missions that applied different methods for gathering and assessing information. Though all MRF mechanism types are tasked with gathering information and drawing conclusions about allegations of violations of international law, the methodologies of fact-finding missions, mapping exercises, and inquiry panels mandated by the UNSG differ from one another. These differences, which bear on the types of sources on which the mission relies and the procedures it adopts for information gathering, allow the Handbook to grapple with the methodologically eclectic nature of the domain of MRF.

Information about the selected missions – listed in reverse chronological order, according to the date of release of the final report – appears below.

1. International Commission of Inquiry on Libya (Libya Commission)

The United Nations Human Rights Council authorized this mission in February 2011 with United Nations Human Rights Council resolution S-15/1. The context of the mission was the Qaddafi regime's crackdown on Arab Spring protesters, though the mission also examined the armed conflict that subsequently emerged. The mission conducted field visits, during which the mission met with over 350 people, and presented its findings at the seventeenth session of the United Nations Human Rights Council. In response, in June 2011, the Council extended the mandate of the mission. The mission presented an oral update during the eighteenth session of the Council in September 2011 and presented the mission's final report at the Council's nineteenth session in March 2012.

2. Bahrain Independent Commission of Inquiry (Bahrain Commission)

The government of Bahrain created this mission by Bahraini royal decree in June 2011. The authorization of the mandate followed a crackdown conducted by the Bahraini government after protests had erupted in the country in February 2011. The mission established an office in Bahrain, conducted on-site visits, and collected statements through interviews with 5,188 individuals. The chair of the commission presented the mission's report to the king of Bahrain in a public ceremony held in Bahrain in November 2011.

3. The Secretary-General's Panel of Inquiry on the 31 May 2010 Flotilla Incident (UNSG Flotilla Panel)

On May 31, 2010, the Israeli Defense Forces boarded a flotilla of six ships in an operation that led to the loss of nine lives and injuries to many others. In response, the United Nations Secretary-General created this panel to examine information related to the incident and "recommend ways of avoiding similar incidents in the future." Based on the mandate, the panel's information gathering focused on reviewing interim and final reports of national investigations undertaken in Israel and Turkey – namely, in Israel, the Public Commission to Examine the Maritime Incident of May 31, 2010 (commonly called the Turkel Commission, after retired Israeli Supreme Court

Judge Jacob Turkel, who chaired the commission), and in Turkey, the Turkish National Commission of Inquiry. The panel produced a final report that is dated September 2011.

4. Independent, International Commission of Inquiry on Côte d'Ivoire (Côte d'Ivoire Commission)

The United Nations Human Rights Council authorized this mission in April 2011 with Council resolution 16/25. The context that prompted the creation of the mission was the armed conflict that erupted after the November 2010 Ivorian presidential election. To implement the mandate, the mission conducted field visits to Côte d'Ivoire and Liberia and presented its findings at the seventeenth session of the Council in June 2011.

5. Kyrgyzstan Inquiry Commission (Kyrgyzstan Commission)

The mandate for this mission arose as a result of the engagement of a wide array of actors. Several Nordic countries prompted the initiative, and the president of Kyrgyzstan officially endorsed the mandate in September 2010 after consultations with the Office of the High Commissioner for Human Rights. The investigative focus of the mission was the internal disturbance that had occurred in Kyrgyzstan – and specifically, in Osh and surrounding provinces – in June 2010. The mission established public offices in Kyrgyzstan and conducted over 750 interviews. The mission released its final report in May 2011.

6. The Secretary-General's Panel of Experts on Accountability in Sri Lanka (Sri Lanka Panel)

Days after the conclusion of the Sri Lankan Civil War in 2009, the United Nations Secretary-General issued a joint statement with the President of Sri Lanka that addressed the importance of accountability for violations of IHL and IHRL that had occurred during the civil war. Then, in June 2010, the Secretary-General announced the creation of a panel "to advise him on the implementation of the said commitment with respect to the final stages of the war."[1] The panel gathered information from a wide array of sources, though the Sri Lankan government denied access to the panel to visit Sri Lanka. Additionally, the

---

[1] "Report of the Secretary-General's Panel of Experts on Accountability in Sri Lanka," March 31, 2011, p. 2, accessed June 14, 2015, http://www.un.org/News/dh/infocus/Sri_Lanka/POE_Report_Full.pdf.

panel's report states of the panel's methodology, "The Panel has not conducted fact-finding as that term is understood in United Nations practice, as it does not reach factual conclusions regarding disputed facts, nor did it carry out a formal investigation that draws conclusions regarding legal liability or culpability of States, non-state actors, or individuals."[2] The panel produced a final report in March 2011.

7. International Fact-Finding Mission to Investigate Violations of International Law, Including International Humanitarian and Human Rights Law, Resulting from the Israeli Attacks on the Flotilla of Ships Carrying Humanitarian Assistance (UNHRC Flotilla Fact-Finding Mission)

The United Nations Human Rights Council created this mission with resolution 14/1, adopted in June 2010. The adoption of this mandate followed the flotilla incident, during which Israeli Defense Forces boarded a flotilla of six ships in an operation that led to the loss of nine lives and injuries to many others. The mission gathered information from a wide array of sources, including eyewitness accounts from witnesses and victims acquired through interviews conducted by the mission. The mission was not granted access to Israel but did travel to Turkey, Jordan, and the United Kingdom, where the mission was able to inspect the *Mavi Marmara*, the ship on which the nine passengers had died. The mission reported its findings at the fifteenth session of the United Nations Human Rights Council in September 2010.

8. United Nations Mapping Exercise in the Democratic Republic of Congo (DRC Mapping Exercise)

Numerous entities – including the United Nations Secretary-General, the Office of the High Commissioner for Human Rights, the Department of Political Affairs, the Office of Legal Affairs, and the Office of the Secretary-General's Special Adviser on the Prevention of Genocide – were involved in the creation of this mission. However, the formal authorization for the mission fell under the umbrella of the mandate for the United Nations Organization Mission in the Democratic Republic of the Congo, with Terms of Reference approved by the Secretary-General. The Terms of Reference authorized the mission to "conduct a mapping exercise of the most serious violations of human rights and international humanitarian law committed within the territory of the Democratic Republic of the Congo between March

---

[2] Ibid., 3.

1993 and June 2003."[3] The mission's final report states that the mission's methodology "has much in common with international commissions of inquiry, commissions of experts and fact-finding commissions" but stresses that mapping is a distinct exercise with its own methodology.[4] The mission's findings were based both on firsthand information gathered by the mission and on pre-existing findings deemed to be credible by the mission. The final report was released in August 2010.

9. International Commission of Inquiry for Guinea (Guinea Commission)

The United Nations Secretary-General established this mission in October 2009. The context that prompted the creation of the investigation was a governmental crackdown on political protesters that occurred in Guinea on September 28, 2009. The mission conducted a field visit to Guinea, during which the mission interviewed 687 individuals. The mission produced a final report that is dated December 2009.

10. Independent International Fact-Finding Mission on the Conflict in Georgia (Georgia Fact-Finding Mission)

The Council of the European Union authorized the creation of this mission in December 2008. The mission was created in response to the Russo-Georgia War that had occurred in August 2008. The implementation of the mandate entailed conducting a field visit to different regions in Georgia to gather information from eyewitnesses. The final report of the mission was released in September 2009.

11. United Nations Fact-Finding Mission on the Gaza Conflict (Gaza Fact-Finding Mission)

In February 2009, the United Nations Human Rights Council authorized the creation of this mission with resolution S-9/1. However, this original mandate focused the mission's investigative attention solely on Israel, excluding other parties to the conflict. The chair of the mission rejected this mandate and

---

[3] "Report of the Mapping Exercise Documenting the Most Serious Violations of Human Rights and International Humanitarian Law Committed within the Territory of the Democratic Republic of the Congo between March 1993 and June 2003," Office of the High Commissioner for Human Rights, August 2010, p. 542, accessed June 14, 2015, http://www. refworld.org/docid/4ca99bc22.html.

[4] Ibid., 36–37.

operated under terms agreed upon with the president of the Council. These renegotiated mandate terms allowed the mission to focus on all relevant parties and also expanded the temporal and territorial scope of the mission. The mission believed that this more expansive scope to constitute the mission's operative mandate. The mission traveled to relevant areas in Gaza but did not receive the cooperation of Israel so was not able to travel to Israel and the West Bank. Additionally, the mission held public hearings in Gaza in June 2009 and in Geneva in July 2009. The mission completed its final report in September 2009.

12. High-Level Fact-Finding Mission to Beit Hanoun Established Under Resolution S-3/1 (Beit Hanoun Fact-Finding Mission)

The United Nations Human Rights Council authorized the creation of this mission in November 2006 with resolution S-3/1. The Council created this mission to gather information related to an incident that had occurred on November 8, 2006, during which Israeli Defense Forces had fired shells into the Gaza Strip that led to the death and injury of many individuals. The mission initially endeavored to gain access to Gaza through Israel but did not receive permission from Israeli authorities to do so. Then, in May 2008, the mission undertook a field visit to Gaza, entering through Egypt. The mission produced a final report in September 2008.

13. Commission of Inquiry on Lebanon (Lebanon Commission)

In August 2006, the United Nations Human Rights Council adopted resolution S-2/1, which authorized the creation of this mission. The focus of the mission was the armed conflict that had occurred between Israel and Lebanon in July and August 2006. The commission sought cooperation from the governments of both Israel and Lebanon, though only the government of Lebanon cooperated with the mission. The mission conducted two field visits to Lebanon and produced a final report that is dated November 2006.

14. United Nations Independent Special Commission of Inquiry for Timor-Leste (Timor-Leste Commission)

In June 2006, the United Nations Secretary-General requested that the United Nations High Commissioner for Human Rights establish this mission. The focus of the mission was the internal disturbance that had occurred in Timor-Leste in April and May 2006. The mission undertook field visits to Timor-Leste, during which the mission conducted interviews with a wide array of actors. The mission completed its final report in October 2006.

15.   International Commission of Inquiry on Darfur
(Darfur Commission)

In September 2004, the United Nations Security Council mandated this mission with resolution 1564. This mission was a component of the Security Council's response to the non-international armed conflict that had begun in Darfur in February 2003. The implementation of the mandate included field visits that the mission took to Sudan in November 2004 and January 2005. The mission completed its final report in January 2005.

INDEX